Just GIVE ME JESUS

ANNE GRAHAM LOTZ

THOMAS NELSON
Since 1798

NASHVILLE DALLAS MEXICO CITY RIO DE JANEIRO BEIJING

Published in Nashville, Tennessee, by Thomas Nelson. Thomas Nelson is a registered trademark of Thomas Nelson, Inc.

Thomas Nelson, Inc., titles may be purchased in bulk for educational, business, fund-raising, or sales promotional use.
For information, please e-mail SpecialMarkets@ThomasNelson.com.

ISBN: 978-0-8499-2093-6

Library of Congress has catalogued the earlier edition as follows:

Lotz, Anne Graham, 1948–
Just give me Jesus / by Anne Graham Lotz.
p. cm.
ISBN 978-0-8499-1646-5 (hardcover)
1. Jesus Christ—Person and offices. 2. Bible. N.T. John—Criticism, interpretation, etc. I. Title.

BS2615.2 .L68 2000
232—dc21

00-024773

Printed in the United States of America
09 10 11 12 RRD 6 5 4 3 2 1

CONTENTS

To those who need
a fresh touch from God

PLEASE . . .

My life in 1999 and 2000 was pressure packed and trouble filled. My husband's dental office, where he had practiced for thirty years, burned to the ground. All three of my children got married within eight months of each other. My son was diagnosed with cancer and went through successful surgery and follow-up radiation. I published two books, *God's Story* and *Daily Light*, as well as *The Daily Light Journal: Morning Readings.* I produced a seven-volume video series with workbooks and study guides for *The Vision of His Glory*. I kept up an intense speaking schedule that included international travel, fulfilled ministry obligations, and gave physical care to my parents, including going through my mother's five emergency hospitalizations within a span of ten months. My ministry, AnGeL Ministries, was going through a transition that increased our yearly budget sixfold so that in the year 2000 we could offer arena events for the purpose of revival—at no charge.

Even now, my duties and responsibilities at times seem overwhelming, and my schedule is overfilled. But I don't want a vacation, I don't want to quit, I don't want sympathy, I don't want money, I don't want recognition, I don't want to escape, I don't even want a miracle!

This book is the cry of my heart—just give me Jesus. *Please!*

AND THANK YOU

To those who have helped and encouraged me as this book took shape and was completed—thank you!

...To dearest Danny, for reflecting Jesus through your unconditional love, gentle strength, and steadfast endurance as you put up with my race to meet yet another manuscript deadline.

... Jonathan and Alicia, Morrow and Traynor, Rachel-Ruth and Steven, for reflecting Jesus through your patient understanding of my distractedness from the family in order to complete this manuscript on time—and for giving me so much joy!

...Marjorie Green, Doris Weathers, Dody Ragsdale, Jean Clark, Bonnie Moore, Debby Morris, Sherry Burrows, and Pam Wilson for reflecting Jesus through your intercession on my behalf as you clothed every stroke of my pen (or tap on my computer) with prayer.

... Helen George for reflecting Jesus through your servant's spirit and faithful assistance in supporting me in ministry, regardless of where or what it has been.

... Brenda Bateman, Ginger Kirby, Carol Cooper, Rachel-Ruth Wright, Ann Whitehurst, Carolyn Holding, Kathie Waldrop, Dana Dixon, Linda Horton, and Pam Catlin for reflecting Jesus through your commitment to do the Father's work, not just talk about it.

... Leigh O'Dell for reflecting Jesus through the gift of yourself to AnGeL Ministries.

... Lee Gessner, Joey Paul, Debbie Wickwire, Laura Kendall, and my Thomas Nelson family for reflecting Jesus through your constant encouragement and consistent excellence.

... Dr. Lewis Drummond for reflecting Jesus through your availability to help me communicate the truth on the written page.

... Sue Ann Jones and Janet Reed for reflecting Jesus through your ability to change an editing plan B to a plan A—on short notice.

INTRODUCTION

Several years ago, Andrew Morton wrote a biography of Diana, Princess of Wales. In his publicity tour for the book, he said his information was based on conversations he had had with some of her closest friends. His book sold thousands of copies.

After Lady Diana's tragic death in a car accident in Paris, Andrew Morton's book was re-released. This time he revealed that the source of his information had not been intimate friends of Diana's, but Diana herself. He then produced hours of taped conversation with the princess as proof. And his book sold hundreds of thousands of copies. It made an enormous difference to the reading public to discover the book was not hearsay but what Diana had said about herself.

In the last several years, the market has been flooded with books about Jesus. His likeness has been on the cover of every major secular newsmagazine. He has been:

romanticized,
sentimentalized,
fictionalized,
criticized,
idolized,
modernized,
popularized,
trivialized,
visualized,
and scrutinized!

So why do we need one more book about Jesus? Because I believe there is a very important and often vast difference between what people say about Him, and what He says about Himself.

Inspired by the same Spirit that lived within Jesus, the apostle John wrote an eyewitness account of His life that is, in effect, what Jesus says about Himself. And this book is my attempt to draw you into His biography, which is also uniquely His autobiography.

Because John's gospel is so rich and space here is limited, I have been unable to include every passage. I selected the passages I did because these were the ones God seemed to lay on my heart—for myself. I have felt desperate for personal revival in my life, and that need has drawn me back to Jesus—to Jesus alone.

John's motivation for writing his gospel is expressed in a brief letter he wrote at the end of the first century to the churches under his leadership. Although he was an old man at the time, his passion for Christ still burned so intensely that it ignited every syllable as he wrote, "That which was from the beginning, which we have heard, which we have seen with our eyes, which we have looked at and our hands have touched—this we proclaim concerning the Word of life. The life appeared; we have seen it and testify to it, and we proclaim to you the eternal life, which was with the Father and has appeared to us."[1]

It is obvious that the thrill of knowing Jesus never fizzled out of John's life but remained vibrant until his faith became sight. With all my heart, that's what I want. I don't want to burn out; I want to burn on—and on and on and on!

While John's *motivation* for writing his eyewitness account of the life of Jesus was his overwhelming, passionate love for Christ, his *purpose* in writing was his love for you. The desire of his heart was, "that you may believe that Jesus is the Christ, the Son of God, and that by believing you may have life in his name."[2]

How did John know that in the twenty-first century, at the beginning of a new millennium,

> our lives would be so busy,
> our schedules would be so crammed,
> our focus would be so divided,
> our bodies would be so tired,
> our minds would be so bombarded,
> our families would be so attacked,

our relationships would be so strained,
our churches would be so programmed,

that we would be desperate for the simplicity and the purity, the freedom and the fulfillment, of "life in his name"? How did John know that with all the "stuff" in the church in this postmodern age, we would be thirsty for the Living Water and starving for the Bread of Life? I don't think he did know. But God did. Which is why He *just gives us Jesus* . . .

JESUS MAKES GOD VISIBLE

He is enduringly strong.
He is entirely sincere.
He is eternally steadfast.
He is immortally gracious.
He is imperially powerful.
He is impartially merciful.
He is the greatest phenomenon that has ever crossed
the horizons of the globe.

He is God's Son.
He is the sinner's Savior.
He is the captive's Ransom.
He is the Breath of Life.
He is the centerpiece of civilization.
He stands in the solitude of Himself.

He is august and He is unique.
He is unparalleled and He is unprecedented.
He is undisputed and He is undefiled.
He is unsurpassed and He is unshakable.

He is the lofty idea in philosophy.
He is the highest personality in psychology.
He is the supreme subject in literature.
He is the unavoidable problem in higher criticism.
He is the fundamental doctrine of theology.
He is the Cornerstone, the Capstone, and the stumbling
Stone of all religion.
He is the miracle of the ages.

Just give me Jesus! He makes God visible!

1

JESUS MAKES GOD VISIBLE . . .

To Me

JOHN 1:1–9

Years ago my mother was invited to a very prestigious dinner party in London, England. The glittering affair included members of the royal family as well as other aristocrats and leaders from British society. The dinner, softened by candlelight, with the tinkle of silver and the sparkle of crystal accompanying the sounds of accented conversation, had an ambiance of elegance.

The occasion might have been intimidating for someone unaccustomed to such a setting, but my mother was as at ease as a queen holding court. Dressed in a simple black gown with a triple strand of pearls around her neck, she looked stylish and sophisticated. Heads turned as people whispered their curious inquiries about who she might be.

But my mother was so interested in the other guests at her table she was oblivious to the small stir she had created. Her expression was not the duly bored, arrogant look adopted by many of the socially elite. Nor were her words stilted and self-conscious. Instead, her eyes danced with the joy of life, and her conversation was lively and peppered with questions as she sought to draw the others at her table into a discussion.

As she conversed, Mother discovered that the distinguished-looking older gentleman seated beside her was the former head of Scotland Yard, Great Britain's equivalent of the FBI. Fascinated, she respectfully began to probe him for anecdotes. As he opened up under her genuine interest, he revealed that the departments under his authority had included those for forgery and counterfeiting. When she surmised that he must have spent a lot of time studying counterfeit signatures, he corrected her. "On the contrary, Mrs. Graham. I spent all of my time studying the genuine thing. That way, when I saw a counterfeit, I could immediately detect it."

Today, our world is cluttered with lies, deceit, hypocrisy, and fraud at almost every level. From government leaders

to salesclerks

to airline ticket agents

to restaurant maître d's

to business associates

to secretaries

to friends

to neighbors

to advertisers,

everyone seems to play loose with the truth.

This "whatever works is right" attitude has even crept into the Christian community. Too often, we focus on methods instead of missions, programs instead of prayer, organization instead of inspiration, pragmatism instead of power. Many preachers preach to be popular, instead of preaching to change lives. Their sermons are 95 percent their own thoughts and 5 percent God's truth. And the average church member *cannot tell the difference* because he or she is biblically illiterate!

Sadly, this also tends to twist our perception of who Jesus is. While some have softened and sentimentalized Him until He is barely recognizable, others have distorted and doubted Him until He is undesirable.

My mother's dinner partner had unwittingly touched on a very important principle. If you and I want to be able to detect counterfeit Christs and counterfeit truth, we need to immerse ourselves in the real thing. We need to saturate ourselves in the truth of the Word of God. This applies to our faith in general, as well as to our understanding of Jesus.

Who is Jesus? He lived just over two thousand years ago, in an obscure town, in an obscure country, during a relatively dark period in human history that was dominated by the Roman Empire. Yet He stands unequaled and unparalleled in the phenomenal greatness of His life as well as in the stunning impact He has had on history.

As we conclude the first decade of the new millennium and gaze back at the last two thousand years, a handful of individuals seem to rise up from our history pages—individuals whose lives or words or accomplishments impacted the entire human race, for good or for bad. Names like Julius Caesar, Martin Luther, Muhammad, Christopher Columbus, Orville and Wilbur Wright, Adolf Hitler, Alexander Graham Bell, Jonas Salk, Joseph Stalin, Mahatma Gandhi, Mao Tse-tung, and David Ben-Gurion come readily to mind. Yet I would heartily agree with Reynolds Price, who in the introduction to his *Time* magazine cover story on Jesus, wrote, "It would require much exotic calculation . . . to deny that the single most powerful figure—not merely in these two millenniums but in all human history—has been Jesus of Nazareth."[1] Even today's date is based on the calculation of the date of His birth.

So *who is Jesus? What is there about Him* that makes Him *so compelling* that . . .

. . . a Yugoslavian nun would give her life to comfort the dying in Calcutta for His sake?

. . . some of the greatest architectural achievements in Europe were built for worship of Him?

. . . some of the world's most beautiful art was created to honor Him?

. . . some of the world's most glorious music was written to praise Him?

. . . 167 years after Rome crucified Him, He was acknowledged as the only God in the Roman Empire?

. . . Aleksandr Solzhenitsyn, rotting in a Siberian work camp, said the very thought of Him was enough to keep his sanity?

. . . in an outburst of physical pain, frustration, anger, or just disagreement with the officials at a ball game, His Name—not Buddha's or Muhammad's—is used in cursing?

. . . two thousand years after He has been physically removed from the world, people from all walks of life say He has saved them from drugs, illness, suicide, depression, and hopelessness?

. . . in His Name, people forsake personal gain to feed the hungry, house the homeless, clothe the naked, heal the sick?

Who is Jesus? How can we know who He *really* is? We know by studying the truth. The only legitimate source of historical information on His life is found in the four New Testament Gospels. This book, *Just Give Me Jesus,* focuses on the fourth gospel, written by John, who witnessed firsthand the events he recorded. And John's gospel is the truth.

So *who is Jesus?* Decide the answer for yourself as you read the apostle John's clear, confident, certain, and compelling biography. His stirring account begins by leaving no doubt that Jesus makes God visible to all, because Jesus is *God as Man.*

Jesus Is Bigger Than I Think

John's Gospel begins with a verbal trumpet flourish: "In the beginning was the Word" (John 1:1). These words immediately take us back to the vastness of eternity before there was anything at all. They also take us back to Genesis, where God began to reveal Himself to all mankind. In Genesis, the Bible itself opens with the exact same phrase, "In the beginning . . . ," as it introduces perhaps the most dramatic chapter of the entire Book.[2] As the passage unfolds the mysteries of creation, the phrase "And God said" is repeated no fewer than ten times in the first chapter.[3] The phrase shows God's awesome creative power as He spoke into existence everything that is or ever has been or ever will be. We might assume that the "word" He spoke, the "word" by which He called everything into being, was a *language* of some sort, with nouns and verbs and pronouns and adverbs conveying His will to empty space.

Not so! John stuns us in the very first verse of his Gospel, which reveals, "In the beginning was the Word, and the Word was with God, and the Word *was* God. *He* was with God in the beginning" (John 1:1–2, emphasis added). How awesome that the "Word" that was in the beginning, by which and through which God created everything, was—and is—a living Person with a mind, will, emotions, and intellect.

He Is Eternal

The gospel of John states this living Person was not *from* the beginning, but that *in* the beginning of time, space, the universe, eternity, and history, He was already there! He is eternal!

John's choice of wording in the Greek language makes his opening declaration astounding. The Greek for "Word," which he emphasized by repeating three times in the first verse, is *logos,* the outward expression of the mind and will that rules the universe. Plato, whose writings were popular in John's day, had said he hoped that someday a "logos" might come forth from God that would make everything about life clear. John, who had perhaps read Plato, began his gospel by stating in Greek that a "logos" *had come* from God. And not just *a* "logos" but the "*Living*

Logos"—an outward revelation of the heart and mind of God expressed perfectly for us in a living Person.

As we meditate on John's words, our sense of awe increases when we realize that "out of the . . . heart, the mouth speaks."[4] So our conclusion is that the Logos who was in the beginning with God is a living Person . . . *but He is more.* He is the living expression of what is on God's mind. But He is more. He is the living expression of what is on God's heart. But He is even more. He is the very heart of the almighty God of the universe laid bare for all to see!

Do you want to know what is on the mind of God? Then look at Jesus! Do you want to know the will of God? Then look at Jesus! Do you want to know what is in the heart of God? *Then look at Jesus!* Jesus is the exact revelation of what is on the mind and heart and in the will of God!

Jesus makes God visible. But that truth does not make Him somehow less than God. He is equally supreme with God.

He Is Equal

Each word John used, including the prepositions, becomes weighty with treasured truth: "He was *with* God in the beginning." Because you really can't be *with* yourself, John implies there were two People, two separate supreme Beings who are equal in power, activity, personality, and intelligence in a face-to-face, eye-to-eye existence. One was not more and One was not less. They were and are equally supreme, sharing the glory and splendor of heaven's throne, because "the Word was *God.*"

What a wondrous mystery! Our God is one God, yet at the same time He is more than one. Throughout the ages people have engaged in an intellectual wrestling match with this astounding truth. But those who do so miss the blessing that comes from simply worshiping an infinite God who is beyond our finite understanding.

He Is Enduringly the Same

As John continued his trumpet flourish, we learn that Jesus, the Living Logos, is enduringly the same today as He always has been: "The same was in the beginning with God" (John 1:2 KJV). There was no personality change in this Person from the beginning of time until John's day to our day to the last day of human history on into eternity.

The One who spoke all things into existence and then transformed planet

Earth from a formless, empty, dark, water-submerged blob dangling in space to a beautiful place that reflected His own image is the same Person who has power today to transform your life and mine.

The One who offered all men salvation from the storm of His judgment if they would come into the ark is the same Person today who offers salvation from His judgment if we would come into Him at the cross.[5]

The One who called Abraham out of Ur of the Chaldees, promising to fully bless him if he would follow Him in a life of faith is the same Person who today calls us out of the world and promises to bless us if we follow Him in a life of faith.[6]

The One who delivered His children from bondage to slavery in Egypt with a titanic display of power is the same Person who was crucified then rose from the dead to deliver His children today from bondage to sin.[7]

The One who halted the entire invasion of Canaan by the Israelites while He extended His grace to one Canaanite prostitute is the same Person today who stops to care for and extend His grace to sinners.[8]

The One who elevated David from a shepherd boy to a shepherd king is the same Person today who places His people in positions of leadership, honor, and authority.[9]

The One who answered Elijah's prayer and sent down the fire to consume the sacrifice on Mount Carmel and then sent down the rain to end the three-year drought in Israel is the same Person today who hears and answers prayer.[10] *Do you know Him?*

If Adam knew Him as a beloved Father,
if Eve knew Him as the original Homemaker,
if Noah knew Him as the Refuge from the storm,
if Abraham knew Him as a Friend,
if Moses knew Him as the Redeemer,
if Rahab knew Him as the gracious Savior,
if David knew Him as his Shepherd,
if Elijah knew Him as the Almighty,
if Daniel knew Him as the Lion Tamer,
if Mary Magdalene knew Him as the Bondage Breaker,
if Martha knew Him as the Promise Keeper,
if Lazarus knew Him as the Resurrection and the Life,
if Bartimaeus knew Him as the Light of the World,

if John knew Him as the glorious King upon the throne,
surely you and I can know Him too!

The living Person whom John heard and saw and touched was the same in ages past as He will be in years to come. There is not one God for the Old Testament, another God for the New Testament, another God for today, and still another God for the future. He is the *same* yesterday, today, and forever.[11] He is enduringly the same! Praise God! You and I *can* know Him!

Around thirty-five years ago, without a crisis experience but with an unexplainable, intense yearning, I made the decision to seek to know God. Personally. Intimately. Accurately. Experientially. I decided that if each of these Bible characters could know Him then I could too.

If God hasn't changed, if He is enduringly the same, then if they knew Him and I didn't, the fault must lie with me. So I began a pilgrimage to know God, and that pilgrimage continues to this day. I don't know Him today as well as I want or should, but I know Him better today than I did all those years ago. I know Him better today than I did one year ago. I am growing in my knowledge of God, and I say without hesitation or qualification that knowing God is my joy and reason for living. He is . . .

the Wind beneath my wings,
the Treasure that I seek,
the Foundation on which I build,
the Song in my heart,
the Object of my desire,
the Breath of my life—
He is my All in all!

Please join with me in this life-changing discovery as, through the gospel of John, God just gives us Jesus. Although we may have many preconceived ideas of who Jesus is, John will show us He is actually bigger than we think and greater than we think.

Jesus Is Greater Than I Think

The One who was with God and was God and is the same today as He was in the beginning is the Creator: "Through him all things were made; without him nothing was made that has been made" (John 1:3).

He Is the Source of Life

It can be mind-boggling to contemplate the vastness of the universe, from the greatest star to the smallest particle.[12] It is so vast that astronomers are now saying that it stretches beyond what we are capable of penetrating, even with sophisticated telescopes like the Hubble. And every bit of it was created by the Living Word of God, who, even as He hung the stars in space, counted them and called them each by name![13]

Not only did He create objects of massive size, but He also created such minute, delicate, intricate things as snowflakes, no two of which are the same. He created:

atoms and angels and ants,
crocodiles and chiggers and clouds,
elephants and eagles and electrons,
orchids and onions and octopuses,
frogs and feathers and sea foam,
diamonds and dust and dinosaurs,
raindrops and sweat drops,
dewdrops and blood drops,
and me! And you!

The greatness of His power to create and design and form and mold and make and build and arrange defies the limits of our imagination. And since He created everything, there is nothing beyond His power to fix or mend or heal or restore.

Years ago, a man was driving his car down the road when the engine coughed and wheezed and sputtered before stalling. Try as he might, the driver could not restart the engine. Finally, he stood glaring at it, and in frustration, kicked the tire. Just then a long, sleek, polished black limousine pulled up beside him. The chauffeur hastily jumped out and opened the back door from which stepped an elegantly dressed gentleman. The gentleman asked the driver what the problem seemed to be. The exasperated man replied that he had no idea; the car had just quit running. The gentleman asked to have a look for himself under the hood of the car. The man scoffed at the idea of such a finely dressed man having any knowledge of the mechanics of a car's engine, but the gentleman persisted in his offer. Since no one else had stopped to help, the driver skeptically accepted the assistance and threw open the hood.

The gentleman leaned over the engine, twisted a few wires, tapped a few cables, and tightened a few plugs. Then he told the driver to try to start the car once again. This time, the engine responded immediately.

As he closed the hood of the car, the driver turned to the gentleman and thanked him profusely. Then he inquired, "By the way, what's your name?"

The gentleman replied simply, "Henry Ford."

Henry Ford had made the car, so he had known exactly what was wrong with it and how to fix it! Jesus Christ is the One by whom, for whom, through whom everything was made. Therefore, He knows what's wrong in your life and how to fix it.

Is your heart broken? Does your life need mending? Who or what do you know that needs "fixing"? Jesus, as the Creator of life, knows how to make it work. Let Him take charge. Give Him the authority to put it right. Having brought everything into existence that exists, He has never become bored with or distracted from or unconcerned about His creation. The living Logos personally hovers over all He has created, giving it His full attention.[14]

He Is the Sustainer of Life

With His unlimited power, the living Logos of God not only created all things but even today He still sustains "all things by his powerful word."[15] Who do you know who says he doesn't need God? Think about it for a moment!

Our planet is ninety-three million miles away from the sun. *If* the sun were any closer to earth, we would burn up. *If* it were any farther away from earth, we would freeze.

Our planet tilts exactly 23 degrees on its axis, giving us four seasons a year. *If* it tilted at any other angle, we would have massive continents of ice.

The moon is the exact distance from earth to give us two ocean tides a day. *If* it were any greater or lesser distance, the earth would be flooded.

The ocean floor is at a depth that gives us oxygen, which sustains human life. *If* the depth were any different, the air we breathe would be poisonous.

The atmosphere is the exact density to keep meteors and space objects from hitting us. *If* it were any thinner, we would be constantly bombarded by objects from outer space.

And *who* keeps all this in perfect order? *Who* keeps Earth from getting sucked into some gigantic black hole, or planets from spinning out of control, or stars from falling from the sky? *Who* keeps people upright on earth while it turns on its axis? The laws of nature? Gravity? And where did gravity come from? *Who* established the laws of nature? *Who* gives people the very breath they breathe?

The answer is none other than the living Logos of almighty God who was in the beginning with God and who was God and who is the same today. He is bigger than we think and greater than we think. Nothing is beyond His ability, whether it's

a problem to solve,
a marriage to reconcile,
a memory to heal,
a guilty conscience to cleanse,
a sin to forgive,
a business to save,
a budget to stretch,
another mouth to feed,
a body to clothe,
a boss to please,
a job to find,
a habit to break,
a captive to free,
a prodigal to return,
an addiction to overcome,
or anything else we could name.

All are within His power to "fix." If the living Logos of God has the power to create and sustain the universe, *how can you think His power is insufficient for you?* He is more than able to sustain your marriage and your ministry, your faith and your finances, your hope and your health.

The smallness of our faith is illustrated by the man who walked into a car dealership and picked out a Silver Cloud Rolls Royce. He paid $250,000 for it and drove it home. He found himself fascinated by the way the car handled. He opened up the hood to look at the gleaming engine, then began to poke around, curious as to the horsepower of such a machine. Search as he did, he could find no indication on the engine or in the owner's manual regarding the horsepower of his car. So he picked up the phone, dialed the car dealership, and inquired about the horsepower of the car he had just purchased. The dealer apologized but said Rolls Royce did not divulge the horsepower of its car engines. For a moment the man was speechless. When he recovered his faculties, he said with astonishment, "You mean I just purchased a car from you for $250,000, yet you will not tell me the horsepower of its engine?" When the dealer affirmed that was correct, the new owner sputtered, "I demand to know the horsepower of this car!" He continued his tirade until finally the dealer agreed to fax the irate customer's inquiry to the Rolls Royce headquarters in London. The fax read, "My customer, who just bought a Silver Cloud Rolls Royce for $250,000, demands to know the horsepower of the engine under the hood of his motorcar." In a short time, the fax machine rang, then began to whir. As a page came slowly through the machine, the logo at the top revealed that it was a reply from the CEO of Rolls Royce. But as the sheet continued to come through the fax, it looked blank. Then a one-word answer appeared: "Adequate."

If you are questioning the sufficiency of God's power to resolve your problems and pressures, your suffering and stress, your crisis and change, His answer is the same. The infinite power of the living Logos of God is adequate for any need you or I will ever have.[16]

We may intellectually grasp the truth that God's power is adequate, but we can never know that by experience if we stay in our comfort zone. If all you ever attempt is what you know you can do yourself, if all your needs seem to be met through someone or something other than God, if you never have any difficulties that are greater than you can bear—how will you know the awesome greatness and personal availability of His infinite power? It's when the Red Sea is before you, the mountains are on one side of you, the desert is on the other side, and you feel the Egyptian army closing in from behind that you experience His power to open up an escape route. Power to do the supernatural, the unthinkable, the impossible.[17]

He Is the Significance of Life

As John progressively leads us to fuller understanding of Jesus as the living Word, He says that in Him is "life," and this "life was the light of men" (John 1:4). In other words, His life is our light—our purpose and meaning and reason for living.

Following creation, Adam and Eve disobeyed God, and as a result, sin entered the human condition. Since that historic and pivotal tragedy,[18] sin has been passed from one generation to another so thoroughly that everyone who has ever been born has been born with sin.[19] And the sin with which we are born makes us incapable of pleasing God or responding to God or communicating with God. In fact, the Bible tells us that when we were born, we were born physically alive but spiritually dead in our sin.[20] And if we continue in the spiritually dead state in which we were born until we die physically, we will go out into eternity separated from God. We will go to hell.[21]

However, the wonderful good news of the gospel was shouted out so clearly by the apostle Paul that it still resounds today: "The wages of sin is death, *but* the gift of God is eternal life in Christ Jesus our Lord."[22] The wages of sin is physical death and spiritual deadness as well. BUT the gift of God is eternal life, spiritual life, abundant life through faith in Jesus Christ, the Living Word of God.

What did you think you had to add to your existence in order to experience real life?

Increasing your investment portfolio?
Traveling to more exotic destinations?
Possessing the latest car or computer?
Achieving public recognition?
Reaching your professional goal?
Wearing the trendiest fashion?
Joining the most coveted club?
Establishing a successful career?
Marrying the perfect spouse?
Raising a model family?

I've been to India twice, and both times I met Westerners who had traveled to meet with various gurus, hoping to find spiritual life in a Hindu homily. I visited with a young man who was convinced he would find real spiritual life when he could accurately articulate the difference between the colors red and black. I sat beside another young man on a plane who was traveling to the Adirondacks to seek life by worshiping the mountains. Where have *you* been looking for spiritual life?

The Westerners in India, the two young men, and you and I could save ourselves a lot of trouble by just seizing the truth John imparted: *Spiritual life is found in the living Word of God!* If you want purpose and meaning and satisfaction and fulfillment and peace and hope and joy and abundant life that lasts forever, *look to Jesus.*

Jesus said, "I am the way, and the truth and the life."[23] His life *is* our light!

Now the verbal trumpet flourish that opened John's eyewitness biography of Jesus Christ reaches a crescendo: "The light shines in the darkness, but the darkness has not understood it" or overcome it (John 1:5). Light is John's symbol for truth and godliness and wisdom. Darkness symbolizes everything that is not light, such as untruth, evil, sin, wrongdoing, injustice, ignorance, and unbelief.

When you and I live lives that reflect Jesus, His light in us reveals the darkness of sin and rebellion and ignorance in the world around us. This may begin to explain why your old friends have rejected you or your coworkers avoid you or your neighbors shun you. If they are living in darkness, the light in you makes them uncomfortable.

Recently, I went to a movie in a large theater. When I walked from the bright sunlight into the viewing room, I was temporarily blinded. I had to grope my way down the aisle. But after a few minutes, my eyes adjusted to the darkness and I could see the rows of seats and other patrons without difficulty. When the movie concluded, I returned to the brilliant sunlit day. The light actually caused me to wince and my eyes to water as I quickly put on sunglasses. After having spent time in the darkness, the light actually hurt my eyes.

Our world lives in spiritual darkness, separated from God. But people have adjusted and, generally speaking, are comfortable in their "twilight zone." They may not be able to "see" God or others or themselves clearly, but they see well enough to get along in life.

When a person who belongs to Jesus Christ lives a life that reflects:

> His integrity and morality and purity,
> His holiness and righteousness and truthfulness,
> His goodness and godliness and grace,

the light of his or her life can cause others to react with spontaneous rejection. The Light reveals the darkness of sin and pride and unbelief and emptiness and meaninglessness. And it "hurts." So the world scurries from the Light or tries to keep it hidden in churches or institutions while "putting it out" in the schools and government and marketplace and even social gatherings. But be encouraged! The Light not only reveals the darkness; it also reigns over it. Light is stronger than darkness—darkness cannot "comprehend" or "overcome" it.

Imagine yourself in a darkened room with no windows and one solid door, sealed shut so that no light penetrates at all. You are surrounded by inky blackness. Then imagine lighting one candle. Just a small one with a tiny flame. While that flame would not give off enough light to illuminate a large room, it would still throw a circle of light around you, enabling you to see your immediate surroundings. And it could be seen from the farthest corners of the room.

Now imagine snuffing out the candle, then taking a paper bag and filling it with the darkness of the room. Open the door and step into a bright room with lamplight and sunshine flooding every nook and cranny. If you opened the bag and let the darkness escape into the lighted room, what would happen? Nothing. Darkness cannot overcome light. Light is stronger and more penetrating than darkness.

The Light cannot be overcome by the darkness, but it can be hidden by us. That's why the Bible says: "You are the light of the world. A city on a hill cannot be hidden. Neither do people light a lamp and put it under a bowl. Instead they put it on its stand, and it gives light to everyone in the house. In the same way, let your light shine before men, that they may see your good deeds and praise your Father in heaven."[24] Your light is the truth of the gospel message itself as well as your witness as to who Jesus is and what He has done for you. Don't hide it!

Are you so intimidated by the majority of darkness that you are hiding your Light under a bowl of fear? Fear of being offensive in a pluralistic society? Fear of failure or rejection? Are you hiding your Light under a bowl of unbelief—doubting that your neighbors and friends and coworkers and family members are going to hell apart from faith in Christ? Do you sincerely doubt that your one little candle flame of testimony, your one little candle flame of a verse of Scripture, will make any real difference in someone else's life?

I live in the southern part of the United States. During the warmer months in particular, if I leave the porch light on at night, all sorts of moths and insects swarm to it. The variety can be fascinating. Everything from large luna moths to beetles to strange green crawly things beat and flutter their way to the light. In fact, I have to be careful when opening an outside door because the little varmints scramble to get inside the house. I have never stood at the door and called these insects to come or set out bait for them. All I have to do is to turn on the light and they come of their own volition—by the hundreds. Moths, in the midst of the darkness, are not attracted to more darkness. They are attracted to the light. They are hungry for the light. They long to be in the light.

People today, living in the midst of "darkness," are not attracted to more darkness; they are attracted to the Light. So let your Light shine! Lift it high! You don't have to have a clever presentation to your witness or learn evangelistic formulas or take a course on communicating to postmodern man. For heaven's sake, *just turn on the Light!*

One night when Robert Louis Stevenson was a small boy, his nanny called him to come to bed. Oblivious to her summons, he was staring at something outside his nursery window. The nanny walked over, stood at his shoulder, and inquired patiently, "Robert, what are you looking at?" The little boy, without taking his eyes away from the window, exclaimed in wonder as he pointed to the lamplighter who was lighting the streetlamps, "Look, Nanny! That man is putting holes in the darkness!"

You and I may not be able to change the world, but surely each of us can put a hole in the darkness! Turn on the Light! Share what Jesus means to you and give God's Word to someone else!

All through the ages, men and women have done just that! They have turned on the Light so that a living faith in God has been passed from generation to generation. Not everyone has been attracted to the Light, but one by one people have come to Him for truth, wisdom, hope, salvation, and eternal life. One outstanding torchbearer who made the transition from turning on the Light by faith to actually introducing Him to others face-to-face was "a man who was sent from God; his name was John. He came as a witness to testify concerning that light, so that through him all men might believe. He himself was not the light; he came only as a witness to the light" (John 1:6–8).

The man referred to is not John the apostle, author of the eyewitness biography of Jesus we know as John's Gospel, but John the Baptist. John the Baptist was the first cousin of Jesus who served as His advance man. He was the last of the fiery Old Testament prophets whose assignment was to prepare God's people to accept and receive God's Messiah.[25] But the light he lifted up, the witness he gave, was so clear and powerful, people thought he was the Light.[26]

John the Baptist overcame the darkness of religious intolerance and public apathy and secular pluralism of his day by boldly proclaiming the truth of God's Word, applying it to the lives of the people around him.[27] And if we want to overcome the darkness of our day, we must do the same.

In a day yet to come, at the very end of human history, when the world reels in the chaos of rebellious blasphemy and profanity and obscenity against God and His people, ordinary men and women will faithfully overcome by lifting up the Light. One last time, in a world of almost total spiritual blackout, they will overcome "him [Satan, the prince of darkness] by the blood of the Lamb and by the word of their testimony."[28]

The world will see friends, neighbors, coworkers, and family members who had been in rebellion against God suddenly changed by the power of the Light!

In the midst of worldwide depression and confusion,
in the midst of worldwide war and hate,
in the midst of worldwide envy and cruelty,
these changed people will have joy!

When confronted with rudeness, they will be patient.
When confronted with meanness, they will be kind.
When confronted with hatefulness, they will be loving.
When confronted with thoughtlessness,
they will be considerate.

And when the evidence of their lives demands a verdict by those who observe them, they will have the thrill of pointing others to the Light of truth in Jesus. Today, in a world where the role models are entertainers, athletes, and politicians, many of whom lack morals, integrity, and even common decency . . . in a world where no one seems to stand for anything unless it is to stand for selfish, self-serving rights . . . in a world where anything is compromised if it impedes success . . . in a world where pleasure takes priority over principles . . . in a world where we care more about public opinion than about what God thinks . . . in a world where there are no absolutes, where what is right is what works or what feels good . . . in a world where character no longer seems to count . . . In such a world, the testimony of *one life* lived for Christ is powerful! *One life* cleansed through faith in the blood of Jesus. *One life* that confesses, "Jesus is Lord."[29] *One life* that has the courage to stand for godly convictions in the midst of moral compromise. *One life* that tells the truth. *One life* that lives the truth. *One life* that lifts high the Light!

You can be that *one life*! John the Baptist was. He was a powerful witness because the Light he lifted up was "the true light that gives light to every man . . . coming into the world" (John 1:9).

Have you ever felt intimidated by other religious beliefs or even a little guilty for sharing your faith, as though you were presumptuous in thinking yours is *the truth*? Do you feel somewhat smug and self-righteous and insensitive to others, accepting that what you believe is good for you and what they believe is good for them? That their religious beliefs are their business and none of yours? That if you are truly loving, you will tolerate the false and compromise the truth so as not to be offensive? Yet a person who really cares about his or her neighbor, a person who genuinely loves others, is a person who bears witness to the truth. John the Baptist was such a person.

The stunning climax of this introductory passage is that Jesus Christ is the true Light that gives light to every man and woman. *The Truth* for *every* man and woman! Think about it for a moment. You may be:

Afghan

American African

Asian Australian

Eskimo Ethiopian

European Indian or Russian or Mexican

Spanish Swedish

South American Saudi Arabian

South African Cuban

Chinese Canadian

Israeli or Pakistani or Iraqi

You may be Hindu or Hare Krishna, Muslim or Mormon, Jewish or Jehovah's Witness, Roman Catholic or Protestant, Buddhist or Baha'i, Baptist or Anglican, or animist or atheist . . . it makes no difference! Jesus Christ is *the* Light for *every* man and woman! There is no other light! Other religions and peoples may have some truth, but only Jesus Christ is *the* truth for everyone who has ever been born into the human race, regardless of culture, age, nationality, generation, heritage, gender, color, or language.

There is not a Light for America and a Light for Africa and a Light for China and a Light for Europe and a Light for India—there is only one Light for the entire world for all time, for every person, and His name is Jesus. That's why John bore witness to the Light. That's why you and I share our faith, present the gospel, and refuse to be intimidated by a multicultural, pluralistic world.

Who do you know who says we can each have our own religion as long as we're sincere? Does that person put a guilt trip on you for what he or she describes as a dogmatic, narrow-minded, intolerant, and exclusive faith? But the gospel wasn't our idea, was it? Jesus Himself declared, "I am the way and the truth and the life. *No one* comes to the Father except through me."[30] We must come to God through Him or we don't come at all. The Bible says emphatically that "salvation is found in *no one* else, for there is *no* other name under heaven given to men by which we must be saved."[31] Just the name Jesus.

And who is Jesus? He is God Himself made visible to all. Praise God! You and I are not condemned to live in the darkness, because He has turned on the Light! Praise God for just giving us Jesus!

A LITTLE BOY was pestering his father, who was desperately trying to get some paperwork done. The father thought he would distract his small son. He handed him a piece of paper and a pencil and told him to draw a picture of a dog. Two minutes later the little boy proudly handed his busy father the picture—a stick figure of a dog. The father, making an extra effort to be patient, gave his little nuisance another piece of paper with the instructions to draw an elephant. Two minutes later, the paper was dutifully handed back with another stick figure drawn on it. The father gave the child one piece of paper after another, telling him to draw a lion, a frog, a dinosaur. Each time, his son handed back the paper within a matter of minutes. Finally the father felt he had a stroke of genius. He knew something that should occupy the boy for hours. He dramatically handed his son what he informed him would be the last piece of paper and told him to draw a picture of God. The father smiled smugly to himself, believing he had outwitted the youngster and would now have some uninterrupted work time. To his astonishment, the little boy began busily drawing and within the usual two minutes was prepared to hand back his paper. The father exclaimed in exasperation, "No one knows what God looks like!" to which the little boy replied with the confidence of youth, "Well, they will now."

The little boy's drawing was, of course, a crude rendition of his own idea. But there was another Father who told His Son to draw a picture of what God looks like, and the Son did. He drew the picture, not with crayons and paper, but with His own flesh and blood. And the picture was drawn so perfectly that it was an exact replica of God's image.[32]

Thank You, dear Son, for drawing the picture so vividly. So accurately. So personally. And thank You, dear Father, for just giving me Jesus!

2

JESUS MAKES GOD VISIBLE . . .

As Man

JOHN 1:10–18

When I was a young girl, almost every Sunday afternoon that my father was home, we would hike to the ridge of the mountain on which we lived. While those afternoon climbs are now just a precious memory, I still enjoy walking with Daddy when I go home. He can't climb as high or walk as swiftly, but the fellowship is just as sweet.

On one of our hikes, Daddy inadvertently stepped on an anthill. When he looked down at his big footprint in the soft dirt, he could see the havoc he had wreaked on the bustling ant colony. Panic had set in as ants scurried in every direction, confused as to what had become of their world. Daddy stooped down to try and reopen the tunnels, scooping away the collapsed soil, but to no avail. His fingers were too big and the ants were so small. In frustration, he mused, if only he could become an ant, even temporarily, he could tell them what was wrong and how to fix it. But he couldn't. There was an impassable barrier between himself and the little creatures because he was a big man and they were tiny insects.

That impassable barrier between my father and those little ants illustrates the impassable barrier between God and mankind. As God looked down from heaven, man scurried around in panic, unable to cope with the confusion and conflict of life—especially when man's whole world seemed to collapse and life dealt unexpected blows. All man's answers to the problems of pain and evil and death were insufficient. Life just didn't make sense. There seemed to be no order or long-term purpose to it all. And so God became a Man, not just to sort out the confusion and rebuild the collapsed world, but also to offer a new life altogether. Jesus came to make God visible *as Man.* And that visibility is irresistibly compelling.

The Visibility Is Compelling

The awesome reality of who Jesus is presents you and me with a compelling and inescapable choice. In fact, every person who has ever been born has the sovereign right to make this same choice—to receive Jesus Christ by faith as God's revelation of Himself or to reject Him.

The Choice to Reject

If we think we can avoid God by pleading indifference toward Him or ignorance of Him, we're mistaken; both choices are indirect rejection. John makes this point when he states, "He was in the world, and though the world was made through him, the world did not recognize him" (John 1:10). It would be easier to imagine Ford Motor Company not recognizing Henry Ford, or Microsoft not recognizing Bill Gates, or the United States of America not recognizing George Washington than to imagine man not recognizing his Creator!

Do you know someone who was made by Jesus Christ and for Jesus Christ, yet who does not know or accept Jesus Christ? Actually, just about everybody you and I know fails to recognize Jesus for who He is. The majority of the world doesn't recognize Him for who He is. The world talks of and teaches evolution as the beginning of all things. The world talks of and teaches about Jesus Christ as a good man or a well-meaning prophet or a revolutionary zealot. But the world does not recognize Jesus Christ for who He really is: *God as Man!*

Rejection because of *ignorance* is one reason Jesus chose and taught and trained twelve men to go into all the world and turn the Light on! He chose twelve to be His disciples in order to carry on His work and spread the truth of His message after His ascension into heaven.

Those twelve men not only gave testimony to what they themselves had heard and seen, but they also preached what Jesus had taught them. They carefully recorded their eyewitness accounts of His life and death and resurrection and ascension in what we know as the Gospels. When others responded to their message of truth about Who Jesus is, they established groups of believers who became known as *Christians.* And these Christians established what became known as the church—a society within society that demonstrates by its words and deeds what society itself would be like under the authority of Jesus Christ. When the disciples couldn't be present in these churches, they wrote letters giving clear understanding of what Jesus meant by His teachings. This written instruction and illumination is preserved for us in the Epistles of the New Testament.

In fact, the entire Bible, the New Testament in particular, was written and preserved to dispel our ignorance of who Jesus is.[1] Very few people today can plead genuine ignorance, especially within America, because God holds us accountable for what we have *opportunity* to know, even if we don't actually know it. With the multitude of Bibles available, especially in modernized countries, and the availability of churches, of Christian television and radio programs, of Bible teaching on cassette tapes and videos, ignorance is just not an excuse for rejecting Jesus.

In his letter to the Romans, the apostle Paul held the entire human race accountable for basic knowledge of God, which he declared "is plain to them, because God has made it plain to them. For since the creation of the world God's invisible qualities—his eternal power and divine nature—have been clearly seen, being understood from what has been made, so that men are without excuse."[2] Even tribal people isolated in jungle huts or desert tents have the fundamental testimony of creation. Through the faithfulness of the sun to rise and set, through the orderly pattern of the stars in the sky, through the miracle of reproduction and birth, through the migratory instincts of animals, and through a myriad of other silent witnesses, the human race has been confronted with the truth.[3] And unless we deliberately repress what we instinctively recognize in the silent witness, we would acknowledge and come to the truth.

The real reason most people reject Jesus, at least in the Western Hemisphere, is not ignorance, but *intolerance*. If John was amazed that the world that Jesus created did not recognize Him, he must have been deeply ashamed that Jesus "came to that which was his own, but his own did not receive him" (John 1:11). Jesus' own people, the Jews, who had the prophets and prophecies and Old Testament Scriptures and religious heritage and symbolic ceremonies and were actually looking for their Messiah, *missed Him*!

The Jews had many preconceived ideas about the Messiah based on their interpretation of Scripture and what they wanted. When Jesus of Nazareth came on the scene with His public ministry, He was neither the Messiah they had been expecting, nor the Messiah they wanted. The Jews wanted someone who would:

raise their standard of living,
give them something for nothing,

rain down riches without work,
grant them privileges without responsibility,
and restore them to the world power they had known under King David and King Solomon. They wanted someone who would meet their physical and material and emotional needs.[4]

They expected a glorious, victorious King who would rid them of the Romans and establish them in national peace and prosperity and prominence. But the first time He came, He came to establish the kingdom of God, not in the world, but in the hearts of men.[5] He was born to die.[6] And so He was rejected.

Years ago, I received a smallpox vaccination before taking a trip overseas. The doctor used a needle to scratch smallpox germs into my skin—not enough to give me a case of smallpox, but enough to cause my body to react and build up an immunity against it. In other words, I had just enough of the disease to keep me from catching a case of the real thing. The Jews seemed to have had just enough religion to keep them from catching real faith. They had an immunity to Jesus.

Today, some of the hardest groups of people to reach are not the Jews but those who have gone to church all their lives, are familiar with the gospel story, converse using spiritual clichés, and sing the traditional hymns of faith from memory, yet have never truly placed their faith in Jesus Christ. They seem to have just enough religion to inoculate them against a personal relationship with God through faith in Jesus Christ.

Many people come to Jesus assuming that because He is able He will answer all their prayers and heal all their diseases and solve all their problems. They come to Him for what they want Him to do for them. When what they want is not His will and He doesn't come through, they reject Him. He's just not what they want.

Have you had the misguided perception that Jesus is some kind of divine genie in a bottle who, if you rub the bottle with the right kind of prayer or the right kind of faith or the right kind of good works, will pop up and grant you your requests? And when you try and try, and rub and rub, and pray and pray, and don't receive what you ask, have you become disillusioned and disappointed to the extent that you have rejected Him too?

When my husband and I were newly married, we lived in a small university town. Every Sunday night we opened our home to the athletes for dessert and Bible study. One of the young men who attended was a strapping six-foot-five, three-hundred-pound starting tackle for the football team. One particular Sunday evening this young athlete bitterly complained after losing the previous night to a fierce rival. They had lost because the team had been unable to convert on fourth down and get the ball across the goal line, just one yard away. They failed to score the goal that would have won the game. His comment as he left our home that evening was that God had let him down on the one-yard line. He never came back to our Bible study. God just wasn't what he wanted. And that was his choice. But there were many young athletes who did want God on *His* terms. They received Jesus Christ by faith and went on to grow into outstanding Christian leaders.

The Choice to Receive

Whether it's to young people or couples or families, my husband and I love to open our home. We treasure our friendships and thoroughly enjoy relaxing around the table over a meal, talking for hours until our stomachs are full, our bodies are stiff, and our conversation winds down. However, during the day, my schedule is so packed that although I love my friends, I resist interruptions. Because of the pressure of time, without meaning to be rude, I come quickly to the point on the phone and must seem almost inhospitable to anyone who shows up unexpectedly at my door. In fact, when someone does ring the doorbell, I often go to the door, stand inside the house with the screen door still fastened, and talk to the person on the other side. If it is a friend, we can laugh or cry or share common experiences in raising a family or discuss the weather or neighborhood news; she may look longingly over my shoulder at the comfortable seating in the living room; she can sniff the coffee brewing in the kitchen, but even though I enjoy her company, I just stand there. I don't invite her in because I know if I do, our visit will involve much more time than I can afford to give. After a little bit, I know she will leave, and I will get back to my work. Even though I love talking with my friend, I don't open the screen door and invite her to step over the threshold and into my house.

Many people seem to have a "screen door" relationship with Jesus. They talk to Him in prayer, and He talks to them through His Word; they can enjoy His presence, but they never invite Him to come into their lives as Savior and Lord. He's on the outside, looking in.[7] So John gave you and me motivation to open the door and invite Him to come in: "Yet to all who received him, to those who believed in his name, he gave the right to become children of God" (John 1:12).

I have heard popular preachers and politicians say that we are all children of God. Although God is the Creator of us all, nowhere does the Bible say we are all

His children. On the contrary, John gave two conditions you and I must meet before we can be called God's children. One is that we must receive Jesus, or open the screen door of our hearts and invite Him to come in. The other is that we must believe in His Name.

Names in Scripture almost always had special meaning and denoted character. For instance, God changed Isaac's son's name from "Jacob," which means manipulator, schemer, supplanter—aptly describing who he was—to "Israel," which means one who has power with God. When Jesus called Andrew's brother to be a disciple, his name was Simon, which means impulsive, compulsive, unstable—again an accurate description of his character. But Jesus changed his name to Peter, which means a rock, steadfast and sure. And both Jacob and Simon, as they matured in their relationship with God, were transformed until their characters matched their new names of Israel and Peter.

One of the two qualifications John gave for membership in God's family is to believe in Jesus' name. Believing in His name means we must be willing to commit our lives to all that He is as represented by His name. And His name is *Lord Jesus Christ.*

Lord is the Greek equivalent of Yahweh, or Jehovah, the God of Abraham, Isaac, and Jacob.[8] Jehovah created everything, then called out of the masses of the world a people

to know Him,
to love Him,
to obey Him,
to serve Him,
to reveal Him

in a unique way to the rest of the world. It means He is Master, Boss, Teacher, our number one Priority. *Jesus* means Savior, revealing His God-ordained mission to present Himself as the Lamb, without spot or blemish, who would make atonement for the sin of the world through the sacrifice of Himself on the altar of the cross.[9] He became our great substitute and bore the full punishment for our sins, satisfying God's justice. He "saved" us from our sin. *Christ* is the Greek equivalent of the Hebrew word for Messiah.[10] It sums up His fulfillment of the Old Testament prophecies that pointed to God's long-awaited Anointed One, who would reign on earth in righteousness and peace.

John's qualification for being a child of God by believing on His name means much more than just head knowledge. It is not just giving intellectual assent to the fact that the name Lord Jesus Christ is the label attached to the person. It means to rest in Jesus, to put all of our trust on Him alone for forgiveness and salvation. John is challenging you and me to believe in the character of Jesus, which is revealed by His name. And what does His name reveal?

It reveals that Jesus of Nazareth is the Creator God, Master of our lives—He is *Lord.* It reveals that He is the only means of our salvation from sin and judgment—He is *Jesus.* It reveals that He is God's Anointed One who will one day reign on this earth—He is *Christ.*

If you and I receive Him, if we open the screen door of our hearts and invite Him to come into the center of our lives, if you and I believe on His name—that He is the Lord, Jesus, Christ—we are promised "the right to become children of God" (John 1:12). Do you meet the qualifications? When have you opened the door of your heart and invited the Lord Jesus Christ to come into the center of your life? When have you claimed Him as your God, your Savior, your Ruler and King?

At the moment you meet the qualifications, you are "born not of natural descent, nor of human decision or a husband's will, but born of God" (John 1:13). If someone *could* be born into God's family by natural descent, maybe it would be me. I had committed Christian maternal and paternal grandparents, committed Christian parents, committed Christian in-laws, a committed Christian husband, and committed Christian children. But entrance into the family of God is not "of natural descent." Entrance into God's family is not something we can inherit. It is not automatic. God has no grandchildren.

My husband has commented that being born in a garage does not make you a car. My being born into a Christian family and living surrounded by a Christian family does not make me a Christian. Just as your being raised in a Christian home or raised in the church does not make you a Christian.

Becoming a child of God is "not of natural descent;" neither is it "of human decision." While becoming a child of God *does* involve our personal decision, it does not rest in that decision alone.

Just because you decide to go to church every Sunday . . . just because you decide to do more good works than bad works . . . just because you decide to adhere to the basic doctrine of the Apostles' Creed . . . just because you decide not to be a Muslim or a Jew or a Buddhist or a Hindu . . . *does not make you a child of God.*

You can decide:
to turn over a new leaf,
to join a Bible study,
to try harder to be good,
to pray every day,
to join a church,
to call yourself a Christian,
to tell others about Jesus,
to buy that recommended book to see how the Christian life is meant to be lived. But that does not make you a child of God. *It is not of human decision.*

Nor do you become a child of God as the result of your "husband's will" or of someone else's decision for you. Someone cannot knock on your door, take you through a gospel formula, then announce that you have become a child of God. You cannot walk the aisle of a church or a revival meeting, sign a card, and be declared a child of God. I cannot say a prayer over you, then declare you a child of God. A pastor or priest cannot baptize you as an infant or an adult, then pronounce you a child of God. Becoming a child of God is not by human will. It cannot be forced on you by anyone else.

When you receive Jesus into your life and believe on His name, at that moment someone may be praying with you or sharing the gospel with you, but that person cannot do it for you. It is a personal, individual transaction that you make yourself with God by faith as you meet His conditions. Only then can you be "born of God" into His family, forever.

When Mary was engaged to be married, she was told by the angel Gabriel that she would be with child and give birth to a son. She asked how that could be possible since she was a virgin. And Gabriel said, "The Holy Spirit will come upon you, and the power of the Most High will overshadow you. So the holy one to be born will be called the Son of God." Then Mary submitted to God's Word through Gabriel, responding, "I am the Lord's servant. May it be to me as you have said."[11] And she conceived within her body the physical life of the Lord Jesus Christ.

When you and I submit to the Word of God by faith, receiving the Lord Jesus Christ into our hearts, believing in all that His name reveals, we spiritually conceive His life within our own bodies. Just as the life of the Lord Jesus Christ was born within Mary physically when she placed her faith in God's Word, so the life of the Lord Jesus Christ is born within you spiritually when you place your faith in His Word. But you don't give birth to a child; *you* become the child of God. It's a miracle. "For nothing is impossible with God."[12]

Are you a child of God? Are you unsure? If I had invited my friend to come into my home and have a cup of coffee with me, I would know that I had opened the screen door and she had stepped over the threshold to come into my home. There would be no doubt in my mind that she was no longer on the porch but was indeed inside the house. If you invite the Lord Jesus Christ into your life, there should be no doubt whatsoever that He has come in.

If you doubt that you are a child of God, there could be several reasons. Unconfessed sin in your life will cause you to doubt. Disobedience to His Word will cause you to doubt. Resisting His will for your life will cause you to doubt. Ignoring Him by neglecting prayer and Bible reading will cause you to doubt. But the biggest reason of all is that *you may not be* a child of God. So if you are plagued by doubt right now, I suggest you slip down on your knees and pray a simple prayer something like this:

> *Dear God,*
>
> *I want to be sure I am Your child. I bow before You stripped of everything—family heritage, religious affiliation, personal decisions, other people's opinions or desires, public reputation and private goals—everything except my need to be sure I am Your child.*
>
> *I open the screen door of my heart and invite the Lord Jesus Christ to come into the center of my life. I am willing to repent, to turn away from all my sin, and to trust in Jesus alone as the sacrifice substituted on the cross for me. By faith, I believe He makes You visible to me, and I claim Him as my* Lord*—my Master and Teacher; my* Jesus*—my Savior from sin and judgment; my* Christ*—my Ruler and King.*
>
> *Amen.*

Are you at this moment even more unsure and discouraged because you have prayed a similar prayer on other occasions but continue to doubt your membership in God's family? If so, perhaps you have never prayed by *faith*. Faith says, "God, You have said, 'To all who receive Him, to those who believe in His Name, He gives the right to become children of God.' I have opened my heart, invited Jesus to come live within me, and I believe by faith based on Your Word that I have received Him. I believe He is the Lord Jesus Christ, with all that is implied by His name. Therefore, based on Your own Word, by faith I am claiming my rights. And right now, by faith, I want to thank You that I am Your child."

At the moment you thank Him by faith, taking Him at His Word, you may still lack assurance. Mary may have lacked assurance as the angel departed after his stunning announcement that she would conceive the Son of God, but she became more sure as the days and weeks went by because the Child within her began to grow and she could see and feel that life. Although you may lack assurance at this moment, as you read your Bible, pray, get into fellowship with other Christians, and yield your life to God's will, His life within you will begin to grow and you, too, will see and feel the difference. Don't settle for less than being absolutely sure that you are a child of God. It's your right!

Your choice to either receive or reject the Lord Jesus Christ will determine where you spend eternity. You can:

resist the choice,
ignore the choice,
put off making the choice,
deny you have the choice,
assume you have made the choice,
close this book and forget about the choice,
ridicule the choice,
but *you are compelled to make a choice!*

All of the above attitudes are actually indirect choices to reject. There is no middle ground. You do not have the option of sidestepping the issue. The consequence of rejecting Him is that He will reject you and you will be separated from Him now and forever. Won't you make sure, right now, without another moment passing, that you have truly received Him by faith and are a genuine child of God?

The choice is compelling because Jesus makes God visible as Man. He is the God-Man, God walking the earth in a human body, God robed in homespun, God come down!

The Visibility Is Clear

Jesus stands at the center of human history like a colossus, with everything dated before Him and after Him. He is the very incarnation of the glory and grace of God.

The Glory of God

The glory of God is not only His character, but also His unique radiance. In the Old Testament, when God was present on Mount Sinai, the mountain glowed with His glory as though it were on fire.[13] When Moses went up on the mountain to meet with God, his face shone so intensely with the reflection of God's glory, he wore a veil to keep people from seeing when it faded.[14] When the priest went into the tabernacle to sprinkle the blood on the altar to make atonement for the sin of the people, the tabernacle was filled with a golden cloud of God's glory that gave evidence of God's presence.[15] When the Israelites wandered in the wilderness for forty years, the glory of God led them during the day as a pillar of cloud and at night as a pillar of fire.[16]

Today countless people look for a god within themselves or in crystals or in trees or in a former life or in some statue or in a religious experience or in the stars. But John declares the awesome truth that the glory of God is not confined in any of those things, just as it is no longer confined on a mountain or in a tabernacle or as a cloud or fire or as a reflection on a face. Instead "the Word became flesh and lived for a while among us. We have seen his glory, the glory of the one and only Son who came from the Father, full of grace and truth" (John 1:14).

John is saying emphatically, "I have seen Him!

"I've seen Him first thing in the morning when He awoke.[17]

"I've seen Him when He was tired and had nowhere to lay His head.[18]

"I've seen Him when He was alone.[19]

"I've seen Him when He was surrounded by a crowd of people.[20]

"I've seen Him when He was so sad He wept.[21]

"I've seen Him when He was feasting and full.[22]

"I've seen Him when He was fasting and hungry.[23]

"I've seen Him when He preached His heart out and the people turned away.[24]

"I've seen Him tenderly touch the eyes of a man born blind and create sight.[25]

"I've seen Him when He was angry.[26]

"I've seen Him when He was rejected as a son of Satan.[27]

"I've seen Him praised as One who came in the name of the Lord.[28]

"I've seen Him dressed in a robe more dazzling than the sun.[29]

"I've seen Him in a loincloth as He washed my feet.[30]

"I've seen Him confound the greatest religious leaders of His day.[31]

"I've seen Him cuddle a little child on His lap.[32]

"I've seen Him when His face was slapped.[33]

"I've seen Him when His feet were wet from Mary's tears and dried with her hair.[34]

"I've seen Him riding a donkey in triumph into Jerusalem.[35]

"I've seen Him when He prayed so earnestly He sweat great drops of blood.[36]

"I've seen Him tortured, carrying His own cross out of Jerusalem.[37]

"I've seen Him dead,[38]

"I've seen Him buried,[39]

"I've seen Him risen,[40]

"I've seen Him ascended.[41]

"I'VE SEEN HIM! *I've seen the glory of God clearly in Jesus Christ!* And in every situation I have seen Him full of grace and full of truth!

"Not once did He lie to get out of a tight spot or flatter to get into a better spot.

"Not once did He complain about His physical deprivation or brag about His superior position.

"Not once did He try to hurt those who had hurt Him or ignore those who had ignored Him.

"What I have seen is not just the clear visibility of God's glory but the clear visibility of God's grace!"

One recent translation puts it in the modern vernacular: "[He] moved into the neigborhood. We saw the glory with our own eyes, the one-of-a-kind glory, like Father, like Son."[42]

The Grace of God

As children of God, we are the primary recipients of His blessing. Regardless of our past failures or present shortcomings, our relationship with Jesus Christ ensures that "from the fullness of his grace we have all received one blessing after another" (John 1:16).

When the Mediterranean Sea evaporates or runs low, the Atlantic Ocean rushes in at the Strait of Gibraltar to replenish it and keep it full. When you and I are related to Jesus Christ, our strength and wisdom and peace and joy and love and hope may run out, but His life rushes in to keep us filled to the brim—not because of anything we have or have not done, but just because of Him we are showered with blessings.

In my earlier book, *God's Story,* I related an incident in my life that made these blessings even more precious to me.

> It was the first day my children were out of school for the summer, and I took all three of them to celebrate at a special downtown restaurant in our city. Two hours later, in the middle of the day, we returned home to find the front door broken down and everything of value gone! I will never forget the sick feeling of walking through my house and seeing the empty places where antique furniture had been, the space where my grandmother's clock had been, the blank wall where the mirror had hung, the drawers of my silver chest partially open to reveal their emptiness. Cameras, jewelry, silverware, and even the little silver baby cups and spoons my children had used as infants that had been displayed on a cabinet—gone!
>
> The police who came and dusted the house for fingerprints said there was nothing that could, or would, prevent thieves from entering when they set their minds to it. Apparently they had "staked out" our house for some time, and once the thieves had decided to rob our home, it was just a question of when.
>
> That night I crawled into my bed—the same bed that the thieves had so neatly turned back so they could take the pillowcases off the pillows to use as sacks in which they carted off my things! As I lay there in the darkness, thinking of what the police had said, I felt myself growing icy cold with the realization that there was nothing I had that could not be taken from me.
>
> My health could be robbed by illness.
> My education could be outdated by more advanced knowledge.
> My house could burn to the ground.
> My children could leave home.
> My husband could drop dead from a heart attack.
> My youth could be robbed by old age.
> My reputation could be robbed by gossip . . .
>
> I could not think of one thing I had that was permanently secure! And then it was as though the light came on in my mind's eye. I knew I had "an inheritance that can never perish, spoil or fade—kept in heaven"[43] for me. I had the blessings of God that could never be robbed from me! As I lay in bed, surrounded by a home

that had been violated, I began to count my blessings. I fell asleep counting my blessings, and when I awoke in the morning they were still on my mind. And my joy was back!

As I drifted off to sleep, I had thought of so many permanent blessings of God in my life that I listed them the next morning on paper in alphabetical order to remember and meditate on them. The list itself has become a blessing! Because I am:

Accepted by God,
Beloved by God,
Chosen by God,
Delivered by God,
Enlightened by God,
Forgiven by God.

I have:

Grace of God
Hope for the future
Inheritance in heaven
Justification
Knowledge of God
Love
Mercy of God
Nearness to God
Oneness with God
Peace
Quickening of the Spirit

I am:

Redeemed
Sealed with the Holy Spirit
Treasured by God
United with other believers
Validated as an authentic child of God

I have:

His Wisdom

And one day I will be **Exalted** with Him to live in heavenly places! Praise God from whom all blessings flow! If He doesn't bless you and me we won't be blessed, because all real, permanent blessing comes from Him![44]

That's the fullness of His grace! We don't deserve it. We can't earn it. We can't bargain for it. We can't buy it. We just open our hearts and hands to receive it. One blessing after another blessing after another blessing. For a lifetime! Forever!

The Christian life is motivated, not by a list of do's and don'ts, but by the gracious outpouring of God's love and blessing. We want to live our lives to please God because before Jesus "the law was given through Moses" (John 1:17a). Think of the law as summed up in the Ten Commandments.

The law didn't make us feel better. It made us feel worse.

The law didn't help us to be good. It revealed how bad we were.

The law didn't give us joy or peace. It made us feel guilty.

The law didn't help us measure up. It showed us we fall short.

The apostle Paul said the law was like our schoolmaster, teaching us how much we need a Savior.[45] But "grace and truth came through Jesus Christ" (John 1:17b) because He perfectly fulfills the law. His life measures up to the standard established by the law, and when we receive Him by faith, His righteousness is credited to us. Therefore *in Christ* we, too, fulfill the law. The law reveals the truth: We need righteousness. The grace of God bestows it through the person of Jesus Christ.

Praise God! What a plan! What grace that brought it down to you and me! What marvelous grace that is greater than all our sin and guilt and shortcomings and mistakes and failures!

The blessings that we access by grace are awesome. But they pale into insignificance when compared to the thrilling revelation of God we see in Jesus. All through the ages people have longed to actually see God. They have drawn pictures

and carved images

and written books

and composed music

and painted masterpieces

and constructed temples,

all for the purpose of unveiling the mystery of what He is like. But we are no longer left to our imaginations, wondering in educated ignorance. We can know for sure. Although "no one has ever seen God, . . . God the One and only [Son], who is at the Father's side, has made him known" (John 1:18).

What a thrilling, firsthand, life-changing, mind-blowing, awe-inspiring testimony! God did not have to reveal Himself to us, but He did. He chose to make

Himself visible in a way we could understand—as Man. This visibility is not only compelling and clear; it is glorious! So . . . just give me Jesus!

AS A MOTHER tucked her small son into bed one night, he began to whimper and cry. Taking his quivering body into her arms, she gently inquired what was wrong. Between sniffles, he explained that he missed his daddy. Knowing that the boy's father, who was away on a business trip, would not be back for several days, the mother hugged the little boy, then laid him back down on his pillow, telling him to wait for just a moment. She then slipped out of the room, and when she returned she held a picture of the little boy's father in her hand. She placed it beside him in the bed and told him that when he was especially lonely for his daddy, he could just look at the picture and be assured his father loved him and was coming back soon.

The little boy gazed at the smiling face of his father staring out at him from the framed photograph. Then the tears began slipping down his cheeks once again as he said simply, "I wish Daddy would just step out of the picture."

Our Father *has* stepped out of the picture, and His name is Jesus!

JESUS MAKES CHANGE POSSIBLE

No means of measure can define His limitless love . . .
No far-seeing telescope can bring into visibility the coastline
of His shoreless supply . . .
No barrier can hinder Him from pouring out His blessings . . .

He forgives and He forgets.
He creates and He cleanses.
He restores and He rebuilds.
He heals and He helps.
He reconciles and He redeems.
He comforts and He carries.
He lifts and He loves.

He is the God of the second chance,
the fat chance,
the slim chance,
the no chance . . .

Just give me Jesus! He makes change possible!

3

JESUS MAKES CHANGE POSSIBLE . . .
When Love Runs Out

JOHN 2:1–11

I was seventeen years old and had just graduated from high school the night I met Danny Lotz. My date for the evening meeting of a Fellowship of Christian Athletes summer conference introduced us. Danny was six feet seven inches of tanned muscles, broad shoulders, ramrod-straight back, and the friendliest, warmest eyes I had ever looked into. Two nights later he invited me to accompany him to the last meeting of the FCA conference, an opportunity I readily accepted, in part because my father had helped to arrange the date. Besides, I wanted to go out with Danny.

My friend who had introduced us had told me about Danny's athletic career. He had been a basketball star on the University of North Carolina team that had gone undefeated for thirty-two games, ending the year of 1957 with a triple-overtime victory over Kansas to win the NCAA championship. When he graduated, he was given a unique scholarship to play football his first year at the UNC dental school. After graduating from dental school, he entered the air force, where he quickly made its all-service basketball team and was invited to try out for the Olympics.

Needless to say, I was impressed and somewhat curious. Because my father had helped arrange the date and because Danny was eleven years my senior, I did not take that first date too seriously. That meant we both relaxed, talked freely, discovered common appreciation for the same kinds of books and music, and just thoroughly enjoyed the evening. In fact, although at seventeen my experience was very limited, it was the best time I had ever had with a guy.

One of the first things that became evident to me was Danny's love for the

Lord Jesus Christ. He had been raised in a strong Christian home by a father who was a preacher in New York City and pastor of a small church in the shadow of Yankee Stadium. Danny had received Jesus Christ as a young boy in Daily Vacation Bible School at his dad's church and had taken a strong, uncompromising stand for his faith since then. He was a man's man and a young girl's dream, and it wasn't long before I fell in love. Fifteen months later, we were married in the same mountain chapel where my parents had married twenty-three years earlier.

After our honeymoon we moved into a small house, and at eighteen years of age, when my friends were well into their college studies and planning their careers, I was grocery shopping, cooking, mopping, and decorating, as well as working part-time. And it was wonderful!

Ten years later, we had moved to a city where Danny practiced dentistry full-time. By then, we had three small children, I did volunteer work in the community, and I had established and taught a weekly Bible class that was attended by five hundred women.

Without my noticing it, the busyness had overtaken me, and I awoke one morning to the realization that I was in a marriage where the love had run out! I will never forget that panicked, trapped feeling as I knelt in prayer with tears streaming down my face, desperately pleading with the Lord for help. I knew there was no way out. When I had pledged my vows to Danny at the marriage altar before God and the assembled witnesses, I knew they were irrevocable. Was I condemned to live the rest of my life in a shell of a marriage relationship, keeping up a superficial front for our children, friends, family, and the general public, while my heart felt lifeless? Would I ever get used to the heaviness and pain? How could I endure? How could I live a life of hypocrisy? What would happen if I was ever found out?

God, in His infinite mercy and love, allowed me to struggle for almost a year. During that time, it was not Danny's shortcomings God revealed to me, but my own.

Do you also feel trapped in a marriage where the love has run out? Have you panicked, looking for escape in an illicit relationship or afternoon fantasies or romance novels or alcohol or divorce? Or have you resigned yourself to your fate, plunging into a demanding career or the lives of your children or church activities or community volunteerism in a desperate effort to manage the pain?

Praise God! There is hope for you just as there was hope for me. My marriage today bears testimony to the truth that Jesus makes change possible, even when the love runs out. The first step in starting over is to invite Jesus into your marriage.

JESUS WAS INVITED TO COME INTO THE MARRIAGE

John has given us glorious eyewitness testimony of the identity of Jesus Christ. Yet that identity was limited by Jesus' humanity, which was like a house of curtains, veiling His deity. However, when He performed miracles or taught the truth, it was as though the curtains parted and the glory streamed through.

What a simple yet profound blessing it is to know that the first time the "curtains" parted and Jesus' glory was revealed was in a home as He celebrated a wedding and participated in a marriage! At the very start of His public ministry,

the One who makes God visible *to* man and visible *as* Man,
the One who was with God at Creation and who was the God of Creation,
the One by whom and for whom and through whom everything was created,
the One who hung the stars in space and sustains the universe today,
the One who formed man and breathed His own life into him,
the One who is the very incarnation of the glory of God and the grace of God . . .
the Creator,
the living Word,
the long-awaited Messiah,
the Jehovah God of the Old Testament,
the Redeemer of Israel,
the Savior of the world,
the Son of God,
the Son of Man,

was invited to a wedding. "On the third day a wedding took place at Cana in Galilee. Jesus' mother was there, and Jesus and his disciples had also been invited to the wedding" (John 2:1–2). And He accepted the invitation!

Have you invited Jesus to come into your home? To be a part of the wedding you are planning? To participate in your marriage? Marriage was His idea. He gave the basic ground rules for it.[1] He knows how it works best. And He longs to be invited to come into yours.

Danny and I invited Jesus to come to our wedding from the first moment we were engaged. In fact, inscribed inside each of our wedding bands is a triangle that signifies there are three of us in this relationship. God is at the apex, Danny and I at the lower corners. Our commitment was that as we grew closer to God individually, we would also draw closer to each other. If you need a miracle in your marriage, start by inviting Jesus into the relationship. You will be blessed, not only by your increased awareness of His Presence, but also by the knowledge that He is there when unexpected problems and crises arise.

Jesus Was Informed of the Crisis

During the first century, when Israel was under Roman occupation, perhaps similar to the situation in France during German occupation, there was little cause for celebration. A wedding created an exception in that oppressive atmosphere. After the evening wedding ceremony, guests would escort the bridegroom and his bride under a portable canopy to their new home, with torches illuminating the way. As the procession wound through the village streets along the most indirect route, friends, neighbors, and passersby would shower the newly married couple with blessings and congratulatory best wishes. When they finally arrived at home, instead of going off on a honeymoon, they would hold an open house for several days of joyful festivities. The bride and bridegroom would entertain lavishly and be treated like a king and queen, their word would be law, and they would be honored at a series of parties, dinners, and feasts.[2]

It was to such a time of celebration in Cana of Galilee that Jesus, His disciples, and His mother were invited. And it was during such a festive occasion that a crisis occurred: "The wine was gone" (John 2:3).

The Shortage

Apparently the young newlyweds were of modest means, perhaps even poor. They obviously had made minimum provision for their guests, hoping for the best. Or possibly more people attended the wedding feast than they had counted on. Whatever the case, the bridegroom was responsible for the food and wine for his guests, however many there were and however long they stayed. And the wine had run out before the wedding festivities had ended!

Having planned and put on two weddings as the mother of the bride, I know the calculated guesswork of determining numbers with the caterer for a reception. Toward the last, I almost closed my eyes, held my breath, and prayed for the best! At one of the receptions a few of the food choices ran out, but overall I escaped any major embarrassment. So the predicament of the young couple seems understandable but not catastrophic. Yet in this case, running out of wine was more than simply running out of a food choice. In that culture and time, to run out of wine was considered the height of rudeness. It would cause the newlyweds such humiliation that they would never be able to lift their heads in public again. It could conceivably open up the bridegroom to a lawsuit by the bride's family. And at the very least, it would ensure a tension-filled, rocky start to their relationship, as the bridegroom would lose respect in the eyes of his bride. This was a marriage in trouble almost from the moment it began.

How long has your marriage been in trouble? Evaluating it, what have you run out of that has precipitated a crisis? And looking back, can you see that the shortage was present almost from day one? Is it a shortage:

of patience?

of understanding?

of kindness?

of thoughtfulness?

of respect?

of time?

Is it a shortage of something practical, like money or physical space or mutual friends?

As a result, has the "wine"—that spirited, sparkling, full-bodied liquid that symbolizes passionate, affectionate, lively love—run out of your marriage? The loss of love can be a quiet, gradual sort of crisis, similar to the way the wine ran out at the wedding in Cana.

At the young couple's wedding feast, I doubt there was any major catastrophe, like the waiter dropping a dozen bottles of wine in the kitchen. I expect the wine ran out one glass at a time until it was gone.

How, I wonder, was the shortage discovered? Did one of the waiters search the kitchen in vain for another jug from which to refill his pitcher, only to find them all empty? Did he slip purposefully back into the banquet hall, urgently whispering the news into the ears of his fellow servants? Did the servants stiffen with shock, turn white with dread, then redden as their faces flushed in humiliation at the soon-to-be obvious lack of wine? How would they handle the angry guests who would demand that they be served more wine when there was none? Were their eyes fearfully riveted on the guests as cups were raised, toasts were made, and sips were taken?

The Solution

Unknown to the servants, Mary, the mother of Jesus, had already learned of the embarrassing shortage. How did she become aware of the crisis when only the servants knew? Was it possible that this marriage feast was for one of her other children?[3] Is that why Jesus and all His disciples had been invited? Was it also why she got involved, taking the initiative to find a solution?

If Mary was involved because this was her family's crisis, it makes the way she responded even more remarkable. When she learned of the crisis, she didn't wring her hands or try to fix it herself. She didn't hyperventilate in panic or run to the neighbors, begging for their extra wine. She didn't apply for a government loan or even run to the local relief agency. Instead she immediately went to Jesus and told Him what was wrong.

Has the "wine" run out, not in your marriage, but in the marriage of one of your children? Is there a crisis in the marriage of someone you love? And has the problem been there almost since the couple shared their wedding vows? What a precious responsibility and privilege it is to go to the Lord on behalf of the marriage of a loved one. It doesn't matter what the problem is or how long it has been there; He can fix it. And from experience, I know He listens attentively to the prayers of a mother; He has listened to my mother's prayers for me, just as He listened to Mary's prayer for this young couple.

Perhaps your unexpected crisis is not in a marriage, but in a home. Is it a small crisis like your boss coming for dinner?

or a personality conflict with a coworker?

or a limited budget for Christmas?

Is it a large one like a rebellious teenager?

or a job layoff?

or a diagnosis of serious illness?

or elderly parents who need full-time care?

I wonder if Mary had been accustomed for years to turning to Jesus for help with a problem, whether it was:

a small, domestic one,
a painful, private one,
a public, obvious one,
or a practical, spiritual, or emotional one.

Since nothing is said of Joseph in Scripture after he took the twelve-year-old Jesus to the temple, we assume Joseph died when Jesus was a young teenager. His death would have left Jesus, as the eldest son in the family, with adult responsibility for His mother and half brothers and half sisters. He would have understood firsthand the needs of a family.[4]

And so Mary, knowing from years of experience her son's compassionate nature, informed Jesus, "They have no more wine" (John 2:3). The crisis was stated simply. There were no exhaustive details of how much wine had been consumed, no lengthy explanation of how the needs had been miscalculated, no financial estimate as to how much money would be needed to purchase additional wine, not even one small suggestion as to how He might fix the problem. Just, "They have no more wine."

When you pray for your marriage or the marriage of a child or loved one, how do you pray? Do you feel compelled not just to go into detail but also to tell God how to fix what's wrong? Do you think you have to use your holy imagination to come up with a plan so you can pray specifically? Perhaps you have that unconscious attitude that "God helps those who help themselves." If so, do you frantically try to add sparkle to your marriage with movies or trips or parties or money or clothes or music? Yet try as creatively as you might, pray as imaginatively as you can, have you found that you just can't re-create the "wine"? It's gone.

Could you do what Mary did? She clearly and simply stated the problem: "They have no more wine." Perhaps in your case your prayer would be simply: "The love has run out," or, "There's no zest or joy or real life in the family anymore."

Jesus responded tenderly to Mary: "Dear woman, why do you involve me? . . . My time has not yet come" (John 2:4). Although kind and respectful, His response also sounds a little aloof, almost indifferent and uncaring. And it gives the impression that He doesn't intend to do anything about the problem.

If you have prayed for your marriage or that of a child or friend, has Jesus' answer seemed confusing? Do you feel that nothing will ever change? Has He appeared indifferent or unwilling to get involved? Sometimes His answer addresses not just the specific need we have brought to His attention but also something deeper.

In Mary's case, Jesus was not just her son but God's Son as well. And as God's Son, He knew what was in her heart. Apparently, she wanted to solve the problem for the young couple, to save their marriage, but she also had a hidden agenda, and it was the hidden agenda that He addressed. Let's listen closely as we read between the lines of their conversation:

"Son, I know who You are. I conceived You when I was a virgin. And I've watched You for thirty years. I've heard Your wisdom, I've witnessed Your patience, I've experienced Your love, I've seen Your joy, I've benefited from Your strength. In the last six weeks, I've heard the town talk about Your baptism by Your cousin John and how he identified You as the Lamb of God who would take away the sin of the world.[5] And there are many witnesses to Your Father's voice reverberating from heaven in approval.[6]

"You've gathered some terrific, tough, thoughtful young men around You. With a mother's intuition, I know You are getting ready to make Your move. After all these years, You are finally going to reveal Yourself and declare who You are. You are not Joseph's son; You are God's Son. You are Israel's long-awaited Messiah. And Jesus, I think this wedding celebration, in the presence of so many friends, would be a wonderful place to begin letting people know who You are. Son, do something about the wine."

"Ma'am,[7] search your heart. What is your real reason for asking Me to help this young couple? Are you trying to manipulate Me into performing a miracle so that your friends will know what you already know, that I am not only your son, but also God's Son? The timing and agenda for My public ministry have been set by God. I can't run ahead of Him or allow Myself to be pushed ahead of Him, even by My own mother."[8]

Are there hidden agendas in your prayers? Are you praying for God to save your marriage to avoid being humiliated or rendered financially devastated by divorce, instead of striving to glorify Him?

Is there a hidden agenda in your prayer for the marriage of your child? Are you praying for that marriage because you're afraid that if your child fails, your own carefully cultivated reputation might be tarnished? Or because you don't want the responsibility of raising your grandchildren?

"Why do you involve Me?" is Jesus' challenge to us to search our hearts for hidden motives in our intercession for ourselves or for others. Why are we really asking for help?

Are you asking for physical healing because you're tired of feeling bad? Are you asking for financial relief because you're tired of budgeting? Are you asking for a better job because you want more prestige?

So many of our requests, when we listen to ourselves closely, are rooted in selfishness and pride. While Jesus understands the feelings of our infirmities[9]—He knows how hard it is to feel sick all the time, He knows the constant struggle of trying to make ends meet, He knows our need to feel worthwhile—glorifying God should be our bottom-line agenda.[10]

Regardless of her hidden agenda, Mary's faith was evident in that she went to Jesus for help. She may not have understood the larger picture of God's timing for His life, but she did understand the potential destruction to the marriage of the young couple if it became public knowledge that the wine had run out. She knew Jesus would do something, even if it wasn't what she expected. How did she know? Because she knew Him well enough to know He cares about the smallest details of our lives as well as the largest details in the world. She knew Him well enough to know He cares about, not just spiritual things like salvation, justification, sanctification, and glorification, but also about everyday, practical things like wine and a wedding party. Intense emotional things. Intimate personal things.

Mary may not have known and understood everything, but she knew Jesus cared. And she knew that in order for Him to have the freedom to make a difference, she would have to place total control of the situation in His hands.

Jesus Was Invested with Full Authority

After speaking with Jesus, Mary immediately called the servants together. I would imagine they were already exchanging knowing looks, rolling their eyes, shaking their heads, but they listened quietly to Mary's instructions: "Do whatever he tells you" (John 2:5). She was so confident Jesus could make a difference in the crisis, she deliberately, consciously placed the situation, the home, and the marriage under His absolute authority.

Have you placed your home, your family, your marriage, your situation under His authority? Until you do, Jesus won't have the freedom He requires to make the necessary changes.

As I wrote this, a middle-aged, newly married couple called me. From the moment they had said their wedding vows, things had started to go wrong. In fact, as they described their situation, all I could think was, *This is all wrong. This marriage should never have taken place.*

As the son of a locally prominent family, the husband brought into the relationship arrogance mingled with a lot of resentment and anger; he believed he had never measured up to his family's expectations. His parents had been so consumed with the family business, he had felt neglected as a child. The wife struggled with memories of abuse and had grown up in a very poor family; both of her parents had been alcoholics. Before their first year of marriage was up, these two were screaming, fighting, pouting, sulking—their wine had run out! I knew, without their specifically saying it, that they were both looking for the door with the exit sign over it.

In prayer, I took this desperate couple to Jesus. I told Him that they had no more wine. No more love for each other. No more patience. No more kindness. No more understanding. No more energy to work out their relationship. Then I told them that God would redeem their marriage if they submitted totally to His control. They had to die to their own rights and desires and feelings and expectations, focus on God, and work at developing their own relationship with God first; then "do whatever He tells you."

The first miracle is that the couple agreed and did it! The second miracle is that God has begun to create new wine in their relationship. Praise His Name!

The same God who performed a miracle at the wedding in Cana is our God today. But we have to give Him absolute authority and freedom to act.

Will you have to run out of wine before you turn over the control of your home and marriage to Christ? Maybe one reason He has allowed you to be in your present crisis is to bring you to the point of complete submission to His will.

I believe that's what happened in my life. After I had been praying daily and continually for several months about my own marriage, I remember getting up early one morning for my quiet time, slipping down on my knees, and tearfully asking God once more what I needed to do and how I could fix the relationship with Danny. I asked Him to pinpoint areas in my life that needed change—even as I pointed out to Him things in my husband's life that I thought needed changing! As I got off my knees, I opened my Bible to 1 John 4 and picked up where I had been reading for the past several weeks. As I meditated, God began to give me verse-by-verse, specific instructions on what I needed to do. And His instructions were not at all what I had expected. Listen as I try to recall His words to me from 1 John that morning long ago:

"You are to love Danny because I first loved you. If you say, 'I love God,' yet you don't love Danny, you are a liar. Because if you don't love your husband, whom you have seen, you cannot love Me, whom you have not seen. So I give you this command: If you love Me, you must—it's not an option—you *must* also love Danny. Dear Anne, love one another, for love comes from Me. Everyone who loves has been born of Me and knows Me."[11]

Through His gentle words, God laid out three very basic principles about my love for Danny. The first is that love comes from God. I don't have within myself the ability to manufacture love for someone when the love has run out.

The second is that those who are able to love others, including their own spouses, are those who have been born of God. I knew I had been born of God when I received Jesus Christ as my Savior. At the moment of conversion, God came to live within me, and since God is love, and He loved Danny, then I had love for Danny inside of me.

The third is that those who are able to love others, even when the love runs out, are those who are not only *born of God* but who also *know God.* A distinction is made between being born again and knowing God. In other words, although God lived within me, His love for Danny was only available to me in proportion to my knowledge of Him. In case this last principle was confusing, He restated it: "If you are not able to love Danny, it's because you do not know Me, because I am love."[12]

I realized that knowing God was more than just being saved or being born again, just as knowing my husband was more than just saying marriage vows at the wedding altar. Knowing God involves an intimate, personal relationship that is developed over time through prayer and getting answers to prayer, through Bible study and applying its teaching to our lives, through obedience and experiencing the power of God, through moment-by-moment submission to Him that results in a moment-by-moment filling of the Holy Spirit.

As tears rolled down my cheeks and splashed on the Bible page, I knew God had given me the key for changing my marriage. I had been trying so hard to please, to adapt, to be the wife Danny seemed to want. I had been reading anything I could get my hands on that might help me in my marriage. But as I had tried harder and harder, the burden had gotten heavier and heavier, until I knew I was miserably failing. However, on that morning years ago, God gave me the key for turning water into wine. *The key was not to focus on my relationship with Danny, but to focus on my relationship with God!*

As I spent time with God, growing in my knowledge of Him through prayer, Bible study, obedience, and submission, He would fill my life. And because God is love and because He would fill me, His love would also fill me. Therefore, since God loved Danny, love for Danny would fill my life and overflow from God, through me, to my husband.

I cannot adequately express the relief and joy that swept over me that morning. The instructions were clear: "Get to know God. Spend more time with God. Grow in your personal relationship with God." I knew what to do. And that morning I relaxed, resting in God's power to turn water into wine while I concentrated on obeying His instructions. Immediately I felt relief from the private burden I had been carrying. It would be weeks, even months after that moment before I could honestly say that the water had been turned into wine, but I was no longer frustrated, tense, or worried. God gave me peace and joy within as I put myself in His hands, trusting Him moment by moment to infuse my life and my marriage with His love.

Looking back, I am so grateful I persevered in prayer for my marriage, even during weeks when I received no answer from God or encouragement from anyone else. I knew my marriage was in God's will, it had His blessing, He had been invited to be the center of it long before the wine had run out, and I just had to wait for Him to tell me what to do.

When the shortage of wine first became known at the wedding feast in Cana, it seemed on the surface that Jesus would do nothing. But Mary knew Him well enough to know that He would act in His own time and in His own way. Her expectancy must have infected the servants who continued to wait quietly for any instructions He might give them.

They didn't have to wait long before Jesus approached them. His attention was directed toward six stone jars that stood by the door. Each jar had a capacity of twenty gallons of water, which was used for ceremonial cleansing as well as for practical washing. As guests came to the wedding feast, a servant greeted them at the door and, using water from these jars, washed their dusty feet before they entered the home. And before the meal, as well as between courses, water from these jars allowed the guests to wash their hands.

Jesus issued a command to the servants that seemed to have nothing to do with the shortage of wine: "Fill the jars with water" (John 2:7). The servants must have stolen furtive looks at each other, but without question, resistance, or argument, "they filled them to the brim" (John 2:7).

I wonder what the servants were thinking as they obediently filled those jars with water. Surely they must have questioned what water had to do with wine. It must have seemed illogical, impractical, and irrelevant to the crisis situation. But they not only filled the jars with water; they filled them to the brim! These servants were used to taking orders, but was there something about the thoughtful demeanor and quiet authority of Mary's Son that impressed them? Something that quickened their hearts in expectancy?

If they wondered to themselves what filling the jars with water had to do with a shortage of wine, what did they think when He told them, "Now draw some out and take it to the master of the banquet" (John 2:8)? Can you imagine the looks on their faces when Jesus gave them those instructions? Can you image the jumbled thoughts that tumbled through their minds: "*Do what?* Take *water* to the master of the banquet when he is expecting *wine?* Do You know how embarrassing that's going to be? Do You know the risks of pulling a stunt like that? Why, I'll probably lose my job! At the very least, I'll be sharply reprimanded. People will laugh at me. Criticize me. What do You take me for? I may be a servant, but I'm no fool."

What thoughts have been running through your mind in response to the instructions Jesus has given you?

"If I submit to my husband,[13] he'll walk all over me."

"If I'm patient and loving with my wife,[14] she'll begin to expect such treatment all the time, and she'll never learn her place."

"If I make the kids go to church now,[15] they'll rebel against God when they get older."

"If I forgive my spouse,[16] he or she will get away with the wrong."

"If I obey the instructions Jesus gives,[17] I'll lose out. I'll be laughed at. I'll be criticized. It just will never work. I may be a servant, but I'm no fool."

What a terrible tragedy, what a shameful waste, what an unnecessary humiliation, what a disastrous crisis was *averted* because the servants simply did what Jesus told them to do!

Why did the servants obey? What made them risk their reputations and their jobs and carry out His instructions? Surely it wasn't just because Mary told them to do whatever He said. It must have been something about Jesus Himself that thrust them out on the limb of risk-taking obedience.

Was it His clear, firm gaze of authority as He surveyed their
trembling forms?
Was it the quiet confidence of His demeanor as He directed their
attention to the water jars?
Was it the unwavering strength of His tone of voice as He
commanded them to fill the water jars with water?
Was it the compassion tinged with the joy of anticipation
twinkling in His eyes as He told them to draw water out and
pour it into the glass of the master of the banquet?

Instead of sullenly dragging their feet, were the servants quickened with expectation as one volunteered, "I'll do it. Let me take the pitcher of water to the head table"? And so one did.

I can imagine all the servants crowding into the doorway between the kitchen and the banquet hall, jostling for position with each other to get an unobstructed view of their coworker as he made his way gingerly through the guests to the master of the banquet. They must have held their collective breath as he carefully poured the liquid from the pitcher into the glass. I wonder as he began to pour if his hand jerked, spilling a few drops, when he saw that although he had put water into the pitcher, *wine came out.* Was he still staring, stupefied, as the master of the banquet gave him a quizzical look, then reached out to wrap his fingers around the glass, lifted it to his lips, and "tasted the water that had been turned into wine" (John 2:9)?

The master of the banquet "did not realize where it had come from, though the servants who had drawn the water knew" (John 2:9). As the servant surely stood wide-eyed and slack-jawed in amazement, he must have overheard the master of the banquet as he "called the bridegroom aside and said, 'Everyone brings out the choice wine first and then the cheaper wine after the guests have had too much to drink; but you have saved the best till now'" (John 2:9–10). The verdict was in! The water had been turned into wine! And not just any wine! The new wine was the best!

As the servant weaved his way back through the tables to the kitchen, was he greeted by the other servants with "high-fives," claps on the back, and a spontaneous celebration over what Mary's Son had done? It had been a miracle! There was no way water could turn into wine! The wine had to have been *created*! But it was such a quiet miracle. Nothing flashy that would have drawn attention to Jesus. Nothing spectacular that would have announced the Messiah had come. Just a quiet change that had saved a young bridegroom's honor and a newlywed couple's marriage—and answered a mother's prayer.

Can you imagine the thrill those servants experienced? It's the same thrill I've experienced again and again as I have climbed down from a pulpit to a standing ovation, acutely conscious of the water I had put into the message—the interrupted prayer time, the scattered thoughts, the flawed outline, the weak delivery—yet the wine had flowed out. People responded to the message, lives were changed, and the demonstration of the power of God was evident. No one in the audience knew what this servant knew—that water had gone in, but wine had come out. And as I outwardly lift my hand in praise to God, inwardly I humbly acknowledge what only He and I know—that a quiet miracle has occurred.

It's the same thrill I get whenever I look at my own children. I know the water that went into my part in raising them. Jonathan was born when I was twenty-one years old. The girls came along shortly thereafter. In my youth, I made mistakes that make me cringe even now as I reflect back. When Jonathan was five years old, Morrow was three, and Rachel-Ruth was ten months old, I established Bible Study Fellowship in our city. I plunged into teaching a weekly class of five hundred women on top of discipling a weekly leadership group of sixty-five women. I was preoccupied and distracted for most of my children's growing-up years. But I've seen the wine come out—three children totally committed to Christ, each one married to a committed Christian, and each one seeking to be a servant of the Lord. And wonder of wonders, they even love me and tell others that they had the greatest childhood ever! It's a miracle!

And it's the thrill I get daily when I look at my beloved husband and remember the water—and the wine! While my marriage is far from perfect, it is living testimony to the power God has today to turn water into the best wine. God's love in me and through me for Danny is so much deeper, stronger, richer, kinder, steadier than I ever had on my own. It's the sort of miracle known only to those who have put water in and seen wine come out.

Is that what you desperately want? Just a quiet miracle in your marriage or your home or even your ministry that would turn the water into wine? Then invite Jesus to come in, inform Him of the problem, and invest Him with full authority. Jesus makes change possible even when the love has run out of your marriage. He invites you to taste and enjoy the "new wine" as from your heart you thank God for just giving you Jesus!

MY FATHER once received a handsome Swiss watch from some good friends. After he had worn and enjoyed it for a while, the watch stopped working. When my mother took it to the local jewelry store, the repairman said that he was very sorry, but he could not fix it. So Mother took it to another repairman and another. They all said the same thing, that it was beyond mending.

Not too long after that, my mother happened to be going to Switzerland, so she tucked the broken watch into her bag. When she arrived, she arranged for the watch to be sent to the company that had made it, explaining that it had broken and no one could fix it.

Within a short period of time, she received the watch in the mail, running like new. The company that had crafted it had no trouble at all in making it work again.

Marriage is God's idea.[18] He "crafted" it. If your marriage is broken, all the "repairmen" or counselors or seminars you take it to will be unable to fix it; take it to Him. The Creator who made it in the first place can make it work again. Which is why God has given you Jesus.

4

JESUS MAKES CHANGE POSSIBLE . . .

When Life Isn't Enough

JOHN 3:1–21

The story is told of a man who, while walking down the street of his town, passed the window of the local pet store. He could see a giant iguana sunning itself on a rock, furry kittens tumbling head over heels as they kick-boxed a small toy back and forth, and doe-eyed puppies excitedly yapping at the kittens. But what caught the man's attention and caused him to stop and stare was the most magnificent bird he had ever seen. It sat regally on a perch in the middle of the window display, haughtily preening its brilliant feathers. Its head was a shimmering cobalt blue, its wings an iridescent yellow, its throat ruby red fading into a misty rose on its chest. The beak and feet gleamed ebony black, as did the fierce, intelligent eyes.

The man couldn't resist. Inside the pet store he noticed a sign posted near the bird that said in large block letters: "This bird is guaranteed to sing." He inquired as to the price and was told he could own the bird for one thousand dollars, which would include the cage.

The man gasped. But in spite of the sticker shock, he paid the price and proudly took the bird in its cage home. The rest of the day, he watched and waited, eagerly anticipating the bird's song.

By the next morning, the bird still had not sung, so the man returned to the pet store. "What could be wrong?" he asked. The clerk apologized, "Sir, didn't I tell you? The bird needs a ladder. He will climb the ladder; then he will sing." The man bought the ladder for twenty dollars, took it home, put it in the bird's cage, and waited expectantly to hear the bird sing. The bird climbed the ladder but sat at the top in silence.

The next morning the man returned to the pet store and told the clerk the bird still had not sung. The clerk apologized again and said, "I'm sorry. I forgot that he needs a little bell. He will climb the ladder and ring the bell; then he will sing." The bell cost twenty-five dollars. Back home when the man put it at the top of the ladder in the bird's cage, the bird climbed the ladder and rang the bell, but that was the only sound that came from the cage.

The next morning he returned to the pet store. This time he learned the bird needed a thirty-dollar mirror beside the bell. Back at home the bird climbed the ladder, rang the bell, and looked into the mirror, but it didn't even chirp.

The next morning the man strode resolutely into the pet store. He pounced on the clerk and angrily recounted his purchases totaling $1,075—$1,075 for a bird that didn't sing!

The clerk answered that the bird would definitely sing if the man installed a thirty-five-dollar swing in the bird's cage. The man pounded his fist on the counter as he paid for the swing and warned that if this didn't work, he would return the bird and expect a full refund!

The man stormed back to his house, put the swing in place, crossed his arms, and stared at the bird. Sure enough, the bird climbed the ladder, rang the bell, looked into the mirror, and swung on the swing—then it fell to the bottom of the cage, dead!

The man was aghast! He grabbed the cage with the dead bird, took it back to the pet store, slammed it on the counter, and yelled hysterically at the clerk: "I bought a bird for a thousand dollars, a ladder for twenty, a bell for twenty-five, a mirror for thirty, and a swing for thirty-five. Not only does this bird not sing, but it's dead! What went wrong?"

"Oh," the clerk responded, "did I forget to tell you? He also needed birdseed."

The bird had everything but the one thing it really needed, not just for a song, but for life itself. It needed birdseed!

What about you? Is something missing in your life, something that you can't define? Perhaps all you know is that life doesn't seem to be enough for you.

Has your search for your "song," for joy and happiness and meaning, caused you to choose a "ladder"—a way of climbing up in your career, seeking a higher position, devoting yourself to greater success in your business? When that didn't work, did you decide you needed a "bell"—a way of drawing attention to yourself by increasing your public reputation, visibility, or fame? Did you become more frustrated when that turned out to be another dead end? Perhaps then you rushed to get a "mirror"—a way of remaking your image through cosmetic surgery, dieting, weightlifting, jogging, an exercise video, or a membership at the spa where you sculpted your body. As a last act of desperation, did you purchase the "swing"—by throwing yourself into pleasurable pursuits, entertainment, fun? As a result, do you find that at this moment you are beyond frustration and totally exhausted in soul and spirit? You've just died on the inside. Hasn't anyone told you? You need "birdseed." You need the basic Necessity for real life. You need Jesus. He makes change possible when life isn't enough.

THE AWAKENING TO OUR NEED

No one would have imagined that Nicodemus lacked the basic Necessity for life and needed a change, including Nicodemus himself. He'd had a heart for God ever since he could remember. He loved the ceremonies and traditions of his religion, finding that rather than being a burden, they were a comfort to him. They made him feel as though he were somehow closer to God. And God was his life.

For more years than he could count, he had been a student of the holy Scriptures. He had saturated himself in the writings of Moses and the writings of the prophets of Israel. He had devoted his life to keeping God's law and all the man-made laws that were attached to it, including fasting two days a week. Becoming a Pharisee, then a ruler of the Pharisees, seemed to be logical steps in his spiritual journey. His dedication to God's law and his meticulous observance of the laws of the day were so pronounced that he stood out among men who were well-known for both.

By the time he was middle-aged, he had become, not only one of the most outstanding religious leaders in Israel under Roman occupation, but one of Israel's premiere religious teachers as well. By the time he was a senior citizen, he was something of a religious statesman, the most outstanding Bible scholar in all of Israel. His name had become a household word. His presence in the local synagogue surely would have guaranteed an overflow crowd. He was known for his lifetime of learning, his enormous insight into the Scriptures and the law, his keen ability to articulate the truth, and his fair-mindedness. So why did this "man of the Pharisees . . . , a member of the Jewish ruling council" slip into the night to talk to Jesus (John 3:1–2)?

Nicodemus seemed to have everything—position,[1] wealth,[2] respect,[3] education,[4] fame[5]—yet he was searching for something more. Now, toward the end of his life, he had begun to experience a gradual awakening to a need that had not been met in who he was, or in what he had accomplished, or in all that he knew, or in everything he possessed.

Awakened by God's Grace

Nicodemus had heard of the young Rabbi from Nazareth. It would have been difficult to find anyone in Israel who had not. Jesus had burst on the scene from nowhere, mobbed by hordes of people wherever He went. As He gave sight to the blind, cleansed the lepers, healed the sick, opened the ears of the deaf, and straightened the limbs of the crippled, His fame spread. Rather than channel His following into a political movement or a power base, however, Jesus had enveloped His miracles with teaching that was equally life changing.

Nicodemus was curious. Finally he could resist the urge no longer, and "he came to Jesus at night" (John 3:2). As he slipped through the deserted alleyways and darted down narrow streets, his heart must have been pounding. He was instantly recognizable throughout the area, and it was frighteningly risky to be seen talking with Jesus. What would people say—what would his *peers* say—if they knew? They would at the very least ask him questions. How could he ever adequately explain that he, a Pharisee, a ruler on the council of the Jews, the premiere teacher in Israel, was dissatisfied with his own religious experience? How could he make them understand that in spite of a lifetime of devotion and dedication to God, he had no real joy or happiness—that life just didn't seem to be enough? Something was missing. Something that perhaps the young Rabbi could help him find.

Are you furtively, inwardly searching for something? Has the search seemed even more unsettling because the world sees you as a religious person? Have you automatically eliminated your restlessness as related to God because, after all, you go to church, read your Bible, pray, and have a reputation as a Christian? Are you beginning to suspect you are having a midlife or some other identity crisis? Are you relatively healthy and wealthy with no major problems in your marriage or family or business—but not happy? What's wrong?

It may very well be that nothing is wrong. In fact, everything may instead be all right. Maybe God in His grace is drawing you to Jesus—without your conscious will, without your intellectual reasoning, without any verbal articulation from you as to what you want or whom you seek. In some way, God used Nicodemus's secondhand knowledge of Jesus to awaken him to his need for something more. That's grace.

Nicodemus's aides must have helped to arrange the clandestine meeting that took place that balmy spring evening. When he arrived at the designated place, the full Passover moon was on the rise, enabling him to see Jesus, who was waiting expectantly. There were no formal introductions or preliminaries since this was a private rendezvous. But as Nicodemus looked into the younger man's face, he must have immediately, instinctively known that all he had heard about Jesus was true. Nicodemus faced a unique man, a great man, but whether He was more than a man had yet to be determined.

Even though he was aware that Jesus had no formal schooling or training, Nicodemus opened the conversation with gracious, deferential respect. "Rabbi, we know you are a teacher who has come from God. For no one could perform the miraculous signs you are doing if God were not with him" (John 3:2). Nicodemus unwittingly had done what Jesus later challenged His disciples to do seriously, to judge people not just by what they say but by the *fruit* of their words and actions.[6] Having heard of the words and actions of Jesus, Nicodemus had assessed their impact, their "fruit." He had come to the not-so-difficult conclusion that Jesus of Nazareth, at the very least, was from God.

But having made this assumption, Nicodemus's faith stopped short of acknowledging Jesus for who He truly was. He expressed his lack of faith when he called Jesus "a" teacher who had come from God, not "the" teacher, that is, the Messiah.

How many people today, especially religious people, do what Nicodemus did? They base their knowledge of Jesus on hearsay—what they have heard their pastor say,

or their parents say,

or a friend say,

or a radio preacher say,

or a book say.

Their superficial examination of the "fruit" leads them to a shallow faith that believes Jesus is a good man, a great man, perhaps even a prophet from God, but they stop short of truly being convinced He is the unique, only-begotten Son of God—God Himself in a man's body. Like Nicodemus, they believe Jesus can help them find what they are looking for, but it never occurs to them that *all* they are looking for can be found in Jesus Himself—Jesus alone.

Awakened by God's Gospel

As Nicodemus waited expectantly for a response from the young Rabbi, was he proud of his affected humility and graciousness in referring to Jesus as a rabbi and a teacher sent from God? Did he think Jesus would respond by blushing just a little as He stuttered His profuse gratitude for being addressed as "Rabbi"? Did he think Jesus would say something like, "I'm flattered that the greatest teacher in Israel thinks that I, a lowly carpenter from Nazareth, could teach him anything." Was he expecting Jesus to thank him for the honor of a personal, private visit while pledging to do all He could to help him? I wonder what thoughts exploded in Nicodemus's mind when Jesus did speak.

The eyes of God looked at this courtly, thoughtful, intellectual, inquisitive, educated, wealthy, respected, religious, searching Pharisee who had never committed a gross sin, and He saw beyond the outward courtesy of Nicodemus's demeanor to the inward cry of his heart. With compassionate gentleness, yet convicting truthfulness, Jesus pinned down Nicodemus's need when He declared in stark simplicity, "I tell you the truth, no one can see the kingdom of God unless a man is born again," (John 3:3). Jesus did not enter into the social games people play during such auspicious meetings. There was no preamble, no preparation for the verbal bombshell He dropped with His opening words, words that have reverberated throughout every generation since then whenever God's gospel is proclaimed. And what is the gospel? The Bible says:

All have sinned and come short of the glory of God.[7]
There is no one righteous, no not one.[8]
The wages of sin is death, but the gift of God is eternal life.[9]
Whoever believes on him shall not perish, but have everlasting life.[10]
If you confess your sin, he is faithful and just to forgive you your sins.[11]
If you open the door to your heart he will come and live within you.[12]
To as many as receive him . . . he gave the power to become his child.[13]

When you heard and believed, you were sealed with the Holy
Spirit.[14]
It is by grace that you have been saved, through faith . . .
not by works.[15]
If you are in Christ you are a new creation.[16]
Your sins are forgiven.
Your guilt is atoned for.
Your past is removed.
Your future is secured.
You have peace in your heart.
You have purpose to your step.
You have a song on your lips.
You are saved from hell.
You are right with God.
You are going to heaven.
BUT . . . *you must be born again!* That's God's gospel!

The simple but sharp edge of that gospel phrase has been dulled as advertisers from Madison Avenue have used Jesus' words to describe everything from the Volkswagen Beetle, which made a comeback after twenty years, to fashions like bell-bottom trousers, which have reemerged in the marketplace. Sports commentators have used it to describe the effort made by rejuvenated teams in their valiant charge for the championship. Political columnists have used it to describe a politician who was defeated at the polls but came back years later to win. News analysts have used it to describe the nation of Israel, which rose from the ashes of history to reestablish itself as a nation after two thousand years of nonexistence. Cynics have used it to mock Christians who believe that the Bible is God's infallible Word and that faith in Jesus is the only way to heaven. The term has become so much of a contemporary cliché that it is in danger of losing the phenomenal impact of the original meaning, and we are in danger of missing the answer to our need.

THE ANSWER TO OUR NEED

What did Jesus mean by the term *born again?* In essence, Jesus was saying, "Nicodemus, you are looking for real life. Eternal life. Abundant life. A personal relationship with God now and heaven when you die. But not only are you not going to heaven when you die; you will not even see heaven unless you start all over again. Unless you have a completely new beginning, totally separated from the past. Unless you are born again. You need to be created again. Spiritual rebirth is the only answer to the unspoken, unconscious need of your heart."

That carefully cultivated expression of studied politeness must have been wiped from Nicodemus's face as the young Rabbi's response pierced through:

all the layers of morality and religiosity,
all the years of thinking and training,
all the accumulated pride and prejudice,
all the complicated reasoning and rationalizing,
all the neatly compartmentalized preconceptions and presumptions.

The Answer Is Not Physical Rebirth

Jesus' words touched the very nerve in Nicodemus's soul, and he cried out with yearning unbelief, "How can a man be born when he is old? . . . Surely he cannot enter a second time into his mother's womb to be born!" (John 3:4). With amazing clarity and simplicity Nicodemus seemed to have grasped that this was exactly what he was searching for, this was the need of his heart; this was the missing piece in his life. Yet at the same time, just as a starving man knows he will never eat again, or a thirsty man knows he will never drink again, or a lost man knows the rescuers have passed him in the night and he will never be found, Nicodemus knew the answer was impossibly unattainable. It was beyond his reach. To be born again as Jesus described was beyond human achievement.

Perhaps for the first time in his life, Nicodemus was aware that he was totally helpless and truly hopeless.

Does that same hopeless despair gnaw at your soul? Perhaps, like Nicodemus's, your life has not been so terrible—it just hasn't been so good. It has not been what you thought. What you dreamed. What you sought. What you worked for. Something has been left out. Something is missing. It seems flat. Empty. Skimpy. You're too old to chart a different course. And so you join a bridge club or learn to play golf. But in the stillness of the night do you wonder, *do you wish,* there were something more?

Or maybe your life has been terrible. You made choices when you were younger that blossomed into bitter fruit. You got trapped in the consequences of those choices, and your life seemed to take a direction of its own. You became caught up in a stream of experiences that you didn't really want. And no one knows the bitterness, the anger, the frustration that imprisons your spirit daily. Moment by moment. *If only* you could start over. *If only* it were possible to truly be different. *If only,* at this stage of life, you could really change.

What did Jesus mean? How could Nicodemus—*how could anyone*—be born again? How is it possible to start life over when you are forty or fifty or sixty or seventy or eighty years of age? It's as impossible as climbing back into your mother's womb and repeating the physical birth process! It just can't be done!

The Answer Is Spiritual Rebirth

The answer is obviously not some sort of reincarnation or physical rebirth. Jesus patiently explained: "I tell you the truth, unless a man is born of water and the Spirit, he cannot enter the kingdom of God" (John 3:5). In other words, in order to experience spiritual rebirth, you must be physically born. You must be a living person. You must be "born of water."[17] It is not possible to pray for someone who has died without Christ and change that person's eternal destiny. Once someone has died, you cannot pray that person out of hell or into heaven. The only people who go to heaven are those who are born of water.[18]

But those who go to heaven must also be born of the Spirit. Just as the Virgin Mary conceived the physical life of the Son of God, you and I conceive the spiritual life of the Son of God when we are "born again." From that moment on, we are essentially two people on the inside. We have the mind, emotions, and will that we were physically born with, but we now also have the mind, emotions, and will of Christ within us.[19] We have a spiritual "implant" of the life of Jesus Christ within our bodies. This is actually Jesus in the person of the Holy Spirit.

This "implanting" of the life of Christ is a supernatural miracle. It is something God does in response to our humble confession and sincere repentance of sin coupled with our deliberate, personal faith in His Son because of His death on the cross as our atoning sacrifice and His resurrection. Only those with this implant will ever see, much less enter into, God's heavenly home. Only those with this implant will receive eternal life because "flesh gives birth to flesh, but the Spirit gives birth to spirit" (John 3:6).

Flesh refers to the natural life we were born with, which includes our will, emotions, and intellect—all that we are on the inside. It is incapable of personally knowing God or truly pleasing God or eventually seeing God. It cannot improve. It will never change. It is permeated with sin and therefore condemned. It is totally separated from the Spirit. So although we can physically reproduce, that which is born to us is just more of the old fleshly nature.

The Spirit, on the other hand, reproduces Himself within us. And the Spirit He reproduces within us knows God intimately because He is God. And He is always pleasing to God. And He sees and understands the things of God. And His life is eternal. This is why we need the spiritual rebirth, which is only made possible by the Spirit of God supernaturally imparting the Spirit or the life of Christ within us. There is no way our flesh can produce a spiritual rebirth. The Spirit and the sinful flesh by nature are totally separate. Neither will ever change and, like oil and water, they will never intermingle.

The evening breeze must have blown gently across the garden and into the room where Jesus and Nicodemus sat. As it rustled the leaves outside and carried the sweet, pungent perfume of early spring blossoms inside, the softness of its movement contrasted with the increasingly puzzled and startled expression Nicodemus must have worn as Jesus described the phenomenon of rebirth. Without giving Nicodemus opportunity to respond, Jesus gently checked the man's incredulity before it could become real unbelief by offering a relevant analogy: "You should not be surprised at my saying, 'You must be born again.' The wind blows wherever it pleases. You hear its sound, but you cannot tell where it comes from or where it is going. So it is with everyone born of the Spirit" (John 3:7–8).

In essence he said, "Nicodemus, rebirth is as real an experience as the evening breeze blowing into the room. You can't see the breeze and you don't know where it is coming from or where it is going or what it is going to do next. But you know it's there when it rustles the leaves or carries the fragrance of garden flowers or blows through your hair or stirs these papers on the table. Rebirth is like the gentle breeze. It's just as mysteriously invisible, yet also just as real."

Although we can't see the wind, we have no doubt that it is there; we can see its effect. And when you experience spiritual rebirth, you will know; you will see its effect as well. For example, when you were physically born, you were consciously aware of life. Although you didn't understand it and couldn't articulate what you felt, you *knew* you were born. This awareness of life increased with your growth, maturity, and age.[20]

When you are born again, you will be consciously aware of your spiritual life. You may not understand it or be able to articulate what has happened to you. But *you will know* you are spiritually alive. And the awareness of this new life within you will also increase with your spiritual growth, maturity, and age.

The answer to the quiet yearning in Nicodemus's heart, and to the cry of every human heart in every generation, is the same. The answer is spiritual rebirth. Why, then, doesn't the world get it? Why do we look to material possessions,

to personal relationships,

to powerful positions,

to pleasurable places,

to sexual experiences,

to eating and entertainment and exercise and education

for what is only found in spiritual rebirth? What about you? Do you get it? Do you know that you have been born again? If not, what are you waiting for? Are you waiting until you can understand it? Then you may never be born again, for who can understand such a thing? It's far more important to experience it than to understand it.

THE AVERSION TO OUR NEED

Nicodemus didn't understand it, either. He knew the Scripture. He knew the facts. But he just didn't grasp their meaning or application for his life. It was all so simple, yet so mind-blowing! It was almost beyond his ability to comprehend because, in spite of his advanced education, he was ignorant of the truth.

Aversion Because of Ignorance

Jesus sought to explain in simple, relevant terms the answer to Nicodemus's question, "How can a man be born when he is old?" But Nicodemus began to resist the truth. He interrupted Jesus' explanation by blurting out incredulously, "How can this be?" (John 3:9). He was pleading ignorance.

Is ignorance your plea? Has no one ever told you that you *must* be born again if you want to receive eternal life and go to heaven when you die? Or have you been told, yet assumed it was a Baptist thing?

Or a Billy Graham thing?

Or a fundamentalist thing?

Or a Protestant thing?

Or a revivalist thing?

While being familiar with the term, have you been ignorant of its implication and application in your life? Has it just never occurred to you that *you* had to be born again? Have you always thought it was for somebody else? Could it be your ignorance borders on pride or arrogance?

I wonder if Nicodemus's answer today might have been something like, "You've got to be kidding! I've never heard such a far-fetched idea! If You are telling the truth, and I could actually receive the Spirit of God, who would give me a new nature, I would have to accept responsibility for living in that new nature. I would no longer have an excuse for my sin. Or any rationalization for my attitudes. Or a hiding place for my pride and my prejudices. Why, if I were born again as You describe, I would lose control of my life. It would change everything about the way I think and feel and plan and perceive and act! You're talking radical change. I'm not sure I'm ready for this."

Nicodemus must have begun to resist in his heart because Jesus didn't accept his defense of ignorance. Instead of entering into polite, intellectual debate on the possibility of new birth, Jesus put His finger on the real problem, the heart of Nicodemus.

Aversion Because of Arrogance

Jesus exposed Nicodemus's resistance when He responded with a forceful question of His own: "You are Israel's teacher . . . and do you not understand these things? I tell you the truth, we speak of what we know, and we testify to what we have seen, but still you people do not accept our testimony" (John 3:10–11). In other words, "Your problem is not ignorance, Nicodemus. It's arrogance. It's a prideful, willful refusal to acknowledge and accept the truth." And Nicodemus had been increasingly confronted with the truth. He not only knew it through the written and spoken Word, but he also had recently seen it demonstrated when Jesus had cleansed the temple.

After the wedding in Cana, Jesus had gone to Jerusalem, where He became outraged at the commercialization of His Father's house. In righteous indignation and judgment, He had driven the merchants, who were cashing in on ministry, out of the temple area. His disciples were deeply impressed by seeing a fulfillment of Old Testament Scripture concerning the Messiah.[21] Nicodemus, as the premiere religious teacher in Israel, would have been fully aware of this incident and the Scriptures that related it to the Messiah and Redeemer of Israel. In response to Jesus' directive, he was repressing the astounding implication of what had taken place in the temple courts as well as resisting what Jesus was explaining to him.

Do you know someone who has used Nicodemus's tactics of aversion? After having explained the gospel to your friend as clearly and simply as you know how, did he or she ask a multitude of questions, then respond by saying, "This just doesn't make sense to me"? Did you go back and explain it again, using different analogies and Bible verses, to no avail? Why? Because the problem wasn't in your explanation or even in your friend's understanding; it was in his or her heart.

I recently presented an opportunity for an evangelistic outreach in another city to a group of leaders who responded with careful attention and dozens of questions. Their questions were very thoughtful and provocative, and I spent hours in prayer and consultation with others in order to answer as thoroughly as I could. When I gave them my answers, which filled sixteen typed pages, their response was another six pages of questions. At that point, even though they were saying they were very interested in the opportunity I was offering, I knew they lacked real desire to follow through. Their questions were a tactical defense to avoid commitment. When I challenged them, sure enough, they withdrew and admitted they were not willing to take the opportunity. And I very much appreciated their honesty in the end.

What questions have you been asking in order to avoid the responsibility and commitment the answers may demand? You may find yourself, like Nicodemus, gently rebuked: "I have spoken to you of earthly things and you do not believe; how then will you believe if I speak of heavenly things?" (John 3:12).

It is obvious that Nicodemus's problem was not a problem of intellect but a problem of unbelief. "You do not believe," Jesus pointedly said. If Nicodemus refused to accept even the analogy of an earthly thing like wind, how could he possibly grasp a spiritual thing like rebirth? He couldn't. So Jesus brought him back to the basics, back to the subject of who He is and what the central issue was: "No one has ever gone into heaven except the one who came from heaven—the Son of Man. Just as Moses lifted up the snake in the desert, so the Son of Man must be lifted up, that everyone who believes in him may have eternal life" (John 3:13–15).

Jesus clearly and bluntly told Nicodemus who He is. The best antidote for unbelief is to focus on the bottom line—that Jesus of Nazareth is the unique Son of God. He came down from heaven, revealing exactly what God is like, offering eternal life and a personal relationship with God, on the condition of our rebirth—a rebirth made possible through His own death on the cross.

Using an Old Testament passage that would be very familiar to Nicodemus, Jesus illustrated His purpose in life. He spoke of the children of Israel, walking in circles in the wilderness, tired, bored, and short-tempered. Day after day they made no headway; day after day they ate the same manna; day after day their complaints grew louder: "Why have you brought us up out of Egypt to die in the desert? There is no bread! There is no water! And we detest this miserable food!"[22]

Finally God's patience with Israel ran out. He removed His hand and exposed the people to the dangers He had protected them from, such as poisonous snakes. Many of the Israelites were bitten, the venom permeated their systems, and they died. If their situation had continued unchecked, the entire nation of Israel would have perished. So they stopped complaining and in desperation cried out to God for salvation—for deliverance from the deadly poison.

And God, in His infinite mercy, heard the cry of the wandering Israelites and made provision for their salvation. He instructed Moses to place a bronze sculpture of a snake on a wooden pole and lift it up high above the people. If those who were dying from the poisonous venom would obey God's Word by looking on the bronze snake and believing they would be healed, they would be saved. If they refused to look, they would die. The provision for salvation was made, but the choice was theirs to claim.[23]

Jesus used that Old Testament story to illustrate the most fundamental truth of the New Testament. Just as Moses lifted up the bronze serpent on the pole so that those who looked and believed would be saved from the poison of the snakes, so Jesus would be lifted up, and those who would look with the eyes of faith would be saved from the deadly poison of sin.

Surely the brilliant Old Testament scholar Nicodemus understood without further explanation. Jesus' dialogue with the great religious leader now challenged Nicodemus to look and to live, as God had previously instucted the children of Israel—to look to the Son of God alone for healing from the poison of sin, for eternal life, and for salvation from God's judgement. The appeal is:

striking in its simplicity,
stunning in its clarity,
supreme in its authority,
solemn in its inescapability,

strong in its necessity,
satisfying in its complexity,
sufficient in its centrality,
successful in its sufficiency,
and scorned for its exclusivity!

THE APPEAL TO OUR NEED

Jesus' appeal to Nicodemus to believe and be born again in order to receive eternal life and be assured of a place in heaven is God's gospel in a nutshell. It's as widely known as anything Jesus ever said. References to it can be seen on posters lining the fields of National Football League games, or on customized automobile license plates, or adorning T-shirts; it can be heard in sermons, homilies, and testimonies. What a wonder it must have been to have heard for the first time, "For God so loved the world that he gave his one and only Son, that whoever believes in him shall not perish but have eternal life" (John 3:16)—from the mouth of God Himself!

Thousands of men and women throughout the ages have experienced the life-changing impact of the words Nicodemus had the privilege of hearing first. But those generations of believers have also had the advantage of New Testament teaching. It's hard to imagine how stunning Jesus' words must have been to a man who heard them with an Old Testament perspective. It's understandable that Nicodemus was unable to quickly grasp such a profound yet basic concept. Even now, two thousand years later, we marvel at the beautiful way God has provided what we need most. Being born again is God's solution to our need for love and life and light.

Our Need for Love

Our world is looking for love. As human beings, we need to love and be loved. But we're looking in all the wrong places. We look for it from a parent,
from a child,
from a sibling,
from a spouse,
from a lover,
from a friend,
from a pet.

But our parents grow old and die,
our children grow up and live their own lives,
our siblings move out and on,
our spouses are too busy or too tired,
our lovers become jealous or bored,
our friends are superficial or selfish,
our pets can't speak or counsel.
Who can truly *understand* the need of the human heart?
Who can *meet* the need of our hearts?
Where is love found?

Jesus revealed to Nicodemus the profound insight that love is found in the heart of God. Man was created by God to know and love Him in a permanent, personal relationship. But man sinned. And that sin broke the relationship with God for which he was created, causing him to be separated from his Creator. The eternal plan to reconcile man with God and bridge the separation, to save him from judgment for that sin, to forgive him of all sins, originated in the heart of God. It was motivated by His great love. *For God so loved you* that He gave His Son, His only Son, the Son Whom He loved—He gave heaven's most precious Treasure—He gave everything He had—in order to offer you eternal life.

Do you doubt the love of God? Why? Because of the bad things that He allows to happen to good people? Because of the unfairness and injustice and unkindness and misery and suffering and pain and cruelty of life? Some questions we won't have answers for until we get to heaven. But one thing we can know for sure is that God loves you and me. How do we know that? We know it by just looking at the cross where He proved His love for the world that mocks Him and ignores Him and despises Him and scorns Him and rejects Him.[24]

We look at the cross and see "I love you" written in red—the red of Christ's blood.[25] Our basic human need for love is met in Jesus.

Our Need for Life

Jesus also meets our need for life. Because of the sinful condition in which we are born, we are not only separated from God now but also condemned by our sin to an eternity of separation from God, which the Bible calls hell: "For God did not send his Son into the world to condemn the world, but to save the world through him. Whoever believes in him is not condemned, but whoever does not believe stands condemned already because he has not believed in the name of God's one and only Son" (John 3:17–18).

The wonderful and familiar Old Testament story of Noah and the ark illustrates how God meets our need for life.[26] In Noah's day, the world became so saturated with evil that God decided to pour out His judgment on the entire human race by sending a flood to wipe every living thing from the face of the earth. Because Noah was the only living person who was right with God, he received instructions to build an ark to save his life and the lives of his wife and children, a select group of animals, and anyone who would claim the ark for salvation from the judgment that God said was coming.

Although it is doubtful that Noah had ever seen a large boat or even a large body of water, he faithfully worked, day in and day out, for 120 years to build the ark in obedience to God's Word. When the ark was completed, God invited Noah and his family to enter. They accepted His invitation, taking with them all the animals God brought to them.

The only reason Noah entered the ark was because God told him to. The only reason he had built the ark in the first place was because God had told him to. There was no indication that judgment was coming except that God had said it was. There was no rumbling thunder, no lightning flash, no ominous clouds. The day Noah entered the ark was a day like any other.

Have you refused God's offer of salvation because you have no awareness that you are in danger? You may have no advance warning before you suddenly find yourself stepping into eternity. The only reason to believe judgment is coming is because God says it is.[27] The only reason to take Him up on His offer of salvation by placing your faith in Jesus Christ is because God's Word says to.[28] On the day Noah entered the ark, there was no reason to do so except God's Word.

The New Testament tells us that Noah was a preacher of righteousness. After he and his family entered the ark, nothing happened for seven days. Did Noah stand in the doorway and preach to the people who surely must have gathered to watch the crazy old fool? While the animals were getting settled in their stalls, was Noah preaching his heart out? Was his long, flowing gray beard unable to absorb the torrent of tears that streamed down his cheeks as he thunderously begged and pleaded for his friends and neighbors to repent? Did he urge them, like the best of the revivalist preachers on the sawdust trail, "Repent! Judgment is coming! Get right with God before it's too late. Repent! Judgment is coming!"

If he did, the record shows that no one believed Noah. None but his immediate family joined him on the ark. Finally, God shut the door. And then the judgment no one believed would come, came! Everyone and everything outside of that ark perished.

Do you know someone who maintains that a loving God would never send anyone to hell? That a loving God will let everyone into heaven? Ask Noah! He was there when God shut the door of the ark. And although technically God doesn't send anyone to hell, you and I are condemned to go there if we refuse to enter through the "door" of the Cross into the safety of the "ark," which is Christ.

God didn't want anyone to perish. He wanted all to repent of their sins and rebellion and enter into the safety of the ark. But the people refused. So He sent the flood as His judgment for the world's wickedness. And when that judgment fell, there was no other hiding place. No other way of salvation. Noah and his family, who chose to accept God's invitation to enter the ark, were saved from judgment. Everyone outside the ark perished.

The God who saved Noah from His judgment by providing an ark is the same God who so loved the world that He sent His only Son as an Ark—a hiding place from the storm of His wrath—who would Himself be our salvation from judgment.

Whosoever believes in Jesus as God's gracious provision for salvation will not perish or come under God's judgment but will be saved and receive eternal life. *But you have to believe or you will perish.*

How cruel God would be if He sent His only beloved Son to die on the cross, to experience excruciating pain, humiliation, alienation, and judgment, if faith in Him for salvation were merely optional. If there were any other way for you and me to be saved, don't you think God would have found it and spared His only Son?[29] But there is no other way to be forgiven of sin, no other way to get right with God, no other way to go to heaven, no other way to escape eternal punishment in hell.

Jesus spoke more often about hell than He did about heaven. But no one talks much about hell today. No one likes to think about hell. No one seems to be informed about hell. Few even really believe in hell. But the Bible teaches that hell is a real place, prepared for the devil and his demons, and those who refuse God's gracious offer of salvation through faith in Jesus Christ.

Just exactly what do we know about hell, the place "outside the ark" where people perish under the judgment of God?

Hell is a place of physical agony, mental suffering, and emotional sorrow. Jesus described it as a place where there is gnashing of teeth and weeping.[30]

Hell is a place of insecurity and fear. The Bible describes it as a bottomless pit, an abyss.[31] Imagine the terror of constantly falling, trying desperately to grab onto something—anything—to stop the fall. Hell is a place where one lives with the constant, conscious awareness of imminent danger.

Hell is a place of instability. It is described as a lake of fire.[32] A lake changes, fluctuates, with no firm surface on which to stand. Hell is a place where every moment is lived in uncertainty.

Hell is a place of darkness.[33] It is totally devoid of light. Have you ever heard people quip that they want to go to hell to be with their friends? You might want to point out that while their friends may be in hell, they will never be seen. It's pitch black in hell; there's nothing to distract people from their suffering and sorrow and fears and insecurities and instability. When we are sick, our suffering seems to intensify in the middle of the night. We long for the daylight to come. Somehow just the light of day makes us feel better. But in hell the dawn never comes.

Hell is a place of loneliness. Each person is there alone. He or she may be able to hear the weeping and gnashing of teeth of others, but there is no one to talk to, no one to cry with, no one to even yell at. Each person is isolated in hate and bitterness and jealousy and pride and selfishness and meanness.

Hell is a place of dissatisfaction. Jesus described it as a fire.[34] It may be a literal fire that creates a physical sensation of burning or just an overwhelming yearning for God, for love, for joy, for peace, for life that will never be. It must be the equivalent of being intensely thirsty yet never having a drop of water. Or intensely hungry with never a crumb to eat.

Hell is a place of eternal separation from God.[35] Each person who goes to hell will be separated forever from the source of life, the heart of love, the very One for whom he or she was created.

God doesn't *send* anyone to hell. You send yourself there when you refuse His gracious offer of salvation: "For God so loved the world that he gave his One and only Son, that whoever believes in him *shall not perish* but have eternal life." BUT if you refuse to believe, you will perish. You will go to hell. The choice is yours.

Our desperate need for eternal life is met in Jesus Christ. All you and I need to do is receive Him.

Our Need for Light

As Jesus spoke with such profound eloquence, did a veil of darkness drop across Nicodemus's face? Looking into his eyes, could Jesus see Nicodemus pulling back and withdrawing from the truth?

Nicodemus must have felt that his entire world was on the verge of shattering into a thousand fragments. All his life he had been convinced that his religion made him right with God. He had taken refuge in the security that his good works would outweigh his bad works, and God would let him into heaven. He was sure his morality and integrity and purity would please God. In fact, he had lived with smugness, believing that his pharisaical religiosity made him better than the average person. It had never occurred to Nicodemus, a Jew, circumcised on the eighth day, incorporated into the nation of Israel, a ruling member of the Sanhedrin, a Pharisee, that he was in danger of perishing! The delusion and deception in his life must have begun to crack and crumble as Jesus verbally pounded away at the barrier of unbelief. And through the cracks, the light of truth penetrated the darkness—light from which Nicodemus recoiled in intense discomfort, even if temporarily.[36]

And so Jesus brought the conversation to a conclusion by issuing a verdict: "Light has come into the world, but men loved darkness instead of light because their deeds were evil. Everyone who does evil hates the light, and will not come into the light for fear that his deeds will be exposed. But whoever lives by the truth comes into the light, so that it may be seen plainly that what he has done has been done through God" (John 3:19–21).

It must have been totally mind-blowing for Nicodemus to be bluntly told:

that his unbelief was evil;

that his good deeds had been exposed by the Light of truth as insufficient to satisfy a perfect God;

that what was really preventing him from believing was the fear of acknowledging that his life had been wasted and he had strayed off track, as far as eternity was concerned;

that his carefully cultivated righteousness and religiosity were as filthy rags in God's sight;

that he was no better than the next sinner who was in danger of God's judgment.

Just as, long before, God had invited Noah to come into the ark, Jesus invited Nicodemus to come into the Light. But Nicodemus, reeling from the shock of the truth applied to his life, with a face that had lost any mask of pretense, must have averted his eyes, bowed his head, and with stooped shoulders slipped away into the darkness . . .

Sometime later, the Sanhedrin became embroiled in open animosity, jealousy, and hostility toward Jesus of Nazareth. With arrogance and eloquence, the rulers of Israel verbally berated the Man and His ministry. Except for one man—Nicodemus. Toward the end of the debate, he stood with quiet dignity and reasoned with his colleagues to do what he had done—meet with Jesus in order to find out for themselves who He was and what He had to say. But Nicodemus, the greatly respected teacher of the Law, the renowned Old Testament scholar, was shouted down for his ignorance and rebuked for his stupidity.[37]

Early one morning some months later, the ruling body of Israel, of which Nicodemus was a member, was hastily called together. As the sleepy-eyed leaders gathered, their attention was directed to a Man standing quietly before them with His hands bound. What a shock it must have been when Nicodemus recognized the young Rabbi who had boldly and bluntly told him during that nighttime conversation so many weeks before how he could receive eternal life.

This time Nicodemus remained silent as he listened to the angry accusations—of tax evasion, insurrection, terrorism, and blasphemy—leveled against Jesus. In the end, the charge of blasphemy was sealed by Jesus Himself. With every eye riveted on Him and every ear straining to hear, He clearly and unmistakably claimed to be the Messiah of Israel and the unique Son of God. As the normally formal and dignified Sanhedrin erupted into an outraged brawl, Nicodemus must have stood in the shadows and watched in horror as Jesus was beaten, slapped, spat upon, and mocked.[38] Even if he had not accepted the radical teaching of spiritual rebirth, surely he must have recognized that Jesus did not merit that kind of brutal treatment.

Did Nicodemus once again slip away to ponder what he had seen and heard? Or did he follow at a distance and watch as Jesus was subjected to three Roman trials? Did he then join the bloodthirsty mob that congregated at the place of crucifixion and watch as Jesus was nailed to a Roman cross? Did he ask himself, "Why? God, *why?* Why did You let this happen? What does this mean? *Who is this Man?*" And did God bring to the Old Testament scholar's mind a familiar passage from the greatest of the prophets, Isaiah?

"He was despised and rejected by men, a man of sorrows, and familiar with suffering. Like one from whom men hide their faces he was despised, and we esteemed him not. Surely he took up our infirmities and carried our sorrows, yet we considered him stricken by God, smitten by him, and afflicted. But he was pierced for our transgressions, he was crushed for our iniquities; the punishment that brought us peace was upon him, and by his wounds we are healed."[39]

Perhaps the light then dawned in the mind of Nicodemus. Jesus of Nazareth *is* the Messiah! But the Messiah was not to be a king in Israel, like David, or a world ruler, like Solomon—not this time. Instead He would be a permanent sacrifice for sin. That's what Jesus had meant when He said He would be lifted up as Moses had lifted up the serpent in the wilderness.

As the almost unthinkable thoughts tumbled through his mind, the hours must have run together. If only he could do something! But it was too late. Friday evening was drawing near, and Jesus' body hung bloodied, limp, and lifeless on the cross. The crowd had long since dispersed. The only ones left were Nicodemus, a small handful of women, and a wealthy businessman from Jerusalem, named Joseph.

Nicodemus must have overheard Joseph's plans to claim the body, for while Joseph made the necessary arrangements with the authorities, Nicodemus put together a small fortune of burial spices. When Joseph returned to take the body down from the cross to bury in his own tomb, Nicodemus boldly assisted.[40] Disregarding the danger from the Romans and his almost certain excommunication from the Sanhedrin, he chose to openly identify with Jesus in His death.[41] And Nicodemus came out of the darkness into the Light.

MY FATHER was seated at a welcoming dinner in his honor attended by the civic, business, religious, and political leaders of the eastern nation that had invited him to hold open evangelistic meetings. The man next to him was the archbishop of the dominant religion in that country. During the course of the dinner conversation, my father asked the archbishop when he had become a Christian. The man's eyes glistened with emotion as he put down his fork and proceeded to tell my father his story.

He had already been installed as the archbishop in his country when he was invited to Chicago to give a lecture in a prominent theological school. He accepted the invitation and found himself in the heart of the Windy City.

One afternoon, in his effort to do some sightseeing, he boarded a city bus. No sooner had he taken his seat when a big black finger tapped him on the shoulder. He turned to look into the full, round, ebony face of an obviously poor woman seated behind him. In a wonderfully rich voice, she asked, "Mister, has you ever been born again?" He frowned, thinking for sure he had misunderstood her question since English was his second language. With polite reserve he asked, "Excuse me?"

The deep, rolling voice repeated, "I says, has you been born again?" The archbishop stiffened his back, straightened his shoulders, and replied with the greatest dignity, "My dear madam, I am the archbishop of the church in my country. I am here to give a lecture at the theological seminary."

As the bus rolled to a stop, the woman rose to get off. She looked at the proud, religious man dressed in his flowing robes bearing the bejeweled insignia of his office and persisted bluntly, "Mister, that ain't what I asked you. I asked you, 'Has you been born again?'" Then she turned and walked off the bus and out of his life.

But, the archbishop said, her words rang in his ears and burned in his soul. He went back to his hotel room, located a Gideon Bible in a dresser drawer, opened it to the gospel of John, and read the familiar story of Nicodemus. With increasing clarity and conviction, he knew that even with all of his religious training and devotion and service and recognition, he had never been born again. So he slipped down on his knees, and that night, in a Chicago hotel room thousands of miles from his home, God answered his heart's cry, and just gave him Jesus.

JESUS MAKES HAPPINESS ATTAINABLE

He discharges the debtors.
He delivers the captives.
He defends the feeble.
He blesses the young.
He serves the unfortunate.
He regards the aged.
He rewards the diligent.
He beautifies the meek.

He is the key to knowledge.
He is the wellspring of wisdom.
He is the foundation of faith.
He is the doorway of deliverance.
He is the pathway to peace.
He is the roadway of righteousness.
He is the gateway to glory.
He is the highway to happiness.

Just give me Jesus! He makes happiness attainable!

5

JESUS MAKES HAPPINESS ATTAINABLE . . .

For the Outcast

JOHN 4:1–42

On September 2, 1966, I exchanged marriage vows with Danny Lotz during an evening candlelight ceremony in the little mountain chapel where my parents had wed. After a lovely, exhausting reception where I stood in line with my new husband and our parents to receive more than seven hundred guests, Danny and I left sometime after midnight to spend our wonderful first night together in a nearby town.

The next day we had a long drive along Interstate 85 to Atlanta. We planned to spend our second night there before catching a plane for Southern California, where we would enjoy our honeymoon. So, on the first day of my life as Mrs. Danny Lotz, as we were driving along, I happened to glance over at the gas gauge. The needle was hovering close to the "E," so I said gently, in my sweetest, most submissive voice, "Danny, darling, the gas is getting low. Don't you think we should stop and fill up?"

"No, no," he replied emphatically. "We have plenty of gas."

After several more miles down the road, I looked at the gas gauge again. The needle pointed below empty. Without wanting to seem obstinate and strong-willed on my first day of marriage, I once more chose a sweet, submissive tone. "Danny, darling, the gas gauge is registering below empty. Why don't we stop and fill up?"

"No, no. This car always has more gas than the gauge indicates. We can go for miles."

His enthusiasm was undimmed and his focus unwavering as we hurtled down the interstate. About ten miles later, the car lurched, popped, and coughed, then glided to a smooth, silent stop beside the road. We had run out of gas!

Running out of gas was no problem to my new husband. Even though it was about 95 degrees and we had come to a stop in an open area that smelled as though every sewer in the county emptied into it, my sweet Danny, wanting to be so protective of his new bride, rolled up all the windows and locked the doors to keep me safe. Then, being the athlete that he is, he jogged down the road out of sight.

Forty-five scorching, smelly minutes later, he reappeared in a tow truck with a can of gas. As the attendant peered at my dripping face through the closed windows, Danny poured the gas into the tank, handed the can back to the mechanic with a large tip to express his appreciation, and waved good-bye as the truck took off, soon disappearing into the distance.

As I gasped for air, Danny opened the door with a big smile, got into the car, and confidently turned the key in the ignition. Nothing happened. Try as hard as he could, he couldn't make the car even turn over. The battery had died! Giving me a loving, apologetic look, my new husband rolled up the windows, bounded out of the car, locked the doors, and, once again, jogged into the distance. For the next forty-five minutes the heat outside the car was nothing compared to the heat inside of me! I was frustrated, miserable, nauseated, and wondering what I had gotten myself into!

The tow truck finally reappeared on the horizon. It stopped beside our car, and the mechanic helped Danny adjust the cables and jump-start the battery. This time the attendant waited until our car was safely running before leaving us. Just as we prepared to continue our journey, another car flying past on the highway suddenly slammed on its brakes, backed up crazily to where we were parked, and screeched to a halt. All four doors of the car burst open at the same time, and out poured Danny's brother, along with other friends who had been at our wedding. I couldn't even crack a smile.

Danny and his brother were clapping each other on the back, bantering back and forth, when his brother said, "Dan, how is married life?" And my husband of less than twenty-four hours replied with a broad grin and undimmed enthusiasm to his oldest, single brother, "Sam, it's wonderful! You ought to try it!" At that moment, I was thankful no one had asked *me*!

But on that first day of marriage I learned a valuable life lesson: Whether you're in a car or in a relationship or just coursing through everyday life, you can't run on empty.

Are you running on empty? Does the gauge in your life point to "E" because your heart is full of misery, or you are barely surviving, or you are just "sweating life out" with no happiness? Or fulfillment? Or satisfaction? Or joy? Or meaning? Or purpose?

Are you someone who just endures life?

Are you someone whose greatest goal is just to make it through one more day?

Are you someone to whom life has been unkind or unjust for whatever reason?

Are you someone who has all the symptoms of emptiness?

Are you someone who feels like the outcast in Samaria?

THE SYMPTOMS THAT REVEAL EMPTINESS

After visiting with Nicodemus, Jesus went searching for the outcast. He headed into the Judean countryside with His small band of disciples. As people began flocking to Him, rumors about His popularity and ministry began to develop into a controversy that threatened to divide His followers from those of His cousin and forerunner, John the Baptist. Rather than lend fuel to the fires of gossip and jealousy, Jesus quietly withdrew, returning to Galilee.

Instead of taking the normal route from Judea to Galilee that circumvented Samaria with its despised, outcast minority, Jesus walked directly to Sychar, Samaria's capital, because "he had to go through Samaria" (John 4:4). There was only one reason "he had to go through Samaria": He had a divine appointment. He knew there was an outcast in Samaria who was running on empty. "So he came to a town in Samaria called Sychar, near the plot of ground Jacob had given to his son Joseph. Jacob's well was there, and Jesus, tired as he was from the journey, sat down by the well" (John 4:5–6).

What an awesome, moving glimpse into the heart of God we see as Jesus—the Creator of the heavens and earth, the Son of God, the King of kings and the Lord of lords, sat by Himself on the stone wall encircling Jacob's well, bone weary after His long walk. He was dusty, dirty, hungry, thirsty—but He was waiting to meet one outcast who had all the symptoms of emptiness and unhappiness. The disciples had gone into town to find food, leaving Jesus alone to wait . . . *And still today* Jesus waits beside the well of water to meet with those who will come to Him.

Have you ever considered that you have a divine appointment when you get up early for your quiet time of prayer and meditation on His Word? . . . That Jesus is patiently, personally waiting to meet with you there?

Have you ever thought of going to church as a divine appointment? . . . That Jesus is patiently, personally waiting to meet with you there?

Have you ever thought of the Bible study you belong to as a divine appointment? . . . That Jesus is patiently, personally waiting to meet with you there?

What a difference it would make in our attitude of expectancy and our habit of consistency if we truly wrapped our hearts around the knowledge that each *is* a divine appointment, that Jesus Himself is waiting to meet with us. Jesus knows:

the small secrets of your heart,
the unspoken dreams of your imagination,
the unrevealed thoughts of your mind,
the emotional shards of your feelings,
the paralyzing fears for your future,
the bitter resentments of your past,
the joys and heartaches,
the pleasures and pain,
the successes and failures,
the honors and humiliations,
the deeds and the doubts.

He knows all about you, inside and out, past, present, and future.[1] And He recognizes the subtle symptoms of emptiness . . . symptoms such as dissatisfaction.

The Dissatisfaction in Freedom

I imagine nothing was moving in the shimmering noonday heat that day in Sychar except perhaps little dust devils that danced once in a while to the tune of a midday breeze. Perhaps a fly or two buzzed or a lizard darted or a distant shepherd called to his sheep. But for the most part, Jesus was alone as He sat by the well, waiting, watching. His face must have softened and a smile may have played at the corners of His mouth as His eyes focused compassionately on the solitary figure approaching the well. As the figure drew nearer, it was easy to see that the "Samaritan woman," with a large water jar balanced deftly on her shoulder, intended to draw water from the public well (John 4:7).

As a Samaritan, the woman's ancestors dated back to 700 BC, when the Assyrians had invaded the Northern Kingdom of Israel and taken all those living there into captivity. Because a few Israelites had escaped and returned to their homeland, the Assyrian king sent some of his countrymen to live in and secure the former Israelite territory, to guard against future revolts. Over the years that followed, the Assyrians who had been sent to Israel intermingled and intermarried with the Israelites who had escaped and returned. The resulting race—half-Israelite and half-Assyrian—were called Samaritans.

The Samaritans were regarded as half-breeds, not only in race but also in religion. The Assyrian king had heard of some unusual problems with his captured territory and had felt he needed to placate Israel's God. So he sent some of the Jewish priests he had captured, along with some of his own pagan Assyrian priests, to the land of Israel. These priests cooperated in an ecumenical movement that mixed half of the truth of Israel with half of the pagan practices of the Assyrians until they were satisfied with the resulting "half-breed" religion. It was a mixture of Assyrian superstition, idolatry, and gods with Jewish ceremonies, traditions, and truth. Thousands of years later, it's still fairly easy to understand why the Jews despised the Samaritans, and why the Samaritans, resentful of being so despised, hated the Jews.

This makes it even more astounding that Jesus, not only a Jew but a rabbi as well, "had to go through Samaria." But what is even more amazing is that He was actually sitting at the well, *waiting to speak* to a Samaritan *woman*! This woman's dissatisfaction was later symbolically revealed when she pleaded with the Lord, "Sir, give me this water so that I won't get thirsty and have to keep coming here to draw water" (John 4:15). She admitted then to an intense thirst that was never completely satisfied.

We know this woman was *dissatisfied spiritually* because she did not know the truth. She had been created in the image of God, with a capacity to enjoy a personal, permanent relationship with her Creator, yet she was separated from Him because of her sin. There must have been a deep yearning in her soul—an emptiness she tried to fill with the cheap substitute of her religion, which mixed the unique revelation of God with false ideas and opinions and rituals. I doubt she had ever searched for truth herself. She just went to her place of worship and believed what she was told. But it didn't satisfy her.

Do you know someone who is dissatisfied spiritually?

Someone who goes to church but has settled for a religious experience instead of a personal relationship with God?

Someone who has never studied the Bible but has let others decide what he or she should believe?

Someone who mixes the truth of God's Word with denominational traditions and rituals?

Someone who mixes the truth of God's Word with popular opinions and cultural ideology?

If that person does not know God in a right, personal, permanent relationship through faith in Jesus Christ, you may safely assume that deep within, he or she is dissatisfied spiritually.

This Samaritan woman was also *dissatisfied emotionally*. Judging from the multiple marriages Jesus eventually revealed, she must have been middle-aged. She was losing her youth, losing her beauty, losing her energy. I expect she felt as though life were passing her by. Was she desperately tired of living, having long ago lost any sense of real purpose and meaning beyond surviving from one day to the next?

Do you know what that feels like? I recently celebrated my fiftieth birthday. What a shock to wake up and realize that I'm middle-aged! And at such a time, if you are like me, you tend to survey your life to assess where you are. Have you recently celebrated a similar milestone in your life? Did you then ask such questions as, "Does my life count? Have I realized all of the things I dreamed of as a young person and a young career professional and a young married partner and a young parent? Do I amount to what I always dreamed I would? Has life been what I expected?" Perhaps it's exactly what you expected. It's just that now that you've experienced it, it's not satisfying. It's not what you thought it would be.

Middle age can bring about tremendous challenges. Very often it involves a forced career change or a lonely empty nest or the exhausting care of elderly parents or unexpected health difficulties or just a traumatic midlife crisis.

The Samaritan woman was dissatisfied emotionally—not only due to middle age but also due to her loneliness, for "it was about the sixth hour . . . when a Samaritan woman came to draw water" (John 4:6–7).[2] It was customary for the women during that era to come to the well in groups either early in the morning or early in the evening. It was a social event equivalent to sitting in a rocking chair on the front porch after a hard day of work, chatting with your neighbor. It was the equivalent of standing a few extra minutes at the water cooler in the office to pass the time of day with a coworker. It was the equivalent of joining friends for a game of cards or talking over the backyard fence or sharing a cup of coffee. It was simply a time to satisfy the emotional needs for friendship and companionship. Yet this woman had come in the middle of the day. Alone. Why? The obvious reason is that she was a social outcast in a nation of outcasts.

The Samaritan woman had no one to confide in,
no one to open her heart to,
no one to relax with,
no one to share with,
no one to laugh with,
no one to cry with.

She had tried, again and again, to have a meaningful relationship (John 4:18). But each effort had met with miserable failure, until her loneliness was surely greater than she could bear. It wasn't just a lack of companionship and friendship. She also had an inner lack of contentment and satisfaction. Surely there must have been a deep loneliness in her soul.

Are you lonely inside? Even surrounded by family, friends, coworkers, neighbors, or church members, are you lonely on the inside because you have no one you can confide in or open your heart to or relax with or share with or laugh with or cry with, no one who understands you or even truly knows you?

Or perhaps this Samaritan woman was something of a radical feminist. It's obvious she had not played by the rules or lived according to the traditional values typical of her gender and generation. Maybe she was defiantly coming to the well in the middle of the day with an in-your-face, I-can-do-as-I-please attitude. Maybe she was asserting her right to exercise her freedom to come and go as she chose in spite of acceptable cultural practices. Maybe she just felt liberated to do what she wanted, when she wanted, how she wanted, where she wanted, with or without whomever she wanted. But it obviously wasn't enough. She was still "thirsty."

In the 1970s, many women of my generation were dissatisfied. Most of them were stay-at-home moms, devoting themselves totally to the responsibility of raising their families and meeting the needs of their husbands. But there was a restlessness of spirit that most husbands, generally speaking, were unaware of, or inattentive to. At that very point in time, a handful of women spoke with a national voice, urging women to leave their homes, families, and husbands in order to discover inner satisfaction and personal fulfillment in a job or career or some type of individual achievement. So a generation of women began looking for satisfaction outside of their homes.

Then in the 1980s we discovered the well was dry. As we juggled our homes and families with a job or career, we couldn't seem to find what we were looking for. The dissatisfaction permeated our lives. We couldn't find it in our homes, and we couldn't find it outside of our homes.

In the 1990s we found women essentially free to do what they chose, when they chose, how they chose, with or without whomever they chose, where they chose. While there have been some positive results, the feminist movement that was supposed to elevate the status of women in society and secure them more respect has essentially been moved aside. In its place there is a flood of feminine freedom expressed by cheapened morality, obscene vulgarity, crude profanity, aggressive sexuality, and competitive equality. All of these symptoms give evidence that many of the women of my generation are dissatisfied in their freedom.

The conversation that followed between the Samaritan woman and Jesus confirms that she was dissatisfied in her freedom. Jesus, who knew these things before she spoke, had quietly watched her approach.[3] As she drew near the well, did she swagger a little with the exaggerated confidence of an insecure person? Did she toss her head in affected casualness that was intended to let Him know she couldn't care less about who He was and why He was there? Did she glare defensively at Him because she thought He might make a rude remark to her? Or, being accustomed to the stares of others, did she just ignore Him as though He weren't even there?

As she silently prepared to draw water, imagine her consternation when He actually spoke to her! Respectfully. Humbly. Sincerely. Inquiring, "Will you give me a drink?" (John 4:7). With that seemingly simple, innocent request, Jesus touched on the greatest need in this woman's life. *She* was the one who was thirsty. *She* was the one who needed a drink. *She* was the one who was deeply dissatisfied with life. But she didn't see it. Her focus was distorted.

The Distortion of Focus

Of all the things the woman might have expected when she first noticed the Jewish Rabbi sitting at the well, the last would have been that He would initiate a conversation. To find Him there at all was profoundly curious since it was unheard-of for a Jew to be in Samaria. To feel His steady gaze on her might have made her uncomfortable. But when He broke the silence with His words, she was genuinely shocked! It was forbidden by law for a Rabbi to address any woman in public, whether she was his mother, sister, wife, or friend. Yet here He was, a Jewish Rabbi, speaking to her, a Samaritan *woman,* in public!

In her amazed consternation, it's a wonder she didn't drop her water jar instead of swinging it gracefully to the ground as she blurted out, "You are a Jew and I am a Samaritan woman. How can you ask me for a drink?" (John 4:9). He had pierced her protective shield with His words, and her response revealed that she was totally *preoccupied with who she was.*

With two thousand years of hindsight, God was speaking to her, and she was so completely focused on racial, sexual, denominational, and cultural differences that she was in danger of missing the blessing He had come to give her. She was caught up in labels. Her response may have been triggered by an instinctive feeling of inferiority since she, the Samaritan, was the outcast. Or it could have stemmed from a feeling of superiority since she was on her home ground and He was the stranger. Either self-centered attitude revealed her deep-seated prejudice.

Even as I wrote this, I wrestled with some of these same attitudes that had surfaced unexpectedly in my speaking ministry. After accepting an invitation to address a large conference for ministers, I was informed I would not be presenting a plenary address, as I had understood; I would instead be leading a workshop. After I agreed to do the workshop, I received further correspondence that said I would not be leading a workshop after all, but holding a women's meeting on the side. At that point my antenna went up. On further inquiry, sure enough, I discovered that some people involved in the planning were balking at having a woman in the pulpit. And I wonder, will they miss the blessing God has for them because their focus is distorted? They are allowing their prejudices to deafen their ears and blind their eyes.

What prejudice is distorting your focus because the speaker is of. . .

another gender

or race

or culture

or denomination

or economic level

or educational background?

Because the messenger . . .

has a different color skin

or speaks with a different accent

or wears funny-looking clothes
or worships with contemporary choruses
or appears in unexpected places—
have you thrown up an invisible barrier? How many blessings from God have you and I missed because we didn't like the packaging?

I imagine the Samaritan woman drew a cup of cool water from the well and handed it to the Jewish Rabbi, just to see what He would do. Her consternation must have been complete when He not only took it from her but also drank it gratefully. Then, with the refreshing drops of water glistening on His lips, He spoke to her again. He didn't get into a defensive argument with her about the Jews and the Samaritans. He just sharpened her focus and whetted her appetite and increased her thirst when He said, somewhat mysteriously, "If you knew the gift of God and who it is that asks you for a drink, you would have asked him and he would have given you living water" (John 4:10).

It's as though Jesus were pleading, "If you knew who is speaking to you, the 'who' would overcome your prejudice! Your focus is distorted. Focus on Me!"

But the woman was preoccupied with who she was and with *what she did.* It was obvious that she knew a lot about this particular well and about drawing water. She missed Jesus' emphasis on the gift of God, she missed His reference to who was speaking, and she missed His description of the water as "living." Instead she only picked up on what He said about something that was familiar to her—water. So she replied very practically, "Sir, . . . you have nothing to draw with and the well is deep. Where can you get this living water? Are you greater than our father Jacob, who gave us the well and drank from it himself, as did also his sons and his flocks and herds?" (John 4:11–12). She was so preoccupied with who she was and what she did that she wasn't a good listener, and she totally missed His point.

How many times have you and I been guilty of the same thing? My children used to burst through the door after school, and as I fixed them a snack, they would chatter about their day—and chatter and chatter. I would find myself nodding from time to time until finally one would wave a hand in my face and say, "Mom, come back to planet Earth." And I knew while they had been talking my mind had been on other things.

How often have I been guilty of that kind of distractedness during my morning quiet times with the Lord? As I read His Word and pray, I have actually found myself eyeing the page while my mind races ahead with the responsibilities and activities of the day. Even as I read the words, I'm planning what I'm going to wear or what I need to fix for dinner or how I'm going to manage all the responsibilities of the day. I might pick up on a word or two, but I discover I'm not really listening to what He has to say. How many blessings have I missed or postponed because, in conversation with Him, I'm preoccupied with myself?

The Samaritan woman seemed very efficient. She knew how to draw water, and she knew something of the history of the well. She was confident in her knowledge of her subject. Like many women, she viewed things very sensibly and practically; she knew it was impossible for Him to draw water from this well unless He had a long rope and some sort of bucket. She was totally preoccupied with her own familiar sphere of knowledge and experience, and her preoccupation caused her to postpone the blessing Jesus wanted to give her.

What is your familiar sphere of knowledge and experience?

Your business?

Your career?

Your investments?

Your home?

Your family?

Your church?

Your ministry?

Your hobbies?

Your exercise?

Your body?

Your diet?

Your volunteerism?

Does your sphere comprise the sum total of your time and attention and money and focus? Do you view everything from the perspective of what is familiar and comfortable to you? There's a bigger world out there than you and I know. There is more to life than what we can see and taste and feel and hear and touch.

Jesus knew the woman had searched for satisfaction and come up short. He knew her heart was empty, without love or self-worth or meaning or fulfillment or happiness. And so He gently but pointedly replied, "Everyone who drinks this water will be thirsty again." (John 4:13). What was "this water"? The woman took it to mean the water in Jacob's well, but Jesus was speaking to her heart. All those who look to draw their satisfaction from the wells of the world—pleasure, popularity, position, possessions, politics, power, prestige, finances, family, friends, fame, fortune, career, children, church, clubs, sports, sex, success, recognition, reputation, religion, education, entertainment, exercise, honors, health, hobbies—*will soon be thirsty again!*

If you look for deep, lasting satisfaction from any of these wells the world offers, you're wasting your time.

The great Catholic theologian Saint Augustine prayed, "Lord, Thou hast made me for Thyself. Therefore my heart is restless till it finds its rest in Thee." Victor Frankl, the Austrian psychologist, wrote, "Each of us has a God-shaped hole in our hearts that only a personal relationship with God can fill."

While the world's wells can temporarily be meaningful and pleasing, they eventually leave the seeker emptier than before, wondering, "Is that all there is?"

The answer is, "No, that isn't all there is." Jesus was specific as He persisted in meeting the need of the Samaritan woman's heart by convincing her that there *was* something more to life, something she was created for, something that would satisfy her deepest longings—and it was available to her through Him. He told her, "Whoever drinks the water I give him will never thirst. Indeed, the water I give him will become in him a spring of water welling up to eternal life" (John 4:14).

At this point the woman jumped at His offer. She was now preoccupied with *what she wanted but didn't have*—an easier life. She revealed the boredom and drudgery of her mundane life when she answered with what surely was a tinge of eager hope, "Sir, give me this water so that I won't get thirsty and have to keep coming here to draw water" (John 4:15). Did she just want Jesus to solve all her problems and make her life a comfortable bed of sweet-smelling roses?

Is that what you want? Do you just want Jesus to give you an easier life? A healthier life? A wealthier life? A problem-free life? You want the answers to prayer and the gifts He gives, but are you overlooking *Him?* Are you preoccupied with what He can do for you, instead of the relationship that He offers you?

Maybe the Samaritan woman was thinking, "Sir, You don't know how hard my life is. I'm just going through the motions. I'd give anything not to be an outcast and have to come here in the middle of the day in order to avoid the gossip and criticism of the other women. I'd give anything to be able to find what I've been looking for all my life. Maybe this is it. I'm so tired of running on empty. It certainly won't hurt to try what You're offering. God knows I've tried just about everything else."

She had begun to be drawn to this unusual Man who seemed attentive and caring. He seemed to understand and know her, unlike anyone she had ever met before. She showed her increasing respect for Him by first calling Him "a Jew," then "Sir." She was drawn to Him, perhaps in spite of herself, and desperately began to want more in life. Her emptiness and unhappiness became suddenly, overwhelmingly unbearable. So in the only way she knew, she humbly asked for the Living Water. Even though she was confused, she reached out to take what He offered.

As He listened not only to the words the woman spoke but also to the thoughts in her mind and the emotions of her heart, He must have been deeply moved. This was why "he had to go through Samaria." At this point, you would think He would give her the Living Water. After all, that was what He *wanted* to do. And she was so close. But one thing still stood in the way of her receiving it. Her sin. So Jesus convicted her in order that she might confess her sin and be forgiven, opening her heart to be filled with Him.

With infinite tenderness yet piercing truthfulness, He confronted her with her sin by instructing her, "Go, call your husband and come back" (John 4:16).

His words must have felt like ice water thrown in her face. She must have stiffened, turned as white as a sheet, and abruptly found herself jerked back to reality, remembering she was nothing but a hopeless outcast. She would never be anything more. Empty. Unhappy. Deeply discouraged by the failures in her life that she now believed would prevent her from ever drinking of the Living Water.

The Discouragement of Failure

The woman did not deny or excuse or rationalize or try to hide her failure. But her reply must have been almost inaudible: "I have no husband" (John 4:17).

I think if Jesus had pressed her, she would have told Him everything at that point. But of course He didn't need to press her. He already knew. Before she could turn away, He spoke to her clearly, with eyes that penetrated into her past, her present, and her future, "You are right when you say you have no husband. The fact is, you have had five husbands, and the man you now have is not your husband. What you have just said is quite true" (John 4:17–18). The woman must have responded in wide-eyed astonishment as this total Stranger put His finger on the greatest sin of her life. *How did He know?*

Jesus didn't condemn her. She was condemned already. But He did open her eyes to see herself as God saw her—a woman who had had five husbands and who was presently living with a man outside of marriage. She was a woman living in sin.

Today as Jesus gazes with those same penetrating eyes into your life, what does He see? What is the greatest sin of your life? Many people think the greatest sins are murder, adultery, theft, and similar gross acts. But Jesus said the greatest commandment was to love the Lord your God with all your heart, mind, soul, and strength.[4] Therefore, it stands to reason that the greatest sin in all the world is breaking the greatest commandment. Could it be that the greatest sin is simply not to love the Lord your God with all your heart, mind, soul, and strength? If so, think of all the moments of all the days of all the weeks of all the months of all the years of your life when you have been guilty of the greatest sin of all! Does God see you as a man or woman living in sin? Before we can be filled with the Living Water, we must be cleansed of sin. Before we can be cleansed of sin, we must be convicted. And sometimes it's painful. And shameful.

Jesus had known the woman didn't have a husband when He told her to go and call him. He was just convicting her of her sin so that she would confess it and be cleansed and be able to receive the Living Water. Is there some sin of which God is convicting you at this moment? What is it? A sin of jealousy, pride, unforgiveness, resentment, anger, selfishness, meanness, lying, worry, judgmentalness, unkindness, unbelief, or immorality?

We cry out, "God, give me the Living Water! Fill me with Your Spirit!" And He says, "*Go,* call your husband and come back"; *go,* confess your sin, and *come to the cross* for cleansing. Unconfessed sin in our lives is one of the single greatest barriers to happiness. So He promises us reassuringly that "if we confess our sins, he is faithful and just and will forgive us our sins and purify us from all unrighteousness."[5]

The Disillusionment with Faith

At this point the Samaritan woman must have been extremely agitated as she then sought to divert attention from the real problem, her sin, by talking about denominational and religious differences. The conversation was becoming too personal. This is the same type of diversionary tactic used by many today when the issue of repentance is brought up as a requirement for rebirth. The classic defense is something like, "What about all the people in Africa who have never heard the gospel?"

As we will see, the Samaritan woman's temporary diversion revealed she was disillusioned with her faith. Her discouragement and despair must have been almost complete, but her eyes were being opened to the fact that Jesus was more than just a man. She must have looked at Him intently as she pointed out, perhaps bitterly, "Sir . . . I can see that you are a prophet. Our fathers worshiped on this mountain, but you Jews claim that the place where we must worship is in Jerusalem" (John 4:19–20). Someone today might say, "God, I've tried religion. It doesn't work for me. I'm sick of all the bickering and fighting and splitting of hairs going on in churches. I'm sick of all the differences and even rivalry between church denominations. I'm sick of all the religious hypocrites. It's been of no personal benefit at all! I've been religious, but I'm still running on empty!"

Who could be more hopelessly disillusioned than someone who has tried God and not found the answers? Who could be more disillusioned than you, as you read this, hoping for answers to your emptiness and unhappiness, only to find that the answer is Jesus? You feel disillusioned because you know you have been born again, you know you have eternal life, you know you are a child of God, you know you're a Christian—but you still seem to be running on empty! You've looked for answers from your church, from your religion, from your denomination, but they just aren't there! It's not working for you!

Or maybe the Samaritan woman had been sincerely asking in a rather confused way, "Where can I find God? How can I get right with God? I know I need to make an acceptable sacrifice for my sin, but where? I've been taught that I can sacrifice here. But maybe I should sacrifice in Jerusalem."

Jesus didn't back down, not even a little, in the face of her defensive challenge. Nor did He get caught up in secondary issues. He dismissed the differences between the Jews and Samaritans by saying, "Believe me, woman, a time is coming when you will worship the Father neither on this mountain nor in Jerusalem" (John 4:21). He then told her plainly, as He may be telling you, that her faith didn't work for two primary reasons. The first reason was that she was *ignorant:* "You Samaritans worship what you do not know; we worship what we do know, for salvation is from the Jews" (John 4:22).

Jesus cut straight to the bottom line. The Samaritans accepted some of the Old Testament truth, but it was intermingled with the ancient Assyrian myths and pagan rituals and their own ideas and opinions. As a Samaritan, she didn't know the truth because what she had been taught was false. She didn't really know what she worshiped and believed. On the other hand, the Jews had been taught the sacrificial system as a means of getting right with God and the law as a means of knowing how to please God. Even though, like Nicodemus, the Jews needed to be born again, their faith was based on the truth of God's revelation.

Do you know what you believe? Can you sort out the truth—based on God's Word—from your church's rituals and traditions and teachings? If your faith is based on hearsay, like the Samaritan woman's was, or on secondhand information or on traditions instead of on your own personal study of the Scriptures, then you, too, will be disillusioned. If you say you have tried Jesus and He just doesn't work, don't overlook the fact that the real problem may be your ignorance of Who He truly is and what He has actually said and how He actively works.

The second reason Jesus gave for why her faith didn't work was *insincerity*. He revealed, "A time is coming and has now come when the true worshipers will worship the Father in spirit and truth, for they are the kind of worshipers the Father seeks. God is spirit, and his worshipers must worship in spirit and in truth" (John 4:23–24).

We *must* worship God as He prescribes or He won't accept it. We can't worship Him any way we choose as long as we're sincere and not hurting anyone else. We can't worship Him the way we want while Muslims worship Him the way they want and Jews worship Him the way they want and Buddhists worship Him the way they want. Jesus said we must worship God as *He* wants.

God wants us to worship Him in *spirit*. What does that mean? It means we must be indwelt by the Holy Spirit. We must be born again. It also means we must worship Him sincerely, earnestly, with a right spirit, with a sweet spirit. We are to worship from the depths of our beings as we are continually occupied with God. Worship is not just the act of going to church because we always have or because it's the thing to do. It is not just putting your body in a pew while your mind is elsewhere. It is not just smiling serenely on the outside while on the inside you are filled with unconfessed sin.

God also wants us to worship Him in *truth*. What does that mean? It means there is no way to God, no way at all, without coming through Jesus Christ who is *the* Truth.[6] It also means that we must base our relationship with Him on His Word, which is the truth. There is no way we can worship God acceptably if we are not reading and getting to know our Bibles so that we might live accordingly. And to worship Him in truth means to worship Him honestly, without hypocrisy, standing open and transparent before Him.

What needs correcting in your worship? Has it been more outward form and ritual than inner desire and love? Has it been based more on your church's rituals or your denomination's traditions or your pastor's say-so than on your personal study of the Bible? If you and I want to be filled with the Living Water, we must worship God in spirit and in truth. If we are disillusioned in our faith, we need to examine our worship. True worship is part of the solution that brings happiness.

THE SOLUTION THAT BRINGS HAPPINESS

In the blistering heat of the noonday sun, looking into the clear, compassionate eyes of this Man who sat attentively and patiently at the well—this Man who understood her so completely—any pride or doubt the Samaritan woman had was broken. She wasn't offended. She was thirstier than she had ever been before. She was more aware than ever of her emptiness and unhappiness and dissatisfaction. She had been confused about the water and religion and even who this Man was, but there was one thing she was not confused about. She expressed the sudden cry of her heart as she declared with absolute certainty, "'I know that Messiah'" (called Christ) "'is coming. When he comes, he will explain everything'" (John 4:25). In other words, *"Oh, God, just give me Jesus! Please!"*

And God did! In fact, He had been there all along! Only she had thought He was just a Jew, or a man, or a prophet sitting at Jacob's well. When He told her simply, "I who speak to you am he," her spiritual eyes were opened (John 4:26).

In a flash she must have known that all she had ever longed for or hoped for or dreamed of was found in this Man who was reaching out to her. He had known all along who she was. He had known about her sinfulness. He had known about her religiousness based on ignorance and insincerity. Yet, wonder of wonders, He had sought her, an outcast among outcasts! He had actually known the worst about her but still offered her Living Water!

And suddenly, miraculously, instantly, she was filled with joy! She was thrilled with the Man beside the well and with her newfound purpose of telling others who He was and how to find Him.

The timing was perfect. At the moment she drank of the Living Water, the disciples returned from town, amazed to find Jesus talking to a Samaritan woman but discreet enough not to ask Him questions (John 4:27). As they approached the well, were they struck by the way the woman's eyes clung to Jesus' face? Were their questions silenced by the rapturous joy that dawned in her eyes then broke out in her radiant smile? As they watched in fascination, the woman turned swiftly and ran toward the town from which they had just come.

As she disappeared in the shimmering heat, all that remained to indicate she had been there was the light in their Master's eye and her abandoned water jar beside the well (John 4:28). The discarded jar was just an ordinary, everyday vessel, but it represented her old way of life and her outcast status and her emptiness of spirit. And she had left it at the feet of Jesus because she was no longer dissatisfied in her freedom; she was filled with joy. She was no longer distorted in her focus; all she could think about or talk about was Jesus. She was no longer discouraged by her failure; she knew she had been forgiven of her sin and accepted by God. She was no longer disillusioned with her faith; it now rested in the truth.

The Samaritan woman had been transformed! Those who knew her best, her friends and her neighbors, were immediately struck by the change in her demeanor. Her words must have tumbled out in an excited rush as she began to tell anyone and everyone about Jesus and how others could find Him for themselves. She invited them to "come, see a man who told me everything I ever did" (John 4:29). And they did. "They came out of the town and made their way toward him" (John 4:30).

As the Samaritans streamed toward Jacob's well to find Jesus for themselves, He told His disciples, "Open your eyes and look at the fields! They are ripe for harvest" (John 4:35). When they looked, they saw hundreds of Samaritans coming toward them. From a distance, with their long, flowing robes, they must have looked like willowy grain. And out in front of the crowd, leading them and urging them onward, was surely a happy woman!

The Samaritan woman who had just met Jesus had sown seeds of truth that blossomed quickly into a genuine spiritual revival in Samaria.[7] "Many of the Samaritans from that town believed in him because of the woman's testimony" (John 4:39). He stayed with them two days, "and because of his words many more became believers. They said to the woman, 'We no longer believe just because of what you said; now we have heard for ourselves, and we know that this man really is the Savior of the world'" (John 4:41–42).

And as the woman went to bed that night, perhaps she whispered softly, over and over again as tears of joy slipped down her cheeks onto her pillow, "Thank You, thank You, thank You, dear God, for giving us, the outcasts of Samaria, *Jesus!*"

WHILE THE WOMAN of Samaria and I have many differences, we have one thing in common. I, too, find myself from time to time running on empty.

In the busyness of ministry,
the pressures of responsibility,
the demands of family,
the weariness of activity,
the excitement of opportunity,

I sometimes wake up and realize, "I am so dry and thirsty." Invariably, when I examine myself, the reason for the dryness of spirit can be traced to one thing. I'm not drinking freely of the Water of Life. I'm neglecting my Bible study. I'm rushing through my prayer time. I'm not listening to the voice of the Lord because I'm just too busy to be still. At those times I carve out quiet interludes to confess my sins and read and meditate and pray and listen and just drink Him in.

Thank You, dear God, for still giving women today—and men—Living Water from the Well that never goes dry. *Thank You for just giving me Jesus!*

6

JESUS MAKES HAPPINESS ATTAINABLE . . .

For the Bypassed

JOHN 5:1–9

Roberto had been raised in the squalid poverty of a third world country. His future was worse than bleak as all he had to look forward to was unrelenting, increasing despair and destitution, primarily because his lower legs were bent forward at the knee in a grotesque right angle to his body. Rather than walk or run like other boys his age, Roberto crawled like a dog on all fours. Because of his deformity, the doors of opportunity and education were closed to him, leaving him hopelessly illiterate and ill equipped to live in a modern world. He was already a teenager, and life was passing him by.

And then God, the Creator and Controller of the universe, who has:

planets to spin and
stars to hang and
nations to judge and
wars to stop and
angels to supervise,

intervened in Roberto's miserable life! Out of the masses of deformed, diseased, destitute, and desperate young people in his country, he was singled out, whisked away to America, and given the opportunity to undergo skillful orthopedic surgery that straightened his legs and changed his life. The lengthy operation produced truly miraculous results, and soon after, Roberto literally danced in the streets of his town! Danced on legs that were straight and nimble! Legs that stood and walked and leaped and ran! Legs that were like keys with feet, unlocking the door to a future of promise and hope! He danced on his new legs in sheer, ecstatic joy.

Several months later, he was invited to return to the American city where his surgery had taken place. Generous benefactors made it possible for him to receive an education with a private tutor as well as job training. And while he diligently studied and worked, he sought out a local church where, on the Easter following his surgery, he participated in a passion play. In simplicity and humility, but with unbridled enthusiasm, he expressed his gratitude to his Benefactor: "My job is to help Jesus carry the cross. I'm happy to help Him, because He has helped me."[1]

Jesus makes happiness attainable for the most unlikely of candidates—physical cripples like Roberto and spiritual or emotional cripples like you and me.

Whoever you are, whatever your condition or circumstance, whatever your past or problem, Jesus can restore you to wholeness just as He did the man beside the pool of Bethesda so long ago.

Sometime after His encounter with the outcast woman of Samaria, Jesus made the uphill trek alone "to Jerusalem for a feast of the Jews" (John 5:1). He went, not because He had to—He didn't—or because it was expected of Him—it wasn't—but surely because worshiping with God's people brought joy to His heart. He must have had an increasingly keen sense of anticipation as the dusty road He traveled wound its way out of the wilderness, through the Jordanian valley, and up to the city of David, which was situated like a crown atop the Judean hills.

At that time, the city would have been packed with pilgrims thronging the narrow streets. It would have swirled with the tantalizing smell of bread baking over open fires, the strident sounds of vendors shouting for attention,

the braying of donkeys
and barking of dogs
and hissing of camels
and squealing of children
and haggling of shopkeepers.

The wild cacophony all added to the festive atmosphere of confusion that was Jerusalem during the days of a national feast.

As Jesus entered the gate of the city that arched high above the teeming crowds, He would have made His way past open stalls that displayed everything from silks . . . to linens . . . to tapestries . . . to carpets . . . to figs . . . to dates . . . to olives . . . to honey . . . to salt . . . to chickens . . . to fish . . . to beads . . . to brass . . . to pots.

The smell of incense mixed with those of unwashed bodies and drying meats and fresh fish and animal dung would have assailed Him. A wide variety of intriguing sights and fascinating sounds would have vied for His attention. So many people and scenes competed to secure His interest. I wonder if He stopped . . .

to toss a ball back to a child who had overthrown his playmate, or
to select a ripe fig from the piles of produce crammed along the street, or
to chat with a shopkeeper about the international makeup of the crowds, or
to sit in the cool shade under an awning while sipping a refreshing drink?

I wonder if He stopped at all? Or did He stride purposefully toward the Sheep Gate to arrive at a "pool, which in Aramaic is called Bethesda and which is surrounded by five covered colonnades" (John 5:2)? The pool was very probably circular but enclosed by five breezeways that formed a pentagon, with each of its five sides made up of a porch covered by an arch. Possibly it was a mineral or sulfur spring that bubbled out of the ground, drawing the attention of the desperately hopeless who believed it to possess healing, curative powers.[2] It was around this pool, under the covered arches, that those who were bypassed by the rest of society gathered, focusing on the legend that said when an angel caused the water to bubble up, the first person into it would be healed.

He Was Neglected by the Crowd

Most passersby would have been hard-pressed to notice the bubbling water of the pool because the scene surrounding it was surely so heartwrenching. Every reject in the city must have gathered at the pool of Bethesda, the "House of Mercy." The emaciated bodies, the pale faces, the pain-deadened eyes, the hollow cheeks all gave silent witness to the helplessness and hopelessness of the diseased and disfigured and dying who lay, crumpled and sprawled, like discarded refuse on the terrace that led to the water's edge. As the eyes of God scanned the mass of misery, He saw "a great number of disabled people . . . the blind, the lame, the paralyzed. From time to time an angel of the Lord would come down and stir up the waters. The first one into the pool after each such disturbance would be cured of whatever disease he had" (John 5:3–4).[3] Each pitiful sufferer focused all attention on the water's surface, desperately pinning his or her hope on being the first to spot the bubbling movement and the first to react by jumping—or falling—into the pool. Each was totally preoccupied with his or her own disability—blindness or lameness or paralysis. So preoccupied that no one saw Jesus, who suddenly appeared among them.

The Crowd's Selfish Preoccupation

The heart-wrenching needs of those lying under the covered colonnades of Bethesda are still reflected in the lives of those we pass by every day—people whose hollow eyes and empty laughter cover up silent fears and secret tears . . .

People who are disabled emotionally because of past or present abuse.

People who are blind to beauty and hope and purpose and truth.

People who are lame as they walk with inconsistency.

People who are paralyzed and incapacitated by fear or addiction or habits of sin.

People who long to be touched by an angel.

People who are preoccupied with themselves and their problems as they focus on a psychiatrist ~ or counselor ~ or doctor ~ or pill ~ or bottle ~ or drug ~ or vacation ~ or promotion ~ or reputation ~ or possessions ~ or education ~ or position ~ or career ~ or spouse ~ or parent ~ or friend ~ or bank account ~ or place ~ or program ~ or agency ~ as their source of hope and deliverance. Today, as in Israel of old, the hopes and prayers of the world have been transferred from "the temple to the pool" as the church sends the needy elsewhere.

Once in a while someone somehow gains help by one of these means just as the pool of Bethesda apparently helped victims in those days of old. But the help is not the deep, inner, permanent miracle that people long for. For most, genuine healing and lasting deliverance seem to be elusive, sending them into a hopeless spiral of self-pity and despair.

One Man's Self-Pity

In the crush of bodies and stretchers and crutches beside the pool of Bethesda, "one who was there had been an invalid for thirty-eight years" (John 5:5).[4] Thirty-eight years is a virtual lifetime of suffering . . . of helplessness . . . of weakness . . . of being by-passed. For thirty-eight years the man had dragged his deadened, weakened limbs to the pool with a hope that diminished day by day. Each time the waters bubbled, the seemingly lifeless crowd suddenly erupted into a frantic scramble as those gathered clambered and tumbled over each other in a desperate attempt to be first into the pool. Out of the mass of confusion someone would shout with ecstatic joy as he or she experienced a measure of relief and healing.

For thirty-eight years this man had watched as his hopes were repeatedly dashed and someone else walked away with the blessing of health and wholeness. Yet still he came, clinging tenaciously to some thread of hope against hope. Or perhaps coming to the colonnaded porches and gazing for hours at the pool had become merely a habit of hope that he had been unable to break.

How long have you been paralyzed beside the pool . . .

Unable to break a habit?

Unable to lead others to Christ?

Unable to take a step of faith and begin serving the Lord?

Unable to step out of your comfort zone and risk all to obey Him?

Unable to establish the consistent spiritual disciplines of daily prayer and Bible reading?

Have you watched somewhat resentfully, yet wistfully, as others have walked off with the blessing of God while you remain incapacitated with no spiritual power or growth or real fruitfulness?

To whom are you looking for help? Where are you going for help? In what have you placed your hope? In a place? Or a program? Or a Person? The paralyzed man and the multitude of the miserable were all focused on the pool, on the water, on the place, on a traditional source of help, even as God Himself stood in their midst!

HE WAS NOTICED BY CHRIST

As Jesus stood on the periphery of the crowd, His eyes scanned the hurting, huddled human forms until they came to rest on the paralyzed man lying inert on his pallet. Out of all the people living on planet Earth, of all the people living in Israel, of all the people jammed into Jerusalem, of all the people huddled around the pool of Bethesda on that particular day, "Jesus saw him lying there" (John 5:6). Why? Why, out of all the people living on Earth, or in your country, or in your state, or in your city, or in your neighborhood, or in your household, why does He notice *you?* And *me?*

Jesus Saw Him

What caught the attention of Christ? With so many gathered that day around the pool of Bethesda, why did Jesus notice this one man? Surely there were others with the same hollow expression, the same gaunt frame, the same desperate dream. When the misery of that place was so total and overwhelming, how would one sufferer stand out over another?

Perhaps it was the man's desperate loneliness or his complex of worthlessness or his persistent hopefulness or his helpless weakness that caught the eye of God. Perhaps for that same reason, Jesus notices you and me. It's our *need* that draws Him to us. He's attracted to our weakness because it gives Him opportunity to glorify His Father by demonstrating His power in our lives.

Jesus Knew about Him

Jesus not only saw the man, but He also "learned that he had been in this condition for a long time" (John 5:6). He knew the man had been paralyzed for thirty-eight years. He knew about the man's deeply depressed emotional state as well as his powerlessness and painful physical condition.

Do you think Jesus doesn't know about you too? Do you think He doesn't know that you have been a spiritual paraplegic for a long time? You're wrong. Think about it. What *does* Jesus know about you?

That for *thirty-eight years* you have been a member of a church
yet have never taken any responsibility in it?
That for *thirty-eight years* you have been a professing Christian
yet have never shared the gospel with another person one on one?
That for *thirty-eight years* you have been an avid reader and
learner, but you have never read and studied the Bible for yourself?
That for *thirty-eight years* you have called yourself a Christian
yet have never established a personal prayer time?
That for *thirty-eight years* you have held on to your bitterness,
resentment, anger, jealousy, worries, and complaints?
That for *thirty-eight years* you have been bound by a habit of pill
popping or overeating or wine drinking or TV watching or
tongue wagging or tobacco smoking?

Does Jesus see you and know you to be a pathetic spiritual invalid?

Does He know that your spiritual weakness has developed into a lifestyle of depending on the prayers and wisdom and insights and Bible knowledge and help of others?

Does He know that you cannot walk by faith on your own? Of course He knows!

He doesn't hold your weakness against you. He loves you in your weakness just as He loved the paralyzed man.

Instead of despising or blaming the paralytic for his weakness, Jesus stopped and spoke to him. Personally. Gently. Inquiringly. Pointedly.

Jesus Spoke to Him

What must it have been like for the pitiful, paralyzed man who was bypassed by everyone else to receive the full gaze of God and hear himself addressed personally by the same Voice that had spoken the worlds into existence? The waiting that had dragged on year after year, the suffering to which he had never grown accustomed, the loneliness that had become more acute as he watched others being helped by friends he didn't have—all must have etched deep lines of sorrow on his face and apathy in his eyes as he returned the look of the Stranger.

Did their eyes hold for a moment as perhaps Jesus squatted down to be closer to the man's level before He asked what seemed a very odd question: "Do you want to get well?" (John 5:6). He didn't ask, "Do you *need* to get well?" But, "Do you *want* to get well?" There was no preliminary introduction or social niceties or even casual conversation, just a Stranger asking a question that would seem to have had a very obvious answer. After all, the man's desire to get well was the reason he came to the pool day after day. Surely, without question, anyone who was a paralytic would *want* to be able to walk.

But Jesus knew that it's easy for physical weakness and mental depression and emotional pain and a lifetime of hopelessness to rob a man of his willingness to do anything about it. It would be less demanding in many ways for the man to be carried about by others. His paralysis absolved him from taking responsibility in life. It was his excuse for not walking. For not working. For not being active. For not helping others.

Do you want to get well? Do you truly want that sin to be cleansed?
that guilt to be removed?
that habit to be broken?
that anger to be dissolved?

that bitterness to be uprooted?
that emptiness to be filled?
that joy to be reconciled?
that relationship to be restored?
that strength to pick up your responsibilities and start walking by faith?

Jesus knows one of the greatest barriers to our faith is often our *unwillingness* to be made whole—our unwillingness to accept responsibility—our unwillingness to live without excuse for our spiritual smallness and immaturity. And so the question He asked was very relevant then and still is today: "Do you want to get well?"

Years of disappointment and discouragement dripped from the man's complaint, "Sir, . . . I have no one to help me into the pool when the water is stirred. While I am trying to get in, someone else goes down ahead of me" (John 5:7). The poor man couldn't drag himself into the water fast enough to be first. Others kept taking advantage of his weakness. Possibly he might have made it if there were someone to help him, but his friends had left him long ago. He had no one. No one cared. He only came to the pool because there was nowhere else to go and there was no one else to turn to. Besides, lying down and looking at the pool had become a habit. And there was some comfort in the fact that everyone around him was doing the same thing.

The man was focused on what he lacked. He lacked a friend to help him. He lacked the strength to do it on his own. But while he was preoccupied with what he didn't have, he totally missed what he did have—*he had Jesus!* Standing right there!

What's your excuse for continuing to lie down on your responsibilities?
What's your excuse for remaining a spiritual child when
you should be mature in your faith?
What's your excuse for sleeping when you should be kneeling in prayer?
What's your excuse for comfortably sitting when
you should be following Christ?
What's your excuse for repeated failure and sin?
What's your excuse?

Is it lack of faith? Lack of willpower? Lack of knowledge? Lack of Christian fellowship? Lack of discipline? Lack of energy? Lack of encouragement?

There is no excuse you or I can come up with that is valid because we have

Jesus! We need to stop focusing on our lacks and stop giving out excuses and start looking at and listening to Jesus.

I wonder—was it with a tender, compassionate gaze that glinted with delightful anticipation of what was about to be, was it with irrepressible joy that played at the corners of His mouth in a gentle smile, was it with a soft but clear, compelling voice that Jesus commanded authoritatively, without any hesitation, "Get up! Pick up your mat and walk" (John 5:8)? In other words, "Dear weak, powerless, paralyzed man, it's your choice. If you put your faith in Me alone and obey My Word absolutely, you will have all the power you need to be different."

How many of us would have responded indignantly, "Mister, who do You think You are? Can't You see my condition? I'm paralyzed! There's no way I can even roll into the water; I certainly can't beat someone else to it. It's impossible for me to get up, much less pick up my mat and walk. Besides, everyone around me is in a similar, weakened condition."

Some time ago, Jesus gave me the very same practical instructions He gave the paralyzed man. He commanded me, "Anne, get up out of your bed early in the morning, pick up your responsibilities of prayer and Bible reading, and walk in step with Me during the day." And I, a Christian leader and Bible teacher, gave every excuse in the book:

"I can't get up this early because I was up so late last night."

"If I get up this early, I won't be able to stay alert all day."

"My calling is not that of a prayer warrior."

"I'm not an early morning person."

"I can't concentrate or even focus that early."

"It will disturb my husband."

"I can pray later in the morning. Or during the day. Or at night."

"My relationship with Christ is not legalistic, it's a love relationship."

"I'm just too tired."

"God understands."

I stayed on my "mat" for so long that I totally lacked even the willpower to get up. My defeat produced deep despair and discouragement, to the extent that I made peace with my sin. I decided that I would always be a spiritual cripple. I rationalized that somehow God would be glorified in my weakness. But all the while, deep down, I knew the truth. I just didn't really *want* to "get well." I wanted to stay in bed and sleep more than I wanted to get up and pray.

Praise God! With all of his being, the man wanted to be different! Something in the face of Jesus or the tone of His voice must have quickened the man's hope and faith. After thirty-eight years of trying to get up and failing and falling again and again, he heard God's Word, obeyed God's Word, and discovered that the power was already his to just do it! Without any question or hesitation, "At once the man was cured; he picked up his mat and walked" (John 5:9).

Was his first step taken almost as an instinctive reaction to the authority of Christ, without really thinking about what he was doing? Was his second step more tentative? Did he begin to shout as he took his third step and fourth step and realized he was walking? Did he then stomp his feet? And jump? And run? And dance? What exhilarating joy must have flooded his heart and burst forth on his face! What abundant blessing and freedom and happiness were his just for the taking!

What would he have missed if he had remained where he was when Jesus came into his life? He would have missed out on the healing, the freedom, the adventure, the blessing, the joy, the fun, the happiness of walking, and the personal experience of the supernatural power of God in his life!

The testimony of the man who had lain paralyzed on his mat beside the pool of Bethesda for thirty-eight years gives powerful, undeniable proof that Jesus makes happiness attainable, even to the bypassed. *But* we have to want it more than our own laziness or comfort or self-pity or hurt feelings or sin or habits or plans or anything. We have to want it enough to be willing to obey His Word: "Get up! Deny yourself! Take up your cross and follow Me!"[5] We have to want more than anything or anyone else for God to just give us Jesus.

BACK IN THE bleak Black Hills of North Dakota during the year 1939, a father eagerly awaited the birth of his first child. He dreamed of a son who would walk beside him on the trails and hunt beside him in the hills and fish beside him in the streams and sleep beside him under the stars and sit beside him around the village fire.

He longed for a baby who would grow into a tall, proud, powerfully built, full-blooded American Indian like himself.

When his wife's time came to give birth, he hovered near for the first glimpse of his dream come true. As the baby boy emerged into the world of the small, cramped cabin, exposed to the scrutiny of his father and the attending doctor, it was immediately apparent that he was not a dream come true, but a nightmare that had become a reality.

The baby's nose hung loosely on the left side of his face, he had no upper lip, and where the roof of his mouth should have been, there was instead a cavernous hole. The doctor threw his hands up in disgust. "Send him away!" he said. "He will never learn or speak like other children." The horror-stricken father ran out of the room, out of the cabin, into the night, into a lifetime of alcoholism.

The distraught mother did all she knew to do. In desperation, she sent the baby she named Donald to a small hospital where his nose was stretched and flattened and spread from the left side to the right side of his face. His face was sewn together under his nose where his upper lip should have been. But no one did anything about the gaping hole in the roof of his mouth.

For seventeen years, Donald's brilliant mind and sensitive spirit were trapped inside a physical body that was ridiculed and mocked by other children, a body that was beaten and rejected by his father, a body that was abused and abandoned by his teachers. Because of the condition of his mouth, he could neither speak nor eat properly. He lived in abject poverty of body, soul, heart, and mind. He rummaged in the city dump for his food and clothing, counting the rats who lived there as his only friends. His misery and loneliness and rejection turned to anger and hate, until he entered a life of juvenile crime with his one goal being that of killing his own father. Donald was not just an outcast; he was also totally, completely, irreconcilably bypassed and discarded by the rest of the world.

But God, the Creator and Controller of the universe, who has planets to spin and stars to hang and nations to judge and wars to stop and angels to supervise, noticed the abused bit of Native American refuse who was neglected by everyone else, just as He had noticed the paralyzed man beside the pool of Bethesda so long ago. And so He leaned out of heaven and intervened in the form of a well-to-do white woman from the valley nearby who asked that Donald be brought to her home. Not knowing what else to do with the teenaged freak who was becoming a menace to the society that had rejected and neglected him, the authorities agreed.

When Donald stood before the woman, she did not recoil in horror as he had expected. Instead, she reached out in tender love and gently touched him. She actually touched him! For the first time in his life, he was deliberately touched without being taunted. He was touched, not in cruelty or mockery, but in kindness and compassion. The woman led him to her dining room table, which had been set with white linen and crystal goblets and porcelain china and sterling flatware. She served him beefsteak and potatoes with gravy and soft cake with icing. She placed her own fingers into his mouth to teach him how to chew his food. She opened her Bible and told him of God's love and of God's Son. She read to him Matthew 7:7, unveiling a world of hope with the strange words, "Ask and it will be given to you; seek and you will find; knock and the door will be opened to you." She explained that this was God's promise to him and that he would understand it later. She arranged for skilled medical help that gave him a new nose and an upper lip and a metal plate to close the roof of his mouth. She provided speech therapy until Donald learned to speak clearly and articulately.

Donald went on to graduate with honors from high school. And college. And graduate school. And eventually he earned his doctorate in education. His mind had been set free! But his heart was still bound in hate and loneliness . . .

Donald tried to fill the vacuum in his heart with a woman whom he married for her exceptional beauty and impressive bank account and respected family name. But the emptiness was still there like an old, wretched wound that refused to be healed. Every bump along the way seemed to reopen it until the blood of real life seeped away and true health was continuously beyond his grasp.

One day he agreed to accompany his wife to a church meeting, dreading the stares of the strangers and the vulnerable feeling of venturing out into unfamiliar territory. When he walked into the church building, the sanctuary was filled with people who reminded him of the well-to-do white woman from the valley who had been God's ministering angel in his past. As he sat in awed silence, his emotions churning within him, a man stood up on the platform before the congregation, stepped behind the pulpit, and began to read and explain Matthew 7:7!

Following the service, Donald fled to his car, jumped inside, and raced down the highway. But he was tired of a lifetime of running. So he pulled the car to the side of the road, rolled down his window, looked up toward the sky, and vehemently challenged, "God, if You're there, I want Jesus Christ!" Immediately, the hate left him, the burden of sin lifted from him, peace filled him, and he felt embraced by the loving arms of his heavenly Father!

On that day, Donald Bartlette, an outcast from his own family, was born again into the family of God. The Native American freak who had been considered an aberration of nature and was bypassed by the world discovered that God loved him and had created him uniquely for an eternal purpose. And for the first time in his life, Donald Bartlette knew what it was to be truly happy . . . *because he had Jesus!*[6]

Jesus Makes Resources Ample

He supplies strength to the weary.
He increases power to the faint.
He offers escape to the tempted.

He sympathizes with the hurting.
He saves the hopeless.
He shields the helpless.
He sustains the homeless.

He gives purpose to the aimless.
He gives reason to the meaningless.
He gives fulfillment to our emptiness.
He gives light in the darkness.
He gives comfort in our loneliness.
He gives fruit in our barrenness.
He gives heaven to the hopeless.
He gives life to the lifeless!

Just give me Jesus! He makes resources ample!

7

JESUS MAKES RESOURCES AMPLE . . .

To Me

JOHN 6:1–14

Corrie ten Boom was a fifty-year-old, unmarried Dutch woman who had lived a somewhat sheltered, uneventful life when Hitler's war machine began systematically eliminating Jews from German-occupied territory. Because she and her family resisted the evil Nazi rampage by aiding Jews who were hiding to escape extermination, they themselves were arrested and sent to the death camps. Corrie's personal, vivid account of heavenly grace in the midst of that earthly hell is one that has been a source of rich blessing for believers and unbelievers alike for several generations.

In her highly acclaimed book, *The Hiding Place,*[1] which was later made into an award-winning film,[2] Corrie described her life in one death camp after another as the Germans reacted to the Allies' advance across Europe by retreating within their own borders, dragging their helpless victims with them. The last Nazi concentration camp she lived in was Ravensbruck, where ninety-six thousand women were slaughtered, including her own sister, Betsie.

When Corrie and Betsie first entered Ravensbruck, they were starving and Betsie was seriously ill. They were two women of fourteen hundred who were packed into a barracks built for four hundred. Their daily ration of food consisted of one slice of black bread in the morning and a gruel made of turnips late in the afternoon.

Corrie had managed to smuggle in a small bottle of liquid multivitamins that she dispensed drop by drop, day by day, on the black bread she and Betsie ate. Knowing they were not being fed enough to sustain life, Corrie wanted to hoard the drops. But so many other women in their lice- and flea-infested dormitory were weak and ill that Corrie began placing a drop of the liquid vitamins on the bread slices of the women nearest them. The number of women begging for the drops of mercy soon grew from fifteen to twenty to twenty-five and more—every morning! It scarcely seemed possible because the bottle was so small, but it continued to produce as many drops as she needed. Corrie was amazed! She held it up to the light to see how much liquid remained, but the dark brown color of the bottle made it impossible to see through. Regardless of how many doses she dispensed, no matter how many times she tilted the little bottle and withdrew the dropper, there was always a droplet of the precious liquid on the tip. It was a miracle!

In the middle of a living nightmare, Corrie experienced the ample provision of God, who had seen the practical need of the women and met it—one drop at a time.

JESUS SEES MY NEEDS

Just as God saw and met the need of Corrie, Betsie, and the other women imprisoned with them, He also saw and met the needs of His disciples. They had been stretched almost beyond endurance. They had just returned from short mission trips that, while exciting, had been exhausting.[3] And the ministry of Jesus was exploding! As word of His preaching and power ricocheted from one end of Galilee to another, the disciples were in such demand that, with "so many people . . . coming and going . . . they did not even have a chance to eat."[4] The religious leaders had become so jealous of the following Jesus attracted, and so enraged by His teaching, that they were already plotting to kill Him.[5]

In the midst of their nonstop busyness and stress, Jesus and the disciples received the shocking news that John the Baptist had been executed. The news must have exploded like a hand grenade thrown into their midst! John the Baptist was dead![6] John the Baptist, first cousin of Jesus, faithful forerunner of the Messiah, fearless prophet of God, had been beheaded by Herod! The small band of disciples must have shaken their heads in disbelief. When the initial shock wore off, they must have been weary with grief and stung by all the "whys?"

John and Andrew in particular were grief stricken. They had been John's disciples before they followed Jesus. They had been devoted to him. And now they had to reconcile his brutal murder with their understanding of the God they served.

The murderous threats, the personal grief, and the never-ending demands of others all added up to pressure that bore down on Jesus and His twelve disciples. Jesus knew the inner turmoil that filled the hearts and minds of His beloved disciples. His own heart was heavy with the burden of grief and the temporary victory the enemy seemed to have achieved. It was time to get away. And so instead of going up to Jerusalem for Passover, He told His disciples, "Come with me by yourselves to a quiet place and get some rest."[7] Jesus knew the time had come for a break in Christian service.

Jesus Sees the Needs of His Friends

What pressure have you recently been under? Are you experiencing the pressure of grief over the loss of a loved one, either through death or divorce, or perhaps one of you has just moved away? Are you living with the pressure of having more to do than you have time for? And while you are grieving, and trying to meet the incessant demands of others, is someone criticizing you or misunderstanding your actions? Do you feel emotionally drained, physically exhausted, and spiritually depleted as well? Jesus sees and understands your needs.

Jesus saw the physical, emotional, and spiritual needs of His friends and knew the solution was a time of quiet rest and reflection. And He knows the solution is the same for you and me today. So He invites us, as He did His disciples, "Come with Me by yourself to a quiet place and get some rest."

Often when I am under stress and pressure, I feel one of my greatest needs is to get a good night's sleep. But I've found that physical rest alone is not enough to revive my flagging spirit. I need the spiritual revival that comes from spending quiet time alone with Jesus in prayer and in thoughtful meditation on His Word.

A careful study of the life of Jesus reveals that as pressed as He was, He "often withdrew to lonely places and prayed."[8] If Jesus felt He needed time alone in prayer with His Father, why do you and I think we can get by without it? How is your prayer life? Could some of the exhaustion you are feeling be the result of simple prayerlessness? How motivating it has been for me to view my early morning devotions as times of retreat alone with Jesus, who desires that I "come with Him by myself to a quiet place" in order to pray, read His Word, listen for His voice, and be renewed in my spirit.

As the disciples slipped out of the village early in the morning, piled into a boat, and rowed softly "to the far shore of the Sea of Galilee"(John 6:1), they must have felt like little boys playing hooky from school. Did Peter muffle the oars while the rest scrunched down inside the boat, hoping against hope that no one would see or hear them leaving so they could escape the crowds? Did they tightly clutch bag lunches as they whispered to each other in excited anticipation of their spontaneous "holiday"? They seemed to have made it across the lake without attracting attention, and then disembarked at Bethsaida Julius, a marshy area where the Jordan River runs into the sea from Mount Hermon.[9]

As they clambered out of the boat and began to hike into the countryside, they must have breathed deeply of the fresh, crisp air as they took in the scenic view. Two miles inland was a large, green, grassy plain covered with wildflowers that surely waved a welcome to their Creator and His frazzled band of men in the early morning breeze. It was a glorious spring day in the Galilean hills.[10]

As "Jesus went up on a mountainside and sat down with his disciples" (John 6:3) they must have collapsed on a carpet of green grass covered with multicolored wildflowers. The snowcapped peak of Mount Hermon would have provided a dramatic backdrop while the glassy blue Sea of Galilee stretched out to the horizon in the spectacular foreground. Their weary, parched spirits must have drunk in the serene beauty like men coming out of a sun-scorched desert who thirstily guzzle water. As they began to rest and relax, surely they began to talk and question and discuss and listen. As they rested together, we have the beautiful picture of the Good Shepherd, making His sheep lie down in green pastures, leading them beside the still waters, that He might restore them on the inside.[11] Jesus knew the demands that would be made on the disciples and Himself that very day, and He knew in order to meet those demands, they had to have some time alone together.

Again and again, I have been amazed to discover that the verse of Scripture or thought or insight that God seems to give me in my early morning quiet time with Him is the very same verse or insight or thought I am called on to give to someone else during the day. Many times I have wondered how I would have been able to speak a "word that sustains the weary," had I not first received it for myself in those brief, early morning retreats.[12] Jesus offers us ample resources, but we have to *receive* them from Him in order to impart them to others.

Jesus Sees the Needs of the Crowd

As the disciples lay back on the hillside, perhaps chewing on long stems of grass, relishing the beauty and the serenity, I wonder which one first spotted the intruders. *Thousands* of them. How had all those people known where to find Jesus? Had the boatman at the dock, or a child peeking out of a window, or a fisherman coming in from the sea, spotted Jesus and His disciples leaving? Someone had informed someone, and the word must have spread like wildfire until "a great crowd of people followed him because they saw the miraculous signs he had performed on the sick" (John 6:2). It was Passover time, it was a national holiday, it was springtime, and it must have seemed the perfect day to join Jesus for a picnic in the hills.

I wonder how the disciples felt as they looked up and saw the trickle of people coming around the end of the lake. I wonder how they felt when they saw the trickle grow into a river that grew into a flood of *five thousand men,* not counting women and children. Did the disciples frantically look around for a bush to crouch behind? Or for any trail that would take them away from the approaching hordes? Or maybe they thought they could just ignore them and they would go away.

How do you react to unexpected interruptions, especially on your day off when you have something definite planned? Do you just refuse to go to the door when someone knocks? Do you let the recorder pick up when the telephone rings? Do you just ignore the needs of others when you are trying to get some desperately needed relaxation? And why is it their phone calls always seem to come at dinnertime? And the neighbor always seems to need you on a Saturday when you wanted to spend time with your family. And your parent always calls on the night you had planned to go out with your spouse. These interruptions are frustrating because we don't want to let go of our time and what we had planned. It's maddening because we see these intruders as an interruption of something that we deem important.

Once in a while I have the cherished opportunity of going out for a meal with my parents. Because my father is so recognizable, we try to slip as inconspicuously as possible into the restaurant. I have developed a self-defensive tactic designed to protect myself from the stares and whispers of onlookers—I just look past everyone as I try to keep my focus on where I am going. Once at a table, I ignore everyone in the room and concentrate on Mother and Daddy. Most people who recognize us are thoughtful and wait until we have finished our meal and are walking out before they approach us. But invariably there are those well-meaning few who want to shake Daddy's hand or get his autograph at their own convenience. When I see them headed for our table, inside I silently resist, steeling myself against this unwanted interruption of our meal and our conversation. Selfishly, I think to myself, *Don't you understand? I just have a brief time to visit with my parents. When you interrupt, you are stealing our time! Please go away!* I want Mother and Daddy all to myself, so I know, if I had been one of the disciples on that grassy hillside, I would have seethed with resentment at the intrusion of so many strangers on "my time" with Jesus. I would have told them to leave, ignored them, or tried to hide from them. While we do not know how the disciples responded to the invasion of their privacy by the seven to ten thousand people, we are told that Jesus "had compassion on them, because they were like sheep without a shepherd."[13]

Jesus looked out at the approaching crowds and saw people who were seeking God but instead had received hundreds of manmade legal burdens.

He saw people who wanted truth but had received political posturing and religious platitudes from the Pharisees.

He saw people who had rowed three miles across the lake or walked seven miles around it while carrying their sick.

He saw people who had made a supreme effort to spend their holiday with Him.

He saw people as more important than His own plans and need for rest.

He saw people not as an interruption, but as an opportunity to reveal His loving care and His Father's compassionate power to meet their deepest needs.

He saw people as sheep who needed a shepherd.

He saw people *as God saw them.*

How do you see people? Especially those who interrupt your family time or your place of business? Do you see just an increasingly senile elderly parent? Or just bratty neighborhood kids? Or just a customer who talks too much? Or just a lonely neighbor? Would you ask God to help you see people through His eyes?

If you and I are going to meet the needs of others, we must not view people as interruptions. We must be willing to see them from God's perspective, and we must be willing to give up some of our own time to help meet their needs. Jesus gave up His time to Himself, He gave up His "holiday," He gave up His "family" time in order to meet the needs of the crowd. He knew that meeting the needs of others invariably requires some personal sacrifice.

JESUS MEETS MY NEEDS

Jesus and His disciples had been on the green-carpeted hillside since early morning. Very likely they had had some precious time to themselves before being invaded by the "sheep," who would not have appeared until late morning or noon. But when the thousands of men, women, and children did arrive, Jesus "began teaching them many things."[14] Before meeting the physical needs of the people, Jesus met their spiritual needs.

Spiritually

From time to time within the church, a heated debate surfaces that on occasion has caused great division. In the words of Dr. E. V. Hill, the great pastor from Watts in Los Angeles, the debate can be summarized as, "Win 'em or feed 'em, feed 'em or win 'em?" In other words, what has priority within the church? Social activism or evangelism? Dr. Hill has elaborated from his personal experience that no meal in the world could ever have satisfied the starvation of his soul.

We can feed the hungry,
and house the homeless,
and clothe the naked,
and heal the sick,
and comfort the dying,
but unless we give them Jesus, they will all go straight to hell!

My grandfather was a medical missionary to China for twenty-five years. He established a three-hundred-bed hospital where he treated just about every type of illness and injury that could be named. Many of his Chinese patients were cured of diseases and saved from death by his skilled ministrations. But in time, every single one of the people who went through his hospital died! If all my grandfather had accomplished was to meet the physical needs of these people, his efforts would have been hopelessly futile. But my grandfather was wise. He knew that "man is destined to die once, and after that to face judgment,"[15] and so all of his ambulatory patients were required to attend chapel every day in the hospital where they were given a Bible lesson and presented with the Gospel of Jesus Christ. Those who were unable to leave their beds were visited personally by someone who would share Christ with them. Hundreds, and even thousands, of Chinese men and women received Jesus Christ as their Lord and Savior at the Love-and-Mercy Hospital in Tsingkiangpu. They had their spiritual needs met while their physical needs were being attended.

Certainly if someone were literally starving to death, we would not be so callous as to present that person with the gospel without first giving him or her something to eat. But I can't help but wonder, on that beautiful spring day in the Galilean hills, if Jesus wasn't giving you and me an object lesson about our priorities in meeting the needs of others. Was He showing us by His own example that the spiritual needs of a person are more important than the physical needs? Jesus met the spiritual needs of the people *first.*

In that crowd of thousands congregating on the hillside, there would have been so many spiritual needs! In that crowd were those who were divorced, depressed, diseased, demon possessed, drug dependent.

In that multitude would have been crabby people, happy people, complaining people, contented people, mean people, kind people, selfish people, thoughtful people, critical people, encouraging people, frightened people, calm people.

There were so many needs to be met! Needs just like those in your neighborhood and your city and your state and your country and our world.

Often, when I arrive in a city to participate in some conference or seminar, the organizers will take me aside and tell me privately about the various people who will be attending. They describe the multitude. People with broken hearts and broken homes and broken dreams and broken hopes. And then they say, "Anne, we want you to know about so-and-so because we're hoping you will say something that will meet his or her needs." If I accepted that burden, I would be crushed under it! There's no way I can meet all those needs, so I usually respond with something like, "That's impossible! There are too many diverse needs. I can't address them all individually. But I can just give them Jesus." And again and again, I have seen Jesus personally meet the spiritual needs of the multitude—one by one.

Jesus has given me ample resources to meet the spiritual needs of others because He has given me Himself and He has given me His Word. But in order to meet the spiritual needs of the multitude, I have to spend hours alone with Him in the prayerful meditation of His Word so that *my* spiritual needs are met. At the same time, I need to remember that Jesus also met the physical needs of the crowd.

Physically

The people had probably packed picnic lunches, but not their dinners. I doubt that any of them had thought they would stay so long. They must have just wanted to linger in His presence, to stay close to Him. As evening drew near, their physical need for something to eat became obvious. There was no dire emergency. No one had fainted from hunger. Perhaps a fussy child, or a crying baby, or a complaining teenager raised a voice here and there. There may have been some elderly people who would have trouble getting home if they didn't have an evening meal to strengthen them for the journey. But everyone would have survived going without one meal. Besides, it was really their fault. They hadn't been invited, and when they had barged in on someone else's vacation, they had overstayed without planning ahead. But Jesus cared.

Did you think Jesus only cares about things like heaven and hell? About forgiveness and sin? About holiness and wickedness? About truth and lies? About salvation and judgment? Jesus does care about those things. But He also cares about your job, about whether your child makes the sports team, about your children's college tuition, about your budget now that you are unexpectedly pregnant, about the roof that leaks, about the cranky transmission in the car, and about all the other physical problems and needs we face.

Jesus cares even if the physical problem we face is largely of our own making. He cares if we are having car trouble, even if it was caused by our not having taken the time to change the oil regularly. He cares if we are having financial struggles, even if they were caused by our having run up massive debts on our charge accounts for things we wanted but did not necessarily need. Jesus cares about your physical needs today, just as He cared for those of the crowd so long ago.

The people who had tagged along, interrupting Jesus' retreat, were people who had first sought to be with Jesus Himself. They had a physical need because they had spent time with Him. And He had promised if they would "seek first his kingdom and his righteousness, . . . all these things will be given to [them] as well."[16]

What are your physical needs? What are the physical needs of those around you in your home, in your neighborhood, in your church, in the hospitals, in the rest homes, in the prisons, in the housing projects?

What would it take to meet those needs practically?

Practically

Jesus pointedly questioned Philip in order to get him to open his eyes to the needs of those around him and how those needs could be met practically: "Where shall we buy bread for these people to eat?" (John 6:5). At this point, the Scripture gives us intriguing insight into the mind of Jesus when it reveals, "He asked this only to test him, for he already had in mind what he was going to do" (John 6:6). Until Jesus questioned Philip, I don't think it had occurred to Philip, or to any of the disciples, that it was their responsibility to feed all those people! Jesus' inquiry began to stir the minds of His disciples and open their eyes to what God wanted to do.

We can imagine what was going on in Philip's mind: "You've got to be kidding! *All these people?* Take a look! There are thousands of them! Do You know how much *just the teenagers alone* would eat? How long has it been since You've been to the grocery store? You're just a little out of touch with what things cost nowadays. It's understandable because You've been so consumed with ministry. Actually, You're a *lot* out of touch with what things cost nowadays!" What he did have the courage to say was what most of us would have said: "Send the people away so they can go to the surrounding countryside and villages and buy themselves something to eat."[17] In other words, "God, this isn't my problem!"

Is that how you respond? If you were truly honest, would you admit that the reason you don't get involved, the reason you don't sacrifice your precious time and resources to help others, is because you just don't see their problems as yours? "Send them away, God. Let the government take care of them. Let the politicians fight over them. Let the church in their neighborhood do something about them." Like Moses, do you respond basically, "Here I am, Lord. Send Aaron!"?[18]

As the late afternoon sun began to sink into the blue water of Galilee, was there a moment of tension among the disciples as Jesus pinned Philip with His gaze? Did the restless sound of the crowd fade into the background as the moment was prolonged and became pregnant? Did a gentle evening breeze stir the strands of His hair but not deter His attention whatsoever from His disciple as He replied gently, but forcefully, "*You* give them something to eat."[19] Jesus made it very clear that the needs of others were indeed the responsibility of His disciples.

Philip's mind must have started to whir in rapid calculation, because he blurted out, "Eight months' wages would not buy enough bread for each one to have a bite!" (John 6:7). Did he mutter under his breath, "And Lord, even if we could afford to buy the bread, where do You think we would find it? Fast-food takeout hasn't come to Galilee. There's not a bakery in this whole region; actually, there's not a bakery *in the whole country* that could produce that much bread on such short notice. It's a nice thought, but put it out of Your mind. *It's impossible!*"

Impossibly

What practical or spiritual needs of others has God brought to your attention? Have you dismissed even the thought of trying to meet those needs as impossible?

Perhaps your resources are too limited and the need is too overwhelming for you to even consider getting involved.

I wonder if Jesus challenged Philip to evaluate the situation so he would come to the obvious conclusion that it was *humanly* impossible to meet the needs of all those people. One of the prerequisites, not only for a miracle but also for meeting the needs of others in a meaningful way that will impact them for eternity, is our total dependence on God. When we face an impossible situation, all self-reliance and self-confidence must melt away; we must be totally dependent on Him for the resources.

When God used my own needs as a young mother to get my attention concerning the spiritual needs of other women in my city, my heart was grieved, but it didn't occur to me to get involved. What could one person do in the face of such overwhelming spiritual emptiness and hunger? Especially when I wasn't even sure the women knew how hungry they were! Twenty-five years ago, just about every self-respecting person in the South went to church on Sunday. It was part of our culture. But I knew the religious pablum the people were being fed didn't even come close to satisfying their emptiness within—because I knew *I* wasn't satisfied.

Looking back, I can plainly see that God was using my need to stir me up and make me aware of the needs of others. When a friend suggested that I do something about the spiritual starvation in our city, I actually laughed and told her she was getting swept up in the emotion of the moment that followed a women's meeting at a local church.

What overwhelming need do you see in your city? Is there a desperate need:

for God's gospel to be presented to the lost?
for God's Word to be taught to the religious?
for God's security to be shared with the homeless?
for God's hope of heaven to be given to the elderly?
for God's forgiveness to be offered to the prisoners?
for God's grace to be demonstrated to the homosexuals?
for God's truth to be proclaimed to the officials?
for God's protection to be assured to the unborn?
for God's love to be poured out upon the children?

There are so many needs, aren't there? But is there *one need* that God has brought to your attention in particular? Perhaps it's a need that is a larger reflection of something lacking in your own life. Would you at least talk to God about it? Describe to Him what you see and how impossible it would be for you to do anything at all to meet that need. Then be alert to what He may reveal to you further.

Almost as soon as Philip's practical protest had left his lips, "Andrew, Simon Peter's brother, spoke up, 'Here is a boy with five small barley loaves and two small fish, but how far will they go among so many?'" (John 6:8–9).[20] While Andrew seemed to agree with Philip about the impossibility of feeding so many, his approach to the need was more positive. Without even realizing it, his faith had found the key to the storehouse of God's ample supply. When he offered Jesus a few loaves and fish, he was offering Jesus *everything* he had!

What do you have? Do you have a little bit of time?

a little bit of Bible knowledge?
a little bit of love?
a little bit of education?
a little bit of money?
a little bit of strength?
a little bit of concern?
a little bit of faith?

Don't concentrate on what you lack, concentrate on what you have. Then give *all of it* to Jesus for His use.

Are you like Philip, convinced that you can never meet the overwhelming needs of those around you with the little bit that you have? Or are you like Andrew, acknowledging that you only have a little bit yet you're willing to *give it all* to Jesus?

Having been in ministry twenty-five years, I have observed another attitude in myself, as well as in others. It's an attitude of fear. There are times I have been afraid to step out and offer Jesus the little bit that I have, because then everyone would know I only have a little bit! As long as I just talk about the needs of others or pray about them or weep over them, I can disguise my inadequacy to actually meet the needs. That fear is rooted in pride. And if I give in to it, that fear will paralyze me, preventing me from serving God, or witnessing for Him, or living out my life in risk-taking obedience to Him. It is very humbling to admit that all I have to offer Jesus is "five loaves and two fish."

But that's what Jesus is waiting for! He never asks us to give Him what we don't have. But He does demand that we give Him all we do have if we want to be a part of what He wishes to do in the lives of those around us!

Remember the servants at the wedding in Cana? They had the thrill of knowing firsthand that water went into the pitcher, but wine came out! They had the unparalleled experience of participating in a miracle! Could you be in danger of missing the thrilling blessing of participating with God in a miracle because, for whatever reason, you won't give Him all that you have? The disciples did not know it at the time, but they were on the verge of participating in a miracle because they gave Jesus everything.

Miraculously

When Andrew offered Jesus the little boy's five loaves and two fish, Jesus must have nodded His acceptance as He began giving His disciples directions "to have all the people sit down in groups on the green grass. So they sat down in groups of hundreds and fifties."[21] There was no chaos or confusion. Instead, there was an orderly, organized cooperation on the part of the people who quietly arranged themselves as they were told.[22] And the arranged groupings enabled the disciples to accurately estimate that there were at least five thousand men, not counting the women and children!

But can you imagine the heightened atmosphere of expectancy as people were not encouraged to trickle off and find food for themselves, but were told to sit down as though they were going to be served a meal? The disciples must have grown almost weak from fear as they looked at all the upturned faces pointing in their direction! What pressure they must have felt as they were confronted by the high, and impossible, expectations of the crowd! A silent stillness must have descended like a soft dew over the outdoor congregation as they waited . . .

Jesus then took the meager offering of five loaves and two fish, "and looking up to heaven, he gave thanks and broke the loaves. Then he gave them to his disciples to set before the people. He also divided the two fish among them all."[23] As people waited and watched quietly, Jesus stood. Every eye must have focused on Him and every ear tuned to listen as His voice rang out in the clear mountain air. But He wasn't speaking to them. The crowd overheard Him speaking to His Father in everyday words, with His familiar tone of voice, thanking God for seeing the needs of the people and meeting them. They heard no pious droning, no religious theatrics, no professional monotone, no singsong incantation, just a simple, "Thank You, Father." Yet how embarrassing it would have been to thank God for the food when it was only five loaves and two fish, an amount totally inadequate to meet the needs of those who expectantly waited.

Before eating a meal in public, do you first bow your head and thank God for the food you have received? Regardless of who else is at your table or in the restaurant? No? Why not? Do you find it embarrassing? If Jesus thanked His Father publicly for the food before eating, why don't you?

Have you become so careless that you don't even take the time to thank God for your food before eating within the privacy of your own home? It's interesting to note that one of the first steps away from God that leads to a totally depraved society is simple ungratefulness, according to the apostle Paul.[24] As we cluck our tongues and shake our heads in dismay over the collapse of our culture, could it be that the fault lies not only with immoral leaders and sinful citizens but also with ungrateful Christians?

Jesus knew that He needed God's blessing if the pitifully inadequate loaves and fish were to become ample enough to feed everyone. And so He prayed within the hearing of the people before breaking the bread and passing it out.

I have tried to follow His example before breaking the Bread of Life and "passing out" God's Word to an audience by always opening a message with prayer. I know, and believe those gathered before me need to know, that I am totally dependent on God to make my pitifully inadequate presentation enough so that everyone present will be fed. Because I can pass out the food and the blessing, but He alone can give it.

After thanking His Father for providing the food and asking for His blessing, Jesus must have taken the first loaf, broken it in half, then fourths, then smaller pieces, then given some to John and some to Peter. Taking another loaf, He must have done the same thing, giving some to Andrew and some to Philip. He continued breaking the bread and passing it out to His disciples who in turn passed it out to the people. When He finished dividing up the loaves, He took the fish, broke them in pieces, and gave the pieces to other disciples to distribute among the people.

As soon as John and Peter ran out of bread, they returned to Jesus, who replenished their baskets. As Andrew and Philip distributed all of their bread, they ran back to Jesus, and He replenished their baskets. There wasn't time to ask Jesus what they were supposed to do when He ran out of food. Philip was probably hoping it wouldn't run out until at least the second row! Back and forth, back and forth the disciples ran, getting the food from Jesus, giving it to the people, going back to get more from Jesus, then passing that out to the people. Not one crumb or morsel was passed out to the people that had not first been received from Jesus.

I wonder who was the first one to think, *You know, those five loaves and two fish stretched further than we would have thought.* I wonder if anyone stopped to really figure out what was happening. Everyone may have been too preoccupied with getting the food, passing it out, getting more food, passing it out, until "they all ate and were satisfied."[25] The people weren't just given a snack or a bite to tide them over until they could get a full meal, they "all had enough to eat" (John 6:12).

When did the reality of what had happened finally get through to the disciples? Was Andrew holding a full basket in his hands when he offered the bread and fish to someone who said, with a mouth already full, "No thanks! I couldn't eat one more bite!"? Did he try passing it to someone else, who also refused it, saying, "I don't know when I've had so much to eat!"? Did Andrew then straighten up, look out over the orderly yet festive crowd that seemed to stretch almost to the horizon, and suddenly realize that *everyone had been fed*? Did he grip the basket with trembling hands, staring hard at the contents, until his thoughts focused? *It's a miracle! It's a miracle! We fed thousands ofpeople with only five loaves and two fish!*

It was such a quiet, unobtrusive miracle. Nothing flashy or showy or manipulative or spectacular. No one would have even known a miracle had taken place, except that Jesus had lifted up five loaves and two fish in front of everyone when He asked His Father's blessing. There had been no adequate resources to feed so many people at once, yet everyone was not only fed but also filled! The only ones who remained hungry were the ones who had refused to stretch out their hands and take the food.

How had He accomplished the miracle? The formula is really quite simple.

The disciples gave it all.
Jesus took it all.
God blessed it all.
Jesus broke it all.
Jesus supplied it all.
The disciples gave it all.
And the entire multitude was fed!

This simple formula is one that I have followed continuously for the past thirty-five years, especially in ministry. I have given Jesus all that I am, as well as all that I have, which isn't much. I am a housewife who does my family's grocery shopping, cooking, cleaning, and laundry. I have very limited education and no formal seminary training or Bible schooling. I have a shy, timid personality that tends to be painfully self-conscious, plus a weak stomach that goes into spasms under too much stress. There have been times when I have had no money of my own, no time to spare, no energy at all. So when I say I have given all to Jesus, I assure you that I make the original five loaves and two fish look plentiful indeed! What I do have is an intense longing to know God, and that longing has given me an insatiable desire to know His Word—for myself. And I have had a sisterly concern for others who are hungry for Him.

The wonder is that when I gave it all to Jesus, He accepted it! He has never rebuked me for my inadequacy, or blamed me for my weaknesses, or accused me of insufficiency. Instead, He has acknowledged that I am not enough in myself to feed anyone or meet anyone else's need. Yet He has blessed what I have given Him, broken and rearranged it to suit Himself until I knew my resources were even more inadequate than I had thought, and given me insights into Him and His Word that only He could give. And I have in turn shared with others through spoken and written words what I have received from Him. As a result, *miracle of miracles,* thousands of people have been fed! Like the disciples, I stand back in awe as I view my life and the people who have been seated expectantly in front of me in audiences that literally have stretched to the horizon of the world and beyond, and *I know* I've participated in a miracle!

If my multitude is those whom God has placed before me in churches and auditoriums and arenas and stadiums and civic centers and my own home and my own church and my own city, who is your "multitude"? Who are the people God wants you to help Him feed? Who are the people you come into contact with who are hungry for the bread of God's Word? And what are your "loaves and fish"? What very limited and inadequate resources do you have? Wouldn't you like to experience the thrill of participating with Him in the miracle of feeding others with what you have received from Him—and finding that it's enough to satisfy their hunger? If all you ever attempt is that which you know you can do or have the resources for, how will you ever discover what He can do? How will you ever know by your own experience that He makes resources ample?

Maybe the disciples looked out over that vast, well-fed crowd, and felt their own stomachs rumbling. Had they fed everyone else, only to go hungry themselves? It was then that they discovered Jesus was ready to meet their needs personally.

Personally

Christian leaders and pastors and missionaries and Bible teachers, as well as disciples, get hungry too. So when all the people had been fed, Jesus instructed His disciples, "Gather the pieces that are left over. Let nothing be wasted" (John 6:12). Was Jesus just being environmentally friendly? Did He just want to make sure that they left the green grassy hillside more or less as they had found it? Was He like a parent who expected His children to clean their plates? *Or was He giving them a final lesson?*

The disciples fanned out over the grassy plain, stooping to gather the uneaten fragments. When they had finished gathering them, they "filled twelve baskets with the pieces of the five barley loaves left over by those who had eaten" (John 6:13). *Twelve baskets* of leftovers! Jesus had been lavish in His generosity and in the abundance of the blessing He had poured out. But there could be no coincidence or mistake in the fact that there was obviously one basket of bread for each of the twelve disciples!

Are you afraid to give Jesus all of your personality? All of your time? All of your money? All of your love? All of your will? All of the control of your life? Are you afraid that if you give everything to Him, and He in turn asks you to give to others, that you will somehow come up short? That you will end up with less?

In the end, the disciples had more than they had had in the beginning! After giving it all away, they had much more than if they had selfishly hoarded their resources for just themselves. The disciples, who had been the channel of so much blessing that day, were in turn blessed beyond anything they could have imagined!

It was a lesson they never forgot. Except instead of giving Jesus all of the bread and fish, they gave Him all of themselves—even though they weren't much to speak of. For the most part, they were just rough, uneducated Galilean fishermen, plus a tax collector and a few others who were equally nondescript. But Jesus took them all and He blessed them all and He broke them all and He gave to them the ministry of imparting the gospel to the world and, as a result, not just five thousand men, not just hundreds of thousands of men and women, but millions of people down through the centuries have been fed! How many will be fed today because Jesus has seen and met their needs through your willingness to give everything to Him?

After all the people had been fed, God was glorified! Jesus was seen in a new, fresh way as they exclaimed, "Surely this is the Prophet who is to come into the world" (John 6:14).[26] But He was more than just a long-expected prophet like Moses who would lead His people out of bondage to sin. He is the Bread of Life who willingly gave all of Himself to His Father. And His Father took all of His life, and blessed all of His life, and broke all of His life, and gave us all of His life, so that "he who comes to me will never go hungry, and he who believes in me will never be thirsty" (John 6:35). *Would you thank God for the Food?*

SEVERAL YEARS AGO I had the privilege of addressing a large convention of pastors. As I began the message, I could feel the stiff coldness of the gender barrier in place between the audience and me. Confident in my call from God to be there, I sent up an arrow prayer asking God to bring down any walls of resistance that would hinder those present from receiving any blessing from His Word that He had for them. As the message progressed, it became very evident that God was answering my prayer. If anything, I had difficulty keeping to my allotted time because of the applause and amens that constantly interrupted my delivery.

After my presentation, a young pastor came up and gave me one of the most beautiful compliments I have ever received in ministry. He said very forthrightly that there had been quite a bit of heated discussion among his peers as to whether I, a woman, should have been invited to speak to their distinguished gathering. He related how he had come to the session with reservations and had taken a seat in the back, unsure of what his position should be. But with an expression I can only describe as that which might be seen on the face of a starving man who had just eaten a full meal, he said humbly, "Mrs. Lotz, it's obvious to me that you have been in the kitchen, preparing the Food. Thank you for serving it to us tonight without messing it up." Then he disappeared into the crowd, leaving me with gratitude in my heart and tears in my eyes and a new perspective on my calling.

And so, dear God, this waitress wants to thank You once again for just giving me Jesus!

8

JESUS MAKES RESOURCES AMPLE . . .

In Me

JOHN 7:37–39 AND 14:15–26

A man walked into a hardware store and told the clerk that as a result of the storm during the night before, an enormous oak tree had crashed into his yard. Although the tree had not hit his house, the main trunk was lying across his driveway, and the huge branches were crisscrossing the front lawn and blocking his view. So he was interested in buying the very best chain saw that the clerk had to sell.

The clerk, who had listened sympathetically to the man's tale of woe, nodded and said he had just the thing. He excused himself for a moment, disappeared into the back stockroom, then reemerged, carrying a huge Stihl chain saw encased in orange plastic housing. The clerk described the features of the saw, but when he said it could cut through the giant oak tree like a knife through soft butter, the man needed no further sales pitch. He opened his wallet, paid for the saw, and lugged it out of the store.

Three days later the man came back into the hardware store, dragging the big chain saw. His hair was disheveled, his face was covered in a bristly three-day-old beard, his clothes were sweaty, dirty, and smelly, and his face was scrunched into an angry scowl. He dropped the saw on the floor. Then he smacked the counter with his fist and in a hoarse, raspy voice, began to yell at the clerk, "I thought you said this was the best saw you had for sale! I thought you said this saw was so good and fast, it would cut through the oak tree like a knife through butter. Well, I've been sawing for three full days, and I've only gotten through two tiny little limbs. I want my money back because the saw doesn't work!"

As other customers stopped and stared, the clerk, who had been standing in shocked amazement at the sudden outburst, moved swiftly to exercise damage control. As he quickly walked around the counter, he responded defensively, "That saw was in perfect working order when I sold it to you." He then reached down to the saw and pulled its little black cord. Immediately the saw sprang to life with a loud roar. The man jerked upright, his eyes wide with astonishment as he exclaimed, "What's that noise?"

The poor man had been trying to use a chain saw to cut wood without ever activating the power! He reminds me of a lot of Christians I know. They are trying to live the Christian life without ever activating the Power. It may be possible to get some things done without Power, but the effort and the struggle will make most want to quit. And the Power is not so much a "what" as a "who." The Power is the person of the Holy Spirit.

There are times when I have gotten the distinct impression from some Christians that the Holy Spirit is an optional extra, reserved primarily for benedictions, baptisms, and those we label "charismatics." Others give the impression that He is more like a heavenly genie in a bottle, who, if you rub Him with the right mixture of prayer and faith, will perform miracles for you. But the Holy Spirit is not an optional extra! He is not to be reserved only for special occasions or exclusive groups, nor is He a trick-performing genie. He is a divine necessity who is imparted to each and every believer at the moment of conversion.

THE PERSON OF THE HOLY SPIRIT

Jesus introduced the Holy Spirit publicly when He went up to Jerusalem for the Feast of the Tabernacles after the miraculous picnic on the hillside of Galilee. The special religious holiday commemorated the time when the Israelites had wandered in the wilderness with no water. They had been so angry and thirsty they had threatened to stone Moses, complaining, "Why did you bring us up out of Egypt to this terrible place? . . . There is no water to drink!" [1]

Moses had been so distressed that he had fallen on his face before the Lord, who had appeared to him and instructed, "Take the staff . . . gather the assembly together. Speak to that rock before their eyes and it will pour out its water."[2] Moses had done as God had commanded, and water had gushed from the rock!

During the Feast of the Tabernacles, the priest would go to the Pool of Siloam each day, fill two golden pitchers with water, and walk back to the temple. Pilgrims who lined the streets along his route shouted, "We will draw water from the well of salvation with joy."[3] The people would then sing psalms as the priest went into the temple and up to the altar. When he actually poured the water, which symbolized God's salvation from Egypt and a deeply satisfied life, on the altar in thanksgiving to God, a great shout would arise from those assembled. On the eighth day of the Feast, the priest did not go through this traditional ritual because it was the last day, and it signified the Israelites' entrance into the promised land, where water was plentiful.

Halfway through this particular feast, Jesus went to the temple courts and began to teach in such an amazing and authoritative way that He was the primary focus of the authorities as well as of the religious pilgrims. Everyone was talking about the Man from Galilee. On the eighth day, "the last and greatest day of the Feast, Jesus stood and said in a loud voice, 'If anyone is thirsty, let him come to me and drink. Whoever believes in me, as the Scripture has said, streams of living water will flow from within him.' By this he meant the Spirit" (John 7:37–39).

Jerusalem was electrified! Public opinion was divided right down the middle, with some proclaiming Jesus as the Messiah and others saying He couldn't possibly be. But everyone understood His message: To a world that was spiritually dry and populated with parched lives scorched by sin, He was the Living Water who would quench the thirsty soul, saving it from "bondage" and filling it with satisfaction and joy and purpose and meaning. He was the Savior who would deliver them not only from bondage to sin but also from meaningless wandering through life. He was the promised land of the fullness of God's blessing.

As John reflects back on Jesus' stunning and dramatic revelation to those at the temple for the Feast of the Tabernacles, he adds his own commentary. He explains that when Jesus spoke of the Living Water that would bring salvation and give satisfaction, He was speaking of the Holy Spirit.

The Holy Spirit Is God

The Holy Spirit is not an "experience" or an "it" or a "dove" or a "flame of fire" or even a "ghost." While He may be symbolized by some of these things, He is an invisible Person with a mind, emotions, intellect, and will. He is God, equal in power and personality to the Father and to the Son.[4] He is sometimes referred to as the third member of the triune God, not because He is the least, but because He is the last to be fully revealed in the Scriptures.[5]

Following supper the night before He was to be crucified, Jesus unburdened His heart to His disciples. With the sun going down on the last day He would be alive on earth, and the moon and stars appearing in the night sky, a deep dread must have descended upon Him. He knew He was going not only to the cross but, after the resurrection, also back to His Father in heaven (John 14:2, 12). His disciples would be like orphans. They would be like sheep without their Shepherd. Had He taught them all they needed to know? Had they learned enough to risk their own lives in passing the truth on to others?

The disciples must have begun to sense His heavy burden and increasing tension. Their feelings must have been very similar to our daughter's the night before we put her on the plane for a six-week mission trip to Rwanda. The small African nation had just experienced a devastating civil war, and Rachel-Ruth was going to help in an orphanage. But as we were preparing to send her so far away, we were all filled with misgivings about her physical safety and emotional security in the aftermath of a war that claimed the lives of hundreds of thousands. Who would she have to protect her, to talk to her, to love her, to comfort her, to pray with her, to listen to her? Like Rachel-Ruth, the disciples must have worried about who would teach them. Or counsel them. Or guide them. Or strengthen them. Or empower them to resist temptation. Without Jesus, how could they *ever* meet their own needs, much less the needs of the multitude? They had given Him *their very lives* for three years. How could they *possibly* manage without Him?

Jesus knew their fears. So He began to tell them how they would go on in His absence. He told them they could live, not just somehow, but triumphantly and powerfully, because "I will not leave you as orphans; I will come to you . . . I will ask the Father, and he will give you *another* Counselor to be with you forever" (John 14:18, 16, emphasis added).

The Holy Spirit Is "Another" Jesus

Jesus described the Holy Spirit as "Another." The Greek word actually means "another who is exactly the same." So although the Holy Spirit is a distinct person, He is exactly the same as Jesus, but without the physical body. He has been described as Jesus without skin. Or, like an FBI agent, He is Jesus undercover.

We know that Jesus is in heaven. As the first martyr, Stephen, was being stoned to death, he looked up and saw heaven open and Jesus standing at God's right hand, preparing to welcome him home![6] Jesus was also seen in heaven by Saul of

Tarsus when he was on his way to Damascus to rid the city of Christians. Saul was suddenly confronted with the living person of Jesus Christ, who leaned out of heaven and dramatically changed Saul's life.[7] And the apostle John testified that when he saw heaven open, Jesus as the Lamb of God was standing in the center of the throne.[8] Even at this present moment, as we begin a new millennium, Jesus is in a man's body, up in heaven.[9]

But that doesn't mean Jesus has left us to stumble through the darkness of the future on our own. He promised His disciples that when He went to heaven, He would ask His Father to send down to earth "Another." One who would have His same mind, will, emotions, and intellect. Jesus called Him the Counselor (John 14:16).

The Holy Spirit Is the Counselor

The Amplified Bible gives six other names that could be equally translated from the word in our text for "Counselor." Each name, as it is defined by Webster's dictionary, describes a different aspect of the person of the Holy Spirit. He is our:

Counselor: One whose profession is to give advice and manage causes.

Comforter: One who relieves another of mental distress.

Helper: One who furnishes with relief or support. One who is of use and who waits upon another.

Intercessor: One who acts between parties to reconcile differences.

Advocate: One who pleads the cause of another.

Strengthener: One who causes another to grow, become stronger, endure, and resist attacks.

Standby: One who can be relied upon either for regular use or in emergencies.

Can you imagine how wonderful it would be to have Someone with these attributes in your life?

Are you distressed today?
Then you need the Comforter.

Are you facing a major decision?
Then you need the Counselor.

Do you need relief from, or support in, your responsibilities?
Then you need the Helper.

Do you have a broken relationship?
Then you need the Intercessor.

Are you being criticized, falsely accused, misunderstood?
Then you need the Advocate.
Are you constantly defeated by habits of sin?
Then you need the Strengthener.
Are you unprepared for an emergency?
Then you need the Standby.

The Holy Spirit is fabulous! He's everything that Jesus is!

Have you ever wished Jesus could be to you what He seemed to be when you were a child? Did He seem so real then, so close, so comforting, so understanding, so strong and protective? Have you ever wished Jesus would come in the flesh, sit next to you, take your hand in His, tell you how much He loves you, talk to you about your problems, and give you wise advice? He *has* come! *He is here* in the person of the Holy Spirit who makes Jesus real to you and me. He is the "Spirit of Christ"![10]

Are you unaware that Jesus is *really* in your life? Is it because you have not consistently been in God's Word? As we spend time reading, applying, and obeying our Bibles, the Spirit of Truth who is also the Spirit of Jesus increasingly reveals Jesus to us.

The Holy Spirit Is the Spirit of Truth

Jesus said the Holy Spirit is not only "Another Me," but He is also the Spirit of Truth (John 14:17). The Holy Spirit is so identified with the Bible, one of His names is Truth! In fact, Peter reveals that the Holy Spirit is the inspirational Author of the Old Testament Scriptures.[11] And Paul wrote to Timothy, encouraging him to stay in the Scriptures because, "all Scripture is God-breathed," referring once again to the Spirit-inspired Word of God.[12]

Have you been trying to work up some kind of emotional feeling? If you lack "it," have you *felt* you didn't have the Holy Spirit? The Holy Spirit is the Spirit of Truth, which means He always works according to and through the Word of God whether you *feel* Him or not. Have you been seeking some ecstatic experience, thinking that would be the Holy Spirit? Remember that He never acts independently; He always works through *the* Truth—the living Word of God, who is Jesus, and the written Word of God, which is your Bible.

One of my first experiences of seeing the Spirit of Truth work in the life of another person occurred during the first year I taught a Bible class. After I had finished giving the message, a woman came up wearing a hostile expression and said in an accusing tone, "Who has been telling you about me?"

I was embarrassed to admit that, in that class of five hundred women, I didn't even know who the woman was, so I simply said, "No one."

She didn't call me a liar, but her expression conveyed that opinion as she drilled me. "Then how did you know . . ." and she went on to describe a rather delicate circumstance in her life.

I assured her I had not known of her situation. With a skeptical, puzzled look, she then repeated some things I had said in the message that had amazingly and specifically addressed the very thing she had just told me about. I looked at her with wonder myself as I replied, "That was the Holy Spirit speaking to you. I knew nothing of what you are going through, but He did. As I explained the morning's passage of Scripture, He quickened it in such a way that you heard His voice speaking to you through it."

That woman's comments were the first of hundreds I have received since then. I never cease to be humbled by them even as they confirm to me the reality and the living presence of the Spirit of Truth who is the Holy Spirit.[13] *He is God,* who *speaks to us* through His Word.

The Holy Spirit Is Holy

Sometimes we overlook the obvious and forget that the Holy Spirit is *holy.* You and I can never assume we are filled with the Holy Spirit if we are not holy, separated from all known sin. One of the first things He does when He comes into your life is to give you a desire to be holy. The very sins you used to enjoy, you begin to hate. And increasingly as you surrender to Him, saturating yourself in the Scripture, He gives you the desire to confess and the power to separate from them.[14]

Quite a few years ago, I was shopping for a pair of pajamas I wanted to give my daughter Morrow for Christmas. I found just what I was looking for with only one problem. The top of one pair looked better with the bottom of another pair. So when the saleslady wasn't looking, I quickly selected the top that I wanted, took the bottom of the other pair off the hanger, and put it with the top I was holding. I then went innocently to the checkout counter and paid for my "custom-made" pair of pajamas. I left the store very pleased with myself. But by the time I got home, I was literally sick to my stomach. The conviction of sin was like a dagger turning inside me until I actually trembled with guilt and shame. I had difficulty sleeping that night, and the next morning, as soon as the store opened, I was back at that lingerie counter with the same salesclerk. When I told her I wanted to return the pajamas, she took out the proper credit slip, then, with her pen poised over the line that said, "reason for return," she asked me, "Why?" So, feeling the blood rush to my face, I told her the truth! I cannot describe the look on her face! All I can say is that it was a long time before I shopped in that department again!

But in one sense that experience was an encouragement to me. It gave me an acute awareness of the activity of the Holy Spirit in my life. My misery was His misery, and He had refused to tolerate that kind of behavior, for which I was, and am, most grateful. As I have continued to grow in my Christian maturity, I have discovered that the Holy Spirit does not let me get by with anything. Whether switching pajama tops and bottoms or snapping at my husband or sharing gossip with a friend or cutting someone off in traffic or hoarding the overhead space in the airplane or pausing the TV remote on an indecent scene, the Holy Spirit lets me know when He is not pleased. In fact, He is the most uncomfortable Comforter I know! He is holy, and He works in my life to make me holy too.

As Jesus described the Holy Spirit, I imagine the disciples became increasingly eager to meet Him! Their tired, grieving faces must have brightened with hope as Jesus told them that although He was going away, "I will come to you. . . . On that day . . . we will come . . ." (John 14:18, 20, 23). What day was He talking about? When would they get to meet Him? When would the Holy Spirit come?

THE PRESENCE OF THE HOLY SPIRIT

The Jews celebrated other feast days besides that of the Tabernacles. One was their Feast of Harvest, similar to our Thanksgiving. Because it fell fifty days after Passover, it was called Pentecost.

Jesus was crucified on Passover. He arose from the dead on the third day, and forty days later, He ascended into heaven. As He had known they would, the disciples did indeed feel "left behind." But they were also filled with expectancy because they knew He had promised that after He left them and returned to His Father, the Holy Spirit would come. So following His ascension, the disciples, joined by more than a hundred other believers, maintained a round-the-clock prayer vigil for ten days.[15] Surely they were praying to claim God's promise of the Holy Spirit

for wisdom to know the next step,
for comfort and peace in His absence,
for opportunities to tell others about Jesus,
for boldness to persuasively present the truth,
for power to change lives.

The tenth day of their prayer coincided with the day of Pentecost. It was before 9:00 a.m. when Peter, John, James, Andrew, and about 120 other believers arrived in what we assume was the temple courtyard in order to worship and keep the Feast.[16] Other pilgrims from around the world were already gathering, and the sight of their colorful native robes as well as their pronounced foreign accents would have given the courtyard the air of an international festival.[17]

As the disciples joined in prayer and praise, "suddenly a sound like the blowing of a violent wind came from heaven and filled the whole house where they were sitting. They saw what seemed to be tongues of fire that separated and came to rest on each of them. All of them were filled with the Holy Spirit."[18]

That day must have started out like any other day for John.

Maybe he had climbed out of bed with a slight headache from the days of fasting.

Maybe as his feet touched the floor he was aware of his hunger and had quickly grabbed a piece of bread.

Maybe as he joined the others for the short walk to the temple grounds, he was oblivious to the early summer heat that was already beginning to rise.

Maybe he had been earnestly praying, asking God to send His Spirit, praising Him for all He had done—especially during the last fifty days.

Maybe he wondered why his sense of anticipation was so keen this morning, as though he were on the verge of something wonderful.

His heart must have been filled to overflowing with just the joy of knowing Jesus when he suddenly heard the sound of a tornado coming! Did his skin prickle and the hair stand up on the back of his neck? Did he crouch behind something for protection? And what did he think when, in spite of the *sound* of the wind, nothing stirred? No scudding leaves, no billowing robes, no dust devils dancing in the street, just absolute stillness made more striking by the noise of the rushing wind! And then, did he do a double take as he looked at Peter? at James? at Andrew? at Matthew? They each had what appeared to be a flame of fire resting on their heads! John didn't have to look at his reflection in a pool or reach up to feel and see if he had one too; he knew he did! And he knew, as surely as he had ever known anything in his life, that *the promised Holy Spirit had come!* And He wasn't just *with* John. He was *in* John! And John was filled with ecstatic joy! And quiet peace. And passionate love. And he had *never, ever felt Jesus so close* to him as he did at that moment. He opened his mouth, and his voice blended with those of the others in a symphony of praise.

Wonder of wonders!

In the garden of Eden, God had been *with* man.
In the Old Testament, God had appeared *to* man.
In the Tabernacle, God had dwelt *among* men.
In the history of Israel, God had spoken *through* man.
In the Gospels, God was visible *as* Man.
But at Pentecost, God became available to dwell in man!

Until that Pentecost two thousand years ago, people were saved by faith in Jesus Christ, even though they didn't know His Name. Their faith was demonstrated by the obedient sacrifices they made at the temple as they symbolically looked forward to the cross. Since Pentecost, we are still saved by faith in Jesus Christ. But our faith looks back to His sacrifice, which has already been made on our behalf at the cross. Additionally, we now have the experience of the indwelling of the Holy Spirit who seals our "rebirth," or "conversion."[19]

Since Pentecost two thousand years ago, the Holy Spirit has been and is available to anyone and everyone in the whole world! But He is a Gentleman! He only comes into, or indwells, the person who deliberately—consciously—specifically—humbly—individually—personally invites Jesus Christ to come in.

When Jesus taught His disciples about the Holy Spirit on that night before His crucifixion so long ago, He explained, "The world cannot accept him, because it neither sees him nor knows him. But you know him, for he lives with you and will be in you" (John 14:17). The disciples must have been puzzled. How did they know the Holy Spirit? When had they been with the Holy Spirit?

The Holy Spirit filled Jesus. In fact, Jesus was so saturated in the Holy Spirit that they were One. So when the disciples had been with Jesus, they had also been with the Holy Spirit without realizing it. However, after Pentecost He would no longer just be with them, but He would also live *in* them, even as He had lived in Jesus.

It's possible today to be *with* the Holy Spirit by just being with someone who is indwelt by Him. You can even feel His presence and His love and His peace and His joy and His power. But when you are separated from that person, you are separated from Him, too, and the sense of His presence disappears, leaving you lonely and depressed. When have you invited the Holy Spirit, Who at times you have been *with,* to come live *inside* you so that you will never be separated from Him?

The Holy Spirit is God's divine Gift to His children. My daughter's birthday is approaching as I write these words, and already she has begun reminding me of it. One day when she has children of her own, she will know that mothers need no reminding. We mothers not only *remember* the births of our children, we will *never forget* the births of our children! My daughter is now grown, married, and working, yet she still gets so excited about birthdays that it's infectious. I am already thinking about what gift I can get her that will make her eyes light up and that she will continue to enjoy.

Jesus used that very example to encourage His disciples. He said, "If you then, . . . know how to give good gifts to your children, how much more will your Father in heaven give the Holy Spirit to those who ask him?"[20] But you have to *ask*![21] When you do invite Him by faith to come into you, He will "be with you forever" (John 14:16). In fact, His presence within you is God's permanent seal on your life that you belong to Him. One reason we can be assured of never losing our salvation is that the seal of God cannot be broken.[22] Praise God! Jesus now lives in you and me in the person of the Holy Spirit; He will never leave or forsake us!

What kind of difference does it make to have *God* living *inside* of us?

The Purpose of the Holy Spirit

What is the purpose of the Holy Spirit's coming? Besides giving us counsel and sealing our salvation and giving us an awareness of the presence of Jesus in our lives, what does He *do*?

Right before Jesus left His disciples to go back to heaven, He instructed them "not [to] leave Jerusalem, but wait for the gift my Father promised, which you have heard me speak about. . . . You will receive power when the Holy Spirit comes on you."[23]

The Holy Spirit Empowers Me

When the Holy Spirit comes into you at your invitation, you receive as much of Him as you will ever have. You do not get a little bit of Him then and a little bit more at later experiences. Since He is a Person, you cannot get Him in pieces. You either have all of the Holy Spirit or you have none of the Holy Spirit. Why is it, then, that He seems to get us in pieces? He comes to us unconditionally, while we surrender to Him conditionally. But He can get more of you!

We give Him our Sundays but not our Mondays.
We give Him our actions but not our attitudes.
We give Him our relationships but not our reputations.
We give Him our time but not our thoughts.
We give Him our burdens but not our bodies.
We give Him our prayers but not our pleasures.
We give Him our crises but not our children.
We give Him our grief but not our goals.
We give Him our health but not our hearts.

The Holy Spirit who now lives in you is the same Holy Spirit in Genesis 1 who hovered over the formless, empty, dark blob of earth that dangled in space. As He powerfully energized and pulsated the atmosphere, He prepared the planet to receive God's Word and be transformed into a place of purpose and beauty that ultimately, in the end, reflected the image of God.

That same Holy Spirit is now powerfully at work in your life, hovering over your heart, preparing you to love God and be fully aware of His love for you. He hovers over your mind, preparing you to understand spiritual things and the truth of His Word. He hovers over your will, preparing you to make decisions that are pleasing to Him. All the power of God—the same power that hung the stars in place and put the planets in their courses and transformed Earth—now resides in you to energize and strengthen you to become the person God created you to be.

When the angel Gabriel appeared to Mary, he gave her the startling announcement that "the Holy Spirit will come upon you, and the power of the Most High will overshadow you. So the holy one to be born will be called the Son of God."[24] When you and I place our faith in Jesus Christ and invite Him to come live within us, the Holy Spirit comes upon us, and the power of God overshadows us, and the life of Jesus is born within us. We do not conceive a physical life, but the spiritual life of Jesus in the person of the Holy Spirit.

It is the indwelling powerful person of the Holy Spirit who sets me free from the habits of sin. But the power I possess to live a life pleasing to God is directly related to how much control of my life I give to the Holy Spirit.

What are you not giving to the Holy Spirit's control? Whatever it is, it will hinder His power in your life.

Beside the road leading to the house where I grew up is a spring of water. Years ago Mother put a pipe into the spring, then placed an old, wooden bucket under the pipe. To this day, water flows through the pipe and into the bucket, which spills over with the clear, cold spring water. A little tin cup is perched on a rock nearby for anyone who is thirsty. But once in a while, the water flowing from the pipe slows to a trickle, then stops altogether. Because no fresh water flows into the bucket, the water that's there gets stagnant and becomes unfit for drinking. When that happens, Mother takes a slender stick and runs it through the pipe, knowing that a small piece of gravel or a little salamander or an accumulation of mud has blocked the water's flow. Sure enough, within minutes, the water starts flowing freely through the pipe and into the bucket once again.

Our lives are like that wooden bucket, with the living water of the Holy Spirit flowing into and spilling from them. God has clearly commanded you and me to "be filled with the Spirit."[25] But an unconfessed sin or resistance to His authority will block the "flow" of His life within us. If we do not deal with it, our spiritual lives become stagnant and we lose our attractiveness and usefulness to God. And we have nothing refreshing about us that would draw other people to Christ.

What is hindering you from being filled with the Holy Spirit? To be filled with the Holy Spirit is to be under His moment-by-moment control. He has not been given to you so that you can keep Him confined to a particular area in your life. Let Him loose! He is Lord! The amount of power you experience to live a victorious, triumphant Christian life is directly proportional to the freedom you give the Spirit to be Lord of your life!

And "where the Spirit [is Lord], there is freedom" for you and me.[26] Freedom from sin and selfishness and spiritual defeat and Satan's snares. Freedom to reflect Jesus as we are "transformed into his likeness with ever-increasing glory, which comes from the Lord, who is the Spirit."[27]

As we live moment by moment under the control of the Spirit, His character, which is the character of Jesus, becomes evident to those around us. The outward evidence of His inward filling of our lives is His "love, joy, peace, patience, kindness, goodness, faithfulness, gentleness and self-control."[28] Is there enough evidence of the Spirit in your life to demand a verdict from your closest friends and family members? The Holy Spirit empowers us, not just to *live* for Jesus, but to be *like* Jesus as He forms Christ within us.[29] Yet we are not just an imitation of Christ but also an *embodiment* of Him.

The Holy Spirit Enlightens Us

As Jesus continued to teach His disciples, He gave them great hope. He promised them, "Before long, the world will not see me anymore, but you will see me" (John 14:19). Their brows must have furrowed as they concentrated on what He was saying, not understanding. How could they *see* Jesus after He was *gone*?

Once again, Jesus was revealing to them a dimension of the Holy Spirit's work.

The world sees Jesus as a man, perhaps even a good or great man and possibly even a prophet, but still a man. It is the Holy Spirit who opens our spiritual eyes of understanding so that we see Jesus as much more than just a man. We see Him as: our Creator ~ the Jehovah of the Old Testament ~ the long-awaited Messiah ~ the only Son of God ~ the Redeemer of Israel ~ the Lamb of God ~ the Savior of the world ~ the Good Shepherd ~ the risen Lord ~ the Judge of all the universe ~ the reigning and ruling King of kings!

The only way we can be convinced of who Jesus is, is through the enlightenment we have received from the Holy Spirit. Jesus explained, "When he, the Spirit of truth, comes, he will guide you into all truth. He will not speak on his own; he will speak only what he hears, and he will tell you what is yet to come. He will bring glory to me by taking from what is mine and making it known to you."[30]

What have you learned about Jesus, just since beginning this book? Although I can attempt to arrange words on a page, only the Holy Spirit can quicken them so that they become personal and meaningful and understandable and applicable to your life. And if my prayer is answered, and you finish this book knowing Jesus better and loving Jesus more and serving Jesus more faithfully than you did when you began reading it, that will be fresh evidence of the Holy Spirit's illuminating power. And both of us will be encouraged!

The Holy Spirit Encourages Me

Even when the Holy Spirit convicts us of sin, it is with the encouragement that He will give us the power to confess it and put it out of our lives. The conviction in itself is evidence that He cares about our Christlikeness, that He is attentive to our spiritual growth, that He is active in transforming us into the people God wants us to be.

The Greek word for "comforter" is *parakletos,* which literally means one called alongside to help. This was beautifully illustrated in the Summer Olympics during a track-and-field event. As the runners in the 440-meter race flew around the oval track, one of them suddenly pulled up on the back stretch, one leg held up and dangling as he limped to a stop. He had pulled a hamstring! As the crowd stood, holding its collective breath, a man ran out of the stands to the young athlete. It was his father! As the television crew relayed the moving scene to the watching world, the microphones picked up the runner's words: "Dad, you've got to help me across the finish line. I've trained all my life for this race." And so the father put his arm around his son, and together, they limped across the finish line to a standing ovation!

In the race of life, God our heavenly Father has come alongside us through the person of the Holy Spirit. And

when we think we can't go one more step,
when the race becomes painful beyond endurance,
when our hearts feel heavy,
when our minds become dull,
when our spirits are burned out,

we have the *Parakletos,* who comes alongside us, puts His everlasting arms around us, and gently walks with us to the finish. The applause you hear is from "the great cloud of witnesses" who rejoice in your victory![31]

The Holy Spirit Equips Me

Our victory means more than we even know, not only to the unseen witnesses in the universe, but also to others who are watching us because we are members of a worldwide family.

When you and I received the Holy Spirit into our lives, we became members of the larger body of Christ that includes other believers. Perhaps without realizing it, at the moment of conversion, we became part of the family of God; Jesus is the Head, and other believers are our brothers and sisters. Paul describes this new identity as being "baptized by one Spirit into one body."[32] But the new privilege of belonging to God's family brings with it new responsibilities to care for and build up the other family members. For that purpose, the Holy Spirit gives us each gifts that enable us to be contributing family members. These gifts are not natural talents although they can enhance what we have developed ourselves. These gifts are supernatural and only come from the Spirit at His discretion.[33]

Because I participate in lots of conferences and seminars, I have shared the platform with all types of musicians and soloists. It is very apparent that some perform with natural talent. They hit all the notes perfectly and clearly, and after their performance, the average comment is something like, "Doesn't he have a splendid voice?" Or, "Have you ever heard that organ played so well?" If, however, the person singing has a spiritual gift, he or she may not hit all the notes, but the impact is one of worship of God and love for Jesus as the hearts of the listeners are stirred beyond a reasonable explanation.

The same can be said of preachers, many of whom stand in the pulpit each Sunday and deliver carefully worded, well-organized presentations of the truth. But lives are not changed, and as soon as the service has concluded, people file out talking about the latest sports event or where they're going for lunch. A gifted preacher may or may not have a carefully crafted sermon, but when he concludes, people are saved, marriages are reconciled, Bibles are read *during* the week, and Jesus is increasingly evident in the congregation.

What is your spiritual gift? The possibilities are endless because there are unlimited combinations of gifts.

Years ago, I remember being in an audience when a Bible teacher asked us what our gifts were. I silently denied having any. As though reading my thoughts, the speaker then stated, "There are no exceptions. Every person who has received Jesus as Lord and Savior has been given at least one gift by the Holy Spirit." I shrank into the shadows and did not get involved in the discussion that followed because I didn't know I had a gift, much less what it was! And I didn't know how to go about finding mine. My discomfort was intensified when the speaker went on to say that God would hold me accountable for discovering and using the gift He had given me—that He had not given it to me to be wasted. But gifts can be difficult to determine because they are given as a potential spiritual ability. They are not fully developed until we discover and exercise them in obedient service to God. So how was I to find my spiritual gift?

One way to find your gift is to ask a godly friend or spouse or pastor who knows you well to tell you what he or she thinks your gift is. Sometimes others see things in us that we can't seem to see ourselves. But when I shyly inquired, my gifts were so well hidden no one seemed to know what they were.

I had one friend who suggested that I go down the list of spiritual gifts Paul describes in Romans and try them all![34] The ones I exercised badly, she said, and got progressively worse at, would not be mine. The ones I exercised badly, then saw some improvement in, would make me grateful for the experience. But there would be some, she encouraged, that I would exercise rather well, and maybe those would be mine. I never even started down the list because it seemed like a lot of trouble, plus I didn't know if I was ready for what I was sure would be a lot of failure.

In the end, I did discover at least one of my spiritual gifts. My discovery took place several years after I learned that I had been given a gift. God had worked in my life, placing me in a position where I had to teach His Word each week to a class of five hundred women. When I first attempted a lesson, I was worse than pitiful! But God was so gracious! He had given me a class filled with women who had never been in a Bible study before and didn't know I couldn't teach. So week by week, I struggled with the assigned passages, doing the best I could to study and dig out the truth as God revealed it to me. And week by week the class patiently listened. In time I improved, and the class grew and multiplied until others began to describe me as a "gifted teacher."

The way I discovered that particular gift, and others I have uncovered since, was simple. I just obeyed God when He opened the door for me to teach the Bible class. I discovered a very basic principle that saved me a lot of time, analysis, and failure. The principle is this: What God commands you and me to do, He equips us for. It's that simple!

If you want to discover your spiritual gifts, start obeying God. Responding to His command with "I can't" is invalid, because He will never command you to do something that He has not equipped and empowered you to do. As you serve Him, you will find that He has given you the gifts that are necessary to follow through in obedience. Any of them. All of them. And if you lack any that you need, God will bring people alongside you who have the gifts that you don't. Working together, you will accomplish the task to the glory of God.

And that's the body of Christ! That's the church. Individual members of the family, each obeying his or her call, exercising the particular gifts the Spirit has given, so that our work is not in vain but produces eternal results.

As exciting and fascinating as the gifts of the Spirit are, we need to be careful that we don't lose our focus on the Giver. The primary responsibility of the Holy Spirit in your life and mine is to glorify Jesus.

While Paul exhorted the Corinthians to "eagerly desire the greater gifts," he also challenged them to a more "excellent way."[35] With passionate eloquence he lifted the standard of the church from that of spiritual giftedness to spiritual fruitfulness as he explained, "If I speak in the tongues of men and of angels, but have not love, I am only a resounding gong or a clanging cymbal. If I have the gift of prophecy and can fathom all mysteries and all knowledge, and if I have a faith that can move mountains, but have not love, I am nothing. If I give all I possess to the poor and surrender my body to the flames, but have not love, I gain nothing."[36] Spiritual gifts without eternal, Spirit-generated fruit mean nothing. That is why, in response to my heart's cry, *God has given me Jesus on the inside!*

SEVERAL YEARS ago, I was privileged to hear Dr. Lloyd Ogilvie, chaplain to the United States Senate, relate the following incident to a group of distinguished evangelical leaders. He recounted that when he had been pastor of the Hollywood Presbyterian Church in Hollywood, California, an elderly woman had taken him by the hand, looked piercingly into his eyes, and said with earnest conviction, "I pray your life will be as wonderful as it was in the mind of God when He created you."

Immediately following the encounter with the woman, Dr. Ogilvie said that he returned to his study, got down on his knees, and pleaded with God, "What did You have in mind when You created me?" In the silence that followed, to his mind clearly came just one word: *Jesus.*

It is the primary responsibility of the Holy Spirit to glorify Jesus by making us like Him—in our character, in our commitment, and in our communion with the Father.

A life that is not increasingly, clearly, personally reflecting Jesus may not be nothing, but it is much less than God intends it to be. And so the prayer of my heart is, *"God, glorify yourself in my life—from the inside out."*

Jesus Makes Suffering Understandable

He guards the young.
He seeks the stray.
He finds the lost.
He guides the faithful.
He rights the wronged.
He avenges the abused.
He defends the weak.
He comforts the oppressed.
He welcomes the prodigal.
He heals the sick.
He cleanses the dirty.
He beautifies the barren.
He restores the failure.
He mends the broken.
He blesses the poor.
He fills the empty.
He clothes the naked.
He satisfies the hungry.
He elevates the humble.
He forgives the sinner.
He raises the dead!

Just give me Jesus! He makes suffering understandable!

9

JESUS MAKES SUFFERING UNDERSTANDABLE . . .

To the Observer

JOHN 9:1–41

Little Hope Lauren Guthrie was ushered into the world on Monday, November 23, 1998, cushioned by the loving prayers and happy plans of her father and mother and brother. Having been eagerly anticipated, she was tenderly embraced as a treasured blessing from God. Within moments of her birth, however, the doctor expressed concern over several physical problems he had detected, including club feet and an inability to suck. His medical alarm was confirmed when a battery of tests determined that Baby Hope had Zellweger syndrome, a unique metabolic disorder. Although Zellweger is rare, it is also relentless and never allows its victims to live more than twelve months.

On June 9, 1999, Hope Lauren Guthrie was once again tenderly embraced—this time by the One who had created her as He welcomed her to her heavenly home. Those of us who'd had the privilege of observing her brief breath of life on Earth were left with tears in our eyes and pain in our heats and questions in our minds. *Why?* Why do the innocent suffer? Why would a good God allow bad things to happen to good people? Why did Baby Hope enter life to experience pain and problems, then exit so swiftly? *Whose fault is this?*

The problem of pain and questions about suffering are as old as the human race. But they remain the clinical subject of philosophical theories and intellectual sparring and theological debate until they become personal, until it's our homes or our children or our loved ones who are hurting. Then we simply have desperate questions that need direct answers.

Our Desperate Questions

Jesus and His disciples had gone up to Jerusalem for the Feast of the Tabernacles, not unlike our harvest of Thanksgiving. For seven days in the fall of the year, the festival commemorated the Jews' return to Israel after seventy years of captivity in Babylon. Those who participated made makeshift "tents" from tree branches and set them up in every conceivable nook and cranny of the city. These booths could be spotted peeking out from doorways and on rooftops, spilling into city parks, crowding the city streets, and lining the roads leading into Jerusalem. The entire population of the city, along with pilgrims from other areas, lived outdoors in these booths for the duration of the festival. Many of the Feast's ceremonies were conducted in remembrance of how the Jews lived in the wilderness, before taking possession of the promised land.

During the national holiday, Jesus had taught openly and passionately in the temple courtyard, interrupted constantly by hecklers who shouted their questions and accusations. In the end, when He clearly proclaimed Himself to be God in the flesh, the heckling turned into hate-filled hysteria as those who heard Him speak tried to stone Him to death.[1]

But the festival concluded without a serious incident, the people went back to their daily routines, and the out-of-town pilgrims went home. Jesus walked through the city with His disciples. Like the morning after a New Year's Eve celebration, or the day after the Fourth of July, there must have been evidence in Jerusalem of the festivities; perhaps an abandoned booth leaned crookedly in a doorway or trash cans tumbled into the streets. Did Jesus have to step over broken, burned-out candles lying on the walkway? Did He pick His way through discarded decorations that blew like trashy tumbleweed through the deserted alleys? We don't know. What we do know is that "as he went along, he saw a man blind from birth" (John 9:1).

It's astounding that Jesus even noticed one of the many beggars who loitered along the streets, much less stopped to get involved, since He had recently had a life-threatening experience.[2] In a similar situation, most of us would have been so preoccupied with our own pressures and problems as we hurriedly tried to escape the danger, we would have been oblivious to who or what was around us. In fact,

I wonder how many opportunities to meet the needs of others God has given me when I was:

too self-absorbed,
too self-centered,
too self-conscious,
too self-defensive,
too self-pitying,
too self-protecting,
to notice.

Who would be helped, who would have his or her needs met, if, as we "went along," we just opened our eyes and really saw those around us?

Like the paralytic at the pool of Bethesda, the blind man was one of hundreds of men and women who littered the streets of Jerusalem like flotsam on a lake's surface after a storm. There was nothing unusual about this man, but something about him caught the attention of Jesus. And because Jesus was interested in him, the disciples were too.[3]

Observing Jesus' gaze and the object of it, they saw a man whose blank face housed vacant eyes that stared, unseeing, as he extended his filthy, clawlike hands in a perpetual, pleading gesture to passersby. Ignoring the pathetic man's persistent begging and personal suffering, the disciples inquired curiously and rather analytically, "Rabbi, who sinned, this man or his parents, that he was born blind?" (John 9:2). Our question might have been something like, "Jesus, whose fault is this man's blindness? Obviously God is punishing him for some sin. What was it?"

When you have observed someone's suffering, have you assumed that it is God's punishment for sin?

Is Suffering Due to God's Punishment for Sin?

In what way are you suffering? Has your suffering actually been increased by a deep-down burden of guilt because you instinctively feel that you have done something wrong? That God is not pleased with you?

The Bible clearly teaches that essentially God's punishment for the guilt of sin is not suffering, but death.[4] Sin is so serious in God's sight that even one sin calls for the death of the sinner.[5] This death sentence that hangs over our heads is the reason that we are totally helpless and utterly hopeless in our sin. There is nothing and no one who can rid us of the guilt of sin in God's sight. There is nothing and no one who can obtain for us forgiveness of sin, eternal life, or a right standing with God. Therefore we are all under God's judgment and destined for His eternal punishment because we are all sinners.[6]

But *Jesus* stepped in and took God's punishment for your sin and mine at the cross! When we claim His death for our sins, we are absolved of guilt, our sins are atoned for, and we are saved, spared from God's wrath and punishment.

Hallelujah!

He has forgiven our sins! All of our sins, *all of our sins,* have been erased from His memory! Through the blood shed at Calvary we have been set free! You and I will never be punished for the guilt of our sins because Jesus has already taken it for us!

Therefore, neither the blind man nor you nor I suffer because of God's punishment for some sin we have committed.

Is Suffering Due to Personal Sin?

The disciples assumed that all suffering was the result of someone's sin. This is true indirectly, since all suffering can be traced back to Genesis 3 and humanity's sin of disobedience to God. On that terrible day at the beginning of human history, God described to Adam and Eve the suffering that would result from their sin.

Standing in the garden, while Adam and Eve cowered in their fig leaves, God turned to His beloved jewels of creation. He addressed Eve first, "I will greatly increase your pains in childbearing; with pain you will give birth to children."[7] As I meditated on the significance of God's judgment, I wrote down my thoughts, which were published in *God's Story.*

> Since the Garden of Eden, women have suffered literal pain associated with childbirth. The physical labor that preceded the birth of my own children lasted more than twenty-four hours in each instance. Yet as excruciating as the physical pain was, it doesn't touch the emotional pain endured in the process of raising children. Every hurt, disappointment, rejection, failure, pain, or heartache they experienced I experienced to an even greater degree than they did. Eve herself not only knew the pain of childbirth but also the severe emotional pain of watching her first two sons grow up with distinctly different natures that clashed with each other, until her eldest murdered her second born. There was another interesting aspect to God's judgment of Eve's sin. He said, "Your desire will be for your husband, and he will

rule over you."[8] Does this mean women were to have a strong tendency to control, manipulate, and manage, yet their position in society and in the family would put them in subjection to their husbands? The greatest oppressor of women is not government policy or male chauvinist attitudes or "good old boy" hierarchy or unfair wage laws. It's just sin!

At the end of this tragic scene, the Father God turned His full attention on Adam. . . . And God held Adam accountable for the direct disobedience to the truth of His Word.

Do you know someone who says God is such a loving Father He will not judge that person's sin? God is a loving Father. He is also a righteous and just and holy Father. He cannot be less than Himself, and His justice demands judgment. So in a voice ringing with His authority as the righteous Judge over all creation, He pronounced the consequences of Adam's sin. "Because you listened to your wife and ate from the tree about which I commanded you, 'You must not eat of it,' cursed is the ground because of you; through painful toil you will eat of it all the days of your life. It will produce thorns and thistles for you, and you will eat the plants of the field. By the sweat of your brow you will eat your food until you return to the ground, since from it you were taken; for dust you are and to dust you will return."[9]

Adam's work had been a delight and joy as he was taught and trained under the loving supervision of the Creator. Each challenge he had faced was an exciting opportunity that he had met consistently with success. Now, as long as he lived, he would be resisted. His life would be filled with struggle and sweat, frustration and failure, disappointment and discouragement.

The consequences of Adam's sin are easily seen around us in our work situations. Nothing comes easily.

In what way is your suffering today linked to Adam's sin? Have you worked hard to maintain your physical health through exercise and good eating habits only to be hindered by old age and the painful limitations it brings? Have you invested days and months and years into a family that has disintegrated in divorce and despair? Have you worked endlessly to further your education only to have the latest technology move you out of your job opportunity? After struggling to work as diligently, faithfully, and heartily as you know how, your work will "produce thorns and thistles." In the end, all you and I have to show for a lifetime of hard work is death and dust.[10]

As a result, all suffering is indirectly related to Adam and Eve's original sin at the beginning of human history.

But suffering can also be the direct result of our own personal sins. I struggle with the pain of a hiatal hernia as well as ulcers on my larynx because of my sin of worry and lack of trust in the Lord. Migraine headaches and psychological stress can be caused by the sin of bitterness, anger, or the refusal to forgive someone who has wronged us. We can suffer injury in a car accident as the result of disobeying the authority of the traffic laws. We can suffer through the pain of divorce because we have refused to live by God's marriage principles.

When we suffer, it's a legitimate response to examine ourselves before God to determine if we are indeed suffering because of personal sin. If you are suffering in this way today, James says to confess your sins to the Lord, pray for release, and ask others to pray for your healing also.[11]

What other thoughts and questions about suffering have gone through your mind?[12] Did you ever wonder if your suffering is due to someone else's sin?

Is Suffering Due to Parental Sin?

Actually, it is possible to suffer because of something our parents have done. Every day babies are born with birth defects or drug addictions that result from a parent's sinful abuse of sex or drugs or alcohol. Children also suffer because of a parent's indifference to God, which causes them to shrug Him off, having been led to believe He's not very important—if He exists at all. Or, through a parent's physical, emotional, or sexual abuse, a child can be scarred for life.

The Bible says that the consequences—not the judgment—of the sins of the parents are visited on the children to the fourth generation.[13] What sin are you committing today that will cause your child to suffer tomorrow?

When I taught a weekly Bible class, one of the young women who attended waited for me rather shyly after the lecture one day. I could see the pain in her eyes as she lifted them pleadingly to mine then quickly looked away. As I gently probed to discover what her question or problem might be, she tearfully confided that she had been pregnant and had lost the baby in a miscarriage. She was convinced the baby had died because God was punishing her for some sin she had committed.

Is a similar thought nagging at your mind, robbing your life of peace and joy? Then open your Bible to the same passage in Ezekiel that I read to her. It emphasizes individual accountability before God: "The soul who sins is the one who will die. The son will not share the guilt of the father, nor will the father share the guilt of the son. The righteousness of the righteous man will be credited to him, and the wickedness of the wicked will be charged against him" (18:20). It was my privilege to see that distraught mother smile through her tears as she was reassured that God had not taken the life of her baby as judgment for her sin.

Although our children may suffer the consequences of our sins, God will never punish them for anything we might have done. Why? Because He has already punished His own Son for our sins. As the disciples paused to observe the man born blind, Jesus gave them several direct answers to human suffering.

JESUS' DIRECT ANSWER

After considering whether your suffering is your fault, or your parent's fault, or someone else's fault, realize it may be that your suffering is no one's fault. The disciples, who were so sure the poor man's handicap was someone's fault, were admonished, "Neither this man nor his parents sinned . . . but this happened so that the work of God might be displayed in his life" (John 9:3).

Suffering Gives God Opportunities to Work

What physical, social, emotional, intellectual, or mental limitation do you have? Instead of blaming it on your doctor or parent or spouse or sibling or teacher or neighbor or boss or pastor or child . . . instead of seeing your handicap as someone's fault or even as an accident, consider that it might be an opportunity for God to display Himself through your life to others.

The apostle Paul was in some way handicapped himself. He referred to it as "a thorn in my flesh, a messenger of Satan" that tormented him. The Greek word for "thorn" used here was not like what we might find on a rosebush, but instead it was more like a stake on which someone could be impaled. Some have conjectured that Paul's "thorn" was physical blindness.[14] Others have guessed it was migraine headaches, or a speech impediment,[15] or a mother-in-law, or even the Jews themselves. Whatever it was, it was debilitating and he felt hindered by it from fully, freely serving the Lord.

So Paul pleaded "with the Lord to take it away from me. But He said to me, 'My grace is sufficient for you, for my power is made perfect in weakness.' Therefore I will boast all the more gladly about my weaknesses, so that Christ's power may rest on me. That is why, for Christ's sake, I delight in weaknesses, in insults, in hardships, in persecutions, in difficulties. For when I am weak, then I am strong."[16] God's grace and power seem to reach their peak when we are at our weakest point. As the great British preacher C. H. Spurgeon noted, "Grace grows best in the winter."

Suffering gives God opportunities to work for His glory. That is why Peter, who himself had been beaten, imprisoned, and persecuted, encouraged other believers while awaiting his own execution, "In this you greatly rejoice, though now for a little while you may have had to suffer grief in all kinds of trials. These have come so that your faith—of greater worth than gold, which perishes even though refined by fire—may be proved genuine and may result in praise, glory and honor when Jesus Christ is revealed."[17]

What kinds of trials have caused you to suffer grief? Could it be God has given you a platform of suffering from which you can be a witness of His power and grace to those who are watching? Because if we always feel good
and look good
and lead a good life;
if our kids always behave
and our boss is always pleased
and our home is always orderly
and our friends are always available
and our bank account is always sufficient
and our car always starts
and our bodies always feel good
and we are patient and kind and thoughtful and happy and loving, others shrug because they're capable of being that way too. On the other hand, if
we have a splitting headache,
the kids are screaming,
the phone is ringing,
the boss is yelling,
the supper is burning,
yet we are still patient, kind, thoughtful, happy, and loving, the world sits up and takes notice. The world knows that kind of behavior is not natural. It's supernatural. And others see Jesus revealed in us. So Peter continues, "Do not be surprised at the painful trial you are suffering, as though something strange were

happening to you. But rejoice that you participate in the sufferings of Christ, so that you may be overjoyed when his glory is revealed. . . . If you suffer as a Christian, do not be ashamed, but praise God that you bear that name. . . . So then, those who suffer according to God's will should commit themselves to their faithful Creator and continue to do good."[18] Because suffering is a gleaming showcase for the display of the precious gems of His character that are reflected in you.[19]

The revelation of God's glory in and through us is illustrated in the story of the little boy who was confused by something the pastor had said one Sunday morning in church. When he saw the pastor in the parking lot, he ran up to him, tugged at his sleeve, and inquired respectfully, "Sir, can I ask you a question about your sermon?" The pastor graciously halted on his way to the car and gave the young parishioner his full attention. "Sure, son, what is it?"

The boy explained, "You said I could ask Jesus to come into my heart."

"That's right," the pastor responded.

"But Jesus is a Man in a man's body," the little boy replied.

"That's right," the pastor patiently answered.

As a frown creased his brow, the youngster persisted, "But I'm just a little boy."

The pastor gravely nodded, "That's right."

The puzzled look on the young boy's face betrayed his total ignorance of the truth he was about to utter. "But if I'm just a little boy and Jesus is a Man, if He comes into me, He'll be sticking out all over."

"That's right," the pastor agreed with a knowing smile.

Suffering is not only the platform for our witness, but it also often seems to be the pressure that pushes the character of Christ to the forefront of our lives so that others see Jesus "sticking out all over."

Has God increased the pressure in your life? Then praise Him, not for the pressure, but for His transforming power at work that will use it to produce His character in you until others can see Him. Paul described it this way: "We have this treasure in jars of clay to show that this all-surpassing power is from God and not from us. We are hard pressed on every side, but not crushed; perplexed, but not in despair; persecuted, but not abandoned; struck down, but not destroyed. We always carry around in our body the death of Jesus, so that the life of Jesus may also be revealed in our body. For we who are alive are always being given over to death for Jesus' sake, so that his life may be revealed in our mortal body."[20]

Our ultimate aim in life is not to be healthy, wealthy, prosperous, or problem free. Our ultimate aim in life is to bring glory to God. So would you start praising God for your "thorns" and limitations and handicaps and suffering and "heat," asking Him to open your eyes to the opportunity He has given you to display His glory and character in your life? So that even your spouse,

even your child,
even your parent,
even your roommate,
even your friend,
even your coworker,
even your pastor,
can see Jesus sticking out all over you!

The disciples had been so sure that suffering was a punishment for someone's fault that it was a totally new thought to consider suffering as a powerful and personal opportunity to glorify God. But before they had had time to mull over this challenge to their preconceived ideas, Jesus continued with His answers to human suffering: "As long as it is day, we must do the work of him who sent me. Night is coming, when no one can work" (John 9:4). In other words, suffering is the "daytime" in our lives that gives God the opportunity to work in a way He cannot when the "night" comes and we either no longer have the opportunity or are not receptive to Him because all is going well.[21]

Our suffering gives God opportunities to work for our good. This principle is illustrated in the life of a friend's brother, named Bob. At fifty-two, Bob had all the trappings of success. He owned his own business as well as a house, boat, cars, and snowmobile. He had a large family—brothers, sisters, parents, wife, and five children—all of whom loved him. But with the success had come a feeling of self-sufficiency and pride that led him away from God. In the midst of his financial wealth, he was spiritually impoverished. It was "nighttime" in Bob's life.

As Bob's family prayed for him, he felt convicted of sin. He had been raised in a Christian home by parents who were committed to Christ, and he knew he had forsaken the faith of his childhood and the God of his fathers. So Bob boldly asked God to do whatever it would take to get him into a right relationship with Him. Three times he received a warning from God that if he did not repent and surrender his life completely to Jesus Christ, he would experience serious consequences. Each time he shrugged it off and let busyness crowd out the conviction and muffle the warning.

Like any red-blooded American male, he was excited when the dealer called and said his new car had come in and was ready to be delivered. Bob rushed to take possession. On one of his first outings, a passing van forced him off the road and beneath a tractor-trailer parked in the median. His hand was scratched, his jaw was broken, and his eyes were torn from his face! In fact, his face was so mangled that medical personnel left him for dead when they arrived on the scene. After he got their attention by flailing his arms, they medevacked him to the closest trauma unit, where the doctors told his family there was nothing they could do for him because he was too far gone. As his brother pleaded with the doctors not to give up their efforts to save his life, Bob's heart was at peace. He knew this tragic disaster was the answer to his prayer for God to bring him back into a right relationship with Him. Although he would never see again, "daytime" had returned in Bob's life. God had used a car accident and the loss of his eyes as an opportunity to work in his life, drawing him to the cross and helping him to grow up into a mature disciple of Jesus Christ.

Today Bob's lack of bitterness and his joy in life, despite his physical handicap, display the work of God in his heart. He gives victorious testimony that "I had to become blind in order to see."

Malcolm Muggeridge, a great British philosopher and convert to Christ, confirmed from his own experience that he'd grown more during times of adversity than he ever had during times of prosperity. What will it take in your life to bring you to the point that you will choose to abandon everything and follow Jesus Christ as His disciple?

As you look back on your life, how have you suffered? What have been your times of adversity? During those times, have you grown bitter—or better? If you submit to God, yielding your life fully to His will even when it includes suffering, you will grow better and better and better until the glory of Jesus is revealed in the clay pot of your life.[22] The "thorn" may not be removed, but His grace is sufficient, the "clay" becomes strong and beautiful, and Jesus sticks out all over!

Having identified Himself by revealing verbally, "While I am in the world, I am the light of the world" (John 9:5), Jesus then gave a visual illustration of who He is and the work He had come to do as "he spit on the ground, made some mud with the saliva, and put it on the man's eyes" (John 9:6).

Can you imagine how this poor blind beggar felt, sitting in one of the many alleyways that twisted around the temple grounds, hearing himself used as an object lesson in a theological discussion? How did he react when the voice of the One he deduced was the Rabbi sounded closer and closer until he could feel His breath in his face and smell the sweat and dust of His robe? Did he try to scuttle back into the shadows, afraid of being poked, mocked, laughed at, and abused by these men as he had been so often by others? Or did he inch forward, leaning toward the Voice in which he could detect an understanding and compassion and authority he had never heard before? A Voice that drew him irresistibly toward the Speaker so that when his face was cradled in a strong, gentle hand and firm fingers smeared something on his eyelids, he remained quiet and still and, for some mysterious reason, very excited and expectant. When the mouth that was now inches from his own spoke, commanding him to "go, wash in the Pool of Siloam" (John 9:7), he scurried off in unhesitating, unquestioning obedience.[23]

What a moment it must have been! Perhaps when we get to heaven we'll be able to see a video replay of the blind man, with his face even dirtier than usual, groping his way to the pool's edge, dipping his hands in the cool water, then splashing so that water cascaded on his forehead, nose, lips, cheeks, chin, and *eyes*! Was there a moment of frozen astonishment as he blinked at the sudden objects and colors and light that appeared before him? It was as though the door of sight that had been shut all of his life had been just a veil that was now lifted. He could see! *He could see*! He "went and washed, and came home seeing" (John 9:7). Jesus hadn't *restored* his sight, since he had never had any. The man had been *born blind.* Jesus had *created* sight!

What would it have been for a man born blind to suddenly, in a moment, receive sight? What would it have been to see for the *first time,*

the blue of the sky,
the leaves of the trees,
the sparkle of the sun,
the green of the grass,
the colors of the flowers,
the crooked alleyway where he lived,
the face of his mother,
the food he put in his mouth,
the people he passed on the street,
the house where he lived?

It's another miracle that he ever even arrived home; each moment of discovery must have been distracting as well as thrilling! Surely the stupendous excitement that was welling up in his chest and spilling out in every pore of his being propelled him to seek out those who knew him that they might share in his incredible joy! But if he was expecting a neighborhood celebration, he was in for a rude awakening! Instead, he encountered hostile, incredulous interrogation.

Suffering Gives Us Opportunities to Witness

As friends and neighbors clamored around him, they seemed to ignore the fact that even though he had been blind, he did have ears to hear what they were saying as well as a mouth to explain what had happened. As they circled him, eyeing him suspiciously, they discussed him as though he weren't there, as though he were an impostor, "'Isn't this the same man who used to sit and beg?' Some claimed that he was. Others said, 'No, he only looks like him.' But he himself insisted, 'I am the man'" (John 9:8–9). These were the same friends and neighbors who had known him all of his life, who saw him every day. They knew him.

Suffering gives us opportunities to witness personally. The formerly blind man witnessed to those around him by just letting them observe the difference Jesus had made in his life. He didn't try to hide it or cover it up or make it inoffensive. They could see for themselves that there was a difference—he was a changed man!

How have you tried to witness to your friends? To the people who see you every day? To the people who know you? Are they gossiping about you behind your back? "I think he's got religion. He used to be so cross and depressed, but just look at him now. He's actually happy! Do you think his stocks have gone up dramatically? Or have things changed at home? Is this for real? I sure hope it lasts."

One of the best ways to witness to family, friends, and neighbors is to let them see the difference Jesus has made in your life, even if it does start their tongues to wag. As they continue to observe your life, they will see that the difference is real and that it does last. That's one reason He has allowed you to suffer. Because it gives you the opportunity to show your friends the change in your life, not just tell them about it.

An old farmer demonstrated the value of firsthand observation when he showed his new, young farmhand around the barn. After he pointed out the stalls, the tack room, and the feed bins, he led the young man to the corral where his prize mule was lazily munching away on some tufts of grass. The old farmer ducked under the pole fence, walked up to the mule, and began to stroke his neck.

The younger man also approached the mule—from behind. In a flash, the mule's hind leg shot out, sending the farmhand twenty feet into the air. In a daze, the young man picked himself up off the ground, staggered toward the farmer, and in a shaky voice, inquired accusingly, "Why didn't you tell me that mule would kick?"

The old farmer shifted the wad of tobacco in his mouth from one side to the other, leaned over, let loose a long stream of brown juice, wiped his mouth on the back of his shirt sleeve, and drawled, "Well . . . showin' is better'n tellin'."

With people who see us every day, sometimes "showin' is better'n tellin'." Often our friends and neighbors and family members will watch what we do much more closely than they will listen to what we say. But our lives should also demand a verdict. We need to back up the difference they see in us with an explanation.

After gossiping about the once-blind man for a while, the neighbors finally demanded, "How then were your eyes opened?" (John 9:10). Their curiosity had led them to question him about the change in his life. And it gave him the ideal opportunity to witness personally by just responding to what they were asking. But what could he say? How could he describe to them that moment in the alleyway when he had heard the Rabbi discussing the problem of human suffering and pain with His disciples, with himself as the object lesson? How could he relate to them the sound of the Rabbi's voice or the feeling of the Rabbi's touch or the authority of the Rabbi's command? How could he relive for them that moment when he had washed his face in the pool of Siloam and opened his eyes to the world around him? *How could he explain a miracle?* So he decided to simply give the facts: "The man they call Jesus made some mud and put it on my eyes. He told me to go to Siloam and wash. So I went and washed, and then I could see" (John 9:11).

There! He had told them! But when they asked a follow-up question, "Where is this man?" (John 9:12), he didn't know enough to tell them how to find Jesus for themselves.

Have you felt defeated in your witness because you couldn't answer all the questions either? Have you been unable to lead others to Christ because you just don't know how? Then God may place you in circumstances where your newfound experience is challenged so that you begin to grow in your faith and knowledge of Him.

Suffering gives us the opportunity to witness publicly. After having heard the man's personal witness, his friends and neighbors apparently felt that the authorities should be informed before this kind of thing got out of hand. So he was dragged before the religious leaders. Did casual bystanders begin to gather around as the friends and neighbors planted him squarely in front of the authorities? Was he the object of dozens of pairs of curious, incredulous, unbelieving eyes?

Under the sharp, critical questioning of the Pharisees, rather than being intimidated, the man's thoughts were stimulated. He used the interrogation as an opportunity to publicly tell others what had happened in his life. As he answered questions, his faith developed rapidly and he came to the conclusion that the One he had thought was just a man was actually a prophet (John 9:11, 17).

What happened next happens all too frequently today. The authorities sent for the man's parents and questioned them with such hostility that they were made to feel they had committed some crime by having a son whose life had been miraculously changed. Although the parents acknowledged their relationship with their son, they were terrified of what others would say. They felt threatened by their son's public witness and the fact that others associated them with Jesus because of his experience. So even though they were very religious people, they backed away, explaining, "We know he is our son . . . and we know he was born blind. But how he can see now, or who opened his eyes, we don't know. Ask him. He is of age; he will speak for himself" (John 9:20–21).

How have your parents reacted to your experience with Jesus?[24] Have they been glad you've been helped and agreeable to the difference it's made in your life as long as you kept it private? But has your public witness made them nervous about what others might say and think and gossip about them behind their backs?

Some years ago, a young couple in our town committed their lives to Christ. Although they had been raised in the church by good, religious parents, when they went home for Christmas following their public profession of faith, their parents sat them down and said emphatically, "Don't ever speak His name in this house. We do not want you coming home if you talk of these things. *What will the neighbors think?*"

How have you reacted to your parents' attitude? The former blind man may have been hurt, but he did not waver in his witness. Perhaps he knew intuitively that if his parents had known Jesus for themselves, they would have been supportive.

So the authorities persisted, becoming ugly as they tried to get the man to change his testimony, to doubt what had just happened to him, by making him take an oath: "Give glory to God" (John 9:24). It was like challenging, "Put your hand on the Bible and swear to tell the truth, the whole truth, and nothing but the truth, so help you God!"

The former blind man could not debate these religious authorities on their level. He did not have all the theological, intellectual, philosophical answers to their questions.[25] But he did have his own experience that no one could take away from him. With what must have been a head held high and eyes that were probably still stinging and watering from the unaccustomed light, he looked straight back at his accusers and declared with simplicity and humility, "One thing I do know. I was blind but now I see!" (John 9:25). As the authorities erupted with ridicule, sarcasm, and insults, the former blind man boldly stood firm on what he knew to be the truth of his experience. And as he did, his faith and understanding grew!

The authorities, referring to Jesus as "this fellow," impugned His character and credibility by declaring, "We know that God spoke to Moses, but as for this fellow, we don't even know where he comes from" (John 9:29). Rather than destroy the former blind man's faith, this public verbal flogging strengthened it. The more the man was questioned, criticized, and challenged, the more he was able to think through his experience and conclude, "Now that is remarkable! You don't know where he comes from, yet he opened my eyes. We know that God does not listen to sinners. He listens to the godly man who does his will. Nobody has ever heard of opening the eyes of a man born blind. If this man were not from God, he could do nothing" (John 9:30–33). Just as his physical eyes had been opened, the man's spiritual eyes were opened with sharp clarity! He knew that the Rabbi who had touched his face and smeared mud on his eyes and told him to go wash was more than a man! He was more than a prophet! He was uniquely from God! The Pharisees rejected this conclusion in a rage, "You were steeped in sin at birth; how dare you lecture us!" (John 9:34).

The former blind beggar had more wisdom and insight than all of the religious leaders who confronted him, whether they acknowledged it or not. What group do you think you can't speak publicly to because you are somehow not on "their level"? Who do you say you can't witness to because he or she is an intellectual, or highly educated, and you are not? Or maybe the person has a seminary degree and you have just started going to church. Remember, it was Joseph, a Hebrew teenager and slave, not the wise men of Egypt, who interpreted Pharaoh's dreams.[26] It was another Hebrew slave, Daniel, not the wise men of Babylon, who deciphered the mysterious writing on the wall of Belshazzar's palace.[27] It was the unlettered fishermen, not the scribes and the Pharisees, who were taken into the confidence of Christ and used of God to build His church.[28]

Do you feel inadequate intellectually, educationally, socially, theologically? Good! God can use you! He states clearly that He "chose the foolish things of the world to shame the wise; God chose the weak things of the world to shame the strong. He chose the lowly things of this world and the despised things—and the things that are not—to nullify the things that are, so that no one may boast before him."[29]

The Pharisees threw the man out of the temple (John 9:34). He was publicly disgraced by the religious leaders of his day and because of the excommunication, he would be considered a moral leper in Jerusalem with no social respectability. How did he feel? Looking back on his day, it must have seemed like a dream that had turned into a nightmare! How could something so fantastically good become something so horribly bad?

Have you ever been "thrown out" because of your witness for Christ? Were you thrown out of a relationship? Or a club? Or a job? Or a church? Or a family? Or a social circle? Or a school?

How did it make you feel to find yourself alone and rejected by what seemed like everyone? Did you indulge in self-pity? Or did the experience draw you even closer to Christ?

My husband, Danny, and I, along with our three children, had belonged to a church in our city for fifteen years. My husband had taught a couples' Sunday school class for at least twelve years and had been chairman of the men's fellowship as well as chairman of the board of deacons. I had served on various committees and for twelve years had taught a Bible class of five hundred women that met in the sanctuary every Wednesday. As the church leaders observed the powerful impact and magnetic influence of Danny's leadership, as well as the increasing popularity of the Bible class, they became threatened and jealous. We were called before a specially formed investigative committee to defend personally what we had been doing. Within weeks, the Bible class was removed from the church facility, and Danny and I were in effect urged to leave the church.

As the local press learned of what had happened, reporter after reporter called to ask questions. Each time I talked to the press, I was able to give a personal witness as to what Jesus meant to me. I remember one reporter asking, "Aren't you bitter?" And I could reply honestly and forthrightly, "No, I'm not. God has simply used this to get our attention, to tell us that He wants us elsewhere. It's obvious we have become a problem to the church. We don't want to hinder it in its walk with

God any more than we want to be hindered in ours. We're looking forward to what God has for us in another church." And I meant it. But it still hurt. To this day, I'm amazed by how quickly friends can become antagonists. I'm amazed at the insidious viciousness of jealousy that festers below the surface and erupts in ugly rhetoric and actions. I'm amazed that a man born blind who had received his sight had not one person to rejoice with him and was instead attacked and accused!

In one day, the former blind man's life had turned upside down and inside out. As he must have wandered in a daze through the narrow, crowded streets, surely he tried to comprehend all he had experienced, realizing that although he had gained his physical sight he had lost any social acceptance he would ever hope to have. Did he wage an almost superhuman battle to force his attention away from all he was seeing for the first time to all the thoughts he was thinking for the first time? And where would he go? Back to the alleyway where he had begged all of his life? Back to his home where his parents resented the disgrace he had brought on the family? Back to his "friends" who had turned him over to the authorities? Since he had received his sight, not one person had congratulated him or shaken his hand or slapped him on the back or even smiled joy and approval. Having lived in a world of darkness all of his life, surely he had never felt so alone as he did in the light.

Until he heard that familiar Voice. It was coming from an ordinary-looking Man standing in front of him—

a Man who had heard of his excommunication from the temple,
a Man who knew what it was to be lonely in a crowd,
a Man who understood how it felt to be treated like a criminal
because of God's presence in His life,
a Man who would experience Himself being outcast, not just from
the temple and the city, but from the hearts of all—
a Man who had heard, who understood, who loved, and
who had searched until He found the formerly blind beggar
to whom He had given sight.

Praise God! Jesus draws near to those who are afflicted and persecuted and criticized and ostracized. Jesus draws near to those who are suffering—especially when the suffering is for His sake.[30]

As the former beggar heard the Voice he would never forget, did his heart leap? Did his newly focused eyes cling to the Man's face, drinking in every detail, listening to every syllable, as the Man gently inquired, "Do you believe in the Son of Man?" Eagerly the man responded, "Who is he, sir? . . . Tell me so that I may believe in him." In other words, "Please, sir. Just give me Jesus." And "Jesus said, 'You have now seen him; in fact, he is the one speaking with you.' Then the man said, 'Lord, I believe,' and he worshiped him" (John 9:35–38).

Jesus then gave a scathing condemnation of the Pharisees who had stood in judgment over the man and were still hounding him. He declared that the man who had been blind could now see, not only physically, but also spiritually because he recognized Jesus as the Son of God and placed his faith in Him. But the Pharisees, who claimed with all of their religious training and knowledge and experience that they could see spiritually, remained blind because they rejected the truth of who Jesus is (John 9:39–41).

Do you *see*? Jesus makes suffering understandable to the observer by answering our questions in a way that challenges our preconceptions and prejudices.

Suffering may be someone's fault or it may not be anyone's fault. But if given to God, our suffering becomes an opportunity to experience the power of God at work in our lives and give glory to Him. Would you open your eyes? God has given us the Answer to human suffering, and His name is Jesus.

AT 3:00 a.m. on August 17, 1999, the very foundation crumbled on which the industrial complex of modern-day Turkey was built. A gigantic earthquake that measured 7.8 on the Richter scale rocked and rolled beneath the earth's surface, and in a matter of forty-five seconds, the nation was plunged into devastating chaos. As the tally of the dead rose quickly to more than seven thousand within two days, and more than fourteen thousand within the week, Prime Minister Bulent Ecevit declared, "It is the biggest natural disaster I have witnessed."[31]

Every day the entire world watched aghast as pictures of inconceivable human suffering were relayed on television and throughout the printed news media. And what we observed were entire cities instantaneously reduced to mass graves with shredded buildings, twisted water and sewer lines, and blazing gas leaks the only grim memorial markers. The images of the dead resembled broken dolls that had been discarded on massive trash heaps. We watched an emotional straitjacket engulf the living in hopelessness and despair until even that which survived was in ruins. Once in a while we smiled through tears as we watched the mangled body of a child being wrenched from the wreckage, still breathing. Or we held our breath until a man, clawing with his bare hands through a mountain of shattered glass and concrete, extracted his loved one from the grasp of hell. But for the most part, the enormity of the nightmare was overwhelming, even to those of us who were simply observing it.

And as we observed the suffering in Turkey from the comfort of our safe homes, we thanked God that it was not our nation that was decimated or our homes that were shattered or our families that were torn to ribbons. As we poured out our hearts in prayer for the sufferers, we couldn't help asking, *"Why?"*

This question was once put to Malcolm Muggeridge by a little boy in a wheelchair during a question-and-answer session. The boy had struggled to say something, but had been unable to do so. Mr. Muggeridge stepped down from the platform and walked to where the boy was seated. Putting his arm reassuringly around the boy's shoulder, he told him to take his time because he wanted to hear what the lad had to say. Finally the boy blurted out, "You say there is a God who loves me."

"Yes," Mr. Muggeridge confidently replied.

"Then—*why me?*" the crippled boy inquired.

For a moment, Mr. Muggeridge, the man whose quick wit and sharp tongue were legendary, was silent. Finally, he asked gently, "If you were fit, would you have come to hear me tonight?"

The boy shook his head no.

Again, Mr. Muggeridge was thoughtfully silent. Finally, he explained, "God has asked a hard thing of you. But remember, He asked something even harder of His Son, Jesus Christ. He asked Jesus to die for you. And He did. Maybe this was His way of making sure you'd hear of His love and come to put your faith in Him."

And the young questioner was introduced personally to God's Answer to his suffering, as he was just given Jesus.

10

JESUS MAKES SUFFERING UNDERSTANDABLE . . .

To the Sufferer

JOHN 11:1–44

When the telephone rang on February 26, 1998, I had no idea the call would precipitate a launch into the wild blue yonder of faith. My son's voice on the other end of the line sounded strong, but serious. "Mom, the doctor thinks I have cancer." With those few words, I was suddenly catapulted into the eye of an unexpected, raging storm of suffering that lashed at every aspect of my life.

Yet in the midst of the storm that hit as suddenly and fiercely as a devastating tornado, I experienced an unprecedented peace—and joy! As I prayed with my son, Jonathan, on the telephone during that initial conversation, I was able to praise God for His divine purpose for Jonathan's life, even if it included cancer. Although we were caught by surprise, we knew God had known about the cancer since before Jonathan's birth. We knew also that Jonathan had been prayed for before his conception, every day of my pregnancy, and every day of his life. He had been born again as a child, and now, as a young adult, was in God's will as far as he understood it. Therefore we had absolute confidence that this suffering would be for Jonathan's good and God's glory.[1] We *knew* God had a plan for Jonathan's life, and this was part of it!

The first doctor's diagnosis was confirmed by a specialist. Within a week of the first diagnosis, and just four weeks before his wedding day, our twenty-eight-year-old son underwent successful surgery to remove a malignant tumor. With the recommended follow-up treatments of radiation, the prognosis of total recovery has been excellent.

What storm of suffering has swept into *your* life? The storm of death? divorce? disease? debt?

Has a feud erupted in your family?
A betrayal in your marriage?
A rebellion to your parenting?
The miscarriage of a pregnancy?
A severance from a job?

How have you reacted to the storm?

A turkey and an eagle react in different ways to the threat of a storm. A turkey reacts by running under the barn, hoping the storm won't come near it. On the other hand, an eagle leaves the security of its nest and spreads its wings to ride the air currents of the approaching storm, knowing the wind will carry it higher in the sky than it could soar on its own. So which are you—a turkey or an eagle—in the way you react to the storms of life?

Within a period of eighteen months, my family experienced one storm after another. From Hurricane Fran, which downed 102 trees in our yard, to the fire that consumed my husband's dental office, to the weddings of *all three of our children,* to Jonathan's cancer and surgery, we reeled from one emergency or crisis to another. In the whirlwind, I discovered I am an emotional turkey. I want to withdraw from the emotional pain and burdensome demands and frenzied activities and unending responsibilities. I want to run under the barn with my wings over my head and hide from friends and family who feel ignored or slighted, misunderstanding my busyness and preoccupation as indifference or arrogance. I want to escape the hurt.

Yet I have chosen to be an eagle in my spirit. And in the midst of the storm, when I have spread my wings of faith to embrace the "Wind," [2] placing my dependency upon Jesus and Jesus alone, I have experienced quiet, "everyday" miracles:

His joy has balanced the pain,
His power has lifted the burden,
His peace has calmed the worries,
and His all-sufficiency has been more than adequate to meet all my responsibilities.

Soaring has become an adventure of discovering just how faithful He can be when I am way out of my comfort zone in the stratosphere over the storm. In fact, soaring has become so exhilarating that I increasingly find I am no longer content to live in the barnyard of familiarity just for its relative security. I want to live by faith! And I imagine a smile of infinite tenderness on His face as the angels in heaven applaud, saying, "Anne, you've finally got it. Now you're beginning to understand."

And to a greater degree than ever before, I do understand. Looking back over that eighteen-month period, my thoughtful, confident conclusion is that those storms of suffering increased and intensified in my life because Jesus wanted me

to soar higher in my relationship with Him—
to fall deeper in love with Him,
to grow stronger in my faith in Him,
to be more consistent in my walk with Him,
to bear more fruit in my service to Him,
to draw closer to His heart,
to keep my focus on His face,
to live for His glory alone!

This growth in depth and strength and consistency and fruitfulness and ultimately in Christlikeness is only possible when the winds of life are contrary to personal comfort. Just as storms make it possible for eagles to soar, so suffering makes it possible for you and me to attain the highest pinnacles in the Christian life. Suffering develops our faith.[3]

SUFFERING DEVELOPS OUR FAITH

Nothing could be more contrary to our personal comfort or more challenging to our faith than death because it is the greatest storm we will ever face, whether it's our own death or that of a loved one. In the story of Lazarus we see Jesus patiently urging Mary and Martha to stop being "turkeys," to leave the barnyard of security and to soar by faith on eagles' wings. But of course it's impossible to soar on our own; for this we need Jesus.

For This We Need Jesus

The trouble that hit the well-to-do[4] home and beloved family without warning didn't appear to be an opportunity to soar, but it became one when "a man named Lazarus was sick. He was from Bethany, the village of Mary and her sister Martha" (John 11:1). Bethany was a small town on the southeastern slope of the Mount of Olives just two miles from Jerusalem. The hot, dusty streets and organized piles of stone that served as houses made it virtually indistinguishable from other villages of its day, with one notable exception: It was in Bethany that Jesus, in effect, had a second home. It was where He relaxed and retreated from the pressures and demands of ministry. It was the starting place of His triumphal entry into Jerusalem as well as the departing place for His ascension into heaven. And each night during His final week before the Cross, after teaching in the temple all day, Jesus and His disciples would slip over to Bethany to rest and be refreshed. What gave it such favor in His eyes? The main attraction seemed to be a particular home in which He felt comfortable and at ease and loved and accepted and honored and enjoyed and trusted.

This place of refuge was the home of Lazarus and his sisters, Mary and Martha. We assume Martha was the eldest because she was like my older sister—bossy! She was bustling, energetic, and practical; she always seemed to be in charge. But she was known to get so caught up in the details of her responsibilities that she would lose her focus.[5] Yet "Jesus loved Martha" (John 11:5).

Mary may have been the middle sibling. She was intuitively sensitive, deeply spiritual, and thoughtfully quiet. She seemed like a still pool that went deep. In spite of household demands, she made the time to sit at Jesus' feet and listen to His Word, a trait for which she received His encouraging, lasting commendation.[6] She was devoted to Him. She "was the same one who poured perfume on the Lord and wiped his feet with her hair" (John 11:2).[7] And Jesus loved Mary (John 11:5).

Lazarus was apparently the youngest. Speculation has suggested that he may have been the rich young ruler who asked Jesus how he could get to heaven.[8] When Jesus replied that he would have to give up everything and follow Him in a life of costly discipleship, the young man turned away sadly because he had many possessions.[9] Yet three times in this chapter we are told that Jesus loved Lazarus (John 11:3, 5, 36). If Lazarus was indeed that same young ruler, it makes his resurrection an even more powerful and poignant story of God's grace poured out on the helpless and the hopeless in a divine answer to the prayer of faith.

This family of three that was so beloved by Jesus experienced a crisis when Lazarus became ill. His sickness was surely more than a summer cold or virus. Perhaps he was stricken with a high fever and splitting migraine and severe dysentery. As he grew weaker and paler, fear and helplessness must have gripped the little family. Think about it. This loved one was desperately ill, but there were no sterile hospitals

or high-tech x-rays

or expensive lab tests
or nurses in white squeaky shoes.
There were no thermometers
or stethoscopes
or antibiotics
or even aspirin.

With all of their wealth and influence, Mary, Martha, and Lazarus were helpless in the face of this silent killer. They became so alarmed that they "sent word to Jesus, 'Lord, the one you love is sick'" (John 11:3). When something bad happened to their little family, they knew they needed Jesus. Their implied request to Him was, "Please, do something about it. Help us. Make Lazarus well."

What bad thing has happened to your family? Is it a physical illness? Or financial collapse? Or severed relationship? Or social exclusion? Do you think that because something bad happened, Jesus doesn't love you or your family? Perhaps that's why this passage repeats again and again that each member of this family was loved by Jesus. *Bad things do happen* to those Jesus loves! You and I need to learn to interpret our circumstances by His love, not interpret His love by our circumstances!

Who is your Lazarus? Who do you know who is not just physically sick, but sick in his or her sin? Someone perhaps who has lost appetite for kindness . . . truthfulness . . . righteousness . . . holiness . . . goodness . . . and responsibility? Someone who has lost appetite for Jesus? Someone who is therefore growing weak morally and spiritually, becoming depressed and discouraged? Is your "Lazarus" your brother? Or sister? Or parent? Or spouse? Or child? Or in-law? When have you told Jesus, "Lord, the one you love is sick"? How has Jesus responded? Has His lack of response caused you to question whether He has heard your prayer?

When Mary and Martha prayed, their sense of helplessness was reinforced; not only because something bad had happened to the family, but when it occurred, God also seemed hidden and out of touch and uncaring and remote and removed from their situation.

Jesus delayed answering. He heard their prayer, "Yet when he heard that Lazarus was sick, he stayed where he was two more days" (John 11:6).

Has your prayer for your "Lazarus" remained unanswered? Does God seem to be hiding Himself from you? *Why does He delay?* Why does He allow you and your loved ones to suffer so? One reason for His delay seems to be to allow us time to exhaust every other avenue of help until we come to the conclusion, without any doubt, that we are totally helpless without Him, and we rest our faith in Him and Him alone.

If Mary and Martha could have heard Jesus' response at the moment their prayer came to Him, they might have been even more confused. "When he heard this, Jesus said, 'This sickness will not end in death. No, it is for God's glory so that God's Son may be glorified through it'" (John 11:4). Yet in reality, Lazarus had already died by the time the message reached Jesus.[10] So what did Jesus mean? He meant that Lazarus's sickness did not have physical death as its ultimate purpose. Jesus was helping His disciples understand suffering—that bad things that happen to those He loves have a greater purpose than the physical or the temporary or the material or the visible. In this case, the greater purpose was to bring Martha to a point of absolute helplessness and hopelessness so that she might put all of her faith in Him, and Him alone, and then soar on eagles' wings as God demonstrated His power and grace and total sufficiency for her need.

Jesus' delay in answering our prayers is never due to preoccupation or indifference with other things or an inability to act. His delay has as its purpose the development of our trust in Him and Him alone for our own good and His glory.

When Jesus did decide to act, His disciples thought the timing was all wrong, and they questioned His wisdom. After delaying for two days, Jesus told them, "Let us go back to Judea" (John 11:7). However, His disciples resisted, protesting, "But Rabbi . . . a short while ago the Jews tried to stone you, and yet you are going back there?" (John 11:8) The disciples were arguing with Jesus!

Have you ever argued with Jesus? Have you ever questioned His wisdom or timing and honestly blurted out that what He seemed to be doing did not appear to be a good idea in your opinion? It's amazing how arrogant we can be, isn't it?

Several years ago I prayed earnestly for a relationship one of my children was in. As I continuously poured out my heart to God in tears and fasting and pleading, He remained silent. For months I could get no answer until finally I just collapsed in a spiritual heap and told Him I didn't know what to do; I was totally helpless. And then the situation got worse, so I began to argue with Him. Every legitimate and imaginary fear I had ever thought came to the surface as, incredibly, I *warned Him* of the dire consequences if this relationship were allowed to progress. I told Him respectfully but in no uncertain terms what I thought He should do.

All I can say from this perspective years later is that I praise God for His patience and sovereignty and for *unanswered* prayers! Although my prayers had been based on my discernment of the facts as I saw them at the time—and I believe my perception was accurate—what I lacked was the big picture. God knew that by His grace people and circumstances change, and that the prayer of my heart would be answered—but in a totally different way than I had asked.

God's delays and His ways can be confusing because the process God uses to accomplish His will can go against human logic and common sense. The reason for this is to focus our faith, not in our friends . . . or ability . . . or resources . . . or knowledge . . . or strength . . . or anything other than Him alone.

Joshua, Moses' successor, led the Israelites out of the wilderness and across the Jordan only to face Jericho, the enemy stronghold that blocked their progress into the promised land. As he surveyed the enemy fortress in planning a military strategy for taking it, God confronted him. He instructed Joshua to lead the Israelites in a silent march around the city once a day for six days. On the seventh day, he was to lead the people around the city seven times. At the end of the seventh lap, the people were to shout as the trumpets were blown, and the walls of the stronghold would collapse. Can you imagine the thoughts that must have crossed Joshua's mind? The instructions surely seemed ludicrous from a military standpoint. But Joshua obeyed, and the walls came tumbling down![11] Why? Because Joshua's faith rested in God alone!

Gideon found himself in a similar situation. He was one of the judges in Israel who faced the daunting task of leading his nation into battle against tens of thousands of Midianites. He gathered together a force of thirty-two thousand troops, but God told him he had too many and cut Gideon's army down to size—three hundred in all! God then told Gideon to instruct his men to each take a trumpet and a lighted torch held under a clay pot, then all should climb to the top of the nearest hill, overlooking the enemy camp. At a prearranged signal from Gideon, they were to break the clay jars, hold up the torches, and shout while blowing the trumpets. The instructions sounded bizarre, to say the least. But Gideon obeyed, and his tiny band of three hundred men was victorious over the enormous Midianite army.[12] Why? Because their faith had been in God alone.

As you pray, where have you placed your faith? Just as He challenged Joshua and Gideon, God challenges you and me to "trust in the LORD with all your heart and lean not on your own understanding; in all your ways acknowledge him, and he will make your paths straight."[13]

Jesus knew Mary and Martha's prayer would be answered, but in a totally different way than they had asked. And Jesus knew much better than His disciples what awaited Him this time in Jerusalem, yet He aslo knew it was for this very time that He had been born. So He addressed their concerns by explaining, "Are there not twelve hours of daylight? A man who walks by day will not stumble, for he sees by this world's light. It is when he walks by night that he stumbles, for he has no light" (John 11:9–10). In other words, "Your life span is like a twelve-hour day. The length is predetermined and fixed. Just as we can't make the sun set one hour earlier, when we are in God's will, we cannot shorten or lengthen our lives from what God has predetermined they should be. The important factor is to walk in the daylight of God's will because then you will be safe; you will not stumble. If, on the other hand, you walk in the darkness—outside of God's will—you remove yourself from His protection and subject yourself to everything and anything that comes along. And that's a dangerous place to be. It is God's will that I go to Jerusalem. Therefore, I will be safer there in the midst of the murderous, plotting Jews than staying here in the tranquillity of the Transjordan outside of His will."

This principle came forcefully to my mind when I was in Madras, India. I had been speaking at a conference of five thousand pastors and evangelists, gathered from every province in the country. One morning, before I went to the scheduled meeting, my traveling companion came rushing into the room, waving a long stream of paper. I recognized it as the news information sheet that was disgorged by the Teletype machine in the lobby for English-speaking people who were interested in what was going on in the rest of the world. Across the paper, in two-inch-high black letters, was the headline, "The War Has Begun!" As our eyes devoured the text, we learned that the United States had actually begun the war in the Persian Gulf in order to evict Saddam Hussein from the oil fields and liberate the tiny kingdom of Kuwait from his tyrannical grip.

As my companion and I looked at each other, we were acutely aware of the distance between us and the safety of our country. We were literally on the other side of the world, in a nation that was not all that sympathetic to the action America had just taken. And we were two women, traveling alone. For all we knew, the entire world would be triggered into a war. It was then that what Jesus told His disciples came clearly to mind. I was confident that my trip to India and my participation in the conference on evangelism were in God's will. Peace flooded my heart. I knew I was safer on that platform in Madras during the Persian Gulf War than I would have been at home. So I began my address that morning by telling the thousands of pastors and evangelists who were packed beneath an outdoor tent—men who I knew faced grave danger as they presented the gospel in a predominantly Hindu culture—that the safest place we can be is in the center of God's will. Because when we are in God's will, He takes full responsibility for us. And although bad things may happen, we have the assurance that they are for our good and His glory.

After Jesus and His disciples had had a lively exchange on the difference that being in God's will makes to our personal safety and security, He informed them, "Our friend Lazarus has fallen asleep; but I am going there to wake him" (John 11:11). And the disciples, so much like you and me, totally misunderstood Him. "'Lord, if he sleeps, he will get better.' Jesus had been speaking of his death, but his disciples thought he meant natural sleep" (John 11:12–13).[14]

When have you totally misunderstood God's Word? When He said, "Love one another," did you think He meant you should tolerate sin?[15] When He said, "Do not judge, or you too will be judged," did you think He meant not to take a stand against unrighteous behavior?[16] Did you think when He said, "In all things God works for the good," that He was saying every story has a happy ending?[17] Did you think when He said, "I will surely bless you," He was promising to make you healthy, wealthy, happy, and problem free?[18] Isn't it amazing how we can misinterpret what He says?

I believe God gave me a promise for my three children. It is from the song of Moses in Exodus 15:1: "I will sing to the LORD, for he is highly exalted. The horse and its rider he has hurled into the sea." The horse and its rider were Pharaoh and his army who were supernaturally overthrown when they tried to prevent God's children from being in the place He wanted them to be, in the place of His blessing. I understood this as God's promise to me that He would supernaturally overthrow anyone or anything that would hinder my children from being in the place of His blessing. But I also interpreted that promise as meaning my children would be safe from those who would harm them. What He said was that He would see that my children would be secure in His place of blessing. But I have discovered that He sometimes allows them to have frightening, traumatic Red Sea experiences of pursuit and danger in the process.

Listening carefully is important, because if we misunderstand what God is saying, we set ourselves up for disappointment, discouragement, and disillusionment. We end up blaming God, becoming offended with Him when He doesn't keep the promise or fulfill His Word as we understand it. Had the disciples remembered their brief dialogue with Jesus, they might have been spared three days of agony. Instead, when Jesus went to Jerusalem and was crucified, the disciples thought it was a tragic mistake. For three days they were lost in hopeless grief and terrified horror. But Sunday came! Then they understood it had not been a tragic mistake but the glorious will of God. His purpose for the life of Jesus was fulfilled, accomplishing our redemption.

Jesus realized that His disciples had misunderstood. Surely, with no twinkle in His eye or smile on His lips but with grave resolution "he told them plainly, 'Lazarus is dead, and for your sake I am glad I was not there, so that you may believe. But let us go to him'" (John 11:14–15). *Jesus was glad? He was glad Lazarus had died,* without Him? What a life lesson to learn! There is a greater miracle than physical healing! It's the miracle of the resurrection! Jesus was glad because He knew not only the joy that was coming but also the leaping strides of faith His disciples, as well as Mary and Martha, would experience because of it. He was glad because He knew God would be glorified to a far greater extent by the death and resurrection of Lazarus than He would have been by Lazarus's healing and recovery from sickness.

Jesus did not enjoy in the least seeing His loved ones suffer. In fact, He wept. But His focus was on the big picture and the purpose of God that would be accomplished and the glory of God that would be revealed. So often our primary ambition is to escape pain or to feel good or to be delivered from a problem when we need to keep our focus on the big picture of what God is doing in our lives through that pain or problem. Our primary aim must be to glorify God, not to be healed or to be healthy or to be happy.

As Jesus started out along the hot, dry, dusty road that would take Him to Bethany, did He walk alone? Did His disciples just sit there, staring at His departing back, totally confused by what all of this meant? Finally Thomas, in a flat voice of discouraged resignation, "said to the rest of the disciples, 'Let us also go, that we may die with him'" (John 11:16). As Thomas rose, his feet must have felt leaden. His entire demeanor was surely tinged with the same hopelessness that permeated the friends and family in Bethany who so desperately needed Jesus.

For This We Have Jesus

After walking all day on rocky roads and over hills turned brown by the heat, Jesus and His disciples came to the little village He had come to love. As soon as He drew near, word spread quickly through all the "many Jews [who] had come to Martha and Mary to comfort them in the loss of their brother" (John 11:19). The sisters must have received the news at the same time together. Jesus had come! But Mary's obvious resentment that He hadn't answered her prayer sooner kept her at home, while Martha ran to meet Him.

Did Martha run to Jesus, fling her arms around Him, sob on His shoulder and pour out her heart? Or did she walk quickly from the house, weaving her way through her friends, until with a more deliberate pace she stood before Him? Was there a hurt, bewildered, accusing light in her eyes as she confronted Him? "Lord . . . if you had been here, my brother would not have died" (John 11:21). Have your thoughts been similar to Martha's? "God, where have You been? Don't You know what we've been going through? Why haven't You answered sooner? Why didn't You intervene? You could have prevented this tragedy. Why didn't You come when we called? We thought You loved us. Why did You let this happen? I just don't understand."

As Martha looked into the attentive, tender face of Jesus, her heart must have softened. After all, He had come! She had His presence in the midst of her grief. Just as the three Hebrew young men knew God's presence with them in the midst of the fiery furnace,[19] just as John knew the presence of God while he was in exile on the isle of Patmos, just as God promises you and me that we will have His presence as we walk through the valley of the shadow of death or deep waters or fiery trials,[20] Martha knew by personal experience the presence of Jesus in her life when she was suffering.

Martha's resentment melted, and a ray of hope pierced through the blackness of her grief. She seemed to have been struck with sudden, startling insight—if this Man could create sight in someone born blind, if He could make the lame walk, if He could feed five thousand people with five loaves and two fish, *why couldn't He . . . ?!* And so she put forth a tiny tendril of faith, "But I know that even now God will give you whatever you ask" (John 11:22).

I wonder if she took a deep breath and held it as she waited for His response. If so, she didn't have to wait long for it this time. He immediately answered her by confirming her hope, revealing to her His intentions, "Your brother will rise again"

(John 11:23). Jesus gave Martha a promise on which to rest her faith. Without His Word, her faith would be just spiritual, wishful thinking. It would be of the "hope-so" variety, which isn't real faith. If you are praying for something or someone, ask God to give you a promise from His Word on which to base your faith.

The morning that my son, Jonathan, went into surgery for his cancer, God gave me several promises from His Word on which to rest my faith as I prayed. He promised to "preserve the way of His saints."[21] He told me that "many are the afflictions of the righteous, but the LORD delivers him out of them all."[22] And finally, I seemed to hear Him almost shout triumphantly, "The LORD your God in your midst, the Mighty One, will save; He will rejoice over you with gladness."[23] And I knew that my son would not only come through the surgery but would also be delivered from his cancer! And he did come through the surgery! And to date, *praise God,* he has been delivered from the cancer!

But I assure you, it made a huge difference in my prayers to know that I wasn't just hoping Jonathan would be all right; I knew, based on God's promises, that he would be all right. Subsequently, my prayers simply became a matter of holding God to His Word.

Even though Jesus gave Martha a promise, her brow must have creased into a frown as she struggled to understand His meaning, "I know he will rise again in the resurrection at the last day" (John 11:24). Is that where your faith is at the present time? "Lord, I know You can answer my prayer because the Bible says all power is yours. But I doubt You will answer it for me now." Do you believe intellectually, based on what the Bible says, that God has the power to answer your prayer but lack the personal faith to believe He will exercise it now on your behalf?

Jesus patiently persisted in developing Martha's faith until it was focused on Him, and Him alone. With eyes that must have seemed to penetrate past her doubting mind and into her bleeding heart to the very depths of her being, He replied with words that have resonated through the centuries, giving hope at the gravesides of thousands of believers of every generation: "I am the resurrection and the life. He who believes in me will live, even though he dies; and whoever lives and believes in me will never die. Do you believe this?" (John 11:25–26). Do *you* believe this? Do you believe that when there is no hope,

when there is no recourse,
when there is no answer,
when there is no help,

when there is no way,
when there is no remedy,
when there is no solution,
when there is nobody,

that there *is* hope if you have Jesus? Do you believe Jesus can make a way when *there is no way?*

Gradually, the light pierced through the depths of Martha's grief and despair, and she affirmed with a beautiful confession of faith, "Yes, Lord . . . I believe that you are the Christ, the Son of God, who was to come into the world" (John 11:27). Martha recognized and acknowledged that apart from Jesus she was totally helpless and totally hopeless.

Jesus had shifted Martha's focus from her own suffering and grief and pain and problems and despair and hopelessness and helplessness *to Himself.*

Are you desperate for your Lazarus? Where is your focus? If you are suffering, is your focus on the pain? Or the problems the pain produces? Or people who don't seem to understand or help as you think they should? Are you desperate enough to place your faith in Jesus alone? One reason Jesus allows us to suffer is so that our faith is developed until it rests in Him alone. But He also allows us to suffer so that we become a display case for His glory.

SUFFERING DISPLAYS HIS GLORY

Just as a diamond seems to sparkle more brilliantly when displayed in a black velvet case, so the radiant beauty of Christlike character seems to shine more splendidly against the backdrop of suffering. Even in Martha's grief, the jewel of hope that seemed to have been birthed in her spirit sparkled. She eagerly went to Mary, drawing her aside privately to tell her, "The Teacher is here . . . and is asking for you" (John 11:28). Mary's broken heart must have crumbled even more as the "if onlys" flooded to the surface. Without thinking of the scene or commotion she would cause, she abruptly got up from where she had collapsed in the house and fled through the door. "When the Jews who had been with Mary in the house, comforting her, noticed how quickly she got up and went out, they followed her, supposing she was going to the tomb to mourn there" (John 11:29–31). As Mary ran through the narrow streets of the little village with almost frantic despair, did she stumble over the sharp stones? Did she cry afresh at the misery of her helplessness, hot tears blinding her eyes and streaming down her cheeks, disheveled hair escaping from beneath her veil and falling over her face?

When she "reached the place where Jesus was and [when she] saw him, she fell at his feet and said, 'Lord, if you had been here, my brother would not have died'" (John 11:32). She wasn't just being emotional. She was totally realistic. Her grief was coupled with a sense of total hopelessness and helplessness because death is so final. While someone has even a thread of life, there is hope. But once that person dies, there is no hope, no help at all. Although Mary's attitude was worshipful and respectful as she fell at Jesus' feet, she just couldn't quite manage to get beyond the despairing defeat of her brother's death. Her mind was focused on the past and what might have been, *if only* . . .

Are you haunted by the ghosts of the "if onlys" in your past?

"If only I hadn't gone there."
"If only I'd never met her."
"If only I had prayed about it."
"If only I had spent more time with him."
"If only I had taken it seriously."
"If only I had known then what I know now."
"If only Jesus had answered my prayer when I asked Him to."
"If only Jesus were here . . ."

Mary thought Jesus had come too late. Do you think that now? Do you think He has shown up . . .

too late to prevent the rape,
too late to prevent the pregnancy,
too late to prevent the abortion,
too late to prevent the wedding,
too late to prevent the accident,
too late to prevent the death?
He's just too late!

Mary thought if He had truly understood their helpless situation He would have acted or answered differently. But as it was, she thought He was too late, and now she was not just helpless, she was *totally* hopeless. And she crumbled, sobbing, at His feet.

As Mary lay with her shoulders shaking and her chest heaving, wracked with pain that was too great to bear, the friends who had followed her voiced their own despair over her grief and they wept as well. The chorus of weeping was a symphony of sympathy. At the sight and sound of the poignant scene, Jesus "was deeply moved in spirit and troubled" (John 11:33). The text indicates He felt more than just grief; He also felt anger.

Several years ago I received an urgent call from someone at the hospital, telling me that one of my dearest friends was dying. I couldn't believe what I was hearing. When I had spoken with my friend the day before, she had been healthy and happy. What could have gone so terribly wrong? As I rushed to the hospital, I kept praying, "Lord, help. The one whom we love is sick—dying!" When I made my way into the waiting room, I found her family huddled in tears and shock. I was told my precious friend had inhaled a virus that had acted like a hand grenade in her body, exploding and destroying her internal organs. In grief and shock myself, I was urged to go into the chapel where her husband and children had gathered to pray. As I slipped into the darkened sanctuary and collapsed onto a pew, I heard the whispered prayers and the sobs of her loved ones. Then the stifled grief erupted in a chilling, heart-wrenching cry as her son yelled out, "God, it's not right. It's not right! It's just not right!" Later, when her family made the decision to disconnect her from the life support and my beloved friend went to her heavenly home, her son's agonized, angry grief echoed in my ears, and I thought, "He was right. This is not right. It's terribly wrong! This was never meant to be."

It wasn't right because in the beginning, we were never intended to die. Death was not a part of God's original plan. He created you and me for Himself. He intended us to live with Him and enjoy Him forever in an uninterrupted, permanent, personal, loving relationship. But sin came into our lives and broke the very relationship with God for which we were created. All of us are affected because all of us are infected with sin.[24] Everyone who is born into the human race has sinned and fallen short of that original purpose of uninterrupted fellowship with God. And the consequence of sin is death—physical death and eternal death.[25] When a believer physically dies, even though she or he has received the gift of eternal life and therefore is saved from eternal death, even though the believer is immediately ushered into the presence of the heavenly Father,[26] the pain and grief and separation inflicted on the loved ones left behind were never meant to be. It's as though sin and Satan have a temporary victory, even though the sting of death and the grave have been removed by the death and resurrection of Christ.[27]

When your loved one dies and your grief is tinged with anger, don't direct it toward God. He's angry too! Direct it toward sin and its devastating consequences. Dedicate yourself to sharing the gospel as often as you can. Pray that through your witness, others who face physical death will choose to escape the second death, which is separation from God—*hell*—by placing their faith in Jesus Christ. As we face death, our only hope is in knowing there is genuine, triumphant, permanent victory over it that is available to us in Jesus' Name!

At my friend's funeral, I had the opportunity to address the hundreds of those gathered, and I shared with them that death was not right, but thanks be to God, because of His Son, Jesus, death is not final. When we place our faith in Him, not only will we go to heaven, but one day, in our flesh, we will also see our loved ones again who have gone before us.[28]

That day in Bethany, as Mary wept and her friends wept with her, a tumult of grief and anger and compassion and empathy welled up within the heart of Jesus until He could no longer contain it. In a voice that must have been choking with emotion, He inquired, "Where have you laid him?" When those around Him replied gently, "'Come and see, Lord.' . . . Jesus wept" (John 11:34–35).

The Glory of His Love

Jesus, the Creator of the universe, the Eternal I Am, so strong, so powerful, so wise, *so human,* stood there with tears running down His cheeks! *Why?* "In all their distress he too was distressed."[29] "For we have not an high priest which cannot be touched with the feeling of our infirmities."[30] In other words, Jesus is emotionally involved in our lives. His love for us is displayed in His understanding of and identification with our suffering to the extent that He weeps with us.

When my youngest daughter, Rachel-Ruth, was small, she wore long braids as a means of controlling her naturally curly hair, which she hated. I will never forget an incident that followed the visit of a beautiful young woman who had long, glossy brown hair. As soon as the door closed behind the young woman, Rachel-Ruth ran into the living room, jerking at her braids, tearing at her bangs, covering her face with her hands, and hysterically sobbing, "I hate my hair! My face is so ugly! I'm not pretty at all!" Not knowing what had triggered this outburst, I just held her and wept with her. I looked up to see my other daughter, Morrow, standing in the doorway, weeping too. We wept because Rachel-Ruth was so distraught and we loved her.

When was the last time you wept into your pillow at night, thinking no one cared? Is the pain so deep and your hurt so great, that you cry night after night? Did you know that *Jesus weeps with you*? Did you know He puts all your tears in a bottle because they are precious to Him?[31] He has said in all of your afflictions, He Himself is afflicted.[32] Why? Because *Jesus loves you*!

Those who had gathered to support and comfort and help the family of Lazarus observed the famous young Rabbi weeping and concluded, "See how he loved him!" (John 11:36). Even though He knew the glory to come, and the heavenly home that was being prepared and the demonstration of God's power that was about to be displayed, Jesus wept! He wept for no other reason than He loved this precious family and they were weeping.[33] He was entering into their suffering even as one day He would ask us to enter into His.

While the overall mood of the crowd was sorrowful, another emotion was also present. Some mourners in the crowd refused to let go of their bitterness and resentment and offense with God because He had not answered their prayers as they thought He should. There were those who wallowed in self-pity and anger that God hadn't conformed to their schedule and given in to their demands. And so they snarled under their breath, "Could not he who opened the eyes of the blind man have kept this man from dying?" (John 11:37). They refused to understand that there is sometimes a greater purpose to suffering than having it end. And they believed the situation at Lazurus' tomb to be beyond anyone's ability to help. After all, if a Man who had created sight in a man born blind could not even manage to come on time and save His friend from dying, surely there was nothing *anyone* could do.

Jesus ignored these muttering cynics and made His way through the crowd to the tomb where Lazarus had been buried. As He stood before the tomb with the blazing sun beating down on His head, "once more [He was] deeply moved" (John 11:38). Was He thinking with a cold chill and deep foreboding and nauseating dread of another death to come? Was He thinking of other friends and family members and disciples who would be numbed with horror and helplessness and hopelessness as they looked on a similar grave near a hillside called Calvary?

Surrounded by a crowd of friends, family, and curious onlookers, Jesus gazed at the scene before Him. Surely Mary and Martha followed His focus fixed so intently on the cave carved out of the hillside that served as the burial place. A large stone sealed off the entrance to the tomb. In this barren, dreary, grief-filled setting, He displayed the glory of His Lordship.

The Glory of His Lordship

Jesus displayed His Lordship in His authority over Martha's doubts and fears as He challenged her to demonstrate her faith through sheer obedience to His Word. Martha was jolted out of any grief-filled reverie by His familiar voice commanding quietly but with absolute authority, "Take away the stone" (John 11:39). At that moment nothing could have been more appalling to her! She cringed at just the thought of such a thing. Her grief had been great but at least there had been closure when her brother was finally buried. To dig him up now seemed to serve no purpose other than to open the fresh wound of her heart. But Jesus knew the stone had to be removed so Lazarus could be set free and so others could see God's power and glory in his life.

What stone is keeping your loved one buried in sin and spiritual death? Is it his or her own pride? Or unbelief? Note that Jesus didn't tell Lazarus to roll away the stone; He told Lazarus's sister Martha to have the stone rolled away. What stone is Jesus commanding you to remove so He can set free from sin and spiritual death:

your brother or your sister,
your husband or your wife,
your child or your parent,
your in-law or your grandparent,
your friend or your neighbor,
your coworker or your boss,
your pastor or your church?

Would your brother experience the power of God in his life
if you removed the stone of rivalry?
Would your sister experience the power of God in her life
if you removed the stone of jealousy?
Would your husband experience the power of God in his life
if you removed the stone of a nagging tongue?
Would your wife experience the power of God in her life
if you removed the stone of unkindness?
Would your parent experience the power of God in their lives
if you removed the stone of unforgiveness?
Would your child experience the power of God in his or her life
if you removed the stone of favoritism?

Would your church experience the power of God in its life
if you removed the stone of hypocrisy?
Would your pastor experience the power of God in his life
if you removed the stone of a critical spirit?
Would your boss experience the power of God in his or her life
if you removed the stone of laziness?
Would your neighbor experience the power of God in his or her life
if you removed the stone of prejudice?
Would our nation experience the power of God in its life
if we removed the stone of prayerlessness?

The stones are endless, aren't they? Piles and piles of stones are heaped over the entrance to the tombs of those around us who are dead and buried in sin. And this whole time, while we've been mourning their death, Jesus says to you and me, "If you want to see Me work in the life of your Lazarus, take away the stone."

The glory of His Lordship is displayed through our obedience. Could it be that one reason we have yet to see the outpouring of God's power and glory in our homes and neighborhoods and cities and states and nations and world is because people like you and me refuse to be obedient? While we should be removing the stones, are we arguing with Jesus about how ineffective such an effort is going to be?

Martha, with what surely was a look of horrified indignation on her face, blurted out, "But, Lord, . . . by this time there is a bad odor, for he has been there four days" (John 11:39).[34] Her immediate, impulsive response was typically practical. She knew that the heat of the days would have hastened the corruption of the body that had been lifeless long enough for decay to set in. And so she argued, "But God, he's been dead too long to be raised!"

Who do you think has been dead too long to be raised to newness of life? Do you have someone on your prayer list like that? Or have you dropped such people off your list and discarded them from your prayers because they've been dead so long, you've lost all hope of possibility that they could ever be raised?

When Jesus seeks to perform a miracle in the life of your loved one, why do you argue with Him about His methods? What is your argument?

"If I submit, my husband will walk all over me."

"If I share the gospel, someone will ask me a question I can't answer."

"If I forgive them, they will get by with what they have done to me."

"If I deny myself, take up my cross, and follow Christ, I'll never
get what I want."

Maybe Martha resisted rolling away the stone because she was afraid of failure, worrying that if she rolled it away, nothing would happen. Such a scene would not only embarrass her but also damage the credibility of Jesus in the eyes of her friends.

Are you embarrassed to lead family devotions? Teach Sunday school? Share your testimony? Witness to a neighbor? Are you afraid God somehow will not be sufficient if you step out in faith, in obedience to His command?

God's help is delayed and His power is bound and His glory is hidden as long as we stand around in disobedience and argue! Martha delayed her own joy as well as the work of God in her brother's life while she stood there and argued with her Lord. What glory and joy are you missing because you refuse to take away the stone? Stop arguing! Stop refusing! Take away the stone! How will you ever experience the power and the glory of God in your life or that of someone else, if you only attempt those things that you are sure you can do? If you stay in your comfort zone?

The gaze Jesus turned onto Martha was most certainly with a look that melted her resistance and silenced her argument. With patient firmness He challenged her, not only to obey, but also to believe: "Did I not tell you that if you believed, you would see the glory of God?" (John 11:40). The glory of His Lordship is displayed, not only in our obedience, but also in our dependence.

It's time to leave low living
and sight walking
and small planning
and smooth knees
and colorless dreams
and tame visions
and mindless talking
and mundane thinking
and cheap giving
and dwarfed goals.[35]

It's time to soar on eagles' wings!

Finally, something in Martha must have been quickened. The spark of faith was suddenly fanned into flame, and without further question or word, she ordered the stone to be rolled away. Just because He said so. Her obedience, her dependence, and her expectance were in Him alone. He was all she had. It was time to demonstrate her faith. The only reason she had for rolling away the stone was that He'd said to. If Martha truly believed, obedience was not an option. And her motivation for obedience was His promise that if she obeyed, she would see His glory displayed in the life of her loved one. What reason do you need before you will obey?

Just as the blind man had to obey the command of Jesus and wash his eyes before he could see,[36] just as the paralyzed man had to get up and take up his bed and walk before he found the power he had been given to do so,[37] just as the man with the shriveled hand had to stretch it forth before it was made whole,[38] so you and I have to demonstrate our faith in God's Word through our obedience if we want to experience the glory of His life-giving power.

The Glory of His Life-Giving Power

The sound of weeping and mourning and whispering must have been hushed in startled amazement. Everyone was staring at Jesus and Martha. It is doubtful anyone could have heard what had been said between them, especially since they were surrounded by the wailing and weeping of the mourners. Then, without any preliminaries, the crowd was suddenly aware that the stone to the tomb was being rolled away. Now, in the heat of the day, there was total silence. There may have been the sound of the grasshoppers whirring in the tall grass or a bird calling its mate from the tree or the rustling of a dried leaf as a breath of hot air blew it across the stones. But the silence must have been deafening except for that one eerie sound, the rumble of the stone as it was ponderously pushed away from the tomb's entrance.

I wonder if Martha was momentarily embarrassed when the stone was rolled away in front of all her friends, knowing that even if the assembled friends could not see Lazarus in the darkened depths, they could smell him. There was no doubt that he was dead.

With every eye fastened on Him ~ the red-rimmed eyes of Mary ~ the hope-filled eyes of Martha ~ the grieving eyes of the friends ~ the hostile eyes of the unbelievers ~ the astonished eyes of the casual observer ~ Jesus boldly, loudly lifted His voice for all to hear: "Father, I thank you that you have heard me. I knew that you always hear me, but I said this for the benefit of the people standing here, that they may believe that you sent me" (John 11:41–42). Jesus was letting everyone know that if Lazarus was raised, the power would come from God.

Then, the same Voice that had brought the worlds into being, the same Voice that had called to Adam as he cowered in the bushes of Eden, the same Voice that had called Abraham from Ur, the same Voice that had reverberated from Mount Sinai, *the same Voice* thundered, "Lazarus, come out!" (John 11:43).[39]

And then, for a moment the heavy silence returned as the sound of His voice echoed from the stone walls and wafted on the gusting breeze and faded into the air. Every eye must have strained toward the cave, peering into the black hole where the stone had been. Then, out of the shadows appeared a mummylike figure "wrapped with strips of linen, and a cloth around his face" (John 11:44). Was there a collective gasp? Did some of the mourners swoon in a faint to the ground? Was everyone frozen in place, temporarily paralyzed by the shock of seeing something that *just couldn't be*? Dead men don't come back to life! But Lazarus did! At the command of the One who is the Resurrection and the Life, he walked out of the tomb![40]

Praise God! Hallelujah! Give Him all the glory! If He can raise Lazarus from the dead after four days of being in the tomb, *what can He do for you and me?*[41] One day that same Voice is going to thunder with a loud command, "and the dead in Christ will rise."[42] Regardless of whether our bodies have been buried for four days or a thousand years, regardless of whether they have been:

burned at the stake,
or eaten by wild animals,
or frozen in an avalanche,
or sunk in the ocean,
or displayed in a velvet-lined casket,
or entombed in a mausoleum,
or sprinkled in the wind,

one day He will call us forth from the dead, and we will rise again! Praise God! *Praise God! PRAISE GOD!*

In the stunned silence, with Lazarus standing bound in the tomb's entrance, Jesus could be heard once again giving Martha instructions. "Take off the grave clothes and let him go" (John 11:44). Lazarus had been raised from the dead, but he was still bound. He needed to be set free from the bonds that hindered him from walking in his new life.

What grave clothes, what bindings of spiritual deadness, are hindering your loved one from walking by faith in the Christian life? Grave clothes can be an old relationship . . . or a habit of sin . . . or an attitude of selfishness . . . or ungodly entertainment . . . or pride . . . or doubt.

Grave clothes hinder our walk and make the Christian life frustrating, robbing us of the joy we were meant to have. The apostle Paul exhorts us to throw off the grave clothes and "everything that hinders and the sin that so easily entangles, and let us run with perseverance the race marked out for us. Let us fix our eyes on Jesus."[43]

Who do you need to help unwrap? How pathetic it would have been had Lazarus been raised from the dead but remained bound. Don't blame or criticize a formerly dead person who has just been raised into life for not walking; start unwrapping! Then rejoice in the glorious display of God's life-giving power. Praise God for just giving us Jesus! There is nothing else—or no one else—we need!

A GOOD FRIEND of ours enjoys making pottery. The process of transforming wet, pliable, dull gray clay into beautiful bowls and vases and jugs and plates is fascinating.

Our friend begins with a shapeless blob, which he places on his potter's wheel. As he spins the wheel, he gently caresses the clay, applying pressure with his fingers and palms. Beneath his skillful touch, the turning clay responds to the varying degrees of pressure until it begins to take the shape of what he has in mind, whether it's a vase or plate or bowl or pitcher.

When the shape pleases him, our friend removes the clay from the wheel. He then paints it with beautiful designs, but the colors are dull and lifeless. At that stage, the quality of the colors makes it unattractive, and the softness of the clay renders it useless. So our friend places it with other vessels into a kiln, where he bakes the pieces for hours in heat that reaches 1,700° F. When the pottery emerges, not only is it strong enough to use, but its colors are also brilliantly vivid. The heat transforms the weak clay into a useful vessel and transforms the dull, ugly colors into radiant beauty.

And so it is with our lives. Jeremiah relates his visit to the potter's house with symbolic description: "So I went down to the potter's house, and I saw him working at the wheel. But the pot he was shaping from the clay was marred in his hands; so the potter formed it into another pot, shaping it as seemed best to him. Then the word of the LORD came to me: '. . . Can I not do with you as this potter does? . . . Like clay in the hand of the potter, so are you in my hand.'"[44]

Jesus makes suffering understandable; as the Potter, He uses suffering as the pressure on the wet "clay" of our lives. Under His gentle, loving touch, our lives are molded into a "shape" that pleases Him. But the shape that is so skillfully wrought is not enough. He not only desires our lives to be useful, but He also wants our character to be radiant. And so He places us in the furnace of affliction until our "colors" are revealed—colors that reflect the beauty of His own character.

Without the preparation of the loving, skillful touch of the Potter's hand, any usefulness or beauty the clay might have would be destroyed by the pressure and heat. But Jesus makes suffering understandable to this blob of clay. In the midst of the pressure and the heat, I am confident His hand is on my life, developing my faith until I display His glory, transforming me into a vessel of honor that pleases Him![45] I don't trust any other potter with my life. So *please, just give me Jesus!*

Jesus Makes Sin Forgivable

His office is manifold,
        and His promise is sure.
His life is matchless,
        and His goodness is limitless.
His mercy is enough,
        and His grace is sufficient.
His reign is righteous, His yoke is easy,
        and His burden is light.

He is indestructible. He is indescribable.
He is incomprehensible. He is inescapable.
He is invincible. He is irresistible. He is irrefutable.

I can't get Him out of my mind . . .
        And I can't get Him out of my heart.
I can't outlive Him . . .
        And I can't live without Him.

The Pharisees couldn't stand Him
        but found they couldn't stop Him.
Satan tried to tempt Him
        but found he couldn't trip Him.
Pilot examined Him on trial
        but found he couldn't fault Him.
The Romans crucified Him
        but found they couldn't take His life.
Death couldn't handle Him,
        and the grave couldn't hold Him.
Just give me Jesus! He makes sin forgivable!

11

JESUS MAKES SIN FORGIVABLE . . .

For Anyone

JOHN 18:1–19:16

It was a beautiful spring day, and the mother's only son was home after finishing his final college exams. Knowing how exhausted he was and how much he loved the beach, the mother packed some sandwiches in a cooler, gathered the beach blankets and chairs, and insisted they go together for a day of sun and relaxation at the shore.

When they arrived, they found a somewhat secluded spot. Although they could hear radios blaring and children squealing and parents calling and friends talking, it was a distant din. The ocean sparkled as it stretched to the horizon, changing shades of color from aqua to royal to navy until it met the cobalt blue of the sky. A few white, puffy clouds floated here and there, a gentle breeze kept the sun's rays from being too intense, the sand stretched out in either direction like wheat-colored velvet trimming a vivid blue dress, and the breakers crashed in the surf in a rhythmic beat like giant drums. Within a few moments both mother and son were laughing and talking and teasing and thoroughly enjoying being with each other.

As they ate the last bites of their sandwiches, they became aware of a piercing sound that penetrated through all the beach activity. They looked up, their eyes searching first the beach itself then the foaming surf for the source of the cry. At almost the same moment, they both focused on a woman beyond the breakers who was flailing her arms and screaming, "Help! Help! I'm drowning!" Without a moment's hesitation, the mother leaped to her feet, urging, "Quick!"

The son raced across the hot sand, splashed through the shallow water, dove through the breakers, and swam swiftly to where the woman was floundering. He put his strong arms around her and pulled her out of the riptide that had been sucking her out to sea. He propelled her through the breakers to safety, but when she stumbled shakily out of the water, she was alone. The mother's son was nowhere to be seen. Sunbathers and surfers gathered, staring at the relatively calm, yet empty sea, whispering that the riptide the woman had escaped had tragically caught the young man and swept him to his death.

The frantic mother became hysterical as she confronted the dripping woman. "My son! My son! My only son died saving you!" The shaking woman pushed wet strands of hair from her face as she shrugged, gave the mother a cold stare, and replied haughtily, "What a pity. It wasn't necessary. I could have saved myself." Then she walked off down the beach.

As the mother of an only son, I can imagine the passionate rage, the furious frustration, the emotional emptiness, the desperate horror of realizing that my beloved son was dead. Period. The agony would be intensified if I felt his death had been in vain or his life had been wasted on an ungrateful, unworthy subject.

With the fierce bond of love that I have for my children, how can I, or any parent, comprehend the heart and mind of God the Father and what He did for us? He enjoyed an eternal, loving fellowship with His only Son yet still sent Him into the treacherous waves of the world to save us from the riptides of sin and guilt. Riptides that relentlessly suck us into personal destruction, judgment, and hell. Riptides from which there is no escape. We are hopelessly doomed unless we have a Rescuer, a Savior. And the only One who can save us is the Father's only Son.

In a voice surely accented by awe, the apostle Paul explained our predicament and God's love in this way: "You see, at just the right time, when we were still powerless, Christ died for the ungodly. Very rarely will anyone die for a righteous man, though for a good man someone might possibly dare to die. But God demonstrates his own love for us in this: While we were still sinners, Christ died for us."[1] What amazing love!

You and I are like the drowning woman floundering in the surf. Not only are we hopelessly doomed in our sin and guilt, not only did God the Father send His only Son to save us, not only did the Son give His life to do so, but we also shrugged off His sacrifice and said it wasn't necessary, boasting, "I can save myself by my own activity, or morality, or religiosity, or sincerity. I don't need a Savior."

We could say that your attitude and mine is like that of the drowning woman.

We are oblivious to what God's Son did. For us. We don't realize we need a Savior much less have any gratitude for our salvation. But God demonstrated His love for us before we were even born by sending His Son to be our Savior. His Son is Jesus, who makes sin forgivable for anyone. Even you. Even me. Even Judas.

Even Those Who Betray Him

The betrayal and arrest of Jesus was preceded by an extended time of prayer in the Garden of Gethsemane. When He stepped out of the garden to present Himself to His enemies, Jesus had been alone, praying and agonizing for hours, wrestling with the will of His Father for His life, sweating what seemed to be great drops of blood in His effort. Throughout His agony He received the personal ministration of angels who helped Him to renew His strength, and He overcame the supreme temptation of the enemy to defy God's purpose, choosing instead to go to the cross. His humble submission to His Father's will must have given Him a mantle of power that cloaked Him for the nine-hour journey that would take Him through six different trials, the inhumane cruelty of physical torture, the ultimate rejection of those He loved, and the climax of His own crucifixion and death on a Roman cross.

The betrayal occurred on the night before Passover. The moon was full, and its shimmering globe could be glimpsed through the olive trees as it rose in the eastern sky. The light that radiated from it was strong enough to cast shadows and turn the unseasonably cool evening into an eerie twilight.

As Jesus stepped from the shadows of the inner garden, the bright moonlight threw the sleeping forms of His disciples into sharp relief against the rocky terrain. Through the trees He could see the Brook Kidron trickling through the valley and in the distance the soft silhouette of the city walls of Jerusalem. As He gazed at the city He loved, He saw the flickering light of hundreds of torches reflected in the polished metal surface of shields, helmets, and spear tips moving steadily toward Him (John 18:3). In the quiet stillness of the crisp night air He could hear the tramping of soldiers' feet, hundreds of them,[2] that made the ground tremble as they drew nearer the secluded garden, and He knew His time had come.[3]

As Jesus calmly surveyed the scene unfolding before Him, He knew the detachment of soldiers, led by Judas, Roman officials, and religious leaders, was coming to arrest Him. Had He been so inclined, He could have swiftly awakened His disciples, urgently whispered to them, then hidden in the bushes to wait until the soldiers returned to Jerusalem empty-handed. Later, He could have slipped back to Galilee unnoticed. It would have required very little real effort to elude this clumsy, noisy, yet deadly mob.

But instead of trying to escape, "Jesus, knowing all that was going to happen to him, went out and asked them, 'Who is it you want?'" (John 18:4). He just stepped forward with the quiet confidence of a king greeting His subjects and demanded they state their business.[4]

The soldiers must have stumbled over each other as they came to an abrupt halt. Instead of having to search for a cowering criminal, they found themselves confronted by an authoritative Man who was giving the orders. As they shifted their heavy spears and shields, lifting the torches a little higher to get a better look, they responded curtly and somewhat sullenly to His inquiry, "Jesus of Nazareth" (John 18:5). What happened next is a scene I hope to see replayed in the video room of my heavenly home. Jesus replied, in a voice that must have reverberated with the power we associate with hurricane winds or Niagara Falls or a tornado funnel or a tidal wave, "'I am he' . . . When Jesus said, 'I am he,' they drew back and fell to the ground" (John 18:5–6). The entire detachment of soldiers, Roman officials, religious leaders, and Judas, who "was standing there with them" (John 18:6), fell flat on their faces before Him!

The Bible says that one day, "at the name of Jesus every knee should bow . . . in heaven, and on earth, and under the earth, and that every tongue should confess that Jesus Christ is Lord, to the glory of God the Father."[5] Whether we want to or not, one day we will *all* bow before God's only Son.

Who do you know who has set him- or herself against Christ?

A school administrator?

A business employer?

A secular corporation?

A religious institution?

A political agenda?

A government policy?

An entire culture?

Whoever, or whatever, sets themselves against Christ will find themselves sooner or later on their faces before Him!

There was no mistake. Jesus was choosing to be arrested as He boldly identified Himself by the name the supreme Elohim of the Old Testament had used to identify Himself.[6] His power must have been impressive to see as it suddenly turned the tables and placed Him squarely in charge of the night's proceedings.

Instead of capturing a quivering coward or a defiant rebel or even a fiery revolutionary, His enemies found themselves facedown before Someone who caused them to grow so weak in the knees they could not remain on their feet. With gasping breath and wildly beating hearts and quaking limbs, they bowed before Him. They heard His ringing voice ask once again, "Who is it you want?" (John 18:7). Was He giving them the opportunity to rethink their part in this evil deed? Was He giving them a chance, now that they had felt His power, to bend to His authority and repent of their wicked purpose?

Whether it was the sinful stubbornness of their hearts or their professional pride or their years of robotlike training, the arresting party clung to their assignment. With bodies prostrate on the ground and faces buried in the dirt they muffled their answer, "Jesus of Nazareth" (John 18:7). Having missed the opportunity He had given them to turn back from a deed so dastardly that they would be held accountable for it for all eternity, they began to pick themselves up off the ground.

As the soldiers groped for their swords and spears and shields, and the officials readjusted their headdresses and dusted off their garments, Jesus responded with a rebuke as well as a command, "I told you that I am he" (John 18:8). At that very moment, Judas, who must have collected his wits more quickly than the others, scrambled up and greeted Jesus in the Middle Eastern custom of good friends . . . with a kiss.

Judas was one of Jesus' very closest friends. He had been handpicked to be a disciple. He had been given the special responsibility of being treasurer for the entire band of disciples—a responsibility he had enjoyed as it gave him access to personal petty cash as well as prestige in the eyes of others.[7] On a grassy hillside, he had passed out portions of five loaves and two fish until more than five thousand people had been fed. He had been in the boat that was swamped and going down during a storm at sea when Jesus, with just a word, had calmed the raging waves and the wind. He had been one of those to question callously why the beggar had been born blind, only to watch as Jesus created sight. He had smelled the odor of death when the tomb of Lazarus had been opened, and he had seen with his own eyes the mummylike figure appear in the gaping hole when Jesus had commanded that he come forth. As recently as that very evening, he had had his feet gently and lovingly bathed by Jesus during dinner in the Upper Room.[8]

During that same meal, he had been singled out for special honor when Jesus had given him the bread dipped in wine.[9]

It was this disciple, this *Judas*, who betrayed his Lord and Friend with a kiss![10] And although Jesus clearly knew the betrayal was coming,[11] it was still a knifelike stab to His heart. His inner wound is poignantly described in Psalm 55:12–14: "If an enemy were insulting me, I could endure it; if a foe were raising himself against me, I could hide from him. But it is you, a man like myself, my companion, my close friend, with whom I once enjoyed sweet fellowship as we walked with the throng at the house of God."

Have you ever been betrayed . . .

by a spouse who has taken a secret lover?
by a sibling who has stolen your inheritance?
by a coworker who has taken the credit for a job you did?
by a company who has fired you just before retirement?
by a friend who has gossiped away your reputation?
by a church that has closed its doors to you?
by a business partner who has progressively shoved you aside?

If you have experienced betrayal, then you understand something of the stabbing pain Judas inflicted at the very outset of Jesus' uphill struggle to the cross.

The arresting officers recognized the kiss as the prearranged signal to confirm that this indeed was the man they had come to seize. To cover their embarrassment at being flat on their faces before Him, and to reassert their control of the situation, they must have surged forward in a threatening assault. The voice of Jesus cracked like a whip over their heads, "If you are looking for me, then let these men go" (John 18:8). The soldiers must have recoiled in silent, unwitting submission to that Voice, allowing the disciples to melt away into the darkness. Except for Peter.

As the disciples, still rubbing sleep from their eyes, had grasped what was happening, they had abruptly reacted by scurrying in every direction. Except for one. Without warning, Peter, who had been sleeping when he should have been praying and therefore did not have a clue what the will of God was in this situation, charged the soldiers with his drawn sword. He swiped viciously at the nearest head but only managed to shave off the right ear of Malchus, servant to the high priest (John 18:10).

What in the world was Peter doing? Did he think he could take on the entire

Roman army? Was he simply making good his earlier vow to Jesus that while others might deny Him, he would die for Him?[12] Did he think that death in a garden scuffle was the inevitable fate of those foolish enough to return to Jerusalem when the climate of hate was so pervasive?[13] Whatever he might have been thinking, the real reason for his rash behavior was *prayerlessness.*

Earlier that evening, Jesus had asked Peter to pray with Him. Instead, Peter had gone to sleep. When Jesus woke him up and asked him once again to pray with Him, Peter rolled over and went back to sleep. When He approached Peter a third time to ask him to pray, Peter was snoring so soundly Jesus didn't even bother to try to wake him.[14]

When have you slept when you should have been praying? Were your subsequent actions, in retrospect, foolish, perhaps even dangerous, causing others to get hurt?

The devilish trap that played out through Peter's actions could have started a scuffle with the soldiers that would have resulted in the slaughter of the disciples in the garden. And our Lord's three-year investment in His disciples' lives would have been lost, along with the gospel message those men would be responsible for proclaiming. If the disciples had died there in the garden, who would have recorded the gospel biographies of Jesus? Who would have prayed for Pentecost? Who would have preached at Pentecost? Who would have established the church? Who would have written the inspired, God-breathed letters that make up our New Testament? *Who would have gone into all the world . . . ?*

Confident the arrest was in His Father's will, Jesus sharply rebuked Peter, "Put your sword away! Shall I not drink the cup the Father has given me?" (John 18:11).[15] He bent down, picked up the severed ear—did He dust it off?—then reached over and gently reattached it to Malchus's bleeding head.[16]

Can you imagine the accountability of the gaping crowd that witnessed that demonstration of the power of God? Was God giving them one more opportunity to recognize their sin, turn away from it, and at the very least, disassociate themselves from the diabolical act of seizing and arresting the Son of God in the middle of the night with the intent to kill Him?

But once again, the soldiers and officials rejected the opportunity to repent. Instead, to cover their earlier embarrassment of having to pick themselves up off the ground, they must have seized Jesus roughly, punching and manhandling Him as they bound Him. *They bound the hands* of the Son of God! *The hands of the Creator!*

Hands that had lifted in authority and calmed the storm at sea.
Hands that had gathered little children on His knee.
Hands that had smeared mud on the blind beggar's eyes and given him sight.
Hands that had touched the leper and cleansed him.
Hands that had broken the fish and the bread and fed five thousand people.
Hands that had hung the worlds in space.
Hands that had formed Adam from the dust of the ground.
Hands that had formed the very men who were now binding Him.

Have you ever felt bound . . .
in a marriage where the love has run out?
in a small home with small children?
in a physical body wracked with pain?
to an elderly parent with Alzheimer's?
by responsibility that isn't really yours?
to a job?
by habits of sin?
by memories of abuse?

Are you struggling with your bindings? Do you find that the more you fight against them, the more pain you inflict on yourself, so that you are miserable in your confinement? Sometimes binding is in the will of God. Jesus was in the center of His Father's will, yet He was bound. He did not resist the tight cords or complain about His confinement. He simply submitted, not to the soldiers, but to His Father's will.

As Jesus was bound and led off to His first religious trial, all the disciples fled. Judas, too, must have slipped away through the darkness. Where did he go? When did he stop running? What finally opened his eyes to the truth—that he had betrayed an innocent man?

Within moments of the betrayal, Judas hated himself for what he had done. But although he felt the pangs of remorse, he never confessed his sin to Jesus. Therefore Judas never received the forgiveness that Jesus later died to give him.

We last see Judas briefly during Jesus' third religious trial, which was interrupted briefly by a commotion at the doorway. Running footsteps sounded in the vaulted hall, a strident voice could be heard arguing with the armed guard at the entrance, and then Judas burst onto the scene. With a face that was surely contorted by the wretchedness of conviction, Judas flung thirty pieces of silver across the temple floor.[17] As the room suddenly grew silent, the clattering coins must have reverberated in the stillness as they skidded and skipped across the marble surface. Thirty pieces of silver! The price that had been paid him by the chief priests for his betrayal! Thirty pieces of silver! The price of a wounded slave![18] Judas sold his Lord for *the price of something that was good for nothing!*

And now Judas regretted it! Had he thought that his betrayal would in some way force Jesus' hand, causing Him to seize power as Judas had wanted? Had he in some way thought he could maneuver or manipulate Jesus into an action that was more in line with his own desires? Had he aimed to set up a confrontation so that the rulers would be removed, Jesus would be installed as King, and he, Judas, would hold a prominent position in the new kingdom? Or had he betrayed Jesus in a moment of petulant anger, seeking revenge for the public rebuke Jesus had given him at the dinner in Lazarus's home?[19] Had Judas ever stopped to consider that, once betrayed, Jesus would actually allow Himself to be put on trial, convicted, and crucified? What was the thought process that led to the climax of betrayal as Satan himself entered into Judas, using him for his own evil purpose?[20]

The horror of Judas's action must have engulfed him in a nauseating wave when he "saw that Jesus was condemned." He reacted with a heart-wrenching cry of confession: "I have sinned . . . for I have betrayed innocent blood."[21] The leaders looked at him coldly and cynically as they dismissed him, "What is that to us? . . . That's your responsibility."[22] And Judas went out and hanged himself! He stepped out of the temple into the night of eternity, lost and separated from God. Judas went to hell.[23]

Why? How could a man who had so much firsthand knowledge and experience of the truth, how could a man who had been so close to Jesus, *wind up in hell*? Because although Judas confessed his sin, *he confessed it to the wrong person.* Judas confessed his sin to the priest!

If only Judas had flung *himself* instead of the silver at the feet of Jesus and cried, "Jesus, I'm sorry. I don't know what got into me. I can't believe what I have done to You. I betrayed You. Please forgive me." Then Jesus would have forgiven Judas!

If only Judas had waited as late as the crucifixion itself and had come to the foot of the cross, pleading, "Jesus, I'm so sorry. I betrayed You. Please forgive me." Then Jesus would have forgiven Judas! Jesus was dying to forgive Judas! But Judas never confessed his sin to Jesus.

To whom have you confessed your sin? Have you confessed it to your priest? . . . your pastor? . . . your counselor? . . . your therapist? . . . your doctor? . . . your attorney? . . . your friend? . . . your spouse? . . . your parent? . . . your child? . . . your neighbor? . . . your bartender? . . . your hairdresser?

Only God in Christ has the power to forgive sin.[24] But you and I must confess it to Him personally, specifically, and honestly if we want to receive forgiveness. God promises, "If we confess our sins, he is faithful and just and will forgive us our sins and purify us from all unrighteousness."[25] That word *confess* means to call sin by the same names that God does, to agree with God about your sin.

You and I often play games with the names we call sin to make it seem less like sin. For example,

We call the sin of unbelief, worry.
We call the sin of lying, exaggeration.
We call the sin of fornication, safe sex.
We call the sin of homosexuality, gay.
We call the sin of murder, the right to choose.

As long as we switch the labels on sin to make it seem less serious, we're being dishonest with ourselves and with God, and we remain unforgiven. *But,* if we say the same thing about our sin that God says—if we say, "God, it's lying. It's jealousy. It's lust. It's revenge. It's hate. It's adultery. It's unforgiveness"—*God will forgive us!* It doesn't matter how big the sin is or how small, it doesn't matter how long ago it was committed or how recently, it doesn't matter whether it was spontaneous or malicious. God will forgive you if you come to Him and confess your sin!

Are you actually guilty of the sin of betrayal? Have you betrayed, not just another person, but also your Lord? You and I betray Jesus when we call ourselves Christians yet give our hearts to money, or material things, or selfish pursuits, or anyone or anything other than Him. We betray Him when we spend more time on the Internet than in prayer. We betray Him when we spend more time reading the morning newspaper than reading the Bible. We betray Him when we exercise our spiritual gift not in a way that serves Christ and His Body, but in a way that serves ourselves. If you have betrayed Jesus, would you come to Him and confess it? Jesus would have forgiven Judas, but tragically, Judas never came to Him and confessed his sin. Jesus died to forgive anyone who comes humbly to Him at the Cross—those like Judas who betray Him, and even those like the religious leaders who attack Him.

Even Those Who Attack Him

As the disciples bolted through the darkness,[26] the soldiers roughly manhandled Jesus "and brought him first to Annas, who was the father-in-law of Caiaphas, the high priest that year. Caiaphas was the one who had advised the Jews that it would be good if one man died for the people" (John 18:13–14). It was quickly obvious that a guilty verdict requiring the death penalty had already been decided, but there was confusion over what charge would obtain it. And so Annas was chosen to do the preliminary deposition.

In the Old Testament, the high priest was a descendant of Aaron, of the tribe of Levi, and was appointed to that position by God. He was a man who mediated between God and the Israelites, made the yearly sacrifice of atonement for the sin of the nation, and interceded on behalf of God's children. The high priest held a sacred, solemn, sanctified position in the eyes of God and in the eyes of the people.

During the Roman occupation, the position of high priest was the most important position of leadership in the nation of Israel since political or government leaders were disallowed. But rather than continue in the historic and biblical mandate as shepherd of Israel, the role of high priest changed drastically. Instead of being filled by God, the high priestly position was opened to the highest bidder. The man who achieved that position was the one who bribed the Romans with the most money, the most promises, and the most collaboration. In exchange he was given a leadership position that was more political than religious, with the expectation that he would keep a tight rein on what the Romans considered a stiff-necked, troublesome nation.

Annas had been the high priest for nine years. He was very wealthy because during his tenure he had stolen from the temple treasury to line his own pockets. He had also used his money to secure the prestigious position of high priest for each of his five sons, who succeeded him in turn. During Jesus' day, Annas's son-in-law, Caiaphas, was the acting high priest. But wily, crafty old Annas was still the power behind the throne and referred to as the high priest.[27]

The First Religious Trial

Because under Roman occupation the Jews had no authority to put anyone to death, it became Annas's responsibility to come up with a charge against Jesus that the Romans would consider serious enough to execute Him. So with great piety and haughtiness, Annas "questioned Jesus about his disciples and his teaching" (John 18:19). I would imagine, as he arranged his brocaded robes around himself and examined his bejeweled fingers with studious indifference, Annas queried in a voice dripping with condescension, "Tell us, Jesus. Who have you been teaching? And where have you been teaching? And when have you been teaching? And what have you been teaching?"

Jesus, with the clear-eyed gaze of Someone who has nothing to hide, answered directly, "I have spoken openly to the world . . . I always taught in synagogues or at the temple, where all the Jews come together. I said nothing in secret. Why question me? Ask those who heard me. Surely they know what I said" (John 18:20–21). In other words, "Annas, where have you been? I've been teaching publicly in the temple every day this week. You're the former high priest. It's your business to know what's being taught on temple property. You should have been directly informed. Go ask someone who heard Me about who I am and what I was saying and to whom I was speaking."

Jesus confronted Annas with the awesome principle that God holds people accountable, not just for what they have heard or know, but for what they have had *opportunity* to hear and know. And in America, with churches on every corner, with religious radio broadcasts, with Christian television programming, with Bible teaching on cassette tapes, with Bible studies on video, with written Bible commentaries and testimonies and stories, with weekly and bimonthly and monthly Christian magazines, with church youth camps and men's fellowships and ladies' luncheons, with evangelistic crusades and festivals and services and movies, *America has enormous accountability before God!*

It doesn't matter if you have ever tuned in to or listened to or read or participated in any of the above. You and I have had the opportunity to do so, and for that we will be held accountable by God.

Annas, who had thought to put Jesus on the defensive by making Him explain Himself as though He had done something wrong, was astounded and offended to find *himself* rebuked and put on the defensive. As the tension in the room intensified, his face must have blanched then turned crimson as anger surged to the surface. Annas's bodyguard reacted swiftly, and "struck [Jesus] in the face. 'Is this the way you answer the high priest?' he demanded. 'If I said something wrong,' Jesus replied, 'testify as to what is wrong. But if I spoke the truth, why did you strike me?'" (John 18:22–23).

The official did not answer; he knew that to strike an unarmed prisoner who had been charged with nothing and was guilty of nothing was against the law. But Annas, who was notorious for disregarding the law as it suited him, ignored the act of injustice. Frustrated and humiliated by the confident authority of Jesus, Annas admitted defeat by sending Him, still bound, to Caiaphas, his son-in-law and the current high priest, without determining a charge against Him (John 18:24). And Jesus allowed Himself to be dragged to His second religious trial.

The Second Religious Trial

Around 3:00 a.m., the cruel and arrogant high priest, Caiaphas, backed by other leaders of the Jewish religious ruling body, found himself facing Jesus of Nazareth. He was "looking for evidence against Jesus so that they could put him to death, but they did not find any. Many testified falsely against him, but their statements did not agree."[28] Caiaphas had arranged a kangaroo court, with false testimony planted in the courtroom. But the witnesses couldn't even agree on their lies. Finally, Caiaphas, in angry frustration, stood up and charged Jesus under oath, "By the living God: Tell us if you are the Christ, the Son of God."[29]

The room must have gone deathly quiet as every eye turned to the Rabbi from Nazareth, as every person waited breathlessly to hear how He would answer the bottom-line, no-holds-barred question. A dropped pin could have been heard as Jesus looked full into a face distorted by all the fury of hell. Knowing with absolute clarity that His answer would give His accusers the charge they had been searching for—a charge that would result in His conviction by the religious courts and condemnation by the Roman courts—Jesus, who had stood silently through the verbal flogging, answered. And His answer shook the world to its foundation: "Yes."

Jesus claimed to be the Son of God! His answer means that believing He is just a man is not an option. It means that believing He is a good man is not an option. It means that believing He is a great man, even a prophet sent from God, is not an option. *He claimed to be the Son of God!* Either He is who He said He is, or He is a liar, or He is a blasphemer and worthy of death under Jewish law, or He is mentally deranged! His answer leaves no middle ground.

Jesus claimed to be the Son of God. *He claimed to be God walking the earth in a man's body! Do you believe Him?* Who do *you* say He is?

Then Jesus continued speaking. He didn't stop with a simple yes. He went on to warn His accusers that there would be a day of reckoning when they would give an account to God for their actions. One day He would be their Judge, when "in the future you will see the Son of Man sitting at the right hand of the Mighty One and coming on the clouds of heaven."[30]

As He wielded the truth like a sharp, double-edged sword, I wonder if there was a chilling moment of fear in the air. Was there a moment of instinctive recognition, the kind of shocked insight that might result from an abrupt slap in the face or a dash of ice-cold water? If there was a moment of stunned silence in that kangaroo courtroom, it didn't last long. Caiaphas unleashed all of his frustration and fury as he tore his clothes and shrieked, "He has spoken blasphemy! Why do we need any more witnesses? Look, now you have heard the blasphemy. What do you think?"[31] And all the false witnesses and pious religious leaders shouted out in unison, "He is worthy of death."[32]

As Caiaphas swept from the room to call together an official meeting of the Sanhedrin, the courtroom erupted in unbridled hysteria and rage. It was as though the very demons of hell possessed the otherwise dignified rulers who "spit in his face and struck him with their fists. Others slapped him and said, 'Prophesy to us, Christ. Who hit you?'"[33] And Jesus, the Son of God, with His hands bound, unable to even block the blows, stood meekly and allowed Himself to be assaulted.

With spit dripping down His face, with bloody flecks springing up where His beard had been yanked from His cheeks,[34] Jesus was jerked and dragged to the third and final religious trial.

The Third Religious Trial

At approximately 5:00 a.m., at an hour when it was unlawful to convene, the full Sanhedrin formally assembled. In sharp contrast to their abusive cruelty just moments before, the leaders now gathered in exaggerated dignity and hypocritical judgment as they officially convicted Jesus of blasphemy and "all the chief priests and the elders of the people came to the decision to put Jesus to death."[35]

Without realizing it, the religious leaders' verdict played into the hands of God, who had predetermined that His Son would die on the cross as a sacrifice for their sin.

Several months later, a young Pharisee named Saul began to viciously attack Jesus by persecuting Christians.[36] In his hate for the followers of Christ, Saul went so far as to hold the coats of those who rioted and stoned to death a leader in the early Jerusalem church.[37] Paul later testified that he had been a "blasphemer and a persecutor and a violent man."[38] With furious, self-righteous indignation, he had requested and received permission from the authorities to travel to Damascus to wipe out the Christians who had fled from his wrath. As he traveled on his diabolical mission, brilliant light flooded his path. The door of heaven opened, and he was confronted with the person of Jesus Christ. And Saul was converted! Years later, he was still overcome with wonder at the grace and forgiveness of God when he exclaimed: "Christ Jesus came into the world to save sinners—of whom I am the worst. But for that very reason I was shown mercy so that in me, the worst of sinners, Christ Jesus might display his unlimited patience as an example for those who would believe on him and receive eternal life."[39]

If God forgave Saul, transforming the chief persecutor of the early church into Paul, the most powerful proclaimer of the gospel the world has ever seen, He can forgive and transform anyone. Would you take a moment now and pray for those you know who are attacking Jesus? Who knows? Maybe in the midst of all the "Sauls," there is a "Paul" just waiting to be confronted with the person of Jesus Christ.

Jesus would have forgiven the very religious leaders who attacked Him if they had come humbly to Him and confessed their sins. In fact, the Scripture indicates that two men, Joseph and Nicodemus, who were members of the Sanhedrin, did repent of their sins and receive forgiveness. Because Jesus makes sin forgivable for anyone—even those who attack Him. And even those like Peter who deny Him.

Even Those Who Deny Him

When Jesus was arrested in the garden, He expressly commanded the soldiers to let His disciples go, which they did. At the same time, He was also indirectly telling His disciples to leave. Nine of them obeyed while two of them did not. One, we assume, was John, a relative of the high priest, and the other was the loyal, bungling, impetuous Peter. They followed at a discreet distance as Jesus was led to the temple compound, which included the house of Annas, for His first religious trial. Because John "was known to the high priest, he went with Jesus into the high priest's courtyard, but Peter had to wait outside at the door. [John] . . . came back, spoke to the girl on duty there and brought Peter in" (John 18:15–16). Then the disastrous drama that Peter would live to regret for the rest of his life began to unfold.

Peter stepped through the outer gate into the inner courtyard. It was surrounded by covered breezeways that connected to the house of Annas on one side, the house of Caiaphas on the other side, and the official temple rooms used for the Sanhedrin on yet another side. As the young servant girl held the gate open for him, she peered at him through the darkness and remarked disparagingly, "You are not one of his disciples, are you?" (John 18:17). Peter must have been somewhat taken aback. The past hour had been like a bad dream. Surely he felt murderous rage toward Judas, anger at the arresting officers, confusion at Jesus' submission to such treatment; he must have also felt terrified for his own safety! Yet it was obvious that he would rather risk exposure and capture than play it safe and totally forsake his best Friend.

But the servant girl's question, coming the moment he stepped into the courtyard, caught him off guard. So he responded in typical Peter fashion, without thinking, in self-defense, "I am not" (John 18:17). As she sauntered away, he must have breathed a slow sigh of relief, ironically thanking God that he had narrowly escaped being cornered so quickly. I wonder if John gave him a curious look.

Peter, who had slept when he should have been praying, not only didn't know the will of God in the situation he now found himself, but also was actually outside of God's will as he warmed himself at the fire of his Lord's enemies (John 18:18). Perhaps he began to relax a little as the servants and officials bantered back and forth. In the flickering firelight, with shadows dancing on the old stone walls, did he furtively try to catch a glimpse of what was transpiring in the house of Annas, then that of Caiaphas? Did the sharp eyes of the servant girl notice Peter's nervous restlessness and furtive glances? Did she whisper to her companions until one of them boldly spoke up, pointing to Peter, "This fellow was with Jesus of Nazareth."[40] Fear must have turned like a knife in Peter's stomach as "he denied it again, with an oath: 'I don't know the man!'"[41] As the tension mounted in the courtyard, he could feel the stares and the whispers and the raised eyebrows. He knew it was just a matter of time before someone nailed him again. He must have hoped against hope that the others would be distracted at least until the trials came to some sort of conclusion so he could know the direction Jesus was going. Then he could slip away into the night with no one the wiser. But at that moment he just couldn't tear himself away from close proximity to Jesus. Not yet.

The whispers and stares seemed to be intensifying, bombarding him from every side until he must have nearly jumped out of his skin as the servants surrounded him, asserting to each other, "Certainly this fellow was with him, for he is a Galilean."[42] He must have cringed as they then turned directly to him with their conclusion: "Surely you are one of them, for your accent gives you away."[43] Seeing denial already on Peter's face, another man stepped up with positive identification. He was a relative of Malchus, whose ear Peter had cut off earlier that evening. With a relentless challenge he pressed his point: "Didn't I see you with him in the olive grove?" (John 18:26).

All of the fear and tension and anger and confusion suddenly exploded in Peter and tumbled out in a stream of curses as he insisted, "I don't know the man!"[44] Yet as he spoke, he heard the unmistakable sound of a rooster crowing in the distance. At that very moment, a commotion in the breezeway got everyone's attention. With the denial and curses still burning his lips, Peter looked up, right into the eyes of Jesus!

Apparently, Jesus was being led from the house of Caiaphas to the trial before the full Sanhedrin. Surrounded by the armed officials and self-righteous religious leaders, Jesus stopped. With a face that was red from having been repeatedly slapped, with blood and spit dripping down His beard, Jesus "turned and looked straight at Peter."[45] For what surely seemed like an eternity, Peter's world stood still as his eyes locked with those of his Lord. The look of Jesus was like a flaming fire, burning away Peter's hypocrisy and sin, bringing the sharp recall of Jesus' words in the garden only hours earlier when He had warned, "Before the rooster crows today, you will disown me three times."[46] Then as the entourage around Jesus roughly pushed and shoved Him forward, the moment passed. Peter stood stunned and stripped and shaken to the core of his being! He fled the courtyard and went into the night, where he "wept bitterly,"[47] sobbing out his confession to God.

Like Judas, Peter experienced deep remorse. But unlike Judas, Peter clung to the Lord. As he wept and cried out to God, did he also recall the words the Lord had spoken to him days before? What wonderful words of encouragement Jesus had given him: "Simon, Simon, Satan has asked to sift you as wheat. But I have prayed for you, Simon, that your faith may not fail. And when you have turned back, strengthen your brothers."[48]

Peter knew Jesus had known he would deny Him. Peter knew Jesus had prayed for him. Peter knew Jesus had said he would turn back and strengthen the other disciples. And that is what Peter did.

Sometime during the following three days, Peter must have slipped back to where the other disciples had gathered in numbed horror.[49] As the survivors of a life-shattering experience, they would have drawn comfort from the presence of those who had also experienced the turmoil and shock. And it may be, because Peter's denial is recorded in each of the four gospels, that he told the other disciples about his miserable conduct. Perhaps they stared silently at him. Perhaps in their grief they didn't fully comprehend his confession. Perhaps they gave him rough pats on the shoulder as they withdrew into their own "if onlys."

I wonder if there were others who also wrestled with "if onlys." As Jesus went through these six trials, accused of blasphemy, tax evasion, and insurrection, where were His defenders?

Where was the paralyzed man who had lain beside the Pool of Bethesda for thirty-eight years before Jesus healed him?

Where were the lepers He had cleansed?

Where was the adulterous woman He had saved from stoning then instructed to sin no more?

Where was the Roman centurion whose servant had been healed at a great distance by the simple word of Jesus?

Where was the woman whose life's blood had seeped from her for twelve years who had been healed by simply touching the hem of His garment?

Where was the nobleman whose daughter arose from death when Jesus took her by the hand?

Where were the mute whose tongues had been loosed at the command of Jesus?

Where was the man who had been born blind to whom Jesus had given sight?

Where were Mary and Martha and Lazarus?

Where were the men and women and children whose lives Jesus had changed?

Where are they still?

Have you ever denied the Lord?

Denied Him with your silence?

Denied Him with your behavior?

Denied Him, exactly as Peter did, with your words?

Denied Him by calling yourself a Christian yet not acting like one?

Denied Him by acting like a Christian, yet refusing to give Jesus the credit when someone commends you?

Denied Him by the priorities and plans and people and places in your life that are Christless?

If you have denied Jesus—and surely all of us have in some way—then you know something of the price Peter paid in shame and humiliation for his denial. But not until you "see" the eyes of the Lord gazing intently at you in the midst of your denial will you know the miry depths of grief for your sin. Instead of repressing your shame and guilt, will you confess it to the Lord so that you can experience the same forgiveness and restoration that Peter did? When you do, you can share the testimony with Peter and the saints down through the ages who know from their own experience that He is precious![50] Because He makes sin forgivable, even for those who deny Him! Even for those like Pilate, Herod, and the Romans who reject Him.

EVEN THOSE WHO REJECT HIM

Having obtained a charge against Jesus that they believed the Romans would accept as legitimate enough for the death penalty, "the whole assembly rose and led him off to Pilate," the Roman governor.[51] Around 6:00 a.m. they arrived on the steps of the Hall of Judgment and sent word to Pilate that an urgent matter had arisen that required his attention.

If it were not so serious, the scenario that John describes for us would be almost humorous: "Then the Jews led Jesus from Caiaphas to the palace of the Roman governor. By now it was early morning, and to avoid ceremonial uncleanness the Jews did not enter the palace; they wanted to be able to eat the Passover" (John 18:28). It was ludicrous that the religious leaders, who were plotting to kill an innocent man, refused to enter the governor's palace for fear of defiling themselves! They were legalistically preoccupied with the traditional law, while in effect smashing the moral law.

So often you and I make secondary issues the priority,
while ignoring the primary ones, as when . . .
We yell at our spouses for not doing what we asked,
while ignoring our own sin of yelling.
We demand that our children dress by a certain code,
while ignoring their disrespect.
We complain about our ill health,
while ignoring our diet and exercise.
We criticize someone for the habits of drinking and smoking,
while ignoring that person's need to be born again.
We raise cash for the church's new building,
while ignoring evangelism and missions.

We hold seminars on racial reconciliation within the church,
while ignoring the low-income projects next door.

The religious leaders were preoccupied with keeping the requirements for Passover, while ignoring honesty and justice. So when Pilate received word that a delegation of religious leaders waited on the doorstep to speak with him, he must have sighed deeply, wondered what he had done to deserve this—and it wasn't even a Monday!—then walked outside to determine what business they had. Standing before him in the early morning light was a group of Jewish officials in the elaborate robes and headdresses depicting their preeminent positions in the occupied nation. Pilate despised these self-righteous, hypocritical, and, to him, obnoxious men, but he dealt gingerly with them because of the trouble with Caesar they could make for him. In their midst was a Man who was obviously a prisoner, with hands tied and blood splotching His seamless robe.

Foregoing any social pleasantries, Pilate abruptly demanded that the religious rulers state their business: "What charges are you bringing against this man?" (John 18:29). The religious leaders, who despised Pilate as the pagan governor of the hated occupying Roman army, had difficulty even pretending any sort of respect: "If he were not a criminal . . . we would not have handed him over to you" (John 18:30). Possibly seeing the disgust and resistance written on Pilate's face, the Jews "began to accuse [Jesus], saying, 'We have found this man subverting our nation. He opposes payment of taxes to Caesar and claims to be Christ, a king.'"[52] Barely able to contain his irritation, Pilate barked, "Take him yourselves and judge him by your own law" (John 18:31). The rulers retorted, "But we have no right to execute anyone" (John 18:31). The rulers made it plain that any trial the Romans conducted would be simply a pretense to enable the Jews to get around the law, since the verdict had been predetermined.

Wanting to end things quickly so he could get on with his day, Pilate turned on his heel and went back into the Hall of Judgment, beckoning Jesus to follow. Pilate then found himself facing Jesus of Nazareth in the first of the Roman trials—the fourth trial overall.

The First Roman Trial

Pilate carefully led Jesus through a series of questions designed to determine any serious threat to Roman sovereignty.[53] His interrogation provoked an agreement from Jesus that He was indeed a king, "In fact," Jesus said, "for this reason I was born, and for this I came into the world, to testify to the truth. Everyone on the side of truth listens to me" (John 18:37). Pilate, satisfied that any claim to authority on the part of Jesus was in the spiritual realm, dismissed Jesus with an exasperated, "What is truth?" without bothering to wait for an answer.

And in turning away, Pilate missed the opportunity of a lifetime—to ask the Truth to explain Himself. Pilate had found the source of all Truth, the summation of all Truth, the supremacy of all Truth, yet he had casually dismissed Him as irrelevant! The Truth was staring him in the face, but Pilate wasn't interested. Pilate has many ideological children today who spend their lives and a lot of money searching for the Truth while dismissing the gospel as irrelevant. The climate today, even within the church, can be so pragmatic, so political, so psychological, so philosophical, that we casually dismiss the Truth as an unnecessary complication to our plans and programs.

The official verdict of the first Roman trial of Jesus was given by Pilate to the religious rulers on the steps of the Hall of Judgment: "I find no basis for a charge against him" (John 18:38). A curious crowd had begun to gather, but the Jews had gone too far in their predetermined course to back down now, so they insisted, "He stirs up the people all over Judea by his teaching. He started in Galilee and has come all the way here."[54]

Pilate, who was becoming uncomfortable with a situation where he felt increasingly cornered, snapped to attention when he heard Jesus was from Galilee. He quickly devised a scheme to rid himself of the entire irritating mess. Since Jesus was from Galilee and Rome had a puppet king named Herod who ruled there, Pilate would turn Jesus over to him. It just so happened that Herod was visiting in Jerusalem at the time, so Pilate sent Jesus to Herod, who conducted the second Roman trial, the fifth trial overall.[55]

The Second Roman Trial

Herod was like a child with a new toy. He was so excited to finally get to meet Jesus of Nazareth—to talk with Him and listen to Him and maybe even see a miracle or two. As he entered the room where Jesus had been brought, he must have rubbed his hands together in gleeful anticipation of the entertaining diversion he expected to have. Perhaps for just a moment he felt a twinge of remorse as he flashed back to his interaction with Jesus' first cousin, John the Baptist. John had been Herod's favorite preacher of all time.[56] He just loved to hear John preach fire and brimstone to all those Pharisees and religious hypocrites.

Herod reminds me of people who tell me they love to hear my daddy preach every time he's on TV. When I press them for any real difference it's made in their lives, they look at me rather blankly and repeat, "I just love to hear your daddy." Similarly, Herod loved to hear John preach. Maybe he even got emotional about it and raised his hands or wept in response. But it didn't make any difference in his life. Not really.

One day John's preaching became somewhat annoying when John boldly told Herod he should not be living with his brother's wife. Herod shrugged it off, but Herodias, his brother's wife, was outraged. To placate her, Herod had John imprisoned, but even there Herod protected him because he knew instinctively John was a prophet of God.

But Herodias did not forget. She silently plotted her revenge and found opportunity to take it on the occasion of Herod's birthday celebration. He threw something of a drunken orgy for himself and invited Herodias's daughter to dance for his guests and himself. Herod became so aroused by the girl's provocative performance that he impulsively promised her anything she wanted, up to half of his kingdom. As a young girl she didn't know what to ask for, so she ran to her mother for advice. With surely the same menacing gleam in her eye as the wicked queen had when Snow White took a bite of her poisoned apple, Herodias commanded her daughter to request not the latest model chariot, or a vacation home at the beach, or a designer wardrobe, or a guaranteed income for life, or even betrothal to Prince Charming—but the head of John the Baptist on a platter! And to satisfy the whim of a little belly dancer, Herod took off the head of a man Jesus had said was as great as any man ever born![57]

Now Jesus of Nazareth stood before that same Herod! And Herod convinced himself that Jesus was John the Baptist raised from the dead![58] So Herod could barely contain himself as he fairly danced around Jesus in his excitement: "Jesus, I've been dying to hear You preach. They say You're as good as John. Some even say You are John who has risen from the dead. I want to hear Your best sermon so I can decide for myself. And by the way, do a few tricks. I would just love to see a miracle or two." Dead silence followed. Finally, Herod asked a stream of questions, with a background chorus of accusations from the religious leaders to guide his interrogation, "but Jesus gave him no answer."[59] Why? Why did Jesus remain silent before Herod, especially since He had responded to the questions of Pilate, Caiaphas, and even Annas?

The Bible says that if we refuse to respond and obey the Truth that we are given, we will not be given any more.[60] And Herod, who had been offered a lot of Truth by John the Baptist, had refused to respond in obedience. So God refused to give him more Truth. God was silent in Herod's life.

Is God silent in your life? Could it be that He has given you Truth to which you have not responded obediently? Has He given you truth through a Bible study,

or your pastor's sermon,

or a Sunday school lesson,

or your daily devotions,

or a radio message,

or an inspirational book,

or a godly friend,

that you have yet to apply and obey? Have you been frustrated because the Bible doesn't seem to make sense to you? And when you pray, is it as though your prayers hit the ceiling of your room and bounce back? Have you felt as though God has abandoned you? Has His silence become deafening? If so, you need to go back to the last thing you can remember that He told you and act on it. If you can't remember, just return to the Cross by faith. In prayer, confess your sin of disobedience whether it was willful or the result of procrastination. Ask God to break His silence in your life.

God remained silent in Herod's life because instead of repenting of his sin, "Herod and his soldiers ridiculed and mocked [Jesus]. Dressing Him in an elegant robe, they sent him back to Pilate."[61] And once again, Pilate inwardly squirmed as he was confronted with making a decision about Jesus he had thought he could avoid.

Who do you know who thinks he or she doesn't have to make a decision about Jesus? Such people can put Him off,

shove Him aside,

ignore Him,

postpone Him,

rationalize Him,

deny Him,

avoid Him,

but sooner or later they are going to have to face Him at the final judgment.

Their own. Which in effect is what Jesus had bluntly told the religious rulers when He warned them, "From now on, the Son of Man will be seated at the right hand of the mighty God."[62] In other words, the next time they faced Him in a legal court, they would be the accused, and He would be the Judge![63]

The Third Roman Trial

Confronted by Jesus once again, Pilate was extremely uneasy. As he presided over the third Roman trial—the sixth and final one overall, his wife sent him a message warning him not to have anything to do with the Jewish plot to murder Jesus.[64] Yet the rulers were relentless in their insistence that Jesus be executed and were becoming vicious in their veiled threats to report an insurrection to Caesar, for which Pilate would be liable. To make matters worse, as the morning progressed, the crowd outside the Hall of Judgment had increased and was threatening to riot.

In consternation at their lynch-mob mentality, Pilate admonished the chief priests, the rulers, and the people, "You brought me this man as one who was inciting the people to rebellion. I have examined him in your presence and have found no basis for your charges against him. Neither has Herod, for he sent him back to us; as you can see, he has done nothing to deserve death. Therefore, I will punish him and then release him."[65] What an indictment on the venerated system of Roman justice! What twisted logic to punish this Man whom the Roman courts had repeatedly pronounced innocent of all charges![66] What diabolical depravity and wicked weakness to hand over an innocent man to the blood-crazed rabble!

Perhaps thinking to satisfy the crowd's thirst for blood without actually going so far as to execute Jesus, Pilate had Him flogged. The soldiers dragged Him into the Praetorium, stripped Him of all but His loincloth, tied Him with His face to a post, and, using a whip of leather thongs tipped with metal bits, whipped Him. The flogging would have ripped the flesh off of His back, exposing His internal organs. History records that flogging victims either passed into unconsciousness, went insane, or died. The miracle is not that Jesus survived the whipping, but that *He submitted to it!* How easy it would have been for Him to defy them and, without cursing but in righteous judgment, send them all to hell!

Why? *Why* would God allow His Son to endure such physical torture? The answer had been given years earlier, when Isaiah solemnly prophesied, "Surely he took up our infirmities and carried our sorrows, yet we considered him stricken by God, smitten by him, and afflicted. But he was pierced for our transgressions, he was crushed for our iniquities; the punishment that brought us peace was upon him, and by his wounds we are healed."[67]

The entire company of soldiers who had watched the flogging of Jesus seemed to become infected with the crazed frenzy of the crowd. Not content with merely flogging Him, they put "a scarlet robe on him, and then twisted together a crown of thorns and set it on his head. They put a staff in his right hand and knelt in front of him and mocked him. 'Hail, king of the Jews!' they said. They spit on him, and took the staff and struck him on the head again and again."[68]

Then Jesus, dripping His own flesh and blood, still wearing the royal robe and the crown of thorns, was dragged once more before the crowd. Surely, for a moment, a hush fell over the crowd as they gazed upon One who was so disfigured by torture it would have been difficult to tell He was a Man, much less determine His identity.[69] How could the crowd manage to keep from gagging and retching collectively at such a sight?

Pilate tried once more to get out of the complicated mess. He told the crowd, "Look, I am bringing him out to you to let you know that I find no basis for a charge against him. . . . Here is the man!" As soon as the chief priests and religious rulers saw Him, they shouted, "Crucify! Crucify!" (John 19:4–6).

Pilate was very quickly losing control of a dangerous and volatile situation. He was desperate to disengage himself from the uprising. The thunderous chanting of the raging mob could now be heard through the walls of his palace. And the hysterically angry religious officials who swirled about him had lost all pretense of dignity as they shrieked their accusations and threats.

In the eye of this storm stood Jesus. With blood flowing from His wounds and streaming down His face from the two-inch thorns embedded in His brow, with hands still bound, was His head still high? Were His eyes still filled with compassion? His demeanor still one of nobility, confidence, and strength? He looked calmly at His frantic accusers and remained silent. Pilate, in exasperation, yelled, "'Don't you hear the testimony they are bringing against you?' . . . Jesus made no reply, not even to a single charge—to the great amazement of the governor."[70]

When Pilate reiterated his verdict of innocence to the leaders and the crowd, the Jews insisted, "We have a law, and according to that law he must die, because he claimed to be the Son of God" (John 19:7). At that remark, Pilate froze. Something must have been triggered down deep within him, and suddenly he suspected the Truth! With genuine terror, he went back inside his palace and demanded Jesus tell him where He came from. When Jesus remained silent, Pilate lost his temper. With eyes that must have been blazing and a face red with fury, Pilate shouted, "Do you refuse to speak to me? . . . Don't you realize I have power either to free you or to crucify you?"(John 19:10). Jesus did not even flinch. With a level gaze and firm authority, His response must have sent another chill down Pilate's spine: "You would have no power over me if it were not given to you from above. Therefore the one who handed me over to you is guilty of a greater sin" (John 19:11).

Pilate was beside himself! He had tried everything he knew to set Jesus free short of simply doing the right thing regardless of what the rulers and the crowd demanded. Finally, the threats got downright dirty as the crowd warned, "If you let this man go, you are no friend of Caesar. Anyone who claims to be a king opposes Caesar" (John 19:12). The gauntlet had been thrown, and Pilate knew his own job security and promising future were on the line.

Pilate caved in with one last, pitiful attempt at compromise. He came up with a solution he believed might satisfy the bloodthirsty crowd and the relentless officials. As part of the Passover celebration, it was his custom to release any prisoner the crowd chose. It just so happened that "at that time they had a notorious prisoner, called Barabbas. So . . . Pilate asked them, 'Which one do you want me to release to you: Barabbas, or Jesus who is called Christ?'"[71]

The pent-up humiliation of being forced to ask a Roman for a favor and the jealous hatred[72] they felt toward Jesus caused the rulers once again to momentarily lose any semblance of dignity that remained as they shouted back, "No, not him! Give us Barabbas!" (John 18:40). *Barabbas!* Barabbas was a thief and a murderer and a rabble-rouser![73] The rulers of the law, the priests of God, the religious leaders of Israel were demanding that Barabbas be set free and Jesus be crucified. They were joined by a raucous chorus that kept shouting, "Away with this man! Release Barabbas to us! . . . Crucify him! Crucify him!"[74]

To clarify their choice, Pilate asked the mob a question that has reverberated through the centuries, "What shall I do, then, with Jesus who is called Christ?" They demanded with one voice, "Crucify him!"

In consternation, Pilate challenged them again, "Why? What crime has he committed?"

But the crowd increased their volume as they shouted back, "Crucify him! Crucify him! Crucify him!"[75]

Pilate, sensing he was losing the battle, mockingly gestured toward Jesus, "'Here is your king.' . . . But they shouted, 'Take him away! Take him away! Crucify him!'

"'Shall I crucify your king?' Pilate asked."

And the Jews, who hated the Romans with a passion, responded vehemently, "We have no king but Caesar" (John 19:14–15).

Finally, realizing the trial was getting nowhere, Pilate motioned for his servant to bring him a basin of water. In front of the entire rioting assembly, he deliberately washed his hands and declared, "'I am innocent of this man's blood. . . . It is your responsibility!' All the people answered, 'Let his blood be on us and on our children!'"[76] With that, Pilate released Barabbas[77] and surrendered Jesus to their will.[78]

And so Jesus, convicted of blasphemy by the religious courts but declared innocent of all charges by the Roman courts, was led off to be crucified. He was rejected by the religious leaders, by the Romans, and by His own people.

Whom do you know who is rejecting Jesus today? Whoever those people are, regardless of the vehemence of their words, or the hardness of their hearts, or the coldness of their eyes, there is still hope.

Because some of the very men who had rejected Jesus on the Friday morning of His crucifixion did repent of their sins and receive His forgiveness and salvation! This astounding turnabout took place fifty days after the rioting mob screamed its rejection of Jesus. In the very place where Jesus had been condemned by the religious leaders, Peter preached a sermon to a crowd of thousands at the Feast of Pentecost. He boldly faced many who had been in the mob that had rejected Jesus and pointedly said, "Therefore let all Israel be assured of this: God has made this Jesus, whom you crucified, both Lord and Christ."[79] Three thousand people responded with deep contrition to Peter's powerful proclamation of the truth. They repented of their sins and claimed Jesus Christ as their own Savior and Lord, receiving His forgiveness.

The rejection of Jesus that led to His crucifixion was not a tragic mistake, or a senseless act of injustice, or a cold-blooded murder, or a lynching. It was the heart of God making sin forgivable for anyone—even Judas . . . even Peter . . . even the religious leaders . . . even Pilate . . . even the soldiers who flogged and mocked Him . . . even the crowd that demanded His blood . . . even me . . . *even you!*

She was an old Gypsy woman wandering through Eastern Europe who happened to pass by an open doorway to an ordinary-looking building in a little village. From within the building came the sound of people singing. Out of curiosity, the old woman stepped inside and found a church service in progress. Drawn by the sound of the music, she stayed and heard the gospel message of God's love and forgiveness that is extended to all through His Son, Jesus. The old woman's heart was touched, and she responded by slipping up to the front of the crowded room at the end of the service in order to speak with the pastor. Sensing her need, he prayed with her and led her to a personal relationship with God through faith in Jesus Christ as her Savior and Lord.

The old Gypsy, a member of a rejected minority in society, was so thrilled by God's love and acceptance that she immediately went out into the street and told everyone, "God loves you." She told those who passed her by, "God loves you." She told the shopkeepers in the stores, "God loves you."

One day soon after her experience with God, she walked past the train station where two drunk men were lounging. Their shoulders slumped, cigarettes dangled from their lips, and their entire demeanor was of such dejected hopelessness that the old woman walked over and repeated what she had been tirelessly telling everyone else, "God loves you." One of the drunks responded by slapping her across the face. As the woman recovered from the emotional shock and physical pain, she blurted out, "God loves you, and I forgive you." The drunk slapped her again. *Again* her response was, "God loves you, and I forgive you." This scene was repeated until, in the end, the woman lay bloodied and senseless on the ground, and the two drunk men ambled off.

Christians in the town heard what had happened to the old woman, and they took her in. For three months they nursed and fed and cared for her until finally she regained her health and strength. She moved into a little room in a dilapidated building. Once again she was on her own, telling everyone of God's love. A year went by, and everyone forgot the ugly incident at the train station.

One day, the old woman heard a knock on her door. When she opened the door, she saw a man standing on the narrow sidewalk. He asked her if she remembered him.

She shook her head—no.

"Do you remember a year ago when you told two drunks at the train station that God loves them?"

"Yes," she replied.

"Well," the man continued, "I am the drunk who slapped you and left you for dead. But for weeks and months afterward, what you said haunted me. So I found someone who could tell me about God. And I told God I was sorry, and He forgave me. I have become a Christian because of what you said. And I've been looking for you ever since because I want to say I'm sorry and ask you to forgive me too."

Because they lived in a repressive society, the old woman became alarmed, thinking perhaps this man was a spy for the secret police. So to verify the truth of his claim, she demanded that he kneel on the public sidewalk and pray, knowing that no KGB agent would ever do such a thing. The man immediately dropped to his knees and prayed, thanking God for His love and mercy and grace. When he got up from his knees, he and the old woman embraced!

Jesus is the *only One* who makes not only our sins but also the sins of others against us forgivable. Praise God for just giving us Jesus!

12

JESUS MAKES SIN FORGIVABLE . . .

For Everyone

JOHN 19:17–30

In the Old Testament, when a person sinned, he was required to take the very best, blue-ribbon lamb he could find, one without any spots or blemishes, to the priest at the temple. There, in front of the priest, the sinner would grasp the lamb with both hands and confess his sin. His guilt was transferred to the lamb as though it had traveled through his arms and hands to the terrified little creature. The priest would then hand the sinner a knife, and the sinner would kill the lamb so that it was obvious the lamb had died as a result of the sinner's action. Then the priest would take the blood of the lamb and sprinkle it on the altar to make atonement for the man's sin.

Throughout the years, fountains of blood and rivers of blood and oceans of blood flowed from the temple altar as God's children sought His forgiveness for their sin. Yet when they walked away from such a sacrifice, their hearts must have remained heavy as the burden of guilt clung like river slime to their souls. The writer to the Hebrews put it bluntly: "It is impossible for the blood of bulls and goats [and lambs] to take away sins."[1] So why the sacrificial slaughter?

The entire bloody ritual was like an IOU note that bought the sinner temporary atonement until a perfect sacrifice would come and pay it off. And the perfect Sacrifice did come.

One day, as John the Baptist was standing beside the River Jordan, a rather ordinary-looking man walked past. John recognized Him as his cousin, Jesus of Nazareth. But John didn't call Him by His given name. Instead, John pointed and identified Him as "the Lamb of God, who takes away the sin of the world!"[2] John was making the most remarkable announcement since the angels had heralded the birth of the Baby in Bethlehem. With razorlike perception, he recognized that Jesus Himself would be the perfect Lamb who would pay off all those IOU notes with the sacrifice of Himself.

The pervasive misconception today is that since Jesus died as a sacrifice for the sins of the world, then we are all automatically forgiven. But we overlook the vital truth that we must grasp the Lamb with our hands of faith and confess our sins. We then must acknowledge that He was slain for our sins as surely as if we had plunged the knife into His heart. At that moment, the Lamb becomes our High Priest and offers His own blood on the altar of the cross on our behalf. And, wonder of wonders! God accepts the sacrifice and we are forgiven! Our guilt is atoned for! We are made right in God's sight! Jesus, the Lamb of God, makes sin forgivable for everyone![3]

THE LAMB WAS SACRIFICED

Following His six trials, Jesus was turned over to the Roman soldiers, who led Him to the place called Calvary for crucifixion.[4] Jesus had been on His feet for nine hours during which time He had been manhandled, spit upon, slapped, flogged, and dragged from place to place. His back was already a mangled, bloody mess from the scourging when the soldiers roughly placed a cross on it, demanding that He carry His own means of execution through the streets of Jerusalem.

Onlookers and bystanders and curiosity seekers pressed in around Jesus as He dragged the heavy cross through the cobbled, narrow city streets. Finally, His strength must have given way, causing His knees to grow weak and sending Him sprawling to the ground. It became apparent that He could not physically carry the cross the distance to Calvary. So the soldiers, who surrounded Him like a human barricade, quickly solved the problem by seizing an unsuspecting gawker to carry the cross for Him.[5]

At that precise moment, a man named Simon stepped out of obscurity and into the pages of history and the hearts of God's children. Not much is known about him except that apparently he came from Cyrene, implying that he was an African and therefore black. He must have had a powerfully built physique for the Romans to have spotted him so quickly and commanded his assistance.

Imagine what it would have been like to be Simon, and to have carried the cross of Christ while following Him up Calvary.

What would it have been like to have endured the jeers and the cheers
that swirled around Him like a golfer's gallery in hell?
What would it have been like to have shared in the humiliation of rejection
as He was cast out of the city as though He wasn't good enough
to remain inside?
What would it have been like to have felt the sticky warmth of His blood
from the cross on your skin?
What would it have been like to have felt the encroaching horror
as the place of execution neared?
What would it have been like to have looked up through the sweat
that trickled down your face, and see the executioners
who stood waiting impassively with hammers in hand?
What would it have been like to have the burden of the cross lifted
from your back as someone said, "This is His cross; you're free to go
now," and He was nailed to it, not you?

Did Jesus catch Simon's eye and whisper a hoarse, "Thank you! Thank you for carrying My cross!"[6] Did those who witnessed such personal involvement and identification with the cross of Christ remember His earlier words, "Anyone who does not carry his cross and follow me cannot be my disciple"?[7] Have you been hiding your identification with Christ because you recoil with repulsion from the shame and suffering of the cross?

Captain Jeremiah Denton was a prisoner of war in North Vietnam for seven years and seven months, including four years in solitary confinement. America watched with unabashed emotion the day Captain Denton was released and returned to his native America. He arrived home in a plane that taxied up to a strip of bright red carpet, banked by hundreds of microphones, reporters, and photographers. When he stepped off the plane and onto the carpet, we all watched with bated breath, anxious to hear his first words. We didn't have to wait long. With a face deeply etched by suffering, yet with a voice that was clear and strong, the captain said, "We are honored to have had the opportunity to serve our country under difficult circumstances"[8]

On that day, Captain Jeremiah Denton gave us a life's lesson. He expressed humble gratitude for having been able to serve his country, even though that service had involved unspeakable suffering. Could that attitude be what Jesus meant when He said we have to take up our cross and follow Him if we want to be His disciples? And when we arrive in our heavenly home, will we step up and say, "We were honored to serve our King, carrying the cross of God's will, even when that service included personal suffering"? Carry the cross. He promises that if you do, you will share in the power of His resurrection and the glory of His crown.[9]

As Jesus struggled to make His way through the narrow streets crowded with the throngs of pilgrims who had come to celebrate the Feast of the Passover, He heard not only cheers and jeers, but also tears. He did not rebuke the mockery, but He did rebuke the misery of a large group of women who wept and wailed for Him. He actually stopped on His way to Calvary and admonished, "Daughters of Jerusalem, do not weep for me; weep for yourselves and for your children" because of the judgment of God that would fall on them because of that day.[10] Jesus flatly rejected their sympathy and pity.

As we meditate on the sacrifice of the Lamb of God, we need to beware of feeling sorry for Him. Instead, our hearts should be crushed from the weight of sorrow for our own sin that cost Him His life—sin that provokes the judgment of God on us unless we confess it and repent of it.

Jesus was not a helpless victim of Roman cruelty or religious jealousy or general apathy. He was the Lamb of God, who was deliberately sacrificed for the sin of the world. Yet He was as human as He was divine, and in His humanity He suffered.

He Suffered Physically

At this point in the Gospel narratives, each writer seems to have turned away. The details are so scant that it gives us the impression the authors could not bear to recall or relate the atrocities they witnessed that day. It's almost as though they drew a protective veil of silence around their beloved Savior, refusing to describe the indescribable. And so we tread reverently and worshipfully on holy ground as we attempt to glimpse something of the price Love paid for you and me.

When Jesus finally arrived at the place of execution around nine o'clock in the morning, if His treatment followed standard procedure in those days, He was stripped of all His clothes.[11] Possibly He was allowed to retain a loincloth. He was then offered, as a humane gesture, a sedative to dull the initial shock and excruciating pain of the spikes being driven through His flesh.[12] However, Jesus refused the offering. Was it because He wanted to "drink the cup the Father had given" Him to the dregs? Did He want to remain fully alert in order to finish the work

He had yet to do from the cross itself—to fulfill prophecy and forgive a dying thief and care for His mother?

Whatever His reasons for refusing the sedative, He was then laid out on the cross, His arms were outstretched on the horizontal beam at right angles to His body, and nails were driven through His wrists, pinning His hands to the rough wood. His knees were then bent slightly as His feet were placed on a block of wood, and spikes were driven through His ankles into the tall center pole. The entire cross, with Jesus pinned to it by the nails through His wrists and ankles, was then raised upright and dropped into a prepared hole, where dirt was tamped around it. Jesus, the Lamb of God, God's own Son, was sacrificed on the altar of a wooden Roman cross.

Normally, crucifixion victims cursed and screamed obscenities and even passed into unconsciousness from the initial pain. Jesus reacted in a stunningly different way—He prayed, "Father, forgive them, for they do not know what they are doing."[13] Fifty days later, when Peter preached at Pentecost, Jesus' prayer was answered when some of the very men who crucified Him repented of their sins, placed their faith in Him, and were baptized in His name![14]

If God could forgive the men who nailed His Son to the cross, why do you think He won't forgive you? What do you think is beyond the forgiveness of God? Abortion? ~ Adultery? ~ Abuse? ~ Abandonment? ~ Homosexuality? ~ Hate? ~ Hypocrisy? ~ Haughtiness? ~ Doubt? ~ Divorce? ~ Drunkenness? ~ Deception? ~ Murder?~ Or theft? ~ Or immorality? ~ Or___________? You fill in the blank.

It stands to reason that if Jesus asked His Father to forgive the very men who crucified Him, *and God did*, then there is *nothing* and *no one* that He cannot or will not forgive when He is humbly asked.

When have *you* asked?

And if Jesus forgave those who nailed Him to the cross, and if God forgives you and me, how can you withhold your forgiveness from someone else? How can you withhold your forgiveness from *yourself?* If God says, "I forgive you," who are you to say, "Thank You, God, but I can't forgive myself"? Are your standards higher than His? Are you more righteous than He is? If God says, "I forgive you," then the only appropriate response is to say, "God, thank You. I don't deserve it, but I accept it. And to express my gratitude, I, in turn, forgive that person who has sinned against me."

We forgive others, not because they deserve it, *but because He deserves it!* The only reason we have to forgive is that He commands us to, and our obedience gives us opportunity to say to Him, "Thank You for forgiving me. I love You." Our forgiveness of others then becomes an act of worship that we would not enter into except for who He is and for the overwhelming debt of love we owe Him.

We will never comprehend what it cost our Lord in physical agony to offer His forgiveness to everyone—no exceptions. But the veil of scriptural silence that shrouds His death in the Gospels is lifted briefly in the Psalms. Psalm 22 gives us an almost eerie insight into how Jesus felt as He hung suspended between heaven and hell, as King David describes a personal experience that was also a prophetic description of Jesus' agony.

The very first words of the psalm are the prayer that was wrenched from our Savior's broken heart and tumbled from His parched lips: "My God, my God, why have you forsaken me? Why are you so far from saving me, so far from the words of my groaning?" (v. 1) The pain was so excruciating that He could not remain silent, but groaned and cried out in physical agony. In the midst of intense physical pain, He experienced mental torture, feeling His prayers were getting nowhere, pleading, "O my God, I cry out by day, but you do not answer" (v. 2).

All of our Lord's dignity and self-respect were shattered by the nails, and He felt like "a worm and not a man, scorned by men and despised by the people" (v. 6). Looking down from His vantage point while suffering such extreme physical and mental anguish, He could see His enemies clustered about, staring, gloating, mocking, taunting, insulting, "shaking their heads: 'He trusts in the LORD; let the LORD rescue him. Let him deliver him, since he delights in him'" (vv. 7–8). Yet instead of succumbing to the pressure of pain and lashing out at His Father, He clung by faith to what He knew had been true from the day He was born, when He prayed, "[I] was cast upon you; from my mother's womb you have been my God. Do not be far from me, for trouble is near and there is no one to help" (vv. 10–11).

The psalm continues the prophetic description, noting that as the morning sun rose in the sky and the heat intensified, His open wounds were scorched and the moisture was sucked from His body until He was totally dehydrated and felt "poured out like water." And with the weight of His body dangling from His wrists, "all my bones are out of joint" (v. 14).

Because of the weight of His body, the only way He could breathe was to push His feet against the block of wood to which they were nailed at a slight angle, raise His body just enough to allow Himself room to gasp for air, then release His weight until once again He hung fully from His wrists. Every movement must have added to His torture, reopening the wounds in His back, tearing at the flesh around the shattered bones in His wrists and ankles, and inflicting even greater pain. But the only way to remain alive was to push up, breathe, then release; push up, breathe, release; push up, breathe, release.[15] Crucifixion was actually a very slow death by suffocation.

The sensation of suffocation would have been overwhelming as His "heart . . . turned to wax; it has melted away within me" (v. 14). After a relatively short period of time, raging fever would have consumed Him until, "My strength is dried up. . . . my tongue sticks to the roof of my mouth; you lay me in the dust of death. Dogs have surrounded me; a band of evil men has encircled me, they have pierced my hands and my feet" (vv. 15–16). His skeleton would have been grotesquely exposed so that "I can count all my bones; people stare and gloat over me. They divide my garments among them and cast lots for my clothing" (vv. 17–18).

Jesus, the Lamb of God, suffered physically as He was sacrificed on the altar of the cross. In what way are you suffering physically?

Do you have migraine headaches?
Think of the crown of thorns embedded on His brow.
Do you have arthritis?
Think of all His bones pulled out of joint.
Do you have heart disease?
Think of His heart melted like wax within Him.
Do you have cancer?
Think of His raging fever and collapsed lungs.

Many questions about human suffering have no answers.[16] But there is one Answer that transcends all the questions: God, *in the flesh,* knows by personal experience what it *feels like* to suffer physically. Any suffering you or I will ever endure is just a shadow of His, whether physical or emotional.

He Suffered Emotionally

Hymn writers and artists have conveyed to us a picture of Jesus hanging on a cross on a hill far away. In fact, the place of execution was just outside the city gate, beside the main road leading into Jerusalem. And those to be crucified were only raised two to eighteen inches above the ground. That meant all the dignity and modesty and purity of Jesus' physical person was stripped away and He was left naked to die in searing, scorching heat, writhing and groaning in agony, at virtually eye level with those who passed by on their way to and from the city.

Have you ever had to disrobe so you could be examined by the probing, prying eyes of others? Even if the eyes belong to doctors or nurses or interns or x-ray technicians, the experience can be humiliating. It may have been even worse if you were raped or in some other way physically abused or used. In such circumstances the bitterness of the emotional destruction is much more severe than the physical pain.

Jesus' emotional pain surely increased as people passed Him by. In their rush to get to the temple area in time to purchase a lamb for sacrifice, did the pilgrims preparing for Passover *even notice* the Lamb that God was sacrificing for their sin? As Jesus poured out His life, people must have passed by without a glance, eagerly discussing bargains at the shops, or the weather, or the latest investment opportunities. Have you ever poured out your life for someone who didn't even notice? Jesus understands that kind of emotional pain.

I wonder if others on their way to market were so wrapped up in their grocery lists and errands that they glanced up, read the sign over His head that declared His "crime"—JESUS OF NAZARETH, THE KING OF THE JEWS—and clucked their tongues as they commented on the pitiful delusion of the riffraff these days (John 19:19). Perhaps others paused to join in the cruel taunts being hurled at Him: "He saved others, . . . but he can't save himself! He's the King of Israel! Let him come down now from the cross, and we will believe in him. He trusts in God. Let God rescue him now if he wants him, for he said, 'I am the Son of God.'"[17]

At the time of His greatest physical torture, instead of having someone bathe His head with a cold cloth, instead of having someone lovingly sympathize with Him, instead of having any tender care at all, He was mocked and tempted almost beyond human endurance—by those for whom He was dying! That's emotional suffering!

Who is taunting you? Is the taunter someone you have given your life to in marriage? Or in business? Or in school? Or in church? Or in the home?

In what way are you being emotionally tortured? The cruelest of all the taunts hurled at Jesus was surely the one that suggested that if God really loved Him, God would never have allowed Him to be in this situation. Is that how you are being taunted? Is that taunt tempting you to doubt God's love? Is it causing you additional pain? Has someone suggested to you that:

If God really loved you, He would heal your disease?

If God really loved you, He would never have allowed you to lose your job?

If God really loved you, He would bring your spouse back home?
If God really loved you, you would be healthy and wealthy
and problem free?

Yet God has said that the proof of His love is none of those things! The proof of His love is that while we were sinners, passing Jesus by on the road of life, He sent His only, beloved Son to die for us.[18]

Even in the blackness of hate and evil swirling around the cross, the love of God broke through like the rays of the sun on a stormy day. That love shone down on the two thieves crucified on each side of Jesus. Their agony and fury boiled over and spewed out in a venom of curses and taunts hurled at Jesus, challenging Him to save Himself and them.[19]

But one of the thieves grew quieter and quieter, until finally he rebuked his partner in crime, "Don't you fear God . . . since you are under the same sentence? We are punished justly, for we are getting what our deeds deserve. But this man has done nothing wrong." And then, in one of the most moving conversion scenes in human history, the thief turned his face toward Jesus and pleaded in humble faith, "Jesus, remember me when you come into your kingdom." And Jesus turned his face toward the thief and promised, "I tell you the truth, today you will be with me in paradise."[20]

In the twinkling of an eye, that thief changed his eternal destiny; he passed from death to life, had his sins forgiven, and was made right with God. There was no formula or ritual or water baptism or good works, just faith in Jesus.

What do you think you have to do to be saved? Do you think you have to be baptized to be saved?[21] Do you think you have to do something to deserve eternal life? The thief was pinned to a cross! He could barely move his head! He was dying, yet when he placed his faith in Jesus, he was made right with God and granted entrance into His heavenly home! He may have just squeaked through the gates of heaven by the skin of his teeth, but he was in! Do you think it is too late to be forgiven? It's never too late! Because the Lamb makes sin forgivable for everyone, even a dying thief!

Under the scorching sun, with blood dried and caked on His face, with flies and gnats feeding on His broken flesh, with His lips cracked and His throat parched, Jesus surveyed the scene below Him through swollen eyelids. His gaze fell on one of His disciples and a pitiful group of women huddled nearby, their haggard faces showing signs of shock. One of the women was His own mother, Mary.

How could she bear to watch her Son tortured? Yet how could she tear herself away? Did her memory flash back to that night so long ago when her time had come and the only available place for delivery was a stable? Did she remember when she first gazed on His tiny face and traced His curling lashes and rosebud mouth with her finger? Could she still feel the grip of His tiny hand clinging to hers? Did she remember frantically searching for Him in Jerusalem, only to find Him in the temple, already confidently going about His Father's business at the age of twelve? Did she remember the expression in His eyes when He looked at her, and the rich tone of His voice when He spoke to her, and the way He called her name, and . . . was that her Son calling her now?

Mary's entire body must have quivered as though from an electric shock as she heard Jesus calling to her from the Cross. Surely her breath caught as she strained to hear His words, yet He spoke clearly, "'Dear woman, here is your son,' and to the disciple [John], 'Here is your mother.' From that time on, this disciple took her into his home" (John 19:26–27). And somehow, even with the horror of the scene before her reflected in her eyes, and the weight of agony pressing against her chest so that her breathing was labored, she knew everything was going to be all right. She didn't understand, but in the midst of the anguish only a mother knows as her heart is shattered by the pain of her child, a quiet peace must have stolen its way within when God spoke directly and personally to her from the cross. God had singled her out, He had noticed her, He had cared for her, and she was comforted.

In His tender, thoughtful care for His mother, Jesus, as He was dying, gives you and me a powerful lesson in how to overcome emotional suffering. Most of us increase our pain by dwelling on it or by analyzing it. We throw a pity party and expect others to join us. We spiral downward into depression, withdrawing into self-preoccupation. But the way to overcome is not to focus on ourselves or on the pain, but to focus on the needs of others.

Would you get your eyes off yourself and your problems and your pressures and your pain and look around? Who do you know who is suffering or struggling in some way? What can you do for them? Ask God to bring to your attention those you can care for. Because as you do, you will find joy in easing their burden, and in the process, you will ease your own. Jesus, at the height of His physical and emotional suffering, looked out for others as He forgave the dying thief and made arrangements for the care of His mother.

Hanging on the cross, Jesus suffered physical pain and emotional torment that are beyond our comprehension. Yet the spiritual suffering He endured was even worse!

He Suffered Spiritually

In our increasingly secularized society, spiritual suffering is often ignored. It seems to get categorized under all sorts of psychosomatic labels. We may try to drug it, drown it, or lock it up, but it doesn't go away, because it is very real. The spiritual suffering of Jesus is not as easily recognizable as His physical and emotional suffering, but it was by far the worst suffering of all. We first glimpse it when Jesus was stripped of His robe and left to hang virtually naked before the world. The emotional shame and humiliation would have been acute for any dignified Jewish rabbi. Yet it wouldn't even have warranted an honorable mention alongside the spiritual humiliation He endured as He was spiritually stripped of His robe of righteousness in God's eyes.

We are first made aware of this type of humiliation in the garden of Eden when Adam and Eve were naked, yet they seemed to feel no shame or self-consciousness. Some scholars believe they may have been clothed in shimmering light, but that was all. But when they disobeyed God and ate of the fruit He had forbidden, "they realized they were naked; so they sewed fig leaves together and made coverings for themselves . . . and they hid from the LORD God among the trees of the garden."[22] In some way, as soon as they sinned, their physical nakedness was associated with shame and guilt. Their clothing, whatever it had been physically, had also been their spiritual right-relationship with God. When they sinned against Him, they lost that righteousness and in the same poignant scene described in my book, *God's Story,* they

> stood before each other, dirty in sin and feeling very exposed. They were ashamed of themselves and ashamed of each other, but that didn't begin to compare with their feeling of shame before God. They were so ashamed that just the thought of having to face Him sent them scurrying for a cover-up. The fig leaves they chose to sew together were totally inadequate. God could see right through them.
>
> What fig leaves have you sewn together as a cover-up for your sin and shame before God? Fig leaves . . .
>
> of good works?
>
> of religiosity?
>
> of church attendance?

of community volunteerism?
of morality?
of philanthropy?

There are no fig leaves thick enough or big enough to hide your sin and shame from God.[23]

Unlike Adam and Eve, when Jesus hung on the cross, He had no fig leaves to use as a covering, inadequate as they were, and He had no bushes to crouch behind. He was totally exposed, not just physically before all people, but also spiritually before God. He didn't just take our sins upon Himself, He *became* those sins for us.[24] Imagine how dirty and vile and evil and guilty and *ashamed* Jesus must have felt as He hung there before a holy God with our sins exposed as *though they were His!*

Jesus' extreme sensitivity to sin can be illustrated by the sensitivity nonsmokers can have to cigarette smoke. For instance, when I check into a hotel room where someone has smoked, even if it was weeks before my arrival, I get a headache. I'm just extremely sensitive to cigarette smoke, a sensitivity that is sharpened by the fact that I've never smoked. If I walk into a room full of smokers, I become nauseated. But my sensitivity to cigarette smoke is just a faint shadow compared to the sensitivity Jesus would have had toward sin and guilt. Jesus had never sinned. Not even once! Can you imagine how exceedingly sensitive He would have been to even the smallest sin? Yet He bore, not just the smallest sins, but *all the sins*—of all the people—of all the generations—of all the ages—of all the worlds—for all time!

Jesus, in His humanity, knew what the guilt and shame of hatred, of murder, of rape, of stealing, of lying, feels like, as well as every other sin, big or small, that's ever been thought of or committed. As He hung on the cross, stripped of His own robe of righteousness, He was exposed, spiritually naked in our sins, with no hiding place from His Father's penetrating gaze of searing holiness.

Have you ever been caught doing something you shouldn't have? Caught breaking the speed limit? Caught sneaking a piece of cake on your diet? Caught in a lie? Caught in gossip? Do you remember the guilty feeling of shame? That's only a glimmer of the emotional trauma Jesus experienced as He was "caught" in your sins and mine.

Yet because Jesus was stripped "naked," you and I can be clothed! The Bible tells us that all of our righteousness, including the very best things we ever do, are so permeated with sin and selfishness that they are like filthy rags in God's sight.[25]

But at the Cross, Jesus gave us His perfect, spotless robe of righteousness and took our filthy garments of sin in exchange.[26] On Judgment Day, you and I will be dressed in His righteousness before God because He wore the filthy garments of our sin.

When Jesus was stripped of His physical clothes, the execution squad of soldiers divided what little He had between them—His belt, sandals, and other things. But when it came to His beautifully woven inner garment, they decided that instead of tearing it into four pieces, they would gamble for it. So while Jesus hung slightly above them, groaning in excruciating pain, fighting for His breath, they callously ignored Him and tossed the dice (John 19:23–24). Their ribald laughter and the clatter of the dice as they were thrown made a sharp contrast to His pain-wracked sobs so near by.

People today still toss the dice for the robe of His righteousness. While coldly ignoring His death on the cross, they gamble for His "robe" by betting their eternal lives on the chance that they can earn acceptance with God through their religiosity, or their sincerity, or their morality, or their philanthropy. They "bet" that

if they read their Bibles every day,
if they just do more good works than bad works,
if they keep the Ten Commandments,
if they go to church regularly,
if they're good,

then they have a "chance" to please God and get to heaven—they have a chance to get His "robe." But His "robe" cannot be gambled for, bought, earned, deserved, inherited, given, bartered, or stolen.

The only way to obtain it is to exchange it for your own filthy shreds of righteousness at the cross. His robe is free, not because it is cheap, but because it is priceless. The guilt of your sin and mine has been removed because it was placed on Him, and His righteousness was placed on us! Praise God! What an exchange!

Jesus hung on the cross for three hours, wracked with white-hot physical pain, tortured mentally and emotionally by the taunting and the tempting and the trauma, crushed by the weight of guilt and shame and sin that was ours but became His. Suddenly, the birds stopped chirping, the vultures stopped circling, the breeze stopped blowing, and everything became deathly still as darkness—pitch-black darkness—descended. The cries that could be heard were no longer just coming from the victims on the crosses but from the bystanders as they cowered, then fled in panic like rats scurrying to leave a sinking ship. Even the hardened soldiers must have shuddered at the supernatural power and anger that permeated the atmosphere.

As terrified people looked up, searching the sky, there were no clouds to block the sun. There was no eclipse. The sun was nowhere to be seen![27] Where it had been was just blackness! Why? Why was the world plunged into what seemed like the very pit of hell?[28]

The eerie darkness that descended was not just nature feeling sorry for the Creator who was nailed to the altar of the cross. It was the very judgment of God for your sins and mine that was poured out on Jesus![29] What He went through is beyond our ability to imagine or describe. I do know that because Jesus is God, as well as Man, He may have entered an eternal state of time as He hung on the cross.

God created time for your benefit and mine—sixty-second minutes and sixty-minute hours and twenty-four-hour days were set in motion by the tides and the rotation of the earth on its axis. But God does not live by our time clocks. He transcends time. That's why Peter said that one day with the Lord is as a thousand years, and a thousand years is as a day.[30] That's why it may be that He created the world in six days on our time clocks, but thousands of years (even millions of years?) on His time clock.[31] Could it be that although Jesus hung on the cross for six hours according to our time clock, it was actually an *eternity of time on His clock?* Did Jesus live through *an eternity of God's judgment* for your sin and my sin as He hung there on the cross? We won't know the answer until we get to heaven, but we do know that He took God's judgment for us. He paid the price in full, and He paid for it with His life.

In the Old Testament, Abraham's faith was tested when God told him to take his son, his only son, the son he loved, and offer him as a sacrifice. And Abraham did. Abraham bound Isaac to the altar and raised his knife to slay him in strict obedience to God's Word. Just before the gleaming knife plunged down, God leaned out of heaven and urgently commanded, "Abraham! Abraham! . . . Do not lay a hand on the boy," and Isaac's life was spared! Abraham looked around; caught in the thicket nearby was a ram. After cutting Isaac loose, Abraham took the ram and offered it on the altar. And I wonder, did Isaac embrace the ram with tears streaming down his cheeks, knowing it was a substitute that would die in his place?[32]

As God's Son, God's only Son, the Son He loved, hung on the cross, the knife of God's fierce wrath against sin was lifted, and there was no one to stay the Father's hand. Instead, "He . . . did not spare his own Son, but gave him up for us all."[33] Jesus was God's Lamb and our Substitute, who endured the full force of God's wrath for your sins and mine when He was bound on the altar in our place.

At midafternoon, the silent darkness was pierced with a heart-wrenching cry that would have sent chills down even the stiffest backs. It came from the cracked lips and the crushed heart of God's Son as His tortured body and fevered mind were pushed to the outer limits of endurance. "My God, my God, why have you forsaken me?"[34] For the first time in eternity, the Father and Son were actually separated.[35] They were separated by all of your sins and my sins, which came between Them. And Jesus, suffocating physically, was smothered spiritually by a blanket of loneliness such as He had never known.

Even when Jesus had been alone in a crowd, or alone on a mountainside, or alone on the lake, or alone in a boat, or alone in a room, He had never truly been *alone!* His Father had always been with Him. He and His Father were so close they were One.[36] To be separated was a spiritual death that was worse than a living nightmare. *It was hell!*

No one on this side of hell will ever know the loneliness Jesus endured on the cross—in your place and mine. When we claim the Lamb as our own sacrifice for sin, we will never be separated from God, because Jesus was. Praise His dear name! He is still Emmanuel—God with us. The sacrifice of the Lamb is absolutely sufficient in itself to take away our sin and reconcile us to God.

The Lamb Is Sufficient

The blood of Jesus is sufficient for the forgiveness of any and all sins[37] because the Cross was two thousand years ago, and all of our sins were still to come. Therefore, all of our sins, whether we committed them yesterday or today or have yet to commit them tomorrow, are covered by His blood—past sins, present sins, future sins, big sins, small sins, or medium-size sins—it makes no difference.

A few years ago, I found myself groping for a way to explain this to a woman who was on death row for multiple murders and was to be executed within ten hours of my visit. Tears glistened in her eyes as she looked at me beseechingly, needing assurance of the salvation she had claimed by faith six years earlier. That very night she would be stepping into eternity, and she was desperate for reassurance of her forgiveness by God.

I asked her if she had ever been to the ocean, and she nodded yes. I asked her if, as she had walked along the shore, she had seen small holes in the sand where ghost crabs had darted in and out. Again she nodded affirmatively. I then asked if she had seen any larger holes, like those made by children digging a deep moat around a sand castle. Beginning to look somewhat puzzled, she said yes, she had seen holes like that. I persisted as I probed gently to see if she had ever seen huge holes created by machines dredging a channel or burying pipe lines on the beach. Her brow began to furrow as she again acknowledged a quiet yes. I then leaned toward her and pressed my point, "Velma, when the tide comes in, what happens to *all* those holes? The little ones made by the crabs, and the medium-size ones made by children, and the great big ones made by machines?"

A soft light began to gleam in her eyes, and a smile played at the corner of her lips as I answered my own question: "All the holes are covered equally by the water, aren't they? The blood of Jesus is like the tide that washes over the 'holes' of your sins and covers all your sins equally." And Velma stepped into eternity reassured of her forgiveness by God and a welcome into her heavenly home based on *nothing but the blood of Jesus!*

Praise God for the blood of Jesus that is sufficient to cover all of our sins! *All of them!* Big sins like murdering your own mother. Little sins like gossip. Medium-size sins like losing your temper. They are all under the blood of Jesus, and we are free just to enjoy our forgiveness! We will never be held accountable for the guilt of our sins because Jesus has taken the punishment for us.

This lesson was brought home to me when a thunderstorm broke one Wednesday morning, deluging everything and everyone with rain as I arrived at the church to teach my weekly Bible class. In just a few moments, the parking lot became a fast-flowing two-inch-deep river, and the steps to the church looked like a multitiered waterfall. As I stood in the narthex looking through the sheets of wind-swept rain, I could see a stream of cars organizing itself into neat rows, their headlights sparkling in the raindrops. As I continued to watch, I noticed one woman make a mad dash from her car to the church, umbrella still tightly folded in her hand. She burst through the door, hair askew, makeup smeared, and clothes dripping with water. I sprang to help her, taking her Bible and notebook while she began to shake herself off. I couldn't help but ask with some astonishment, "You have an umbrella. Why didn't you put it up?"

She laughingly replied, "I thought it was just too much trouble."

The rain that fell on everyone and everything that morning is like the wrath of

God that falls on all of us because we have all sinned.[38] It is inevitable that sooner or later we will come under His wrath and get "wet." But God has given us an "umbrella" in the blood of Jesus. When we "put it up" by claiming His death for our sins, the umbrella of His blood covers us. God's wrath still falls on our sins, but now our sins are on Jesus; under the umbrella of His blood, we stay dry, and we are saved from the rain of God's wrath.

There is only one umbrella that is sufficient to save us or keep us dry in the midst of the storm of God's wrath. God gave you and me the umbrella when He sent Jesus to the cross to shed His blood for you. Are you still clutching it tightly, unopened? Why? Do you think it's just too much trouble to confess your sins, to repent, to claim Jesus as your Savior and surrender your life to Him as Lord? *Please! Go to the trouble!* The umbrella of the blood of Jesus is absolutely sufficient to save you from the rain of God's wrath, but you have to deliberately, consciously, personally put it up! *Put it up!*

As Jesus cried out from the cross, we can hear Him still clinging by faith to whom He knew His beloved Father to be—*My* God. Even as the sound left His lips, the darkness lifted and He called out hoarsely, "I am thirsty" (John 19:28). He wasn't asking for a sedative, but something to moisten His swollen tongue and cracked lips. He had something He wanted to say, and He wanted to say it so the angels in heaven would hear it, and the demons in hell would hear it, and people throughout the ages would hear it, and you would hear it, and I would hear it. One of the soldiers standing guard soaked a sponge in wine vinegar, "put the sponge on a stalk of the hyssop plant, and lifted it to Jesus' lips" (John 19:29).

After nine hours of standing on His feet, after being scourged, slapped, and manhandled, after six hours of hanging on the cross, the average person would have barely had enough life and breath left to even whisper. But Jesus, the Lamb of God, with life still fully flowing through His body, shouted out in a clear, ringing, triumphant voice, "It is finished" (John 19:30).[39] The price for our redemption had been paid! The sacrifice for our sin had been made! Sin was forgiven! Guilt was atoned for! Eternal life was now offered! Heaven has been opened! *It is finished!*

You don't have to do more good works than bad works.
You don't have to go to church every time the door opens.
You don't have to count beads.
You don't have to climb the stairs to some statue.
You don't have to lie on a bed of nails.

You don't have to be religious.

You don't even have to be good!

It is finished! Sin is forgivable for everyone! The price has been paid! *Jesus paid it all!*

Hallelujah!

Hallelujah!

HALLELUJAH!

HALLELUJAH!

As the clarion shout of victory still echoed in the air, Jesus irrevocably handed His life to His Father as He uttered His last words in a ringing declaration of faith: "Father, into your hands I commit my spirit."[40] Then He bowed His head and deliberately refused to take the next breath. He just refused to push up. The One who is the Lord of life,

the Resurrection and the Life,

the Creator of life,

the Source of all life,

gave His life for you and me!

And the blood of the Lamb that was shed on the altar of the cross that day ran down the wooden beam, down a hill called Calvary, and down through the years until it reaches us, where it has become a river that is deep enough to bathe in. Isn't it time you plunged in and took a bath? If you agree, pray this simple prayer by faith:

Dear God,

I choose to grasp the Lamb with my hands of faith and confess to You the hardness of my heart, the meanness of my thoughts, the coldness of my spirit, and the sinfulness of my life. I'm so sorry. I know it was for me—and because of me—that Jesus died. Please forgive me of all of my sins—big sins, medium sins, and small sins; past sins, present sins, and future sins. I choose deliberately to put up my umbrella right now. And I want to exchange my filthy garments for His spotless robe.

Thank You for the cleansing fountain of the blood of Jesus that washes me white as snow. I know even now that I am clean and forgiven and "dressed" for heaven.

Thank You! Thank You! Thank You for just giving me Jesus!

Jesus Makes Heaven Available

He had no predecessor,
and He will have no successor.

He is the Lion,
and He is the Lamb.

He is God,
and He is Man.

He is the seven-way King:

He is the King of the Jews . . .
that's a racial King.

He is the King of Israel . . .
that's a national King.

He is the King of righteousness . . .
that's a moral King.

He is the King of the ages . . .
that's an eternal King.

He is the King of heaven . . .
that's a universal King.

He is the King of glory . . .
that's a celestial King.

HE IS THE KING OF KINGS AND THE LORD OF LORDS!

Just give me Jesus! He makes heaven available!

13

JESUS MAKES HEAVEN AVAILABLE . . .
To the Sinner

JOHN 19:38–20:18

He was just a young boy living on the streets in the slums of London. But Geoffrey had heard that a fiery American evangelist named D. L. Moody would preach in the evening service of a church on the other side of the city, and he wanted to hear him. On the day of the meeting, Geoffrey set out to find the church. He dodged rumbling carriage wheels, slipped through crowded thoroughfares, and wove his way through hordes of scurrying pedestrians. Along the way, he helped himself to an apple from a grocer's cart, narrowly escaping the irate shopkeeper's angry grasp. Finally, just as the sun began to set, he looked up and saw his destination. He halted in his tracks to gape at it in awe. The church was regally situated on a hill, its stained-glass windows reflecting the setting sun with a golden iridescent glow that looked like the very glory of heaven. In the stillness of the early evening air, he could hear hundreds of voices rising and falling with the thunderous swell of organ pipes in a stirring cadence of praise. The sight and sound seemed to reach out and envelop his fiercely independent, yet lonely little heart, awakening a longing that felt like homesickness.

Geoffrey didn't hesitate. He bounded up the long, sweeping staircase that led to the massive wooden front door. Just as he was about to enter, a big hand descended out of nowhere, grabbed him by the shoulder, spun him around, and inquired sharply, "Just where do you think you're going, laddie?" Geoffrey responded stiffly but truthfully, "I heard Dr. Moody was going to preach here tonight. I've walked all the way across London to hear him." The big doorman looked down at the little boy with uncombed hair, unwashed face, unclean clothes, and unshod feet, then stated emphatically, "Not you! You're too dirty to go inside!"

The doorman then folded his arms across his big chest, spread his thick legs, and stood squarely in front of the door, blocking the entrance.

Geoffrey lifted his little chin, squared his little shoulders, glared back at the doorkeeper, then stalked off the front steps. He was confident he could find another way into the church. But as he walked around the building, he found all the other doors solidly locked, and the windows were too high for him to even attempt an entry. He ended up back on the front steps where he plopped down in weariness and discouragement. In spite of his street-cultivated toughness, tears began to trickle down his grimy cheeks.

Suddenly his attention was caught by a black carriage that pulled up to the foot of the steps. A very distinguished-looking gentleman in topcoat and hat climbed out, brandishing a walking cane, and began to briskly climb the stairs. When he reached Geoffrey's step, he glanced over and noticed the curious interest in the young boy's eyes and the tearstains on his cheeks. He stopped abruptly and inquired, "What's wrong?"

For a moment Geoffrey started to shrug and say, "Nothin'." But something in the man's demeanor caused Geoffrey to blurt out, "I came to hear Dr. Moody preach, but he says I'm too dirty to go inside," and he gestured toward the doorman.

The big man looked down at the little boy, then extended his hand. "Here, take my hand," the man offered. Geoffrey took a long, hard look at the man, then let his eyes focus on the man's extended hand. Slowly, he lifted his grimy little hand and placed it in that of the stranger, who clasped it tightly and invited Geoffrey to "come with me." And Geoffrey did.

Hand in hand they walked up the long, sweeping staircase. When they came to the huge door, the very same doorkeeper who had formerly forbidden the boy to enter now hastily opened the door wide. With the man still gripping his hand, Geoffrey walked through the open door and down the center aisle of the church already filled with worshipers, until they came to the very front row. With every eye on them, the big man seated Geoffrey there in front of the entire congregation. Then the big man walked on up the steps to the platform, stood behind the pulpit, and began to preach! The man was D. L. Moody![1]

The only reason Geoffrey was allowed inside the church that evening was because he was holding the hand of D. L. Moody. His acceptance in that church was based solely on his identification and relationship with the great preacher.

After the long journey of life, we are going to look up and see heaven. We're going to hear voices lifted in songs of praise. We're going to see the glory of God radiating from within, and we're going to long for home. But we will be forbidden to enter. Heaven is closed to us because we are too dirty in our sin to enter it.

However, because Jesus found us in our hopeless, helpless state and offered us His hand at the cross, we can be welcomed into heaven. If we accept His offer and put our hand of faith in His, He will walk with us hand in hand, not only through the remainder of our journey, but through the gates of heaven that will be opened wide for us. We will be as welcomed and accepted in heaven as He is, solely because of our relationship and identification with Him. Praise God! Jesus is the One, and the *only One,* who makes heaven available to the sinner, not only through the cross, but also through His resurrection.[2] Come and see the facts.

Come and See the Empty Tomb

Following a crucifixion, the dead bodies were torn from the crosses on which they had been executed and rudely dumped on the ground for dogs or vultures to consume. If the dead were more fortunate, they would be thrown into a common grave. In this case, "Joseph of Arimathea asked Pilate for the body of Jesus" (John 19:38). Because Jesus had just been executed as a criminal and an enemy of Rome, Joseph's request was exceedingly bold. As a prominent member of the religious community, he ran the risk of provoking not only Pilate but also the other Jewish leaders who then could have excommunicated him from the Sanhedrin and the temple itself. He also placed himself in jeopardy by handling a dead body that would defile him, effectively preventing him from participating in the Passover celebration.

Joseph's action was especially astounding since previously he had been so timid and fearful of the opinions of others that he had kept his belief in Jesus as the Messiah a secret. Now, however, he came out of the closet and "with Pilate's permission, he came and took the body." What was even more astonishing, "he was accompanied by Nicodemus, the man who earlier had visited Jesus at night" (John 19:38–39).

The Father's heart must have been deeply moved and heaven's host must have applauded with joy to see these two careful, fearful, prideful Jewish men throw caution to the wind. They had been silent when they should have spoken. They had remained seated when they should have taken a stand. They had denied their faith when they should have asserted it. But no more! Even though it seemed too late to make any difference, they were sick of playing it safe and chose to identify with Jesus in His death because they had missed the opportunity to identify with Him during His life.

Are you a closet Christian? Are you hiding your light under a bushel for fear of what others might say if you publicly gave allegiance to Jesus Christ?[3] Aren't you sick of it? Sick of being a phony? Sick of playing it safe when others are being criticized and ostracized for the very same faith you believe but are too afraid to confess? Isn't it time you threw caution to the wind and joined the fellowship of the unashamed?

In 1836, Colonel William Barret Travis commanded a ragtag army of 189 patriots who were defending the Alamo against the onslaught of the Mexican general, Santa Anna. With a Mexican army of four thousand troops surrounding the small mission outpost, General Santa Anna gave Colonel Travis an ultimatum—surrender or die. Travis assembled his weary men and, in a voice trembling with emotion, explained the total hopelessness of their predicament. He gave each one the opportunity to leave the Alamo and return safely to his home and family. Then, unsheathing his sword, he drew a line in the sand and challenged, "Those prepared to give their lives in freedom's cause, come over to me."[4] Without a moment's hesitation, every man who could do so stepped over the line. One man, Colonel James Bowie, lay sick with pneumonia, incapacitated on a cot and unable to stand or walk in his own strength. So Colonel Bowie, the one man who had not stepped over the line, asked that he be carried over. And so he was!

Colonel Travis then answered the general's ultimatum with a cannon shot. Twelve days later, all those inside the Alamo were massacred. They had crossed the line and given their lives to their cause.

In a similar way, Joseph and Nicodemus, by going to Pilate and requesting the body of Jesus, were crossing the line. They were giving their lives and reputations to Christ. Isn't it time you crossed the line too?

There must have been something very impressive about the "in-your-face" boldness of Joseph and Nicodemus as they made their request, because Pilate granted it without question or argument. Once he was assured that Jesus was indeed dead, Pilate released the body to them.[5]

As evening drew near, Joseph and Nicodemus went together to Calvary, the grim place of execution, and approached the cross on which the body of Jesus hung, limp and lifeless. Did they stand there at the foot of the cross, just for a moment, looking up at the mangled, blood-caked form, gazing on the face that even in death had not lost the deep, haggard furrows of agonized struggle and suffering? Were they overcome with the turmoil of their emotions—horror and gratitude and repulsion and love and rage and regret and the deepest grief they had ever known and the greatest sense of loss they had ever felt? Did they quietly pray, "Jesus, we thought You were the Messiah. We thought You were the Redeemer of Israel. We had even begun to believe You were God walking the earth in a man's body. Never did a Man speak like You,

or act like You,
or love like You,
or live like You,
or die like You!"

Perhaps they continued, "In a way we can't explain, even to ourselves, we feel we are indebted to You. What will the world do without You? *What will we do without You?* As late as our commitment is, we want to cross the line. Because of Your death, we give You our lives in service. Please accept us because we love You."

First, they would have gently extracted the spikes from His ankles. Then, using a ladder, they probably reached up to carefully pull the nails from His wrists, allowing His body to slump over onto their shoulders as they lovingly lowered Him to the ground. Using a veritable fortune of ointments Nicodemus had brought, "the two of them wrapped [the body], with the spices, in strips of linen." They must have carried the body of Jesus the short distance to a garden tomb "in which no one had ever been laid" (John 19:39–41). Lifting that precious burden, "Joseph took the body . . . and placed it in his own new tomb that he had cut out of the rock. He rolled a big stone in front of the entrance to the tomb and went away."[6]

The Facts Are Confirmed

Watching Joseph and Nicodemus from the shadows were several pairs of loving, red-rimmed eyes. Mary Magdalene, whose heart and lifestyle had been radically changed by Jesus; the apostle John's mother, Salome; Mary, the mother of James the younger and of Joses; and Mary, the mother of Jesus. All had kept a lonely vigil at the cross,[7] unable to tear themselves away from the gruesome, hellish scene. Not able to intervene, they simply huddled helplessly as close to Him in His suffering as they could, perhaps praying that their very presence would in some way be a source of comfort to Him in His agony.

The moment Jesus had bowed His head and given His life, a giant earthquake had shaken the earth and split the rocks in two. The terrified women had observed the reaction of the chief executioner. He had presided at countless crucifixions and had grown calloused to human suffering, yet, "when the centurion and those with him who were guarding Jesus saw the earthquake and all that had happened, they were terrified, and exclaimed, 'Surely he was the Son of God!'"[8]

Did Jesus' mother raise her hands and her face and cry to heaven in agreement, saying, "Yes! He *was* the Son of God! He was! I know He was! God, what are You doing? What does all this mean? Surely our hopes don't end here?" Deep down, in the farthest recesses of her spirit, was there a stirring, an impression, a thought, the whisper of a still, small Voice assuring her, "This isn't the end. This is just the beginning, Mary. This is Friday. Just you wait! *Sunday is coming!*"

Mary and the other women had waited for what must have seemed like forever. All the other bystanders had long since fled. Then, in the distance, they saw two men walking hurriedly toward the cross. Fresh fear must have momentarily gripped their hearts as they recognized two of the most prominent religious leaders in Israel—members of the very ruling body that had convicted Jesus of blasphemy and turned Him over to the Romans for execution! Surely the hatred of the Jews had been satisfied by His crucifixion! Surely they were not coming to abuse His lifeless body!

The women watched with sharply attentive eyes as Joseph and Nicodemus claimed the body. They could not have missed the tenderness with which the body was handled. Did they glance at each other wide-eyed, with unspoken questions on their lips? Surely they felt not only curious but also protective of the beloved body. So they followed silently as He was carried to the garden and laid in the tomb. They had not abandoned Him while He was on the cross, and they would not abandon Him now. They quietly observed that Joseph and Nicodemus were in a hurry, because "it was Preparation Day, and the Sabbath was about to begin."[9] With women's eyes for detail, they noted that because Joseph and Nicodemus were rushed, the anointing of the body had not been as meticulous as they felt it should have been. So, "they went home and prepared spices and perfumes. But they rested on the Sabbath in obedience to the commandment."[10] They tore themselves away from the close proximity to His body, with plans to return to the tomb early on the morning after the Sabbath and finish what Joseph and Nicodemus had done so hurriedly. As they slipped away into the encroaching gloom and darkness, they left Jesus not only dead but also buried—His body cold and silent and still.

All night long, the religious leaders must have tossed and turned on their wretched beds. They had a nagging thought, a preposterous premonition, that they weren't finished with Jesus. It had all been too easy for them. Sure, He had died the most agonizing death ever devised, and there was no doubt that He was dead. The Roman centurion, a professional at such things, had officially pronounced Him dead.[11] But somehow, some way, *could it be possible that . . . ?*

First thing Saturday morning, the religious leaders once again showed up on Pilate's doorstep. It's doubtful Pilate himself had slept very well, either, so he was willing to listen to their request, "Sir . . . we remember that while he was still alive that deceiver said, 'After three days I will rise again.' So give the order for the tomb to be made secure until the third day. Otherwise, his disciples may come and steal the body and tell the people that he has been raised from the dead. This last deception will be worse than the first."[12]

Did Pilate's heart skip a beat when he heard the Jews quote Jesus' words about the resurrection? Did he experience a white-hot pang of fear and sudden knowledge as the recent events seemed to click into place and make sense for the first time?

Quickly, almost urgently, before it became too late, Pilate gave instructions, "Take a guard. . . . Go, make the tomb as secure as you know how."[13] The religious leaders must have almost stumbled over each other in their haste to carry out his orders. They selected an elite Roman guard of four soldiers and posted them at the tomb with strict orders to keep watch twenty-four hours a day. The tomb itself was sealed by a rope that stretched across the stone covering the entrance. Each end of the rope was secured by clay to both sides of the opening. If anyone even tampered with the stone, from within or without, the clay would crack and the deed would be known. The religious leaders then left the guarded and sealed tomb, confidently satisfied that everything humanly possible had been done to ensure that Jesus remained buried within.

If the visible enemies of Jesus went to such extreme lengths to prevent even the rumor of His resurrection, what do you think was going on in the world of His invisible enemies? After all, Satan had been trying to stamp out the Son of God since the beginning of the human race.

Think about it: After Adam and Eve had sinned in the garden of Eden, God pronounced judgment, not just on them, but also on Satan, who had led them into it. He had said that in time, there would come the Seed of a woman who would crush Satan's head, delivering to him a fatal blow.[14] Since that prophecy, Satan had watched the sons of men with the predator's eye of a hawk. In the very next generation, he had orchestrated events by sowing discord and jealousy, until one of Eve's sons murdered the other one. Satan was after the Seed. But he missed. Abel wasn't the One.[15]

Satan then supernaturally mingled his own seed with that of the daughters of men until an evil race of beings provoked God's judgment, almost eradicating the entire human race in one disastrous, worldwide flood. Satan was after the Seed, but again he missed. Instead, Noah found favor in the eyes of the Lord, and the human race was preserved.[16]

Within a few generations, Satan mesmerized the human race through the charismatic leadership of Nimrod, who led the entire world in rebellion against God at the Tower of Babel. Once again God's judgment was provoked. But this time, instead of sending a flood, God effectively scattered the human race all over the globe so it could not continue to unite in rebellion against Him. He then singled out one man, Abraham, and called him to live a life of faith. If Abraham obeyed, God promised He would send a Seed through Abraham's family, through whom all the families of the earth would be blessed.[17]

Satan immediately began to focus his efforts on eradicating the Seed of Abraham's family. He set Ishmael against Isaac,[18] Esau against Jacob,[19] eleven brothers against Joseph,[20] and Pharaoh against all the children of Israel until they were enslaved and put into a position where all their male children were to be murdered.[21] Satan was after the Seed. But he missed. Next, God raised up a deliverer from Pharaoh's own household named Moses, who was used of God to save the Israelites and set them free.[22]

But Satan is a persistent devil! He attacked God's children through other nations, through idolatry, and finally, through captivity in Assyria and Babylon. Once again, he hatched a wicked scheme to massacre the entire exiled nation of Israel because he was still after the Seed. Once again he missed. Queen Esther's beauty and bravery were used for just such a time, and God's people effectively defended themselves from slaughter.[23]

As recently as Bethlehem, in reaction to a rumor that a king had been born, Satan had moved Herod to kill all the male babies two years old and younger in a sweeping ethnic cleansing that would surely net any little King.[24] Satan was after the Seed. But he missed—again!

Can you imagine the intense, cold-eyed gleam of concentrated attention Satan gave to the scene at the River Jordan, when an ordinary-looking Man presented Himself to John for baptism? As the young Carpenter from Nazareth came up out of the water, "at that moment heaven was opened, . . . and a voice from heaven said, 'This is my Son, whom I love; with him I am well pleased.'"[25] That Voice that sounded like thunder,[26] that Voice that sounded like rushing waters,[27] that Voice that was terrifyingly familiar to Satan, identified Jesus of Nazareth as the Seed!

Immediately, Satan went after Him in the wilderness. When Jesus resisted his temptations, Satan fled for a season,[28] but he continued to stab and thrust at Him through the religious leaders, fanning their jealousy into murderous hatred. In the end, Satan entered one of Jesus' own disciples, manipulating him to betray Jesus to those who would kill Him.[29] Perhaps fearful that Jesus would somehow once again slip through his death grip, Satan went after Him in the Garden of Gethsemane and came close to achieving his goal. But God sent an angel to strengthen Jesus against the onslaught, so that once again, Satan missed in his carefully aimed attack.[30]

When Satan finally managed to have Jesus pinned to the cross, he challenged and chided and commanded Him through others to come down.[31] But Jesus remained steadfastly on the cross until He had finished His Father's will. Now He was dead and buried. And we can only imagine the intensity—the energy—the immensity—the complexity—the enormity of Satan's effort to keep Jesus where He was! Every evil principality and power in the unseen world must have been massed over and under and around that garden tomb! Satan was no fool! He could remember God's pronouncement of judgment as if it had occurred yesterday! And he knew in his slippery, evil mind that *if* Jesus were raised from the dead, his own head would be bruised and his power would be destroyed for all time! He would be totally, absolutely, finally defeated,

God would have won the battle of the ages,
the sting of death would be removed,
the victory of the grave would be denied,
and Jesus would reign in absolute authority over everything!
Forever!

Today, the visible and invisible enemies of Jesus are still trying to keep Him buried even though they have been defeated. What efforts to keep Jesus buried have you seen?

Our modern-day culture tries to keep Him buried in the church.

The church keeps Him buried in traditions or rituals.

Churchgoers keep Him buried on the weekend like a holy hobby.

The religious masses keep Him buried as an icon of history.

The religious leaders keep Him buried in their programs.

The intellectuals keep Him buried in debate.

The agnostics keep Him buried in doubt.

Without consciously trying, have you been keeping Him buried yourself . . .

in neglect?

in excuses for sin?

in unbelief?

in selfishness and pride?

in alcohol?

in drugs?

in unconfessed sin?

The enemies of Jesus tried then, and are still trying today, to keep Him buried. *But . . .*

Early Sunday morning, before dawn, in the inky blackness of night, the soldiers stood guard over the tomb. Knowing that to go to sleep on duty was an offense punishable by death, the highly trained unit remained alert. Some may have been rolling dice, or telling ribald war stories, or stoking the fire to keep warm in the chilly predawn hours, but there was no question that all were awake and on duty. Their lives depended on it.

Suddenly, without warning, "there was a violent earthquake."[32] If, by chance, the soldiers had been distracted in their night watch, God now had their undivided attention! With the very ground on which they stood rocking and rolling beneath their cleated sandals, they anxiously looked around, swords unsheathed and ready. Almost simultaneously, the predawn darkness was split by a light so brilliant it looked like a laser of lightning! The "lightning" took the shape of an angel who seemed to reach from heaven to earth. Against the inky blackness of the night, the terrifyingly awesome being fearlessly descended, walked over to the stone that blocked the tomb's entrance, flicked it away as though it were dust,[33] and then sat on it![34] And the gaping hole where the stone had been, revealed there was nothing inside the tomb! *The tomb was empty!* Jesus had been buried in the tomb late Friday afternoon, but when the stone was rolled away early Sunday morning, *the tomb was empty!*

While no one saw or recorded exactly what must have taken place, the apostle Paul gives us a glimpse into what occurred. In his prayer for believers to know by their own experience God's "incomparably great power for us who believe," he penned a thrilling insight into the resurrection when he wrote, "That power is like the working of his mighty strength, which he exerted in Christ when he raised him from the dead and seated him at his right hand in the heavenly realms, far above all rule and authority, power and dominion, and every title that can be given, not only in the present age but also in the one to come."[35] God the Father split history in two when He flexed the divine, eternal muscle of His will and exerted His power on His Son's behalf! How He must have eagerly anticipated and rejoiced in the vindication and resurrection of His Son! His power was so mightily tremendous that Jesus was:

Raised up from the dead!
Raised up without our sin!
Raised up to life!
Raised up through the walls of the tomb!
Raised up past the guards!
Raised up through all His invisible enemies!
Raised up to a position of authority over the entire universe!
Raised up to be seated at the right hand of God!

Jesus was raised up!

He's alive!

HE'S ALIVE!

HE'S ALIVE!

PRAISE GOD! HE'S ALIVE! And nothing can ever be the same again!

The guards, an elite Roman unit chosen because they were hardened professionals who could not be bribed, intimidated, or frightened, "were so afraid . . . that they shook and became like dead men."[36] Whether they became frozen in fear at the stunning sight of the angel or they were knocked to the ground, unconscious, perhaps by the force of the resurrection or the radiation that may have been associated with it, the soldiers were totally incapacitated. Maybe they were struck immobile because of what they saw: Nothing! Nothing was inside the tomb! It was empty! Regardless of the reason, their ineffectiveness allowed God's handpicked witnesses to come and see the empty tomb, to confront the facts of the resurrection of Jesus Christ.

The Facts Are Confronted

The women who had been so faithfully vigilant at the cross during Jesus' six long hours of suffering returned together first thing Sunday morning to complete the embalming process that Joseph and Nicodemus had hastily done late Friday afternoon. "Just after sunrise, they were on their way to the tomb and they asked each other, 'Who will roll the stone away from the entrance of the tomb?'"[37]

More than likely, the tomb was a cave, carved out of rock, with a trenchlike groove running parallel to the front. The groove would have sloped down in such a way that the lower portion ended in front of the cave's entrance. A stone that was six to eight feet in diameter and one to two feet thick could easily be rolled like a giant wheel down the groove until it rested at the door of the tomb. A single person could have rolled the stone into place, since it would be a downhill effort. But to roll the stone away would have required several able-bodied men.

The sound of the women's voices could be heard on the brisk early morning air as they discussed the problem of how they would roll the stone away. They knew it would be impossible for them to accomplish, even if all of them pushed together. What stone, what *obstacle* is ahead of you that you think you can't move or get around, that blocks you from fulfilling your commitment to the Lord? Is it the stone of

financial limitations?
practical inexperience?
physical weakness?
intellectual smallness?
emotional instability?
social rejection?
professional inability?
personal inadequacy?
racial prejudice?

If we steadfastly cling to our faith in Him, persevering in our commitment to follow through with real obedience to His direction and call in our lives, He will roll away the stones for us! He will remove anything that hinders or blocks us from carrying out His will.

On that early spring morning so long ago, with the birds beginning to stir as they sang and called and chirped their greeting to that first Easter day, the women entered the garden and "saw that the stone had been removed from the entrance" (John 20:1). A gaping black hole existed where the stone should have been! They must have halted in midstride, their voices silenced in midsentence, as they stared at the impossible. Surely they let out a collective gasp, pointing with trembling fingers to what they could hardly believe they were seeing, clutching each other as they began to walk swiftly to the tomb. All but one.

Mary Magdalene took one look at that gaping hole, jumped to the conclusion that someone had stolen the body, turned on her heels, and ran all the way back to Jerusalem. If she had continued with the other women, she would have spared herself the added distress of imagining that His body had been stolen. Thus she did not know that "when they entered, they did not find the body of the Lord Jesus. While they were wondering about this, suddenly two men in clothes that gleamed like lightning stood beside them. In their fright the women bowed down with their faces to the ground, but the men said to them, 'Why do you look for the living among the dead? He is not here; he has risen!'"[38]

Come and see for yourself! Examine the facts for the resurrection! Here are just a few for your consideration:

- The guards saw the evidence and gave an independent report to the religious leaders, verifying it.[39]
- The religious leaders bribed the guards to lie, which would have been unnecessary if the tomb were not empty or if they could have produced the body.[40]
- The women, going early Sunday morning to anoint the body, met the risen Christ.[41]
- John and Peter saw the empty grave clothes in the tomb.[42] If someone had stolen the body, why would they have bothered to take the time to unwrap it first?
- Jesus appeared to Mary Magdalene, to Peter, to two disciples on the Emmaus Road, to ten disciples in an Upper Room, then to eleven disciples in an Upper Room on another occasion, and to five hundred at

once—all of whom were still living when the report was published and could have refuted it if it were untrue.[43]

- Jesus ate fish and bread, and allowed His disciples to touch Him to verify that He was not a spirit, but flesh and bone.[44]
- His resurrection was totally unexpected by His disciples. They were cowering in fear behind locked doors when He appeared to them, yet they were so convinced of the truth of His resurrection that they were willing to die for proclaiming it.[45] If the story were untrue and Jesus had not been raised from the dead, why would they have died for a lie? Or died for gossip?
- He was seen in heaven by Stephen just before Stephen was crushed to death by stones, and He was seen in heaven by Saul of Tarsus on the Damascus Road.[46]

Examine the evidence! Come and see for yourself the facts that confirm the bodily, historical resurrection of Jesus of Nazareth. There is more evidence for it than for any other historical event of that time period. And the evidence demands your verdict.

Mary Magdalene saw only one fact: The stone had been rolled away. It never entered her grief-stricken mind that Jesus had risen from the dead. So she ran all the way back to Jerusalem without bothering to examine the details. There, she banged furiously on the door to the Upper Room. When Peter and John opened the door, she breathlessly exclaimed, "They have taken the Lord out of the tomb, and we don't know where they have put him!" (John 20:2).

Without thoughtfully or prayerfully meditating on the facts she had confronted, Mary was quick to proclaim that what she had seen was not of God because it was so unexpected. God had intervened in a miraculous way, but she saw it as man's interference.

What practical evidence has God given you this past week as proof that Jesus is alive? Has He given you a specific answer to prayer? Has He spoken to you personally through His Word? And have you proclaimed it just a coincidence?

When Mary burst through the door, hysterically stammering something about grave robbers and the tomb being empty, Peter and John looked at each other in horrified astonishment. They both had the same thought and tore out the door, running through the early morning streets of Jerusalem until they came to the garden. John "outran Peter and reached the tomb first. He bent over and looked in at the strips of linen lying there but did not go in" (John 20:4–5). In a matter of moments, Peter charged up and into the tomb. Panting heavily, he looked wildly around and "saw the strips of linen lying there, as well as the burial cloth that had been around Jesus' head. The cloth was folded up by itself, separate from the linen" (John 20:6–7). Peter confronted the evidence, but he was confused. At that instant, he must have been angrier than ever. He must have surmised that the enemies of Jesus had dared to crucify Him, and now they had cruelly taken the body for who knew what purpose! Peter was like a keg of dynamite, ready to explode as he left the scene without any comprehension of what had really taken place.

As Peter exited, John quietly looked around. He noticed that the grave clothes were totally unlike those of Lazarus, which had been just a pile of stinking rags by the time Martha had finished unwrapping him. These grave clothes were lying, not as though someone had removed them from the body, but as though the body were still inside! The face cloth was situated where the face would have been, with the few inches of the neck separating it from the rest of the shroud. As he thoughtfully studied the evidence, it must have gradually dawned on him that the grave clothes looked like an empty cocoon! They looked as though the body had just evaporated up through them! *Then John knew!* (John 20:8). The body hadn't evaporated. Jesus had risen from the dead! *He was alive!*

Even though he had seen the facts, John was still confused. He just "did not understand from Scripture that Jesus had to rise from the dead" (John 20:9). It's not enough to come and see the facts of the resurrection. You can have lots of head knowledge of Bible truth, you can be raised in a Christian home and have heard it all your life, you can even have theological seminary degrees and still come to the wrong conclusion and be more confused than ever if you stop with just the facts. You must meet and know the risen Christ personally.

MEET AND KNOW THE RISEN CHRIST

Following Peter, John left the tomb and went back to join the other disciples. In the meantime, Mary walked slowly back from Jerusalem to the garden. Her feet must have felt like leaded weights, her heart must have felt as though it were constricted in a vise, and her eyes must have stared glassily ahead without seeing. The past few hours had commenced and concluded so suddenly! So swiftly! So shockingly! She must have had a huge struggle just adjusting to the surprise of it all. As she walked, did she look back over the memories of the last few years . . . ?

She had once been possessed of seven demons.[47] Was she remembering the fear . . . the rage . . . the torment . . . the depression . . . the jealousy . . . the immorality . . . the misery that had been hers in a lifetime of bondage that had seemed so far, far away but was now returning with an acute awareness? Did the old burden of filthy guilt, the old impulse of self-destruction, the old bondage of enslavement by evil come back to her as she trudged to the garden tomb? Were the sin and memories of her past beginning to cling to her once again like loathsome things?

Mary Magdalene had been set free from her sin and her tormentors and her self the day she met Jesus. Was she already beginning to feel the loss of her freedom? With His death, she had no peace and purpose in her life. She knew without Him she would never be anything other than what she had been—a desperate, hopeless, helpless, hell-bent sinner.

As she worked her way through the crowds that were packing up and beginning to trudge home after the Passover celebration, did she reflect on the first time she had met Jesus? How, among the throngs of people, had He happened to notice her? And would she ever forget the searing hope that gripped her heart as she came under His gaze? Had she trembled in fear as she sensed the supernatural power of His Person? Had she spewed uncontrollable venom in His direction as the demons within her frantically squirmed and resisted His authority, which they also recognized?[48] Yet when He had addressed them in a Voice that was terrifyingly familiar, commanding them to leave, they had! Just like that!

The struggle of a lifetime had ceased, and she had been set free. Free to love God and enjoy Him and serve Him and follow Him in the person of His dear Son. For the first time in her horrible, dysfunctional life, she had known real peace and joy and fulfillment and understanding and acceptance. Jesus had seen her—a person who was spiritually deformed and twisted by the enemy—yet He had looked past the obvious to the potential of the person she was meant to be. And He had loved her. For the first time in her life she had a reason for living. And *He was her reason . . .*

Following that first encounter, He had never again brought up her past. Instead, He had given her the feeling He had forgotten about it.[49] He had convinced her she was of great value and precious in God's sight.[50] He had lifted her up from the quicksand of sin that had kept her mired in defeat and depression, He had set her feet on a firm foundation of God's grace and mercy, and He had caused her to walk with her head held high under the banner of His truth and love![51] Oh, how she loved her Lord![52]

All that He had done for her and all that He was to her had made her nightmare that much blacker when she had heard the rioting early Friday morning at the Hall of Judgment. She had recognized some of the voices. They were sickeningly familiar. They were the voices of her seven former tormentors, joined by a legion of others, all shouting, "Crucify Him! Crucify Him!" And she had fallen into a whirlpool that threatened to suck out her insides when she learned that it was His blood for which they were screaming! As she ran to the city center, stumbling over the uneven cobblestones, tripping over the hem of her own garments, had she desperately sobbed, "God, no! No! Don't let it be so! God, help us!"?

She had plunged into the bloodthirsty mob until she was caught up in the flow of it, pressed in on all sides by heaving, shoving, angry bodies as they followed His bloody trail up Calvary. Here and there, she had glimpsed other horror-stricken faces, but any protest they might have made was drowned out by the rising tidal wave of maniacal hate. She had stood at a distance from the cross, unable to bear a closer look at the inhuman brutality and cruelty of His execution.[53] The humiliating shame and excruciating pain that He bore were like a living thing that lacerated her very soul. She could not bear to watch, yet she had been unable to tear herself away. She was still there when the air was split by the startling strength and clarity of His triumphant cry, "It is finished!" She had seen His body go limp—and with it her entire life. Her hope, her joy, her peace, her reason for living had crashed and shattered at the foot of that blood-stained cross.

Yet she had stayed. She had joined the other women in their lonely vigil of grief. She had watched with anxious worry as Joseph and Nicodemus had taken the beloved body from the cross, and she had followed them, slipping softly through the darkness to learn where His body would be laid. When the embalming process had seemed rushed, her grieving heart had seized on something she could do for Him in His death, and she had planned some way, somehow, to finish the process as soon as she was able on Sunday morning. All Friday evening and Saturday and Saturday evening she must have comforted herself by looking forward to Sunday morning when she could do something for Him, even if only to pay final homage to Him by anointing His dead body.

But now, *now,* her world that had been smashed on a Roman cross was trampled into a thousand pieces by the violation of Jesus' tomb! As she neared the garden, her eyes swam with tears. She knew she was on the verge of total emotional disintegration as she "stood outside the tomb crying. As she wept, she bent over to look into the tomb and saw two angels in white, seated where Jesus' body had been" (John 20:11–12). While the angels may have paralyzed the elite Roman guard, they didn't seem to faze Mary when they inquired, "Woman, why are you crying?" (John 20:13).

Mary's reply is one that is echoed by God's people throughout the church today, "They have taken my Lord away . . . and I don't know where they have put him" (John 20:13). Have you heard the heart cries of those like Mary, even within the church, sobbing out, "God, You used to be in my life—where are You now? I long to be near You. I long to know Your presence and feel Your love in my life, but they have taken You away and I no longer know where to find You." Is her cry, *your* cry? "God, just give me Jesus. *Please!*"

The angels didn't verbally respond to Mary. Instead, they must have looked intently past her, watching something over her shoulder. Sensing Someone standing behind her, she followed their gaze, and saw "Jesus standing there, but she did not realize that it was Jesus" (John 20:14). He was right there, in her life, and she didn't know it! He had come to her, and she didn't recognize Him!

Could it be, as you search for Jesus, that He is with you? Now? Beside you as you read this, drawing your attention to His Word that He might reveal Himself to you?

Mary straightened up as she turned to face Him, and the question Jesus challenged her with is one that resounds in our day: "Woman . . . why are you crying? Who is it you are looking for?" (John 20:15).

Today, with all of our liberation and feminization and equalization and assertion and recognition, women are still unhappy! We are still "crying." The high rate of divorce and drug dependency, of abortion and alcoholism, of immorality and therapy reflect the tears of a generation of women who are looking for Someone. And our Lord's gentle voice still prods, "Woman, why are you crying? What's missing in your life? Why are you so empty? What are you looking for? *Who* are you looking for?"

With tears running down her cheeks and blurring her vision, Mary jumped to another conclusion. She thought He was just a man.[54] She thought "he was the gardener." She begged Him, "Sir, if you have carried him away, tell me where you have put him, and I will get him" (John 20:15). How she expected to do that, only Mary knew! She just wanted to be near the body of her beloved Lord.

Then the One who was her Shepherd called her by name, "Mary" (John 20:16). Her head must have snapped up as her eyes focused sharply on the "gardener." We can only imagine the electrified shock that caused every taut, frayed nerve in her body to tingle as she recognized her Shepherd's voice and saw, with her own eyes, her Shepherd's face!

There, standing before her, was *Jesus! Alive!* In His physical body, with the fresh wounds on His brow where the thorns had been and the fresh wounds in His hands and feet where the nails had been! *He was alive!* How could it be? But He was! And she flung her arms around Him, and cried, "Rabboni!" (John 20:16).

As she clung to Him and felt His flesh and bones and *life*, she knew He was more than she ever had thought Him to be! Never again would she be empty or lonely, loveless or lifeless, hopeless or helpless, captured or condemned because He was alive! Heaven was opened for her!

And that's where many of us long to be—in the arms of the risen Lord. That's where many of us long to *stay*! But when we truly come and see the facts of the resurrection for ourselves, when we meet and know the risen Christ personally, we are compelled to go and tell the glorious good news to someone else.

Go and Tell the Good News

As Mary clung to Him, Jesus must have gently unwound her arms from around His neck as He instructed, "Do not hold on to me, for I have not yet returned to the Father. Go instead to my brothers and tell them, 'I am returning to my Father and your Father, to my God and your God'" (John 20:17). In other words, "Mary, go tell My brothers I'm going home! My home is your home because My Father is your Father, and My God is your God. Mary, go tell my brothers—'welcome to the family!'"

What unbearable agony it must have been to tear herself away from the comfort and sweetness of His presence, but she had been commanded to go and tell. He was alive, and He was her Lord. She had no option!

I wonder if Mary had any recollection of her return to Jerusalem? With her feet racing in her excitement to tell others, her mind still tumbling with astonished thoughts, her heart overflowing in ecstatic joy, her face radiating in the reflected glow of His risen glory, she burst into that Upper Room where eleven desperate men had gathered. And Mary's day, which had begun with such hopeless despair, ended with the thrilling proclamation of her personal discovery: "I have seen the Lord!" (John 20:18).

Nothing would ever be the same again! When Jesus died on the cross, He took our sins upon Himself, offering us forgiveness through His shed blood and eternal life through His resurrection! All we have to do is place our hands of faith in His hand at the cross as we claim Him as our Savior, then follow Him as our Lord—right through heaven's gate! Praise God! Jesus makes heaven available to sinners like Mary and you and me! Heaven is our home because we are now members of His family!

When was the last time that you, like Mary, shared the glorious good news of the gospel of Jesus Christ? Have you felt inadequate and ill prepared because you don't have a seminary degree? Did you think you had to have a pat on the head from some bishop in your church? All Mary had in order to be qualified to share the gospel was a personal encounter with the risen Lord Jesus Christ and a command to tell others that He's alive and He's Lord!

We *cannot* have a genuine, personal encounter with the risen Christ and either remain the same or remain silent. We are not only commanded, but we are also *compelled* to go and tell a despairing, depressed, doomed world . . .

Our sins are all forgiven,
heaven's gates are opened wide!
He's alive! *He's alive! HE'S ALIVE!*
Praise God for giving us the *living* Lord Jesus Christ!

Unlike Mary's encounter with the risen Christ, my own initial encounter was by faith, but it was just as real as Mary's. I don't remember the exact date, but I know that I was a young girl. I had watched an old black-and-white Cecil B. De Mille film on the life of Jesus titled *King of Kings*. As I watched the crucifixion scene unfold on an Easter Sunday long ago, I began to weep. I knew Jesus had died for me. My wise mother recognized my tears, not as those of pity for a brutalized man, but as tears of conviction in a little girl's heart for the sin that had nailed Him to the cross. And so my mother led me in prayer as I confessed my sin to God and told Him I was sorry. I thanked Jesus for dying for my sin and asked God to forgive me and cleanse me with the blood of Jesus.[55] I told Him I believed Jesus had risen from the dead, and I invited Him to come live in my heart. I don't remember any dramatic sensation afterward. But I knew my sin had been forgiven, I knew I had been born again, and I knew I would go to heaven when I died. And that prayer began a love relationship with Jesus that is more real to me than any other.

Yet as a young bride and young mother, I drifted from the Lord I loved. I didn't drift intentionally or willfully but just because I was busy and distracted by all the responsibilities that were mine. I was immersed in small talk and small toys and small clothes and small, sticky fingerprints. One day as I lost my patience with my oldest child, I was shocked to realize, like Mary, that "they have taken my Lord away and I don't know where they have put him." I had become so preoccupied with my family, so wrapped up in myself, that I had neglected my relationship with Him. And it seemed as though He had become lost to me.

As I cried out with an overwhelming feeling of homesickness for God, He caused me to see others, who, for various reasons, were in my same predicament. I saw friends and neighbors who seemed to have it all together on the outside, but I questioned their serenity on the inside. I wondered if they felt the Lord was lost to them too.

Around the same time, my husband and I were invited to the Lausanne Congress on Evangelism in Switzerland. As we attended the plenary sessions and mingled with evangelical leaders from all over the world who were exploring ways to take the gospel to the ends of the earth, I was ashamed to admit I had never taken it to my next-door neighbors!

When I returned home, I acted quickly before I lost the nerve. I invited a dozen neighbors to my home for coffee with the intention of telling them about God's love in Christ. Only four showed up! After an hour of small talk, I nervously presented such an awkward testimony that to this day, none of them remember it! But it was a watershed experience for me. I had crossed over the line.

Following that day, I began reading my Bible and praying on a regular basis. One afternoon I was led to the passage of Revelation 3:8 by my godly mother-in-law. The words almost sprang off the page as God seemed to speak to me, calling me into service, "Anne, I know your deeds, and you haven't done much. Like all young mothers, you only have a little strength. But you have kept My word and have not denied your identification with Me. Therefore, I am placing before you an open door for service that no one can shut." I knew the open door was an opportunity to establish and teach a weekly Bible class for women in my city. I also knew that when God sets before us an open door, He means for us to walk through it. Which I did. The class immediately exploded as five hundred women came to study God's Word together. As a result of the hours of disciplined study that I had to give in order to teach, my love relationship with the Lord was reestablished. I had found Him where He had been all the time—in His Word.

I had been teaching that weekly Bible class for twelve years when God seemed to speak dramatically to me through Deuteronomy 1:3, 6–7: "Anne, in your fortieth year, on the first day of the eleventh month, . . . tell these people you have stayed long enough at this mountain. Break camp and advance." I knew He was telling me to leave the class. But because I knew I had been in God's will as I taught the class, and because it had become so entwined with my love relationship with Him, I asked God to confirm His call. He led me to Acts 26:16–18: "Now get up and stand on your feet. I have appeared to you to appoint you as a servant and as a witness of what you have seen of me and what I will show you . . . I am sending you out . . . into an itinerant ministry that will take you around the world" (my paraphrase). And I knew if He was my Lord, I had no option but to obey. And so on the first day of the eleventh month of my fortieth year, April 1, 1988, I announced to the class I would be leaving. And at the close of that class year, I did.

For twelve years I have gone wherever I felt God was sending me, given out messages from His Word I felt He has put on my heart, and addressed whomever He has placed in front of me. I know I am called to be His servant first, then a witness of the things He has shown me from His Word.

As I went into the world in answer to His call, one of the first opportunities I took was to address a pastors' convention. There were approximately eight hundred pastors in attendance although at the time it looked to me like eight thousand. They were seated around tables in a banquet-type setting that seemed to stretch as far as the eye could see. When I stood up in the pulpit, many of them turned their chairs around and put their backs to me! Those who faced me did so with such hostile expressions of rejection that I was confused and ashamed. When I concluded my message, I was shaking. I crawled away in my spirit. I was hurt and surprised that godly men would find what I was doing so offensive that they would stage such a demonstration, especially when I was an invited guest.

When I went home, I told the Lord that I had never had a problem with women in ministry, or with women sharing God's Word when men were present, but now I did. The problem those pastors obviously had was now my problem too. And so I humbly asked God to convict me if I was out of His will, or to confirm His call once again. The story of Mary Magdalene came to mind. When she encountered the risen Christ, He told her to go to Jerusalem and tell eleven *men* what she had seen and heard. Jesus also commanded the other women who had gone to the tomb that early Sunday morning, to go and tell the disciples not only their personal testimony about their experience with the risen Christ but also His Word instructing them to go to Galilee.[56] I concluded, therefore, that Jesus Himself did not have a problem with women either sharing their personal testimony or His Word when men were in the audience.

Then God led me to Jeremiah 1:9, 17–19, where once again I heard His voice say, "I have put My words in your mouth. . . . You are not responsible for the reaction of the audience, you are only responsible for your faithfulness to give out the message I have put on your heart. Prepare yourself and arise, and speak to them all that I command you. Do not be dismayed before their faces or their backs, lest I dismay you before them. Anne, you are not accountable to your audience; you are accountable to Me . . . They will fight against you, but they will not prevail against you, for I am with you to deliver you." I felt rebuked, encouraged, and challenged as God once again confirmed His call in my life.

God had seemed to answer my questions clearly. But before putting the matter behind me, I asked Him for help in understanding 1 Timothy 2:12, where Paul forbids "a woman to teach or to have authority over a man." As I meditated prayerfully on that passage, God revealed to me that the emphasis was on the "authority over a man." Therefore, I believe He has forbidden me to teach or preach from a *position of authority* over a man. Practically speaking, this means He has closed the door to me for ordination in ministry or for the senior pastorate. So when I speak, I speak as a woman who is not *in authority*. Instead, I am a woman who is *under authority*! And I speak with the authority that comes, not from any position I hold, but from the Person I know—the risen, living Lord who has commanded me to go and tell!

Not only has Jesus Christ set me free to go and tell, not only has He called me to go and tell, but I am *compelled* by the very fact that He's alive! *And He is Lord!*

Heaven is now available to the sinner! *Anyone* can take His hand at the cross and enter heaven's gate! Like Jeremiah, I cry out, "His word is in my heart like a burning fire shut up in my bones. I am weary of holding it in; indeed, I cannot."[57] And I testify with Peter and John to any religious authority, "I cannot help speaking about what I have seen and heard."[58] Because He's alive!

He's alive!

HE'S ALIVE!

HE'S ALIVE!

HE'S ALIVE!

14

JESUS MAKES HEAVEN AVAILABLE . . .

To the Failure

JOHN 21

At the beginning of my teaching ministry, I had the opportunity to attend an institute for Christian leaders. As I sat in the first session, not knowing what to expect, I studied those who were sitting around me. Each one, I noted, was physically attractive, stylishly dressed, and efficiently equipped with Bible, notebook, and pen. Everyone seemed friendly, knowledgeable, and eager to sharpen his or her leadership skills. When we broke into smaller groups, the quality of the men and women in attendance became apparent in the lively intellectual exchange of biblical insights, coupled with heart knowledge of God. As I became more and more aware of those around me, I became less and less confident of myself. What was I doing in such gifted spiritual company? I felt woefully inadequate and out of place.

The primary speaker at the institute was a godly, elderly Bible teacher whose British accent made anything he said sound profound. As I listened to him present God's Word, I became increasingly alert to the fact that God seemed to be speaking through him. There was no longer any doubt of it in my mind when he asked those of us gathered what we thought God expected of us. As he paused for us to consider our answers, I was thinking to myself, "obedience," "holiness," "faithfulness," along with other characteristics and fruit of the Spirit. In that brief moment, I reflected on my life's journey—a journey in which I have been confronted not only with the expectations of God, but also with the expectations of others. Even after a casual introduction, I have had people argue over whether I looked more like my mother or my father, then express disappointment that I had been different from what they had *expected.* And then there are those who expect me to speak with a certain delivery, dress with a certain style, mingle with a particular group, know certain facts; the list of expectations is endless. Increasingly during my teenage years, I came to realize how difficult it is to try and measure up to the expectations of others.

By the summer of my seventeenth year, I found myself bound and frustrated by the expectations of others. I was living my life to please everybody and disappoint nobody. Finally, a friend got hold of me and told me I was looking at God through a prism. He explained that my relationship with God was colored and distorted by the opinions of other people. He encouraged me to look at God directly. From that day forward, I decided to live to please God, and God alone. I knew if He was pleased with me, those I cared most about, such as my parents and grandparents and siblings and closest friends, would be pleased too. Other people might not be pleased, but I was already learning through hard experience that I couldn't please everyone anyway.

Years later, during that institute for Christian leaders, I was intrigued when the elderly Bible teacher asked, "What do you think God expects of you?" I truly wanted to know because I was living my life to please God. I desperately cared about trying to live up to His expectations.

After allowing us just a moment to meditate, the speaker once again inquired, "Do you know what God expects of you?" After another pause, he answered his own question in a way I have never forgotten. To a hushed audience, he replied simply, "Failure!"

I was stunned! I just stared at him in wide-eyed astonishment. Surely he would explain himself! He then repeated, "All God ever expects of *you* is failure."

I wanted to raise my hand, wave it wildly, and shout, "I can live up to the expectations of God! I know how to fail!" But before I could respond so enthusiastically, with a smile tugging at the corners of his mouth and a twinkle in his eye, he said firmly, "*But* . . . God has given you the Holy Spirit so that you need never fail."

Bingo! I knew he had nailed the secret to living the Christian life successfully. God would never expect more from me than the Holy Spirit would do in and through me if I would allow Him the freedom.

What a blessed relief to be reminded that God knows me—in fact, He knows me so well He understands that apart from Him I can do nothing.[1]

I don't have to prove myself to God.

I don't have to worry about disappointing God.

I don't have to earn His respect.

I don't have to deserve His blessings.
I don't have to work hard to be accepted.
I don't have to produce a quota.
I don't have to be successful.

He created me in the first place. "He knows how [I] am formed, he remembers that [I] am dust."[2] I am just a little dust person infused with the very breath of God![3]

Just like me, Peter was a failure. He had failed miserably to grasp the will of God when it was revealed to him, and he had brashly told Jesus He wasn't going to the Cross.[4] He had slept when he should have prayed, and he had almost provoked a massacre in the garden when he single-handedly tried to take on the Roman army and sliced off Malchus's ear.[5] He had repeatedly sworn that even if all the other disciples forsook Jesus, he would die for Him—then he denied three times that very day that he even knew Him.[6] There was no doubt in his mind or anyone else's that he was a miserable, habitual failure.

Do you feel like a failure? Have you been discouraged in your Christian life or your Christian leadership to the point of quitting? Do you feel you're just not cut out for this sort of thing? Then praise God! He has a place for you in His kingdom, because Jesus makes heaven available to the failure.

RECALLED AFTER FAILURE

Following Peter's dismal display of disloyalty during the trials of Jesus, his spirit had been shattered by guilt and bitterness.[7] In his misery and humiliation, he had isolated himself from the other disciples. But early Sunday morning, when the women discovered the empty tomb, they were instructed by the angel to, "Go, tell his disciples *and Peter*" that He is risen.[8] And when Cleopas and his companion encountered the risen Christ on the road to Emmaus, they ran all the way back to Jerusalem to breathlessly announce to the disciples gathered, "It is true! The Lord has risen and has appeared *to Simon*."[9]

God made a concerted effort to tenderly reassure Peter individually that he was not only loved by God but that he would still be used by God as a channel of blessing to others. So following the resurrection, Peter was instructed, along with the other disciples, to meet Jesus in Galilee, where he was recalled to a life of discipleship.

Peter and the other disciples obeyed the Lord's instructions and went to Galilee where they waited for Jesus to join them. And they waited. And they waited. And they *waited*... Finally, impulsive, compulsive Peter had had enough! He was not the type to sit idly around, reading magazines, completing crossword puzzles, clipping coupons, watching ESPN, and just chilling out. He hated to wait. So he announced to the others, "I'm going out to fish." And since they had grown tired of waiting, too, they said, "'We'll go with you.' So they went out and got into the boat, but that night they caught nothing" (John 21:3).

I hate to wait too. I hate to wait for a traffic light to turn green,
for the doctor to see me,
for the telephone to ring,
for investments to produce,
for the copier to warm up,
for seeds to grow,
for the fax to go through,
for answers to prayer . . .

I just hate to wait. Period. Waiting is so hard, especially when I am waiting on the Lord. Sometimes He seems to be *s-o-o-o s-l-o-w*. But waiting is an essential part of spiritual discipline. It can be the ultimate test of our faith.

If we wait on God, we will be blessed. If we grow impatient with waiting and take matters into our own hands, we will be in trouble. Isaiah wisely encouraged those who are waiting on God to consider others who have waited on Him when he pointed out, "Since ancient times no one has heard, no ear has perceived, no eye has seen any God besides you, who acts on behalf of those who wait for him."[10]

Throughout the Bible, we are given examples of those who waited and were blessed, as well as those who refused to wait and suffered the consequences. For instance:

Abraham had to wait for the birth of Isaac; he grew so impatient, he tried to help God out and had Ishmael instead. His impatience delayed God's blessing for another fourteen years and produced turmoil that exists to this day.

Jacob had to wait for God to bless him. His impatience that had caused him to steal the birthright from his brother almost cost him his life, and it did cost him twenty years in exile.

Joseph had to wait thirteen years in slavery and imprisonment for God's deliverance. But God rewarded his patience by elevating him to the second highest position in Egypt.

Joshua had to wait seven days as he obediently marched around Jericho before God rewarded his patience and brought the walls down.

David, an anointed king, waited fourteen years in exile before God rewarded his patience by placing him on the throne as the greatest king of Israel. From personal experience he testified, "I am still confident of this: I will see the goodness of the LORD in the land of the living. Wait for the LORD; be strong and take heart and wait for the LORD."[11]

Israel waited for the Messiah to come. Mary waited nine months for Jesus' birth. Jesus waited for the woman of Samaria to come to the well, Mary and Martha waited for Jesus to come to Bethany, and Jesus Himself waited three days in the tomb for the resurrection. A person who lives in submissive obedience to Christ is a person who is often called to wait.

Are you waiting on God for something? What plans have you made in the meantime? Who else have you involved in those plans? Is there someone else, a mother-in-law or pastor or best friend, who is leading you to join him or her in decisive action? Instead of blindly saying, "I'll go with you," take a moment to pray and ask God for His direction. Be alert, especially if it involves something that was closely identified with your life before you became a disciple of Jesus.

I wonder if Jesus delayed joining His disciples in Galilee on purpose in order to test their patience and obedient commitment to His call in their lives. If so, Peter failed the test. Because he returned to his old lifestyle.

Recalled after Returning to the Past

As Peter pushed the boat off from shore, heaving in the anchor, did he hear the creak of the wooden timbers and the snap of the billowing sails? Did he breathe deeply of the fresh sea air and feel the cool spray of water in his face? Did he smell the pungent odor of fish and feel the coarse texture of the nets and remember all those earlier years of fishing on the Sea of Galilee with a nostalgia that bordered on longing? Peter seems to have gone back to the old lifestyle from which Jesus had called him.

After dramatic failure in your commitment to live for Christ, have you slipped back into your old lifestyle? Have you begun hanging out in the old clubs, spending time with your old friends, speaking with your old vocabulary, getting involved in some old projects, and just generally going backward? And have you enjoyed your initial return, feeling at home among the old and familiar things of your past?

Very probably Peter immensely enjoyed those first moments back on the boat. It must have felt good to be back on those rolling decks again. But the joy was short-lived. As the hours went by, Peter found himself fishing all night, yet catching nothing (John 21:3). He must have begun to have an uneasy feeling of "déjà vu." He had been there, done that three years earlier. Now here he was again, repeatedly repositioning the boat as he held the torchlight high and peered futilely through the night darkness into the water, casting the nets and pulling them in empty again and again, all to no avail. Except that the fruitless effort must have served to jar his memory . . .

Three years earlier, Peter had been washing his nets when Jesus had interrupted his life. After using his boat as a floating pulpit in order to speak to the crowds that lined the shore, Jesus told Peter, "Put out into deep water, and let down the nets for a catch."[12] Peter protested because he knew the fish weren't biting that day because he had been out all night and hadn't caught a thing. Besides that, he was a professional fisherman who knew his business. But because it was Jesus who asked, Peter finally agreed. And when he followed the Lord's instructions, he caught so many fish that his boat began to sink. His reaction was unexpected. He fell on his knees before Jesus and begged Him to get out of his life! He knew Jesus was more than a man and was so impacted by the demonstration of His power that he felt an overwhelming conviction of sin. Jesus comforted the guilt-ridden Peter and told him not to be afraid because He had a plan for his life.

Later, Jesus was passing by when Peter and his brother Andrew were casting their nets into the lake. He issued a life-changing challenge: "Come, follow me . . . and I will make you fishers of men."[13] And Peter, without even a moment's hesitation, dropped his nets, jumped out of his boat, left everything, and followed Jesus.

So much had happened since that day. He had seen the lame walk, and the blind see, and the hungry fed, and the lepers cleansed, and the demoniacs set free, and the dead raised. How could he go *back*? Back to *where* he had been before, back to *what* he had been before, back to *who* he had been before. Fishing wasn't a sport or a hobby to Peter; it was a business. It was the way he had made his living. And Jesus had clearly called him to leave it in order to follow Him in a life of faith and discipleship. Now, what was Peter doing, going *back*? Did he think that with Jesus gone he would have to depend on himself for his needs and this would be a good way to bring in the necessary income? Whatever Peter may have thought, it is obvious he was in danger of sliding out of God's will and dragging at least six other disciples with him.

It had been a long, weary, frustrating, fruitless night. Did Peter increasingly come to the conviction during the night that this was *not* what he wanted or was called to do? He no longer found even a shred of satisfaction in fishing and going about his business as usual. His life had changed radically in the last three years, and it was not for the purpose of going *backward.* He did not ever again want to do anything without Jesus! Had God allowed Peter to get into this situation in order to bring him to the clear, firm, once-and-for-all decision to reject his old way of life?

Even as you read this, are you frustrated with the emptiness and weariness and fruitlessness of where you are? Have you increasingly lost your joy in the things that used to give you pleasure? Is there a nagging dissatisfaction in your soul and an intense longing to feel the presence of Jesus once again in your life? Could it be that God is preparing your heart to hear His call to discipleship once again?

Recalled after Rejecting the Past

As Peter and the other disciples headed back toward land, their weariness must have been more than just physical. As they scanned the shoreline through the early morning mist, they noticed a Man standing at the edge of the sea, but "did not realize that it was Jesus" (John 21:4). Were they blinded by their sweat? Were they trying so hard to be good fishermen, trying so hard to be successful on their own, that they just didn't notice Him?

Like any interested bystander, the Man "called out to them, 'Friends, haven't you any fish?'" (John 21:5). Peter must have felt like cursing under his breath. Leave it to a stranger to rub it in! The last thing he needed was someone pointing out another failure in his life. But he answered civilly, as well as honestly, "No" (John 21:5).[14]

If Peter's memory of his first encounter with Christ had not already been jarred, it surely was when the Man commanded, "Throw your net on the right side of the boat and you will find some" (John 21:6). Peter did not receive any intellectual, philosophical, theological, or technical explanation about water currents and wind velocity and net design and fish bait. The Man's instructions were simple and to the point: "Just fish My way. Obey My Word if you want to be successful. I know where the fish are."

The disciples had tried everything else, so Peter must have shrugged, thinking, *Why not? What have we got to lose?* When they followed the Man's instructions, "they were unable to haul the net in because of the large number of fish" (John 21:6).

With bodies sweating
and nets bulging
and fish flapping
and men yelling

and general pandemonium breaking out on the little fishing vessel, John stood and stared hard at the Man on the shore. And it came to him in a flash of understanding. This was no ordinary catch and this was no ordinary Man! Then he blurted out, "It's the Lord!" (John 21:7). Peter's head must have snapped to attention, and with one motion he "wrapped his outer garment around him (for he had taken it off) and jumped into the water" in his haste to be with Jesus (John 21:7). Was Peter's swift reaction the result of wrestling all night, not just with the nets, but also with himself and his purpose in life? Did it reflect his adamant rejection of ever going back to fishing for *fish* instead of fishing for *men*? Was he now ready to put his past failure behind him and eagerly seize the opportunity to wholeheartedly recommit his life to live for Jesus?

As Peter splashed eagerly to shore, "the other disciples followed in the boat, towing the net full of fish" (John 21:8). All of them must have realized how empty and futile their attempt at fishing had been. They needed to be refilled by Jesus Himself.

REFILLED AFTER FAILURE

As the disciples guided the boat, they would have felt it bump and scrape bottom in the shallow water. Jumping out, they must have pulled and hauled on the ropes, dragging the boat that had become exceptionally heavy with the enormous catch of fish, until they had it safely secured on the beach. Looking up, "they saw a fire of burning coals there with fish on it, and some bread" (John 21:9). Where did that fish come from? And was that the wonderful aroma of bread baking? Who made it? Before they could ask, the familiar, beloved Voice they knew so well instructed, "Bring some of the fish you have just caught" (John 21:10).

Refilled through Fellowship

Peter quickly obeyed. He plunged back into the water and dragged the net bursting with fish toward the shore. We can imagine the disciples laughing and jostling each other as they gathered around, grabbed the slippery fish, and tossed them one by one onto the sandy shore, counting as they did so. To their astonishment, their catch totaled 153 large fish! What was even more astounding was the fact that with such a heavy load, the net had not been broken or even torn (John 21:11). Their night of frustration and defeat had ended in incredible success. Yet it must have been obvious to each of them that the difference between their failure and success was Jesus.

As Peter enjoyed the moment with the other disciples in Jesus' presence, there must have been a sweetly satisfying sense of fellowship. Peter had been on a roller-coaster ride that had carried him from the shameful depths of his denial, from the agony of the cross, and the despair of the tomb to the ecstasy of the resurrection. His emotions must have been, at the very least, fractured. Surely, the triumph of the successful catch, the teamwork that was necessary to haul it in, and the joy of savoring the special moment with his best friends must have been like a balm to Peter's wounded spirit.

If you have failed, have you given in to your shame by withdrawing from other believers? Have you stopped going to church or attending Bible study? One of the ways God refills us after failure is through the blessing of Christian fellowship. Just experiencing the joy of simple activities shared with other children of God can have a healing effect on us.

Peter was refilled, not only by fellowship with the Lord and the other disciples, but also by the food Jesus prepared for him, including some of the fish he had caught himself.

Refilled by the Food

Jesus must have taken a few of the fish the men had just hauled in and added them to the others He already was broiling over the crackling fire. The disciples were then invited to "come and have breakfast" (John 21:12). With furtive glances and downcast faces, "none of the disciples dared ask him, 'Who are you?'" as they came quietly to the fire (John 21:12). They knew. And on that early spring morning beside the sparkling sea that stretched out like a blue mirror before them, with the rays of the sun just peeking over the hills, Jesus took the bread and fish from the fire and fed His disciples breakfast! They feasted and were satisfied, not only by the food He had provided, but also by the fish they had caught.

The disciples surely remembered back to that day when Jesus had served a similar meal, not to the twelve of them, but to more than five thousand people. On that day He had multiplied five loaves of bread and two fish until they were sufficient, and everyone was filled. When the crowd had dispersed, the disciples had collected twelve baskets of leftovers, one for each of them. And Jesus had used the experience as an object lesson as He declared, "I am the bread of life. He who comes to me will never go hungry."[15] He was promising deep, lasting satisfaction for the soul through a personal relationship with Himself.

Once again Jesus was teaching His disciples a life lesson. They had been out in the boat, apparently trying to meet their own needs, doing what they were naturally good at, but basically living their lives without Him. And they had come up empty. Unfulfilled. Dissatisfied. But when He was in their lives, and they obeyed His Word, and they served Him in His way, not only were they successful, but they were also satisfied!

Are you a Christian who is saved, but not satisfied? Could it be that even though you are assured, through your faith in Christ, that your sins are forgiven and you are going to heaven, you have been living for yourself? Have you left God . . .

out of your plans?
out of your activities?
out of your spare time?
out of your business?
out of your decisions?

Has your past failure made you shy about including God in *everything*? And although you may be very busy, are you still coming up empty on the inside? There is a richness and depth of satisfaction reserved for those who not only know Jesus as their Savior but also totally live for Him as their Lord.

My husband, Danny, played college basketball for the University of North Carolina. After going undefeated for thirty-two games, his team won the NCAA national championship his sophomore year in a title game against Kansas that went into triple overtime. During that game, Danny played opposite Wilt Chamberlain and successfully held him to a total of only sixteen points. Danny still vividly remembers the swish of the final bucket, the sound of the final buzzer, and the total pandemonium of the crowd rushing the floor like a human tidal wave to celebrate the North Carolina victory. The announcer was yelling into the PA system trying to restore order, the television commentators were screaming, flashbulbs were popping, players were crying, coaches were beaming, parents were fainting . . . And then it was over. Just like that. Danny recalls several days later wondering if that was all there was. He had achieved the athletic goal of a lifetime, but what did it really mean? His team was immortalized in the history books, but what did that mean? The thrill of victory and the satisfaction of accomplishment were exciting, but they did not last.

During that same time, Danny helped accomplish something that did last when he started a chapter of the Fellowship of Christian Athletes on campus. Today, several hundred young men and women meet each Monday night to pray and praise and proclaim the name of Jesus at what is fondly referred to as FCA. And Danny has never lost the thrill of being involved in a ministry that has changed the lives of hundreds of young people at that university. The satisfaction of seeing student athletes graduate to become Christian leaders in their respective fields is impossible to adequately express. His involvement in their lives has been an eternal investment that pays huge dividends for a lifetime.

When you and I serve the Lord in His way, according to His will, in obedience to His Word, for His glory and kingdom alone, we are satisfied! Others may be blessed through our service but not any more than we ourselves are blessed.

Once a year I lead training sessions for men and women, teaching them simple principles on how to read, study, and teach the Bible. These workshops require active participation and, although many participants have never truly studied the Scriptures for themselves, their responses are always a blessing. But I always follow each workshop with a message that requires nothing but a listening ear. In other words, the men and women are fed by what they "catch" or dig out for themselves from the Word of God in the workshops, as well as by what I provide for them in the messages. And student after student has testified to being refilled to overflowing!

If the "food" hasn't been satisfying to you, could it be that you have settled for half a meal? Have you eaten what others have provided—through a pastor's sermon or a Sunday school lesson or a book or a tape—but neglected to feed yourself with what you have "caught" through your own study of God's Word? Peter was refilled after his failure by food that combined what Jesus had provided with the fish he himself had caught. Both are necessary if you and I, as well as Peter, are to be refilled.

As Jesus illustrated this truth to the disciples by using some of the fish they had caught in the meal He provided, Peter must have looked troubled. I wonder if he was wrestling with secret doubts and fears. How could Jesus ever trust Peter to serve Him after what he had done? How could he ever be used as a blessing to others? Was Peter angrily, silently berating himself for his failure, which he thought had effectively destroyed any future opportunity he might have had to serve Christ in a meaningful way?

As Peter sat beside the Sea of Galilee, gazing into the crackling fire, munching on the baked bread and broiled fish, was he thinking of what might have been *if only . . .* ?

Peter knew Jesus had forgiven him. But Peter just couldn't get over his failure. He must have had an extremely difficult time forgiving himself. He desperately needed restoring.

RESTORED AFTER FAILURE

The sun was rising in the morning sky, the fire was burning down, and the last morsels of fish and crumbs of bread had been consumed when Peter found himself the center of the Lord's attention. I wonder if he felt uncomfortable under that gaze. Or had he been anxiously hoping Jesus would say something that would help him get a grip on the rest of his life? If so, he may have been puzzled by the first question Jesus asked, because the question wasn't about his mission in life. It was about his motivation.

Restored in His Motivation

With the other disciples quietly listening, Jesus turned and spoke directly to Peter. In His eyes there must have been an expression of complete understanding and deep love as He gently began to question Peter, "Simon son of John, do you truly love me more than these?" (John 21:15). Perhaps even as Jesus asked the question, He glanced meaningfully around at the circle of disciples just finishing their breakfast.

Peter didn't have to ask, "More than these what, Lord?" He knew Jesus meant his brother, Andrew, and James and John and Matthew and Thomas and

Nathaniel—those who had just gone fishing with him, as well as the others. The question really was, "Peter, do you love Me more than *anyone else*?"

Peter didn't even have to think that one through. He knew he loved Jesus more than anyone. So he replied simply, "Yes, Lord, . . . you know that I love you" (John 21:15).

What about you? Do you love Jesus . . .

more than the other "disciples"?
more than your Christian friends?
more than your family?
more than your church and ministry coworkers?
more than your pastor?
more than your Bible teacher?
more than anyone?

Jesus continued His questions: "Simon son of John, do you truly love me?" (John 21:16). Perhaps this time Jesus stared significantly at the fishing boat that had just been dragged to shore, bulging with a very profitable catch of fish.

Peter must have known Jesus was asking him to examine himself to determine whether he loved Jesus more than his old way of life. Did he love Jesus more than an opportunity for a profitable secular business? More than any plans he may have made for his life? More than any activity in his life? Did he love Jesus more than *anything else*?

Do you? Do you love Jesus . . .

more than your "fishing boat"?
more than your business or profession?
more than your career or hopes for a career?
more than your position or desire for a position?
more than material things and status symbols?
more than your own plans and dreams for the future?
more than your current cash flow and your investments?
more than your profit margin and projected gross income?
more than your leisure activities and pastimes?
more than anything?

Jesus looked straight at Peter without glancing at anyone or anything else, and asked persistently for the third time, "Simon son of John, do you love me?" (John 21:17). Under the direct, searching gaze of his Lord, Peter must have known he was being asked whether he loved Jesus more than himself. This time did Peter squirm uncomfortably? Did he love Jesus more than the opinions of others, such as the servant girl in the courtyard? More than his own safety and comfort, as he would now be dangerously identified with Someone who had been executed as an enemy of Rome? More than his own reputation? More than his memories of sin and failure?

Again, what about you? Do you love Jesus . . .

more than the opinions of others?
more than your own popularity and position?
more than your own safety and comfort and convenience?
more than your own reputation?
more than your memories of past sin and failure?
more than your private hurts and grievances and bitterness?
more than your own beauty and body?
more than your own diet and exercise regimen?
more than yourself?

The first two times Jesus questioned Peter, He used the word *agape* for "love," which is defined as the fullest, highest, richest, most unconditional love we will ever know. Peter's responses are very revealing; although in the English language, Peter repeatedly affirmed his love for the Lord, the Greek word he used was not *agape* but *phileo*, which is more equivalent to "like." The third time Jesus questioned Peter, He dropped down to the word Peter was using for love, and asked Peter if he *liked* Him. Jesus was pinpointing the contrast between His questions and Peter's answers, which perhaps is why Peter was hurt. So the conversation between Jesus and Peter was actually something like this:

"Simon, son of John, do you truly love Me more than these?"
"Yes, Lord, you know that I *like* You."
"Simon, son of John, do you truly love Me?"
"Yes, Lord, you know that I *like* You."
"Simon, son of John, do you like Me?"
"Lord, you know all things; You know that I *like* You."[16]

In response to his Lord's questions, why didn't Peter confess *agape* love for Jesus? Maybe when he was questioned for the third time, his response meant something like this: "Lord, You know all things. You know how I've failed. You know how I told You that while others may abandon You, I never would. You know how I told

You that the Cross was not for You because I had better plans for Your life. You know how I went to sleep when You begged me to watch and pray with You. You know that I denied even knowing You three times while You were being brutally treated. With all the sin and guilt and failure in my life, I just don't dare say I love You. But You know my heart. I love You as much as I'm capable of at this moment, but not nearly as much as I should or as much as I want to. So Lord, to be honest, *compared to Your love for me*, I can only say I *like* You as a Friend." It's interesting that Jesus didn't seem to need any more than that honest confession from Peter in order to restore him and reinstate him in service.

What did you think Jesus required from you before He could use you? Again and again, from the Samaritan woman, to the paralyzed man beside the pool of Bethesda, to the blind man, to Lazarus, we've seen that Jesus meets us where we are. But He doesn't leave us there. He draws us to Himself and lifts us above our circumstances and even beyond our own potential.

Jesus reached into Peter's heart and put His finger on Peter's motivation for service. Peter's motivation to live for Jesus and to serve Jesus was not to be . . .

an attempt to stave off guilt,
an attempt to earn forgiveness,
an attempt to avoid criticism,
an attempt to measure up to the opinions of others,
an attempt to prove something to someone,
an attempt to gain approval or recognition,
an attempt to accumulate more good works than bad works.

Peter's sole motivation in service was to be his love for Jesus, pure and simple. If he did love Jesus, even a little, his mission was to do something about it. He was to get involved in the lives of others.

Restored in His Mission

Do you love Jesus? Do you even like Him at all? If so, Jesus gives to you the same threefold mission He gave to Peter. The first is to "feed my lambs" (John 21:15).

Who or what are "lambs"? Obviously, Jesus wasn't speaking of baby sheep. And yet, in a spiritual sense, He was. Previously, He had picked up on an Old Testament theme and taught the disciples that He was the Good Shepherd[17] while they and other believers were the sheep. Therefore, "lambs" are either the children of "sheep" or they are new believers. His directive was to feed the "lambs."

Several years ago I had the opportunity to go to Australia with my daughter Rachel-Ruth. We were the invited guests of the Anglican Archbishop and Mrs. Donald Robinson. The schedule they had set for my speaking was intense, yet considerate. Every three days, I was able to take a day off. And after the second week, I had a weekend off.

I took advantage of the extra free time and traveled to the Snowy Mountains where Rachel-Ruth and I stayed at a working homestead. The first day there, after riding horses all over the mountains, spotting kangaroos and wallabies and platypuses, we came into the sprawling house where dinner was being prepared. Going into the kitchen, I asked the hostess if I could help. She laughed and said, "Yes, help me get Bobby out of here." To my delighted consternation, Bobby was a wee lamb who kept entwining himself in her legs. The hostess took a bottle of warm milk, placed it in front of Bobby's nose, and used it as bait to get him out of the kitchen and onto the patio in front of the house. Then she handed me the bottle and told me to feed him. I looked rather skeptically at Bobby, and he looked rather eagerly at me. So I squatted down, picked him up in my arms, and stuck the bottle in his mouth! He got his supper, and I learned something about feeding lambs!

Lambs can't eat on their own. They don't graze or nibble. They have to be bottle-fed. New believers or young children are like that too. They can't enter into theological debates or get involved in word studies or argue the value of lexicons or even interpret the parables. They have a difficult time digging out truth from Scripture for themselves because it is totally unfamiliar to them. So they need to be "bottle-fed" or "spoon-fed." Someone needs to sit down with them and teach them the stories and simple truths of the Bible. They need someone like you, who gets involved in their lives for no reason other than that you love Jesus, and He has given you "lambs" as your mission.

What "lambs" do you know? Have you seen lambs who are interfering with someone attempting to "feed sheep," just as Bobby was interfering with the hostess as she attempted to prepare our dinner? Do the lambs keep interrupting the Bible study with questions that everyone else knows the answers to? Are others even getting irritated and frustrated with what appears to be resistance to the truth, when actually it's ignorance? Wouldn't it make a difference if you just met with those people individually one on one and answered each one's questions, and led each through a study of basic Bible truths and doctrines?

Or maybe the "lambs" are the children who keep flocking into your backyard to play with your children, or they may be the children who come with their parents to your church then get dumped in Sunday school as more of a babysitting facility than a teaching time. Couldn't you take the opportunity to volunteer to read Bible stories to them or start a backyard Bible Club?

Years ago in my Bible class, a lovely Asian woman shared how she got involved in feeding lambs. She had two young daughters who went to the public school. The bus they rode stopped right in front of her house, so every morning about a dozen children gathered there to wait for it. One morning it was pouring rain, so she invited all the children to come out of the rain and wait just inside the front door of her house. That morning the bus happened to be late, so while they waited, my friend read the children a Bible verse and prayed for them. The bus came, and the children bounded out the door and clambered aboard.

The next morning, it wasn't raining, but the children were at my friend's door, asking if they could wait inside and have another prayer. My friend was thrilled as she welcomed her little "flock" inside her home. Each morning thereafter, she shared a verse with her "lambs" and prayed God's blessing on their day—just because she loved Jesus.

You can feed lambs by establishing family devotions in your home. Or by helping out with the children's Sunday school at church. Or by sharing a verse with your children's friends when they sleep over. Ask God to give you creativity in getting the "bottle" into their little mouths—and minds!

The second time Jesus inquired of Peter, "Do you truly love me?" and Peter affirmed, "Yes, Lord, you know that I [like] you," Jesus instructed him, "Take care of my sheep" (John 21:16). Sheep can get into all sorts of difficulty, from wandering away from the flock and becoming lost, to getting brambles embedded in their wool, to suffering nose flies or attacks from wolves. They need constant attention and care from the shepherd.

What "sheep" do you know? Believers in your church, your home, your community, your Bible study, your school, your workplace, your club, have so many needs! Are they wandering away from church, drifting from the fellowship of other Christians as they are lured by the sirens of popularity, prestige, position, power, *and just things*?

Are they entangled with the thorns of . . .

personal responsibilities,

financial worries,

marital infidelity,
professional pressures,
physical illness,
emotional stress,
parental care,
and a thousand other things?

Are they constantly battling the "nose flies" of . . .
sickness and ill health,
doctors offices and hospitals,
medical bills and health insurance?

Is Satan himself attacking them in the area of their relationships, robbing them of their joy, tempting them to doubt God's love, luring them to seek a quick fix to a long-term problem or be dissatisfied in their current situations?

Sheep need a shepherd! Surely you can tend just one sheep. Call him, write him, encourage him, pray for him, invite him to a ball game. Meet her for lunch, babysit her kids, make her dinner, or just help in practical ways. Caring for the sheep is the second mission Jesus gave Peter. And you. And me. Just because we love Him.

For the third time, Jesus asked Peter, "Do you even like Me at all?"

When Peter answered, his face must have flushed with shame. How he wanted to love Jesus with all of his heart as he knew he should. But all he could honestly muster was, "Lord, You know I like You." This time, Jesus commanded Peter, "Feed My sheep" (John 21:17, paraphrase).

When I was growing up in the mountains, we had a section of land cleared and planted with grass. The entire area was encircled by a barbed-wire fence, so that the mountain pasture was secured. My mother had three ewes and a little ram that she fed by simply turning them loose in the pasture she had prepared. Because they were mature sheep, they fed themselves.

Unlike lambs that need to be bottle-fed, mature sheep just need to be provided with a green pasture. Open your home for a Bible study, help facilitate a Sunday school class, teach your children to have their own quiet times of prayer and Bible reading. Just look around and see what you can do to make sure each sheep is in a green pasture, grazing on the Word of God for himself or herself.

Several years ago, my daughter Rachel-Ruth and my nephew's bride, Kendra, prayed together each week, asking God to bring women to them who wanted to be in a Bible study. Within five months, God had brought seventeen women to them. Never having led an adult Bible study before, they used a video series.[18] The one they selected required each participant to use her Bible at home in order to complete a weekly lesson, then every Monday night all the women came together to share what they had learned. Following their discussion, they watched the lecture for that week's lesson on video. Week after week, it was thrilling to hear of the impact God's Word was making in the lives of these women who were not only feeding themselves but also being fed. Rachel-Ruth and Kendra had provided the green pasture.

Hungry sheep are everywhere. In fact, the "sheep" are starving! They are sick of junk food—games and musicals and entertainment and self-help seminars and books about the Bible. Instead, they are ravenous for real food! Jesus has offered Himself as the Bread of Life that comes down from heaven to satisfy the hungry soul. When His disciples said that was hard to understand—did He mean they were to eat *Him*?—Jesus replied that He was speaking of His Word.[19]

Why would Rachel-Ruth, who worked as an office manager's assistant and at the same time was learning to cook and be a homemaker for her new husband, and why would Kendra, who was a bride working full-time as a nurse and was also learning to cook and make a home for my nephew—why would they go to the trouble and time and expense of conducting a Bible study for women, many of whom they didn't even know well? For one reason only: They love Jesus. Loving Jesus and serving Jesus go hand in hand. One is your motivation; the other is your mission.

Do you love Jesus? Do you even *like Jesus at all?* Then Jesus said your mission is clear. You are to feed the lambs and tend the sheep and feed the sheep. You do love Jesus, don't you?

Early that morning beside the fire on the shore of Galilee, Jesus asked Peter to publicly confess his love for Him three different times. It was an obvious parallel to the earlier morning beside the fire in the courtyard of the temple when Peter had denied Him publicly three times. Jesus was reinstating Peter in the eyes of the other disciples as well as in Peter's own eyes. He was restoring Peter's soul![20] And Peter *was* restored! At the end of his life, he whispered passionately, "To those of us who believe, He is so precious!"[21]

After finishing breakfast and leading Peter in his public confession of love, Jesus must have stood up and motioned for Peter to join Him in a stroll down the beach. He had something to reveal to Peter that would help the disciple refocus after his failure and remain focused for the rest of his life. John concludes his wonderful eyewitness account of the life of Jesus with one of the last challenges Jesus gave to Peter before returning to His Father.

Refocused After Failure

As they walked slowly down the beach, could they hear the waves lapping gently on the shore and feel the soft sand giving way beneath their sandals? Did a gull call to its mate before joining a flock of seabirds as they circled the fishing boats heading out to the deeper water? Did Jesus dread to tell Peter what He knew He must? It must have been an ominous moment, for when Peter turned to look into the eyes of Jesus, he saw a cross!

Refocused on the Cross

Peter had been so repulsed by the cross that he had contradicted Jesus when he learned God's will for Jesus included it. Now, Jesus told Peter the truth—that God's will for Peter's life also included a cross: "When you were younger you dressed yourself and went where you wanted; but when you are old you will stretch out your hands, and someone else will dress you and lead you where you do not want to go" (John 21:18). While His words may seem vague to us, the one who penned them specifically indicated Peter understood that "Jesus said this to indicate the kind of death by which Peter would glorify God" (John 21:19). This time, instead of being overwhelmed or frightened, I wonder if Peter felt truly honored to be singled out to endure the cross for Jesus because Jesus had endured the Cross for him.

Tradition records that at the end of Peter's life he was arrested for his bold proclamation of the gospel, imprisoned by the authorities, and condemned to die on a Roman cross. As he was stripped of his clothes in preparation for execution and led to the cross, Peter, who had been so afraid of being identified with Christ that he had denied knowing Him, begged to be crucified upside down because he did not feel worthy to be crucified in the same manner as his beloved Lord. The executioner agreed. And God was glorified by Peter's humble obedience to death, even death on a cross.[22]

Are you repulsed by the thought of crucifixion? I am. But I also know that when I look into the eyes of Jesus, I see a cross! And He has said to me, "Anne, if you want to be My disciple, if you want to follow Me, you must deny yourself, take up your cross and follow Me. Because if you want to save your life, you're going to lose it in the end. If you choose to lose your life for Me, you will find it. For what good will it do you if you gain the whole world, yet forfeit your soul?"[23]

The cross that Jesus commands you and me to carry is the cross of submissive obedience to the will of God, even when His will includes suffering and hardship and things we don't want to do. It is a willingness to totally, absolutely, irrevocably, and finally yield our lives to Him because we want what He wants more than what we want.

The cross is not just a symbol of love or a fashion statement. The cross is your daily decision to deny yourself,

your rights,
your wants,
your dreams,
your plans,
your goals,

and deliberately, wholeheartedly, unreservedly live out your commitment to His will and His way and His Word and His wisdom. The cross is your decision to live for Jesus. Period. No ifs, ands, buts, or maybes.

Crucifixion became real to me years ago when I was struggling with trying to balance my time. I spent hours in preparation for my responsibilities in the Bible class I was teaching, plus I had three small children and a husband who needed lots of loving attention, a house to clean and meals to cook and shopping to do and laundry to wash. I remember one morning, having already accomplished almost an entire day's agenda by 9:00 a.m., sitting down to catch my breath and enjoy a quick cup of coffee while I scanned the headlines in the newspaper. No sooner had I sat down than my four-year-old daughter, Morrow, interrupted me for something she needed. The anger and frustration at never having time to myself erupted from within, and as I cut loose to scold her, it struck me that the problem wasn't Morrow; it was me! My anger stemmed from the fact I could never seem to divide up my time so that I had enough of it for all I needed to do. And I resented Morrow for intruding on time that I had allotted, not for her, but for myself.

Instead of yelling at Morrow, I quickly got up to attend to what she wanted, then went back to the kitchen, dropped to my knees, and told God I was sorry. Furthermore, I told Him I could no longer manage my time, so I was going to give it all to Him to manage for me. And then I went a step further and told God I was tired of trying to decide on a daily basis what I would give to Him and what I would keep to myself, so I was giving Him everything.

There was no lightning bolt or voice from the sky or even a special verse to let me know He acknowledged the decision I had made. I got up from my knees and nothing seemed dramatically different. But the next time I was interrupted, I handled it without anger or resentment. The next time I had more to do than I had time for, I just told God I would do what I could, and He would have to take care of the rest. I *relaxed* under His management! To this day, with all the pressures and problems in my life, I sleep soundly at night, I am not easily frustrated, and I live in the confidence that God will make time for all He has for me to do, even if I am unable to do all that I had planned. It is a peace that comes from a moment-by-moment yielding to Him that began, for me, on my knees on the kitchen floor.

But I will tell you honestly from experience that crucifixion is a slow, painful death to your *self*. And it is impossible for victims to crucify themselves. Crucifixion is the result of our decision to yield ourselves to God as He allows various pressures and problems and pain into our lives.[24] These things are often a part of life anyway, but in the life of a disciple of Jesus Christ, they are not wasted. They are used to put us to death that we might be raised to an abundant . . . victorious . . . blessed . . . fruitful . . . powerful . . . Christlike . . . Spirit-filled life.

Don't forget that the resurrection followed His death! You and I need to remember that when Jesus commands us to deny ourselves, take up our crosses daily, and follow Him, He leads us not only to the cross, but also to the crown! Don't become so morbidly preoccupied with the cross that you overlook the resurrection and the glory and the power and the crown to come! But in order to get to the glory and the crown, we must first go through the cross.

God has used pressures and pain and problems in my life as the nails that have pinned me to the cross. By submitting to Him in those things, I have entered into an experience of death to myself. Some of the "nails" He has used include losing a baby, being removed from a church, experiencing a robbery, witnessing the execution of my friend, stepping out in faith to establish AnGeL Ministries, traveling the world, speaking in a broad variety of settings to an even broader variety of people, enduring—and learning to enjoy—an empty nest, caring for my son through his struggle with cancer, and marrying off all three children within eight months of each other. A "nail" can also be another person in your life who irritates, aggravates, and frustrates you—someone whose very presence forces you to choose between living in the spirit or in the flesh. The list of nails could go on, but the apostle Paul articulated it best when he personally testified, "I have been crucified with Christ and I no longer live, but Christ lives in me. The life I live in the body, I live by faith in the Son of God, who loved me and gave himself for me."[25]

The apostle John had a similar experience when he glimpsed the vision of the glory of Jesus and fell at His feet as though dead.[26] As a "dead" man, he was *silent*—no longer was he arguing with God's plan for his life, or making excuses for his sin, or telling God what he wanted Him to do, or rationalizing his behavior or insisting on his way. And as a "dead" man he was *still*—no longer wrestling against God's will for his life, or going off in his own direction, or impatiently running ahead of God, dragging his feet when God called. John was describing his "crucifixion."

Jesus challenges you and me, even as He did Peter and Paul and John, to keep our focus daily on the cross of His will if we want to be His disciples. And as you focus on the cross, don't take your eyes off of Christ!

Refocus on Christ

As soon as Jesus had told Peter that his life would include the cross, Jesus turned to him and said, "Follow me!" (John 21:19). Peter knew Jesus wasn't referring to their walk down the beach but to his journey through life. He was being challenged to live for Jesus regardless of the sacrifice or cost or final outcome.

As Peter continued walking with Jesus along the shoreline, he happened to glance back and see John following them. He must have wondered if living for Jesus was going to be as costly for John as it was for him. And so Peter, with his characteristic, impetuous honesty, asked, "Lord, what about him?" (John 21:21).

Is Peter's question on the tip of your tongue? What about your sister or brother or parent or spouse or pastor or friend or fellow church member or Bible study leader? Do you see . . .

> selfishness in the way that person spends his or her time?
> manipulation in that person's dealings with others?
> temper tantrums when that person doesn't get his or her way?
> political maneuvering when that person wants to achieve his or her goal?

strong-arming in a committee to get the decision that person wants?
public posturing as that person tries to impress others with
an affected spirituality?
greed as that person cashes in on ministry?
dishonesty as that person steals the credit for something someone
else has done?!

And all of this *within the church!* Do you see no real evidence of the crucified life in *any believer you know?*

In response to Peter's question, "What about him?" Jesus said bluntly, "If I want him to remain alive until I return, what is that to you? You must follow me" (John 21:22).

And Jesus says just as bluntly to you and me, "How I work in other people's lives and how they respond to Me is basically none of your business. You are not to live your life in comparison with others. They are accountable to Me and to Me alone, just as you are. Keep your focus on Me!"

What is your focus? Have you been deeply disturbed and discouraged and even depressed as you have looked at the lives of those who say they are disciples and the community that calls itself the church, yet not seen Jesus? Do you look at these people or churches and wonder . . .

Where is the beauty of His character?
Where is the purity of His holiness?
Where is the authority of His Word?
Where is the sovereignty of His purpose?
Where is the majesty of His name?
Where is the security of His promise?
Where is the victory of His power?
Where is the glory of His presence?
Where is Jesus?

My prayer is that if Jesus can be seen nowhere else, He might be seen in your life and mine. Because He is the One—*the only One*—who makes:

God visible
and change possible
and happiness attainable
and resources ample
and suffering understandable

and sin forgivable
and heaven available!
Which is why our hearts' cry is, *"Just give me Jesus!" AND GOD HAS!*

MISS AMY CARMICHAEL established a home for girls in one of the southern provinces of India. At that time, and even to this day, young girls were sold or bartered to the local temple to serve as prostitutes. The life expectancy of one of these little girls was twelve years of age. Miss Carmichael rescued as many of these tragic victims as she could. She then raised them in the Christian atmosphere of Dohnavur that was like a secret garden of God's blessing in the midst of a terrifying jungle of evil.

One day Miss Carmichael was at her desk when one of these little girls came and stood shyly at the door. When Miss Carmichael looked up, the little girl announced very simply, yet in a quivering voice, "I have come." Miss Carmichael stretched out her arm to welcome the young child to her side and gently inquired, "Why have you come?" With large, dark eyes that clung to Miss Carmichael's face, the one who had been rescued softly whispered, "Just to love you."[27]

God's glorious love and saving grace in the person of Jesus Christ draw us to Himself like the little rescued Indian girl was drawn to Miss Carmichael. Love wants to draw near and linger in the presence of the One who is loved.

So just give me Jesus! He is not only our Savior, He is God, who so loved you and me that He drew near and lingered just to say, *"I love you!"*

For God so loved the world
that
He gave
His one and only Son,
that whoever believes in Him
shall not perish
but have eternal life.[28]

"Jesus did many other miraculous signs
in the presence of his disciples,
which are not recorded in this book.
But these are written
that *you may believe*
that Jesus is the Christ
the Son of God,
and
that by believing
you may have
life
in His name."[29]

NOTES

Introduction

1. 1 John 1:1–2.
2. John 20:31.

Poetry

Some time ago, I received a homemade cassette tape with the handwritten title "My King Is . . ." From what I could gather, a man named Lockridge had been called to the platform during a church service to tell the congregation who his King is. The tape was a recording of his eloquent answer. In a rich voice that resonated with passion and increased in volume and tempo as he warmed to his subject, he thundered his description of his King, Jesus—in three minutes!

When the tape ended, I rewound it and replayed it. This unknown brother in Christ had absolutely thrilled my soul with his description of *my* King, Jesus!

I have taken Mr. Lockridge's idea—and, at times, some of his very phrases—and written descriptions of Jesus that appear at the beginning of each couplet of chapters in this book. Even as I pray that these descriptions of our King Jesus will be a blessing to you, I pray for Mr. Lockridge: *God bless you always, sir, for the blessing you have been to this servant of the King!*

Chapter 1: Jesus Makes God Visible . . . to Me

1. *Time*, December 6, 1999, 86.
2. Genesis 1:1.
3. Genesis 1:3, 6, 9, 11, 14, 20, 24, 26, 28, 29.
4. Matthew 12:34.
5. John 3:16.
6. Matthew 16:24–25.
7. Romans 8:1–2.
8. Ephesians 2:8.
9. Romans 13:1; James 4:10.
10. 1 Kings 18:36–45.
11. Hebrews 13:8.
12. Our sun is so massive that 1.2 million planets the size of earth could fit inside it, leaving room for 4.3 million moons. Our sun is the nearest star to our planet—the next nearest star is four times larger than our sun! Our galaxy includes more than 100 billion stars (I wonder who counted?), and the last observation said our galaxy is only one of more than 100 billion galaxies!
13. Colossians 1:15–16; Psalm 147:4.
14. Colossians 1:17.
15. Hebrews 1:3.

16. Philippians 4:19; Ephesians 1:18–21, 3:20.
17. Exodus 14–15.
18. Genesis 3.
19. Romans 3:23.
20. Ephesians 2:1.
21. John 3:18.
22. Romans 6:23, emphasis added.
23. John 14:6.
24. Matthew 5:14–16.
25. Isaiah 40:3.
26. Luke 3:15.
27. John 1:23.
28. Revelation 12:11.
29. Romans 10:9.
30. John 14:6, emphasis added.
31. Acts 4:12, emphasis added.
32. Hebrews 1:3.

Chapter 2: Jesus Makes God Visible . . . as Man

1. Luke 24:27, 44–47.
2. Romans 1:19–20.
3. Psalm 19:1–6.
4. John 6:14–15, 51–66.
5. John 18:36.
6. John 12:23–33.
7. Revelation 3:20.
8. John 20:28.
9. Matthew 1:21.
10. Matthew 16:16; John 11:27.
11. Luke 1:31, 34, 35, 38.
12. Luke 1:37.
13. Exodus 19:18; Hebrews 12:18.
14. Exodus 34:29–35.
15. Exodus 40:34–35.
16. Exodus 13:21.
17. Mark 1:35.
18. Matthew 8:20.
19. John 6:15; Mark 9:2, 8.
20. Matthew 4:25.
21. John 11:35.
22. Mark 2:15.
23. Matthew 4:1–2.
24. John 6:60–66.
25. John 9:6–7.

26. John 2:13–16.
27. John 10:20.
28. John 12:13.
29. Mark 9:2–3.
30. John 13:4–5.
31. Matthew 21:23–27.
32. Matthew 19:13–15.
33. Matthew 26:67.
34. Luke 7:36–50.
35. Matthew 21:6–11.
36. Luke 22:44.
37. John 19:16–17.
38. John 19:30.
39. John 19:38–41.
40. John 20:1–8, 19–20.
41. Acts 1:9.
42. John 1:14; in Eugene Peterson, *The Message* (Colorado Springs, CO: NavPress, 2000), 162.
43. 1 Peter 1:4.
44. Anne Graham Lotz, *God's Story* (Nashville: Word, 1997, 1999), 23–25.
45. Galatians 3:24.

Chapter 3: Jesus Makes Change Possible . . . When Love Runs Out

1. Genesis 2:18–24.
2. See William Barclay, *The Gospel of John* (Philadelphia: Westminster Press, 1956), 81–82.
3. Matthew 12:46–47, 13:55–56.
4. James was one of Jesus' half brothers. It has been said that James's practical doctrine in the book that bears his name was drawn from watching his older Brother in the home.
5. John 1:29.
6. Matthew 3:16–17.
7. "Woman" is the equivalent of our courteous southern title of respect, "ma'am."
8. "My time has not yet come," "the time is coming," and "the time has come" are used by and about Jesus repeatedly in John's gospel (see John 7:6, 8:20, 13:1, 16:32, 17:1). They refer to His time of suffering and humiliation when He entered Jerusalem and was publicly proclaimed Israel's Messiah on Sunday, yet was crucified on Friday of that same week, followed by His burial and resurrection. It was a time when He was revealed to the world as the Lamb of God, who takes away the sin of the world.
9. Hebrews 4:15.
10. John 17:1, 4.
11. 1 John 4:19–21, 4:7.
12. 1 John 4:8.

13. Ephesians 5:22.
14. Ephesians 5:25.
15. Proverbs 22:6.
16. Matthew 6:14; Romans 12:19.
17. Psalm 25:3; Proverbs 1:7, 9:10.
18. Genesis 2:18–25; Matthew 19:3–6.

Chapter 4: Jesus Makes Change Possible . . . When Life Isn't Enough

1. Nicodemus was a member of the Jewish ruling council (see John 3:1).
2. Nicodemus brought a fortune in spices for Jesus' burial (see John 19:39).
3. Nicodemus was Israel's teacher (see John 3:10).
4. Nicodemus was a Pharisee (see John 3:1).
5. This is implied by the fact that Nicodemus met Jesus at night (see John 3:2).
6. Matthew 7:15–23.
7. See Romans 3:23.
8. See Romans 3:10.
9. See Romans 6:23.
10. See John 3:16.
11. See 1 John 1:9.
12. See Revelation 3:20.
13. See John 1:12.
14. See Ephesians 1:13.
15. See Ephesians 2:8–9.
16. See 2 Corinthians 5:17.
17. Another accepted explanation of being "born of water" draws application from the preaching of John the Baptist. Nicodemus would have been very familiar with the words of the forerunner of Jesus to preach repentance from sin as necessary preparation for receiving the Messiah. The outward sign of inward repentance was water baptism (see Matthew 3:1–6). Jesus could have been emphasizing the necessity of repentance in order to be born again.
18. Could this be the true horror of the abortion industry? Since abortionists prevent a child from being born of water, or born physically, does this mean that all the aborted babies "cannot enter the kingdom of God"? Do abortionists actually take the life of the children they abort twice—once when they deny them physical life, and once again when they deny them the opportunity of spiritual life? God have mercy on us if this is so!
19. 2 Corinthians 5:17.
20. Romans 8:16; John 20:31.
21. John 2:17; Psalm 69:9. Apparently Jesus cleansed the temple twice—once at the beginning of His ministry and once at the end. Compare John 2:12–17 with Matthew 21:12–13.
22. Numbers 21:5.
23. Numbers 21:4–9.
24. Romans 5:8.

25. 1 John 4:9–10.
26. The story of Noah and the ark is found in Genesis 6, 7, and 8.
27. Hebrews 9:27.
28. Romans 10:9–10; Acts 4:12.
29. Romans 8:32.
30. Matthew 13:50.
31. Revelation 20:1.
32. Revelation 20:15.
33. Jude 13.
34. Matthew 5:22.
35. Matthew 7:23.
36. John 19:38–42.
37. John 7:45–52.
38. Matthew 26:57–68.
39. Isaiah 53:3–5.
40. John 19:38–42.
41. Nicodemus's action of identifying with the death of Jesus has spiritual application for you and me. Jesus said that unless we deny ourselves, take up our cross, and follow Him, we cannot be His disciples (Matthew 16:24). Paul also instructs us to identify with the death of Jesus that we might experience His life (see Romans 6:1–8).

Chapter 5: Jesus Makes Happiness Attainable . . . for the Outcast

1. Psalm 139:1–6.
2. The sixth hour is about noon.
3. John 2:25.
4. Matthew 22:37–38.
5. 1 John 1:9.
6. John 14:6.
7. Months later, after Jesus had been crucified and buried, had risen from the dead, and had ascended into heaven—and after Pentecost and after the gift of the Holy Spirit was given to each believer—persecution broke out in Jerusalem. The same authorities who had executed the Son of God were determined to wipe out His followers. But instead of wiping them out, the persecution actually caused them to spread throughout the world. One of the first places the early believers went when they fled Jerusalem was Samaria. Philip, one of Jesus' disciples, preached the gospel there, and "there was great joy in that city" (Acts 8:4–8). The well of Living Water that Jesus had given the woman was indeed a spring of water that welled up and brought eternal life in His name to her entire city.

Chapter 6: Jesus Makes Happiness Attainable . . . for the Bypassed

1. *Life* magazine, Editor's Note, May 1999.
2. Ivor Powell, *John's Wonderful Gospel* (Grand Rapids, MI: Kregel Publications, 1962), 118–19.
3. Verse 4 is not included in all manuscripts.

4. The Greek word for "invalid" is *neurosemia,* which means a missing connection between the head and the body. Apparently this man had severed his spinal cord in an accident thirty-eight years earlier and was therefore a paraplegic.
5. See Matthew 16:24.
6. The story of Dr. Donald Bartlette is a true one. I first heard it on a *Focus on the Family* radio program, which is available on two cassette tapes—#CS 344. I have since been privileged to hear Dr. Bartlette in person. His testimony is to the praise of God's glorious grace!

Chapter 7: Jesus Makes Resources Ample . . . to Me

1. Corrie ten Boom with John and Elizabeth Sherrill, *The Hiding Place* (Washington Depot, CT: Chosen Books, 1971).
2. The film, also called *The Hiding Place*, was produced by World Wide Pictures. Jeannette Clift-George played the part of Corrie, and Julie Harris played the part of her sister, Betsie.
3. Mark 6:7–13, 30.
4. Mark 6:31.
5. John 5:18.
6. Mark 6:14–29.
7. Mark 6:31. The following year, Jesus would be the Passover Lamb.
8. Luke 5:16.
9. The Lake of Galilee, also called the Sea of Galilee, is eight miles long and three miles wide.
10. John 6:4 tells us it was Passover time, which would have been our Easter time. The weather must have been conducive to being outdoors because Jesus and the disciples were joined by at least five thousand others in a short period of time.
11. Psalm 23:1–3.
12. Isaiah 50:4.
13. Mark 6:34.
14. Mark 6:34.
15. Hebrews 9:27.
16. Matthew 6:33.
17. Mark 6:36.
18. See Exodus 4:13.
19. Mark 6:37, emphasis added.
20. It has been said that the first miracle on that day was getting the five loaves and two fish away from the little boy!
21. Mark 6:39–40.
22. It has been said that the second miracle that day was getting the people to sit down before they had been given something to eat!
23. Mark 6:41.
24. Romans 1:21 compared with Romans 1:28–32.
25. Mark 6:42.
26. Deuteronomy 18:18.

Chapter 8: Jesus Makes Resources Ample . . . in Me

1. Numbers 20:5.
2. Numbers 20:8.
3. The people's chant was based on Isaiah 12:3.
4. The first verses of the Bible unveil a mystery when they declare, "In the beginning God [God the Father] created the heavens and the earth. Now the earth was formless and empty, darkness was over the surface of the deep, and the Spirit of God [God the Holy Spirit] was hovering over the waters. And God said, 'Let there be light'" [God the Son—see John 1:1]. Farther down in that same passage, God said, "Let *us* make man in *our* image, in *our* likeness" (Genesis 1:26, emphasis added). Notice the plural pronouns, which then switch to singular pronouns: "So God created man in *his* own image, in the image of God *he* created him; male and female *he* created them" (v. 27, emphasis added).

   This rather technical and confusing passage means that our God is one God, yet within His deity, He is three separate, distinct individuals. Like water that can take the form of ice, steam, or liquid yet still retain its same qualities, God is three Persons in one. He is God the Father, God the Son, and God the Holy Spirit. He is beyond our ability to understand, and we just need to worship, placing absolute faith in God's revelation of Himself through the Bible.
5. In a general outline form of emphasis, the Old Testament reveals God the Father, the Gospels reveal God the Son, and Acts and the Epistles reveal God the Holy Spirit. But the entire Trinity is found throughout all of Scripture.
6. Acts 7:56.
7. Acts 9:1–5.
8. Revelation 4:1; 5:6.
9. Acts 1:11.
10. Romans 8:9.
11. 2 Peter 1:20–21.
12. 2 Timothy 3:16.
13. I actually had a woman come up to me after a message and accuse me of peeking in the windows of her home because what I had said had so specifically addressed her own situation!
14. 1 John 1:9; James 5:16; Matthew 5:23–24.
15. Acts 1:12–14.
16. Acts 1:15; 2:1, 15.
17. Acts 2:9–11.
18. Acts 2:2–4.
19. Were John, Peter, James, and the other disciples saved before the Cross, resurrection, ascension, and Pentecost? Yes, but only in the Old Testament sense. It was not until after the historical day of Pentecost, when they received the personal indwelling of the Holy Spirit, that they were saved in a New Testament sense. Their lives bridge the Old and New Testament experience of faith and salvation.
20. Luke 11:13.
21. To ask Jesus to come into your heart is the same thing as asking the Holy Spirit to

come in. Even though at the time of the invitation you may not have understood that Jesus is in heaven, He would have honored your sincere invitation and come in, *in the person of the Holy Spirit.* The Holy Spirit is, in effect, Jesus in you.

22. Ephesians 1:13.
23. Acts 1:4, 8.
24. Luke 1:35.
25. Ephesians 5:18.
26. 2 Corinthians 3:17.
27. 2 Corinthians 3:18.
28. Galatians 5:22.
29. Galatians 4:19.
30. John 16:13–14.
31. Hebrews 12:1.
32. 1 Corinthians 12:13. This baptism of the Spirit is *simultaneous* with our conversion. Every person who has been born again has been baptized by the Holy Spirit.
33. 1 Corinthians 12:11.
34. Romans 12:6–8. Other lists of gifts are given in 1 Corinthians 12:27–31 and Ephesians 4:10–13.
35. 1 Corinthians 12:31.
36. 1 Corinthians 13:1–3.

Chapter 9: Jesus Makes Suffering Understandable . . . to the Observer

1. John 8:59.
2. John 8:59.
3. Who are you interested in because Jesus is?
4. Romans 6:23.
5. James 2:10.
6. Romans 3:23; 1 John 1:8–10.
7. Genesis 3:16.
8. Genesis 3:16.
9. Genesis 3:17–19.
10. Lotz, *God's Story*, 81–83.
11. James 5:14–16.
12. Some other questions might be: Is suffering due to a prenatal sin? Since the beggar was born blind, and the disciples asked if his blindness was due to his sin, they were implying that the man may have sinned before he was born. Jews believed that a fetus within a mother's womb was actually capable of entering into her sin so that if a mother worshiped idols while pregnant, the unborn baby was also guilty of idolatry. But this is not supported by Scripture at all.

    Another question tries to attribute an implication of reincarnation to the disciples' inquiry. In other words, had the man sinned in some previous life and been punished by being reincarnated blind? But Scripture emphatically denies any theory of reincarnation, so we know this was not what the disciples were asking. See Hebrews 9:27.

13. Exodus 20:5, 34:7; Numbers 14:18; Deuteronomy 5:9. Please note the punishment God speaks of is not *judgment for* the guilt of sin but the *consequences of* sin.
14. Galatians 6:11 implies that Paul had difficulty with his eyesight.
15. 1 Corinthians 2:3–4.
16. 2 Corinthians 12:8–10.
17. 1 Peter 1:6–7.
18. 1 Peter 4:12–13, 16, 19.
19. Romans 5:3–5.
20. 2 Corinthians 4:7–11.
21. Jesus' words also obviously and simply point us to the urgency of working when God gives us the opportunity (the daytime) because we may not always have it (nighttime comes).
22. 2 Corinthians 3:18.
23. There was nothing miraculous about the mud Jesus smeared on the blind man's sightless eyes. The mud simply gave the man an opportunity to demonstrate his faith in Jesus' Word when he was told to go wash. In some mysterious way, our obedience to God's Word releases His power in our lives.
24. How have you reacted to your child's experience with Jesus? Have you denied it because you believe he or she is too young to know Jesus or understand salvation? Have you discouraged it because you're embarrassed by what others may say? Are you afraid your child will lose popularity and not be accepted by the children and families you want to be in good standing with?
25. Have you resisted giving public testimony to what God has done for you because you are afraid someone will ask you a question for which you don't have an answer? Has your pride kept you from taking the opportunities God has given you to witness because you're afraid your ignorance will make you look foolish in someone else's eyes?
26. Genesis 41:1–40.
27. Daniel 5.
28. Matthew 16:18.
29. 1 Corinthians 1:27–29.
30. Isaiah 43:1–2; Psalm 23:4; Revelation 1:9, 12–13.
31. *World Magazine,* August 28, 1999, 9.

Chapter 10: Jesus Makes Suffering Understandable . . . to the Sufferer

1. Romans 8:28.
2. John 3:8.
3. 1 Peter 1:6–9; 4:12–13, 19; Romans 8:28.
4. The evidence for the wealth of Mary, Martha, and Lazarus is in the fact that they possessed their own private burial cave (John 11:38), they threw a feast for their friends and neighbors (John 12:2), and Mary poured very expensive ointment on the feet of Jesus (John 12:3).
5. Luke 10:41–42.
6. Matthew 26:13.

7. John 12:1–11.
8. One reason for the speculation that Lazarus may have been the rich young ruler is Mark 10:21, which says that "Jesus looked at him and loved him." Compare with John 11:3, 5.
9. Luke 18:18–23.
10. When Jesus received the message, He was in the Transjordan, a day's journey from Bethany. So if the messenger took one day to get to Jesus and Jesus delayed for two days then took one more to travel to Bethany, a total of four days had passed between the messenger's departure from Bethany and Jesus' arrival. When He got there, He was told Lazarus had been dead four days (John 11:17). Apparently, Lazarus died shortly after the messenger left Bethany to go to Jesus in the Transjordan.
11. Joshua 5:13–6:27.
12. Judges 7.
13. Proverbs 3:5–6.
14. The disciples made another common mistake. They were basing their decision not to go to Jerusalem on the circumstances of Lazarus's health, not on the will of God. In other words, "Lord, if he sleeps, he will get better. Therefore, we don't need to go." The necessity of going to Jerusalem should have been determined not by Lazarus's condition, but by God's will.
15. 1 John 4:7.
16. Matthew 7:1.
17. Romans 8:28.
18. Hebrews 6:14.
19. Daniel 3:24–25.
20. Psalm 23:4; Isaiah 43:2.
21. Proverbs 2:8 NKJV.
22. Psalm 34:19 NKJV.
23. Zephaniah 3:17 NKJV.
24. Romans 3:23.
25. Romans 6:23.
26. 2 Corinthians 5:8.
27. 1 Corinthians 15:54–57.
28. Job 19:26; 1 Thessalonians 4:13–18.
29. Isaiah 63:9.
30. Hebrews 4:15 KJV.
31. Psalm 56:8 KJV.
32. Isaiah 63:9.
33. It has been suggested that one reason Jesus wept was that He knew the glory of where Lazarus was in comparison to where he would be when he returned. And although Jesus did raise Lazarus from the dead, Lazarus would die again.
34. "But Lord" is an oxymoron!
35. This is an anonymous quote I took from the bulletin of Pawley's Island Baptist Church, in Pawley's Island, South Carolina, pastored by Bob Barrows.
36. John 9:7.

37. John 5:8–9.
38. Mark 3:5.
39. It has been said that Jesus called Lazarus by name because if He had merely said, "Come forth," all the dead would have been raised!
40. Out of all the people buried in Judea, why did Jesus choose to raise Lazarus and not others? I've heard this story used to explain the Calvinistic doctrine that some people are predestined to be raised to eternal life, while others are not. It may be that doctrine can be argued from other passages of Scripture, but I reject that reasoning based on this story. It is very obvious from this passage that Lazarus was raised from the dead because he had two sisters praying for him.
41. Can we believe in miracles? We know Jesus did miracles, and we know miracles occurred with some frequency in the early church, but do they still happen today? Several years ago *Time* magazine ran a cover story on miracles that included the entire spectrum of opinion, from Cicero, who concluded pessimistically that "what was incapable of happening never happened, and what was capable of happening is not a miracle. . . . Consequently, there are no miracles," to Thomas Aquinas, who stated emphatically, "Christ was either liar, lunatic, or Lord," to Walt Whitman, who sentimentalized, "To me every hour of the light and dark is a miracle, every cubic inch of space is a miracle."

    A miracle has been described as a "morsel of grace, offered by a merciful God willing to meddle with the laws of His universe." Jesus called miracles "signs" to draw attention to the fact that miracles are not an end in themselves but a means to a greater end. They serve as a "sign" directing us to a deeper, broader, more important truth that God is teaching. "Touch me, heal me, the crowds demanded of their Messiah, and so even as He went about touching and healing, He acknowledged that miracles, if produced on demand, could sabotage the faith they were meant to strengthen. For the truly faithful, no miracle is necessary; for those who must doubt, no miracle is sufficient" (*Time*, April 10, 1995, 64–73).

    We seem the most desperate for a miracle when we are suffering either physically or emotionally or mentally or relationally. Miracles spell relief and deliverance and escape and victory. The story of Lazarus is the story of perhaps the most magnificent miracle Jesus performed while here on earth. But the story of Lazarus is the story of faith and the necessity of placing it in Jesus alone if we are to understand and overcome our suffering—if we are to live life, not just somehow, but triumphantly. If we are to pass from spiritual death to eternal life.
42. 1 Thessalonians 4:16.
43. Hebrews 12:1–2.
44. Jeremiah 18:3–6.
45. Romans 9:21 KJV.

Chapter 11: Jesus Makes Sin Forgivable . . . for Anyone

1. Romans 5:6–8.
2. A detachment of soldiers was between two hundred and six hundred men.
3. John 17:1.

4. Isaiah 32:17.
5. Philippians 2:10–11 NASB.
6. Deuteronomy 32:39; Isaiah 41:4, 43:10, 43:13, 46:4, 48:12.
7. John 12:6.
8. John 13:2–5.
9. When a dinner host wished to honor a special guest, he handed that guest a "sop," or a piece of bread dipped in wine; see John 13:26.
10. Matthew 26:48–50.
11. John 13:21–30.
12. Mark 14:29, 31.
13. John 11:7–8, 16.
14. Matthew 26:37–44.
15. It is noteworthy that the arrest that led to the trials and crucifixion of Jesus was Satan's finest hour. Yet Jesus clearly says that this was the cup that the Father had given Him. Such a clear perspective teaches you and me that when we are in God's will, even Satan's attacks can be taken from the Father's hand, knowing that He has allowed them for our good and His glory. See Romans 8:28.
16. Luke 22:51.
17. Matthew 27:3–5.
18. Exodus 21:32.
19. John 12:7–8.
20. John 13:27.
21. Matthew 27:3–4.
22. Matthew 27:4.
23. John 13:27; Mark 14:21.
24. Matthew 9:1–8.
25. 1 John 1:9.
26. Mark 14:50–52.
27. Acts 4:6.
28. Mark 14:55–56.
29. Matthew 26:63.
30. Matthew 26:64.
31. Matthew 26:65–66.
32. If Jesus was not who He claimed to be, then He was indeed worthy of death under Jewish law, since blasphemy carried with it the death penalty. See Leviticus 24:16.
33. Matthew 26:67.
34. Isaiah 50:6.
35. Matthew 27:1.
36. Acts 9:5.
37. Acts 7:58–59, 8:1.
38. 1 Timothy 1:13.
39. 1 Timothy 1:15–16.
40. Matthew 26:71.
41. Matthew 26:72.

42. Luke 22:59.
43. Matthew 26:73.
44. Matthew 26:74.
45. Luke 22:61.
46. Ibid.
47. Luke 22:62.
48. Luke 22:31–32.
49. John 20:1–2.
50. 1 Peter 2:7.
51. Luke 23:1.
52. Luke 23:2.
53. Five days earlier, on Sunday, Jesus had entered Jerusalem to the acclamation of thousands of Jewish pilgrims who had publicly acknowledged Him as the King of Israel. See John 12:13.
54. Luke 23:5.
55. Luke 23:7.
56. The story of Herod and his relationship with John the Baptist, as well as his reasons for having John beheaded, is found in Mark 6:14–29.
57. Matthew 11:11.
58. Mark 6:16.
59. Luke 23:8–10.
60. Matthew 13:12.
61. Luke 23:11.
62. Luke 22:69.
63. Revelation 19:11, 20:11–15.
64. Matthew 27:19.
65. Luke 23:14–16.
66. Luke 23:4, 14, 15 (two times), 22; John 18:38, 19:4, 6.
67. Isaiah 53:4–5. When I was a young girl, my mother took a pen and showed me how to mark through the personal plural pronouns and insert my name in their place. So the verses, including verse 6, would read: "Surely He took up *Anne's* infirmities and carried *Anne's* sorrows, yet *Anne* considered Him stricken by God, smitten by Him, and afflicted. But He was pierced for *Anne's* transgressions, He was crushed for *Anne's* iniquities; the punishment that brought *Anne* peace was upon Him, and by His wounds *Anne* is healed. *Anne*, like sheep, has gone astray, *Anne* has turned to *her* own way; and the Lord has laid on Him the iniquity of *Anne*." Try putting your name in.
68. Matthew 27:28–30.
69. Isaiah 52:14.
70. Matthew 27:13–14.
71. Matthew 27:16–17.
72. Matthew 27:18.
73. Mark 15:7.
74. Luke 23:18, 21.
75. Selected verses and phrases from Matthew 27:15–23.

76. Matthew 27:24–25. The voices of the mob at the Hall of Judgment during the last and final trial of Jesus seem to echo throughout history, "Let His blood be on us and on our children." Forty years after the crucifixion of Jesus, in AD 70, the Romans crushed Jerusalem. Not one stone was left on top of another. So many Jews were crucified, there wasn't enough wood for all the crosses, requiring two victims to be executed on each cross.
77. Barabbas was the first of many men whose life would be saved because of the death of Jesus Christ.
78. Luke 23:25.
79. Acts 2:36.

Chapter 12: Jesus Makes Sin Forgivable . . . for Everyone

1. Hebrews 10:4.
2. John 1:29.
3. Although this chapter is based primarily on John 19, I have included portions from the other three gospels in order to convey a more complete picture of these events. Each place where I have drawn from the other gospels is endnoted for your information.
4. Luke 23:33 KJV.
5. Luke 23:27; Mark 15:21.
6. Simon's brief brush with the blood of Christ changed his life. How could it not? His entire family became involved in the work of the gospel to the extent that his wife was considered like a mother to the apostle Paul, and his sons Rufus and Alexander became leaders in the early church. See Mark 15:21 and Romans 16:13.
7. Luke 14:27.
8. The biography of Jeremiah A. Denton Jr., can be found at http://www.nff.org.
9. Romans 8:17.
10. Luke 23:28.
11. Mark 15:24.
12. Mark 15:23.
13. Luke 23:34.
14. Acts 2:36, 38, 41.
15. Medical doctors tell us that the strongest instinct we possess is the instinct to breathe. Therefore a crucified victim could not just willfully collapse and refuse to breathe because his instinct took over and forced him to continue pushing up until physical weakness overcame him and he could not. History records that some victims survived as long as nine days on a cross. In this particular case, on Friday evening the guards were told to take down the crucified bodies of Jesus and the thieves on each side of Him so they wouldn't be hanging there on Passover. When the guards checked the bodies, they were amazed that Jesus was already dead. And in order to hasten the death of the two thieves, the guards broke their legs so that they could no longer push up and breathe. See John 19:31–33.

16. Some of the unanswerable questions about human suffering are: Why do the innocent suffer? Why do bad things happen to good people? Why does hate seem to triumph over love? Why does evil seem to win out over good? Why do the wicked seem to prosper while the righteous are defeated?
17. Matthew 27:41–43.
18. Romans 5:8.
19. Luke 23:39.
20. Luke 23:40–43.
21. Water baptism is essentially a symbolic "work" that gives outward testimony to our inward decision to receive Jesus Christ as our Savior. It is necessary for obedience to God's Word, but not for salvation, since the Bible clearly tells us we are saved by faith in Jesus alone. Compare Acts 2:38 with Ephesians 2:8–9.
22. Genesis 3:7–8.
23. Lotz, *God's Story*, 76.
24. 2 Corinthians 5:21.
25. Isaiah 64:6.
26. 2 Corinthians 5:21; Philippians 3:9; 1 Corinthians 1:30; Romans 10:4.
27. Luke 23:44–45.
28. The Bible describes hell as a place God has prepared for the devil, his angels (or demons), and those who refuse His gracious offer of salvation through faith in Jesus Christ. See Revelation 19:20, 20:10, 15. But we also think of hell, not just as a place, but as a state of eternal separation from God, which is what Jesus experienced at the Cross for us.
29. Once before, in Egypt, God's judgment had taken on the form of darkness. See Exodus 10:21–22. And at the end of human history, God's judgment will once again take the form of darkness. See Joel 2:31.
30. 2 Peter 3:8.
31. For a more complete explanation, see Lotz, *God's Story,* xx–xxii.
32. Genesis 22:1–14.
33. Romans 8:32.
34. Matthew 27:46.
35. In a conversation I had with a very godly woman about our Lord's heart-wrenching prayer from the cross, she emphatically told me she believed Jesus was not forsaken but only *felt* forsaken. I responded by pointing out to her that Jesus is the Truth. And He did not cease being the Truth when He hung on the cross. Jesus did not say, "God, I feel so forsaken." He clearly said, "My God, why have You forsaken Me?" Jesus was experiencing the very depths of the pit of hell and judgment as your sins and mine became a barrier between His Father and Himself that caused Them to be truly separated.
36. John 10:30.
37. 1 John 1:7.
38. Romans 3:23; Ephesians 2:1–3.
39. Matthew 27:50; Mark 15:37.
40. Luke 23:46.

Chapter 13: Jesus Makes Heaven Available . . . to the Sinner

1. This true story was told to my mother by an old gentleman who had been the little boy I've chosen to call Geoffrey.
2. The Cross and resurrection are inseparable. Together, they comprise a beautiful unity of God's love.
3. Matthew 5:15.
4. This statement comes from a pamphlet prepared by the Daughters of the Republic of Texas and given to those who tour the Alamo in San Antonio, Texas.
5. Mark 15:44–45.
6. Matthew 27:59–60. It is impossible to have a resurrection without a death. Therefore, the death and burial of Jesus of Nazareth are primary facts that confirm His resurrection three days later.
7. Matthew 27:56; Mark 15:40.
8. Matthew 27:54.
9. Luke 23:54; the Preparation Day referred to Friday, the day before the Sabbath. For an excellent, full treatment of the seeming contradiction between the Gospels on the time of the Last Supper and the crucifixion, please see "Introduction to John's Gospel, Interpretive Challenges," *The MacArthur Study Bible* (Nashville: Word Bibles, 1997), 1570–71.
10. Luke 23:56.
11. Mark 15:45.
12. Matthew 27:62–64.
13. Matthew 27:65.
14. Genesis 3:15.
15. Genesis 4:8.
16. Genesis 6:1–8.
17. Genesis 12:1–3; Galatians 3:16.
18. Genesis 21:8–9.
19. Genesis 27:41.
20. Genesis 37:18–20.
21. Exodus 1:8–22.
22. Exodus 2–12.
23. The book of Esther.
24. Matthew 2:1–8, 16–18.
25. Matthew 3:16–17.
26. Revelation 14:2.
27. Revelation 1:15.
28. Matthew 4:11.
29. John 13:21–30.
30. Luke 22:42–44.
31. Mark 15:31–32.
32. Did the earth quake from the force of the resurrection, similar to the way the earth trembles for miles around the launch of a rocket at Cape Canaveral? Or was the

earthquake associated with the descent of the angel? Or was it just to get the guards' undivided attention? (See Matthew 28:2.)

33. The stone was not rolled away to let Jesus out, because the tomb was already empty. It was rolled away to let the guards—and you and me—see in.
34. The stone was probably six to eight feet in diameter in order to adequately cover the entrance of the tomb. The very fact that the angel sat on it gives us an idea of the angel's size!
35. Ephesians 1:19–21.
36. Matthew 28:4.
37. Mark 16:2–3.
38. Luke 24:3–6.
39. Matthew 28:11.
40. Matthew 28:12–15.
41. Matthew 28:8–9.
42. John 20:6–7.
43. John 20:16–18, 21:7–19; Luke 24:13–35; John 20:19–20, 20:26–28; 1 Corinthians 15:6.
44. Luke 24:39–43.
45. Acts 4:20. According to church history, all of the disciples, except for John, were put to death for their faith in and proclamation of the risen Christ.
46. Acts 7:56, 9:1–6.
47. Luke 8:2.
48. Luke 4:41; James 2:19.
49. Psalm 103:12.
50. Malachi 3:17; Isaiah 43:4.
51. Psalm 40:2; Song of Solomon 2:4.
52. Luke 7:47.
53. Mark 15:40.
54. Like Mary, so many people today read their Bibles without ever recognizing the Voice of the living God behind the words.
55. At such a young age, my list of sins may have been brief. But, like any other daughter of Eve or son of Adam, I have a sin nature—a root of sin—that in time would grow and bear the ugly fruit of specific sins. When I confessed my sin to Jesus, I confessed not just specific sins, but also the very fact that I am a sinner. Praise God! I was, and am, forgiven!
56. Matthew 28:9–10.
57. Jeremiah 20:9.
58. Acts 4:20.

Chapter 14: Jesus Makes Heaven Available . . . to the Failure

1. See John 15:5.
2. Psalm 103:14.
3. John 20:22.
4. Matthew 16:22.

5. Matthew 26:45, 51; John 18:10.
6. Matthew 26:33–35; John 18:15–18, 25–27.
7. Luke 22:62.
8. Mark 16:7, emphasis added.
9. Luke 24:34, emphasis added.
10. Isaiah 64:4.
11. Psalm 27:13–14.
12. Luke 5:4.
13. Mark 1:17.
14. When Jesus called Peter to be a fisher of men, He used fishing as an analogy for evangelism. How successful have you been in sharing the gospel and leading people to faith in Jesus Christ? When Jesus asked Peter if he had caught any "fish," Peter readily admitted, "No." Are you ready to admit your failure in "fishing"? Are you tired, frustrated, and ready to quit even trying to present the gospel and share your faith, because you have yet to even get a "nibble" of interest, much less catch a "fish"? Could it be that God is waiting for you to admit your failure before He will let you know where the fish are? For instance, have you been so focused on your coworker that you haven't even noticed your neighbor? But maybe it's your neighbor who is ready to be "caught." Only God knows where the fish are, which is why it's important to pray and seek His direction and follow His instructions.
15. John 6:35.
16. Some New Testament scholars say that John used the Greek words *phileo* and *agape* as synonyms. Therefore there would be no distinction between the word for love in Jesus' questions and the word for love in Peter's answers.
17. Psalm 23; Isaiah 53:6; John 10:1–16.
18. What a blessing! They chose mine, which is titled *The Vision of His Glory*, and is based on the book of Revelation. It is a seven-session study that includes a workshop and six messages on video, plus a workbook with instructions, worksheets, message outlines, and leader's guide. For further information, contact AnGeL Ministries, P.O. Box 31167, Raleigh, NC 27622, or call 919-787-6606.
19. John 6:35, 51, 60, 63.
20. Psalm 23:3.
21. 1 Peter 2:7, paraphrased.
22. Philippians 2:5–8.
23. Matthew 16:24–26, paraphrased.
24. Romans 6:1–12 teaches us that we are already crucified with Christ. Our part is to claim it by faith as we are presented with the various choices that life presents.
25. Galatians 2:20.
26. Revelation 1:17.
27. Elizabeth Elliot, *A Chance to Die* (Old Tappan, NJ: Fleming H. Revell 1987).
28. John 3:16
29. John 20:30–31, emphasis added.

A Devotional Guide for

Daily Studies for
Personal or Group Use

A PERSONAL WORD FROM ANNE

My beloved friend, Jill Briscoe, once visited what had been an extremely poverty-stricken country in Africa. As she flew in, she looked down on miles and miles of African veldt that had previously been covered by a lush grasslike crop, but was now an unbroken, brown, dusty plain stretching all the way to the horizon. As Jill traveled to the mission station where she would be staying, mile after mile of barren, dry, poverty-stricken land passed by her window. Little dust devils danced in the hot afternoon sun, while shimmering heat waves made the emaciated, dust-covered people walking listlessly beside the road look more like ghostly apparitions than humans.

The relief workers told her the sad story: The veldt had once been a beautifully green, rolling expanse covered by a newly discovered crop that adapted easily to the climate and soil of the area. Within a few short years, this crop had promised to make the people in the area totally self-sufficient as it became the main, and plentiful, staple of their diet.

Sadly, the relief workers shook their heads as they explained what had happened: The crop had, indeed, become the main staple in the diet of the local people, but too late it had been found to have no nutritional value at all. The tragedy was that hundreds of people had starved to death—with their stomachs full!

Those pitiful African people seem to symbolize many church members in America today who are spiritually starving to death with their stomachs full! We have made the main staples of our "diet" those things that have no real nutritional value—political agendas, social issues, human rights, books about God's Word, musical videos, theological formulas for reaching the postmodern man, and marketing strategies for the local church, along with a myriad of conferences, seminars, retreats, dramas, and "special events." None of these things is harmful in itself, but when substituted for the nutrition of daily Bible reading and prayer, the result is increasing spiritual starvation.

For the past twenty years as I have crisscrossed America speaking in arenas, to conventions and churches, I have become convinced of one thing: the average church member is desperately hungry for God's Word. While we read books about it and hear sermons on it and live by principles from it, we are sadly devoid of it on a daily basis. When our lives begin to unravel due to pressure, problems, or pain, we don't seem to know how to access its power and truth in a personal, relevant way that makes a difference. As a result, thousands have spirits that are shriveling even while they are sobbing, "Please, just give me Jesus!"

What does your spiritual diet consist of? Although you may be an active church member and a committed Christian, could it be that you are actually starving for the Bread of Life? Are you starving for the Bread, which is Jesus Himself, offered to you and me through God's Word?

If so, then this workbook is for you! It has been designed to take you directly into God's Word. There is no middleman. There are no blanks to fill in. There is not even any cross-referencing required. The simple format for meditation has been developed from my own daily personal time in God's Word as a means of reading a passage in order to hear Him speaking to me personally through it. Day after day, as I use this method in my Bible reading, God has fed me and filled me to overflowing!

As you begin this Bible study, pray this simple prayer: "Dear God, *please, just give me Jesus!*" Then open your Bible and enjoy the Food!

Anne Graham Lotz

GETTING STARTED

These worksheets are designed to be used as a companion to *Just Give Me Jesus.* Used together, they will provide a format for Bible study that is effective for group discussion (Sunday school classes, women's or men's church groups, home or neighborhood Bible classes, one-on-one discipleship) as well as for your private devotions. Believing that God speaks to us through His Word, we have designed these worksheets to lead you through a series of questions concerning the designated Scripture passage. The exercises enable you to not only discover for yourself the eternal truths revealed by God in the Bible, but also to hear God speaking personally to you through His Word and thus have a fresh encounter with Him.

Getting Started on Your Own

It is suggested that *Getting Started, Tips for Success, Take One Step at a Time,* and the Sample Chapter be used as an initial lesson, in order to familiarize yourself with the format to be used. The worksheets are subsequently divided to correspond with the chapters of the book. If you make your way through this study using one set of worksheets each day, you will complete a chapter a week. The Scripture passage for each worksheet corresponds with the Scripture passage in the divisions of the book chapters. Each set of worksheets will provide a very rich, meaningful pathway for your daily walk with Jesus.

Getting Started in a Group

If you embark on this study through John's gospel in a group, you may want to meet once a week to share the insights you've gained. It is suggested that *Getting*

Started, Tips for Success, Take One Step at a Time, and the Sample Chapter be used as an initial lesson, in order to familiarize yourself with the format to be used. The worksheets are subsequently divided to correspond with the chapters of the book. If you make your way through this study using one set of worksheets each day, you will complete a chapter a week. Ideally, your group will gather each week under the leadership of a facilitator who will lead you through a meaningful discussion of what you've individually discovered. If the group is large (twelve or more), you may need to divide into smaller groups for discussion time, with moderators being chosen to lead each one.

The facilitator may offer a summation at the end of the group study, emphasizing specific applications from the gospel of John to meet the needs and characteristics of your particular group, depending on age, sex, and interests of the members.

Whether you choose to get started on your own or in a group, I pray that your time spent exploring John's gospel will result in your own fresh encounter with Jesus!

TIPS FOR SUCCESS

I have taken countless trips in my lifetime—some long, some short, some far, some near. But every single trip involves a certain amount of preparation in order to be successful. And the preparation itself requires a measure of discipline. This Bible study is no exception.

Spiritual discipline is an essential part of an individual's ability to grow in his or her personal relationship with God through knowledge and understanding of His Word. It is my sincere prayer that whether you use these worksheets as a private daily devotion or in a weekly group Bible study, it will provide you with an easy, meaningful format for this growth to occur.

To stay on track and make this study most effective and meaningful to your life, I offer these specific suggestions:

- Set aside a regular *place* for your daily Bible study.
- Set aside a regular *time* for your daily Bible study.
- Pray before beginning each day's study, asking God to speak to you through His Word.
- Write out your answers for each step of the worksheets in sequence. Do not skip a step.
- Make the time to be still and listen, reflecting thoughtfully on your responses, especially in Step 5.

TAKE ONE STEP AT A TIME

Step 1. LOOK IN GOD'S WORD: Begin by reading the designated passage of Scripture. This is printed for you on each day's devotional section. When you have finished reading the passage, move to Step 2.

Step 2. LIST THE FACTS: Make a verse-by-verse list of the outstanding facts. Don't get caught up in the details; just pinpoint the most obvious facts. As you make your list, do not paraphrase but use actual words from the passage itself. Take a moment to read the completed example of a worksheet on the following pages. When you have read the passage in Step 1, look over the facts listed in Step 2 so that you understand these instructions more clearly.

Step 3. LEARN THE LESSONS: After looking at the passage and listing the facts, you are ready for Step 3. Go back to the list of facts in Step 2 and look for a lesson to learn from each fact. Ask yourself who is speaking, what the subject is, where the action is taking place, when it happened, and so on. Ask, *What are the people in this passage doing that I should be doing? Is there a command I should obey? A promise I should claim? A warning I should heed? An example I should follow?* Look again at the completed example on the following pages. Note that you may have more than one lesson for each verse.

Step 4. LISTEN TO HIS VOICE: The fourth step is the most meaningful, but you cannot do it until Steps 1, 2, and 3 have been completed. In order to complete Step 4, rephrase the lessons you found in Step 3 and put them in the form of questions you could ask yourself, your spouse, your child, your friend, your neighbor, or your coworker. As you write out the questions, listen for God to communicate to you personally through His Word.

There are some challenging passages in the gospel of John. Don't get hung up on what you don't understand. Look for the general principles and lessons that can be learned. Remember, don't rush. It may take you several moments of prayerful meditation to discover meaningful lessons and hear God speak to you. The object of these devotional studies is not to get through the study, but to develop your personal relationship with God in order to satisfy your spiritual hunger and increase your spiritual health.

Step 5. LIVE IT OUT: Read the assigned Scripture passage prayerfully, objectively, thoughtfully, and attentively as you listen for God to speak. He may not speak to you through every verse, but He *will* speak. When He does, record in Step 5 the verse number, what it is He seems to be saying to you, and your response to Him. You might like to date it as a means not only of keeping a spiritual journal but also of holding yourself accountable to following through in obedience.

God bless you as you seek to learn this simple yet effective method of reading His Word, that you might hear His voice speaking to you personally through it. My prayer is that as you walk daily in this study through the gospel of John you will learn to love the Bread of Life.

1 **LOOK IN GOD'S WORD:**
Feel free to underline, circle, or otherwise mark text if it will aid your study.

Isaiah 55:1 "Come, all you who are thirsty, come to the waters; and you who have no money, come, buy and eat! Come, buy wine and milk without money and without cost.

2 Why spend money on what is not bread, and your labor on what does not satisfy? Listen, listen to me, and eat what is good, and your soul will delight in the richest of fare.

3 Give ear and come to me; hear me, that your soul may live. I will make an everlasting covenant with you, my faithful love promised to David."

2 **LIST THE FACTS:**
Make a verse-by-verse list of the most obvious facts. What does the passage say? Do not paraphrase.

55:1 You who are thirsty, who have no money, come, buy milk without cost.

55:2 Why spend money or labor on what is not bread? Listen, eat what is good.

55:3 Hear me, that your soul may live, I will make a covenant with you.

3 LEARN THE LESSONS:

What lessons can be learned from these facts? What do the facts mean? Is there an example to follow? Warning to heed? Promise to claim? Command to obey?

55:1 God freely invites us to come to Him through His Word in order to satisfy our spiritual hunger and thirst, cost-free.

55:2 Listening to God's voice speak to us personally as we read His Word is worth the time, money, and effort.

55:3 Our spiritual health depends upon our Bible reading.

4 LISTEN TO HIS VOICE:

What does this passage mean to you? Rewrite the lessons from Step 3 in the form of a question to ask yourself or another.

55:1 How thirsty am I spiritually?
Am I thirsty enough to accept God's invitation to drink the milk of His Word through my active, daily use of this study?

55:2 What time and effort am I willing to put into this study?
Will I use this study as the "utensil" that makes it possible for me to "eat right"?

55:3 Am I physically alive but spiritually starving because I have neglected my Bible reading?

LIVE IT OUT:

Pinpoint what God is saying to you from the passage. How will you respond? Write down today's date and what you will do now to live it out.

I commit to completing this study as a means of satisfying my hunger as I listen for God to speak to me personally through His Word.

CHAPTER 1

Jesus Makes God Visible . . . to Me

Who is Jesus? How can we know who He really is? We know by studying the truth. One of the few legitimate sources of historical information on His life is found in the four New Testament Gospels, including John's gospel, which we are studying.

So who is Jesus? Decide the answer for yourself as you read the apostle John's clear, confident, certain, and compelling biography. His stirring account begins by leaving no doubt that Jesus makes God visible to all, because Jesus is God as Man . . .

1 **LOOK IN GOD'S WORD:**
Feel free to underline, circle, or otherwise mark text if it will aid your study.

2 **LIST THE FACTS:**
Make a verse-by-verse list of the most obvious facts. What does the passage say? Do not paraphrase.

JOHN 1:1

1 In the beginning was the Word, and the Word was with God, and the Word was God.

3 **LEARN THE LESSONS:**
What lessons can be learned from these facts? What do the facts mean? Is there an example to follow? Warning to heed? Promise to claim? Command to obey?

4 **LISTEN TO HIS VOICE:**
What does this passage mean to you? Rewrite the lessons from Step 3 in the form of a question to ask yourself or another.

5 **LIVE IT OUT:**
Pinpoint what God is saying to you from the passage. How will you respond? Write down today's date and what you will do now to live it out.

1 **LOOK IN GOD'S WORD:**

2 **LIST THE FACTS:**

John 1:2–3
2 He was with God in the beginning.
3 Through him all things were made;
without him nothing was made that
has been made.

3 **LEARN THE LESSONS:**

4 **LISTEN TO HIS VOICE:**

5 **LIVE IT OUT:**

1 LOOK IN GOD'S WORD:

2 LIST THE FACTS:

JOHN 1:4–5

4 In him was life, and that life was the
light of men. **5** The light shines in the
darkness, but the darkness has not
understood it.

3 LEARN THE LESSONS:

4 LISTEN TO HIS VOICE:

5 LIVE IT OUT:

1 **LOOK IN GOD'S WORD:**

2 **LIST THE FACTS:**

John 1:6–8

6 There came a man who was sent
from God; his name was John. **7** He
came as a witness to testify concerning that light, so that through him all
men might believe. **8** He himself was
not the light; he came only as a witness to the light.

3 LEARN THE LESSONS:

4 LISTEN TO HIS VOICE:

5 LIVE IT OUT:

1 **LOOK IN GOD'S WORD:**

2 **LIST THE FACTS:**

JOHN 1:9

9 The true light that gives light to
every man was coming into the world.

3 **LEARN THE LESSONS:**

4 **LISTEN TO HIS VOICE:**

5 **LIVE IT OUT:**

COMMITMENT:

What was the most meaningful lesson to you from each day's study this week?

Study #1

Study #2

Study #3

Study #4

Study #5

As you reflect on all the lessons, what one thing has God seemed to say to you from John 1:1–9? Take a moment now to write out what He has said.

What has been your response?

Is there anything else you need to do in order to follow through completely?

Date your answer—then do it. Be committed!

CHAPTER 2

Jesus Makes God Visible . . . as Man

Before Jesus came, God looked down from heaven as man scurried around in panic, unable to cope with the confusion and conflict of life—especially when man's whole world seemed to collapse and life dealt unexpected blows. All man's answers to the problems of pain and evil and death were insufficient. Life just didn't make sense. There seemed to be no order or long-term purpose to it all. And so God became a Man, not just to sort out the confusion and rebuild the collapsed world, but also to offer a new life altogether. Jesus came to make God visible as Man. And that visibility is irresistibly compelling . . .

1 **LOOK IN GOD'S WORD:** Feel free to underline, circle, or otherwise mark text if it will aid your study.

2 **LIST THE FACTS:** Make a verse-by-verse list of the most obvious facts. What does the passage say? Do not paraphrase.

JOHN 1:10–11
10 He was in the world, and though
the world was made through him, the
world did not recognize him. **11** He
came to that which was his own, but
his own did not receive him.

3

LEARN THE LESSONS:
What lessons can be learned from these facts? What do the facts mean? Is there an example to follow? Warning to heed? Promise to claim? Command to obey?

4

LISTEN TO HIS VOICE:
What does this passage mean to you? Rewrite the lessons from Step 3 in the form of a question to ask yourself or another.

5

LIVE IT OUT:
Pinpoint what God is saying to you from the passage. How will you respond? Write down today's date and what you will do now to live it out.

1 LOOK IN GOD'S WORD:

2 LIST THE FACTS:

JOHN 1:12–13
12 Yet to all who received him, to
those who believed in his name, he
gave the right to become children of
God— **13** children born not of natural descent, nor of human decision or
a husband's will, but born of God.

3 **LEARN THE LESSONS:**

4 **LISTEN TO HIS VOICE:**

5 **LIVE IT OUT:**

1 LOOK IN GOD'S WORD:

2 LIST THE FACTS:

JOHN 1:14

14 The Word became flesh and made
his dwelling among us. We have seen
his glory, the glory of the One and
Only, who came from the Father, full
of grace and truth.

3 LEARN THE LESSONS:

4 LISTEN TO HIS VOICE:

5 LIVE IT OUT:

1 **LOOK IN GOD'S WORD:**

2 **LIST THE FACTS:**

John 1:15

15 John testifies concerning him. He
cries out, saying, "This was he of
whom I said, 'He who comes after me
has surpassed me because he was
before me.'"

3 LEARN THE LESSONS:

4 LISTEN TO HIS VOICE:

5 LIVE IT OUT:

1 LOOK IN GOD'S WORD:

2 LIST THE FACTS:

John 1:16–18

16 From the fullness of his grace we have all received one blessing after another. **17** For the law was given through Moses; grace and truth came through Jesus Christ. **18** No one has ever seen God, but God the One and Only, who is at the Father's side, has made him known.

3 LEARN THE LESSONS:

4 LISTEN TO HIS VOICE:

5 LIVE IT OUT:

COMMITMENT:

What was the most meaningful lesson to you from each day's study this week?

Study #1

Study #2

Study #3

Study #4

Study #5

As you reflect on all the lessons, what one thing has God seemed to say to you from John 1:10–18? Take a moment now to write out what He has said.

What has been your response?

Is there anything else you need to do in order to follow through completely?

Date your answer—then do it. Be committed!

CHAPTER 3

Jesus Makes Change Possible . . . When Love Runs Out

Do you feel trapped in a marriage where the love has run out? Have you panicked, looking for escape in an illicit relationship, afternoon fantasies, romance novels, alcohol, or divorce? Or have you resigned yourself to your fate, plunging into a demanding career, the lives of your children, church activities, or community volunteerism in a desperate effort to manage the pain?

Praise God! There is hope. Jesus makes change possible, even when the love runs out.

Marriage is God's idea. If your marriage is broken, take it to Him. The Creator who made it in the first place can make it work again, which is one reason why God has given you Jesus . . .

1 **LOOK IN GOD'S WORD:**
Feel free to underline, circle, or otherwise mark text if it will aid your study.

2 **LIST THE FACTS:**
Make a verse-by-verse list of the most obvious facts. What does the passage say? Do not paraphrase.

JOHN 2:1–2
1 On the third day a wedding took
place at Cana in Galilee. Jesus' mother
was there, **2** and Jesus and his disciples
had also been invited to the wedding.

3 **LEARN THE LESSONS:**
What lessons can be learned from these facts? What do the facts mean? Is there an example to follow? Warning to heed? Promise to claim? Command to obey?

4 **LISTEN TO HIS VOICE:**
What does this passage mean to you? Rewrite the lessons from Step 3 in the form of a question to ask yourself or another.

5 **LIVE IT OUT:**
Pinpoint what God is saying to you from the passage. How will you respond? Write down today's date and what you will do now to live it out.

1 LOOK IN GOD'S WORD:

2 LIST THE FACTS:

John 2:3–4

3 When the wine was gone,
Jesus'mother said to him, "They have
no more wine." **4** "Dear woman, why
do you involve me?" Jesus replied, "My
time has not yet come."

3 **LEARN THE LESSONS:**

4 **LISTEN TO HIS VOICE:**

5 **LIVE IT OUT:**

1 LOOK IN GOD'S WORD:

John 2:5
5 His mother said to the servants,
"Do whatever he tells you."

2 LIST THE FACTS:

3 **LEARN THE LESSONS:**

4 **LISTEN TO HIS VOICE:**

5 **LIVE IT OUT:**

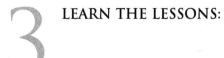

1 LOOK IN GOD'S WORD:

JOHN 2:6–8
6 Nearby stood six stone water jars,
the kind used by the Jews for ceremonial washing, each holding from
twenty to thirty gallons. **7** Jesus said
to the servants, "Fill the jars with
water"; so they filled them to the
brim. **8** Then he told them, "Now
draw some out and take it to the master of the banquet." They did so.

2 LIST THE FACTS:

3 LEARN THE LESSONS:

4 LISTEN TO HIS VOICE:

5 LIVE IT OUT:

1 LOOK IN GOD'S WORD:

2 LIST THE FACTS:

JOHN 2:9–11

9 and the master of the banquet
tasted the water that had been turned
into wine. He did not realize where it
had come from, though the servants
who had drawn the water knew. Then
he called the bridegroom aside **10** and
said, "Everyone brings out the choice
wine first and then the cheaper wine
after the guests have had too much to
drink; but you have saved the best till
now." **11** This, the first of his miraculous signs, Jesus performed in Cana of
Galilee. He thus revealed his glory,
and his disciples put their faith in
him.

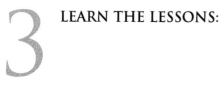

3 LEARN THE LESSONS:

4 LISTEN TO HIS VOICE:

5 LIVE IT OUT:

COMMITMENT:

What was the most meaningful lesson to you from each day's study this week?

Study #1

Study #2

Study #3

Study #4

Study #5

As you reflect on all the lessons, what one thing has God seemed to say to you from John 2:1–11? Take a moment now to write out what He has said.

What has been your response?

Is there anything else you need to do in order to follow through completely?

Date your answer—then do it. Be committed!

CHAPTER 4

Jesus Makes Change Possible . . . When Life Isn't Enough

Is something missing in your life, something you can't define? Perhaps all you know is that life doesn't seem to be enough for you.

Has your search for joy, happiness, and meaning caused you to climb upward in your career, seek a higher position, devote yourself to greater success in your business? When that didn't work, did you decide you needed a way of drawing attention to yourself by increasing your public reputation, visibility, or fame? Did you become more frustrated when that turned out to be another dead end? Perhaps then you rushed to find a way of remaking your image through cosmetic surgery, dieting, weightlifting, jogging, an exercise video, or a membership at the spa where you sculpted your body? As a last act of desperation, did you throw yourself into pleasurable pursuits, entertainment, fun? As a result, do you find that at this moment you are beyond frustration and totally exhausted in soul and spirit? You've just died on the inside. Hasn't anyone told you? You need the basic Necessity for real life. You need Jesus. He makes change possible when life isn't enough . . .

1 **LOOK IN GOD'S WORD:**
Feel free to underline, circle, or otherwise mark text if it will aid your study.

2 **LIST THE FACTS:**
Make a verse-by-verse list of the most obvious facts. What does the passage say? Do not paraphrase.

JOHN 3:1–4

1 Now there was a man of the
Pharisees named Nicodemus, a member of the Jewish ruling council. **2** He
came to Jesus at night and said,
"Rabbi, we know you are a teacher
who has come from God. For no one
could perform the miraculous signs
you are doing if God were not with
him." **3** In reply Jesus declared, "I tell
you the truth, no one can see the
kingdom of God unless he is born
again." **4** "How can a man be born
when he is old?" Nicodemus asked.
"Surely he cannot enter a second time
into his mother's womb to be born!"

3

LEARN THE LESSONS:
What lessons can be learned from these facts? What do the facts mean? Is there an example to follow? Warning to heed? Promise to claim? Command to obey?

4

LISTEN TO HIS VOICE:
What does this passage mean to you? Rewrite the lessons from Step 3 in the form of a question to ask yourself or another.

5

LIVE IT OUT:
Pinpoint what God is saying to you from the passage. How will you respond? Write down today's date and what you will do now to live it out.

1 LOOK IN GOD'S WORD:

2 LIST THE FACTS:

JOHN 3:5–9

5 Jesus answered, "I tell you the truth,
no one can enter the kingdom of God
unless he is born of water and the
Spirit. **6** Flesh gives birth to flesh,
but the Spirit gives birth to spirit. **7**
You should not be surprised at my
saying, 'You must be born again.' **8**
The wind blows wherever it pleases.
You hear its sound, but you cannot tell
where it comes from or where it is
going. So it is with everyone born of
the Spirit." **9** "How can this be?"
Nicodemus asked.

3 **LEARN THE LESSONS:**

4 **LISTEN TO HIS VOICE:**

5 **LIVE IT OUT:**

1 LOOK IN GOD'S WORD:

2 LIST THE FACTS:

John 3:10–15

10 "You are Israel's teacher," said
Jesus, "and do you not understand
these things? **11** I tell you the truth,
we speak of what we know, and we
testify to what we have seen, but still
you people do not accept our testimony. **12** I have spoken to you of
earthly things and you do not believe;
how then will you believe if I speak of
heavenly things? **13** No one has ever
gone into heaven except the one who
came from heaven—the Son of Man.
14 Just as Moses lifted up the snake
in the desert, so the Son of Man must
be lifted up, **15** that everyone who
believes in him may have eternal life."

3 **LEARN THE LESSONS:**

4 **LISTEN TO HIS VOICE:**

5 **LIVE IT OUT:**

1 **LOOK IN GOD'S WORD:**

2 **LIST THE FACTS:**

JOHN 3:16–18
16 "For God so loved the world that
he gave his one and only Son, that
whoever believes in him shall not perish but have eternal life. **17** For God
did not send his Son into the world to
condemn the world, but to save the
world through him. **18** Whoever
believes in him is not condemned, but
whoever does not believe stands condemned already because he has not
believed in the name of God's one
and only Son."

3 LEARN THE LESSONS:

4 LISTEN TO HIS VOICE:

5 LIVE IT OUT:

1 LOOK IN GOD'S WORD:

2 LIST THE FACTS:

JOHN 3:19–21

19 "This is the verdict: Light has
come into the world, but men loved
darkness instead of light because their
deeds were evil. **20** Everyone who
does evil hates the light, and will not
come into the light for fear that his
deeds will be exposed. **21** But whoever lives by the truth comes into the
light, so that it may be seen plainly
that what he has done has been done
through God."

3 **LEARN THE LESSONS:**

4 **LISTEN TO HIS VOICE:**

5 **LIVE IT OUT:**

COMMITMENT:

What was the most meaningful lesson to you from each day's study this week?

Study #1

Study #2

Study #3

Study #4

Study #5

As you reflect on all the lessons, what one thing has God seemed to say to you from John 3:1–21? Take a moment now to write out what He has said.

What has been your response?

Is there anything else you need to do in order to follow through completely?

Date your answer—then do it. Be committed!

CHAPTER 5

Jesus Makes Happiness Attainable . . . For the Outcast

After visiting with Nicodemus, Jesus headed into the Judean countryside with His small band of disciples. As people began flocking to Him, rumors about His popularity and ministry began to develop into a controversy that threatened to divide His followers from those of His cousin and forerunner, John the Baptist. Rather than lend fuel to the fires of gossip and jealousy, Jesus quietly withdrew, returning to Galilee. On His journey through Samaria, He had a divine appointment with one woman—an outcast from society—who was running on empty.

I find myself from time to time running on empty.
In the busyness of ministry,
the pressures of responsibility,
the demands of family,
the weariness of activity,
the excitement of opportunity,
I sometimes wake up and realize, I am so dry and thirsty. Invariably, when I examine myself, the reason for the dryness of spirit can be traced to one thing: I'm not drinking freely of the Water of Life. I'm neglecting my Bible study. I'm rushing through my prayer time. I'm not listening to the voice of the Lord because I'm just too busy to be still. At those times I carve out quiet interludes to confess my sins and read and meditate and pray and listen and just drink Him in.

Thank You, dear God, for still giving Living Water from the Well that never goes dry . . .

Note: Some Scripture verses were omitted on the worksheets for this chapter due to space restraints. But you are encouraged to go back and study the entire passage for the fullest blessing.

1 **LOOK IN GOD'S WORD:**
Feel free to underline, circle, or otherwise mark text if it will aid your study.

2 **LIST THE FACTS:**
Make a verse-by-verse list of the most obvious facts. What does the passage say? Do not paraphrase.

JOHN 4:1–6

1 The Pharisees heard that Jesus was
gaining and baptizing more disciples
than John, **2** although in fact it was
not Jesus who baptized, but his disciples. **3** When the Lord learned of
this, he left Judea and went back once
more to Galilee. **4** Now he had to go
through Samaria. **5** So he came to a
town in Samaria called Sychar, near
the plot of ground Jacob had given to
his son Joseph. **6** Jacob's well was
there, and Jesus, tired as he was from
the journey, sat down by the well. It
was about the sixth hour.

3

LEARN THE LESSONS:
What lessons can be learned from these facts? What do the facts mean? Is there an example to follow? Warning to heed? Promise to claim? Command to obey?

4

LISTEN TO HIS VOICE:
What does this passage mean to you? Rewrite the lessons from Step 3 in the form of a question to ask yourself or another.

LIVE IT OUT:
Pinpoint what God is saying to you from the passage. How will you respond? Write down today's date and what you will do now to live it out.

1 LOOK IN GOD'S WORD:

JOHN 4:7–11; 13–14

7 When a Samaritan woman came to
draw water, Jesus said to her, "Will you
give me a drink?" **8** (His disciples had
gone into the town to buy food.) **9** The
Samaritan woman said to him, "You
are a Jew and I am a Samaritan
woman. How can you ask me for a
drink?" (For Jews do not associate with
Samaritans.) **10** Jesus answered her, "If
you knew the gift of God and who it
is that asks you for a drink, you would
have asked him and he would have
given you living water." **11** "Sir," the
woman said, "you have nothing to draw
with and the well is deep. Where can
you get this living water?

13 Jesus answered, "Everyone who
drinks this water will be thirsty again,
14 but whoever drinks the water I give
him will never thirst. Indeed, the water
I give him will become in him a spring
of water welling up to eternal life."

2 LIST THE FACTS:

3 **LEARN THE LESSONS:**

4 **LISTEN TO HIS VOICE:**

5 **LIVE IT OUT:**

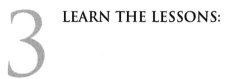

1 LOOK IN GOD'S WORD:

2 LIST THE FACTS:

JOHN 4:16–21; 24–26

16 He told her, "Go, call your husband and come back." **17** "I have no
husband," she replied. Jesus said to
her, "You are right when you say you
have no husband. **18** The fact is, you
have had five husbands, and the man
you now have is not your husband.
What you have just said is quite true."
19 "Sir," the woman said, "I can see
that you are a prophet. **20** Our fathers
worshiped on this mountain, but you
Jews claim that the place where we
must worship is in Jerusalem." **21**
Jesus declared, "Believe me, woman, a
time is coming when you will worship
the Father neither on this mountain
nor in Jerusalem.

24 God is spirit, and his worshipers
must worship in spirit and in truth."
25 The woman said, "I know that
Messiah" (called Christ) "is coming.
When he comes, he will explain
everything to us." **26** Then Jesus
declared, "I who speak to you am he."

3 LEARN THE LESSONS:

4 LISTEN TO HIS VOICE:

5 LIVE IT OUT:

1 LOOK IN GOD'S WORD:

2 LIST THE FACTS:

JOHN 4:27–34
27 Just then his disciples returned and
were surprised to find him talking
with a woman. But no one asked,
"What do you want?" or "Why are
you talking with her?" **28** Then, leaving her water jar, the woman went
back to the town and said to the
people, **29** "Come, see a man who told
me everything I ever did. Could this
be the Christ?" **30** They came out of
the town and made their way toward
him. **31** Meanwhile his disciples urged
him, "Rabbi, eat something." **32** But
he said to them, "I have food to eat
that you know nothing about." **33**
Then his disciples said to each other,
"Could someone have brought him
food?" **34** "My food," said Jesus, "is to
do the will of him who sent me and
to finish his work."

3 LEARN THE LESSONS:

4 LISTEN TO HIS VOICE:

5 LIVE IT OUT:

1 LOOK IN GOD'S WORD:

2 LIST THE FACTS:

JOHN 4:35–42

35 "Do you not say, 'Four months
more and then the harvest'? I tell you,
open your eyes and look at the fields!
They are ripe for harvest. **36** Even
now the reaper draws his wages, even
now he harvests the crop for eternal
life, so that the sower and the reaper
may be glad together. **37** Thus the
saying 'One sows and another reaps' is
true. **38** I sent you to reap what you
have not worked for. Others have
done the hard work, and you have
reaped the benefits of their labor." **39**
Many of the Samaritans from that
town believed in him because of the
woman's testimony, "He told me
everything I ever did." **40** So when
the Samaritans came to him, they
urged him to stay with them, and he
stayed two days. **41** And because of
his words many more became believers. **42** They said to the woman, "We
no longer believe just because of what
you said; now we have heard for ourselves, and we know that this man
really is the Savior of the world."

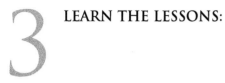

3 **LEARN THE LESSONS:**

4 **LISTEN TO HIS VOICE:**

5 **LIVE IT OUT:**

COMMITMENT:

What was the most meaningful lesson to you from each day's study this week?

Study #1

Study #2

Study #3

Study #4

Study #5

As you reflect on all the lessons, what one thing has God seemed to say to you from John 4:1–42? Take a moment now to write out what He has said.

What has been your response?

Is there anything else you need to do in order to follow through completely?

Date your answer—then do it. Be committed!

CHAPTER 6

Jesus Makes Happiness Attainable . . . for the Bypassed

The pool by the Sheep Gate in Jerusalem was very probably circular but enclosed by five breezeways that formed a pentagon, with each of its five sides made up of a porch covered by an arch. Possibly it was a mineral or sulfur spring that bubbled out of the ground, drawing the attention of the desperately hopeless who believed it to possess healing, curative powers. It was around this pool, under the covered arches, that those who were bypassed by the rest of society gathered, focusing on the legend that said when an angel caused the water to bubble up, the first person into it would be healed . . .

1 **LOOK IN GOD'S WORD:**
Feel free to underline, circle, or otherwise mark text if it will aid your study.

2 **LIST THE FACTS:**
Make a verse-by-verse list of the most obvious facts. What does the passage say? Do not paraphrase.

JOHN 5:1
1 Some time later, Jesus went up to Jerusalem for a feast of the Jews.

3

LEARN THE LESSONS:
What lessons can be learned from these facts? What do the facts mean? Is there an example to follow? Warning to heed? Promise to claim? Command to obey?

4

LISTEN TO HIS VOICE:
What does this passage mean to you? Rewrite the lessons from Step 3 in the form of a question to ask yourself or another.

5

LIVE IT OUT:
Pinpoint what God is saying to you from the passage. How will you respond? Write down today's date and what you will do now to live it out.

1 LOOK IN GOD'S WORD:

2 LIST THE FACTS:

JOHN 5:2–3

2 Now there is in Jerusalem near the
Sheep Gate a pool, which in Aramaic
is called Bethesda and which is surrounded by five covered colonnades.
3 Here a great number of disabled
people used to lie—the blind, the
lame, the paralyzed.

3 **LEARN THE LESSONS:**

4 **LISTEN TO HIS VOICE:**

5 **LIVE IT OUT:**

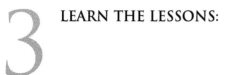

1 LOOK IN GOD'S WORD:

2 LIST THE FACTS:

JOHN 5:5–6

5 One who was there had been an
invalid for thirty-eight years. **6** When
Jesus saw him lying there and learned
that he had been in this condition for
a long time, he asked him, "Do you
want to get well?"

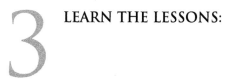

3 **LEARN THE LESSONS:**

4 **LISTEN TO HIS VOICE:**

5 **LIVE IT OUT:**

1 LOOK IN GOD'S WORD:

2 LIST THE FACTS:

JOHN 5:7

7 "Sir," the invalid replied, "I have no one to help me into the pool when the water is stirred. While I am trying to get in, someone else goes down ahead of me."

3 **LEARN THE LESSONS:**

4 **LISTEN TO HIS VOICE:**

5 **LIVE IT OUT:**

1 LOOK IN GOD'S WORD:

2 LIST THE FACTS:

JOHN 5:8–9

8 Then Jesus said to him, "Get up!
Pick up your mat and walk." **9** At
once the man was cured; he picked up
his mat and walked. The day on
which this took place was a Sabbath.

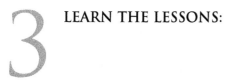

3 **LEARN THE LESSONS:**

4 **LISTEN TO HIS VOICE:**

5 **LIVE IT OUT:**

COMMITMENT:

What was the most meaningful lesson to you from each day's study this week?

Study #1

Study #2

Study #3

Study #4

Study #5

As you reflect on all the lessons, what one thing has God seemed to say to you from John 5:1–9? Take a moment now to write out what He has said.

What has been your response?

Is there anything else you need to do in order to follow through completely?

Date your answer—then do it. Be committed!

CHAPTER 7

Jesus Makes Resources Ample . . . to Me

Jesus saw the physical, emotional, and spiritual needs of His friends and knew the solution was a time of quiet rest and reflection. And He knows the solution is the same for you and me today. So He invites us, as He did His disciples, "Come with Me by yourself to a quiet place and get some rest."

It was Passover time, it was a national holiday, it was springtime, and it must have seemed the perfect day to join Jesus for a picnic in the hills.

I wonder how the disciples felt as they looked up and saw the trickle of people coming around the end of the lake. I wonder how they felt when they saw the trickle grow into a river that grew into a flood of five thousand men, not counting women and children. Jesus gave up His time to Himself. He gave up His "holiday." He gave up His "family" time in order to meet the needs of the crowd. He knew that meeting the needs of others invariably requires some personal sacrifice.

1 **LOOK IN GOD'S WORD:**
Feel free to underline, circle, or otherwise mark text if it will aid your study.

2 **LIST THE FACTS:**
Make a verse-by-verse list of the most obvious facts. What does the passage say? Do not paraphrase.

JOHN 6:1–4
1 Some time after this, Jesus crossed
to the far shore of the Sea of Galilee
(that is, the Sea of Tiberias), **2** and a
great crowd of people followed him
because they saw the miraculous signs
he had performed on the sick. **3** Then
Jesus went up on a mountainside and
sat down with his disciples. **4** The
Jewish Passover Feast was near.

3 **LEARN THE LESSONS:**
What lessons can be learned from these facts? What do the facts mean? Is there an example to follow? Warning to heed? Promise to claim? Command to obey?

4 **LISTEN TO HIS VOICE:**
What does this passage mean to you? Rewrite the lessons from Step 3 in the form of a question to ask yourself or another.

5 **LIVE IT OUT:**
Pinpoint what God is saying to you from the passage. How will you respond? Write down today's date and what you will do now to live it out.

1 LOOK IN GOD'S WORD:

JOHN 6:5–6
5 When Jesus looked up and saw a
great crowd coming toward him, he
said to Philip, "Where shall we buy
bread for these people to eat?" **6** He
asked this only to test him, for he
already had in mind what he was
going to do.

2 LIST THE FACTS:

3 **LEARN THE LESSONS:**

4 **LISTEN TO HIS VOICE:**

5 **LIVE IT OUT:**

1 LOOK IN GOD'S WORD:

2 LIST THE FACTS:

JOHN 6:7–9

7 Philip answered him, "Eight
months' wages would not buy enough
bread for each one to have a bite!" **8**
Another of his disciples, Andrew,
Simon Peter's brother, spoke up, **9**
"Here is a boy with five small barley
loaves and two small fish, but how far
will they go among so many?"

3 **LEARN THE LESSONS:**

4 **LISTEN TO HIS VOICE:**

5 **LIVE IT OUT:**

1 LOOK IN GOD'S WORD:

2 LIST THE FACTS:

JOHN 6:10–11

10 Jesus said, "Have the people sit
down." There was plenty of grass in
that place, and the men sat down,
about five thousand of them. **11** Jesus
then took the loaves, gave thanks, and
distributed to those who were seated
as much as they wanted. He did the
same with the fish.

3 LEARN THE LESSONS:

4 LISTEN TO HIS VOICE:

5 LIVE IT OUT:

1 **LOOK IN GOD'S WORD:**

2 **LIST THE FACTS:**

JOHN 6:12–14
12 When they had all had enough to
eat, he said to his disciples, "Gather
the pieces that are left over. Let nothing be wasted." **13** So they gathered
them and filled twelve baskets with
the pieces of the five barley loaves left
over by those who had eaten. **14** After
the people saw the miraculous sign
that Jesus did, they began to say,
"Surely this is the Prophet who is to
come into the world."

3 **LEARN THE LESSONS:**

4 **LISTEN TO HIS VOICE:**

5 **LIVE IT OUT:**

COMMITMENT:

What was the most meaningful lesson to you from each day's study this week?

Study #1

Study #2

Study #3

Study #4

Study #5

As you reflect on all the lessons, what one thing has God seemed to say to you from John 6:1–14? Take a moment now to write out what He has said.

What has been your response?

Is there anything else you need to do in order to follow through completely?

Date your answer—then do it. Be committed!

CHAPTER 8

Jesus Makes Resources Ample . . . in Me

A lot of Christians I know are trying to live the Christian life without ever activating the power. It may be possible to get some things done without power, but the effort and the struggle will make most want to quit. And the power is not so much a "what" as a "who." The power is the person of the Holy Spirit.

There are times when I have gotten the distinct impression from some Christians that the Holy Spirit is an optional extra, reserved primarily for benedictions, baptisms, and those we label "charismatics." Others give the impression that He is more like a heavenly genie in a bottle, Who, if you rub Him with the right mixture of prayer and faith, will perform miracles for you. But the Holy Spirit is not an optional extra! He is not to be reserved only for special occasions or exclusive groups, nor is He a trick-performing genie. He is a divine necessity who is imparted to each and every believer at the moment of conversion. He is Jesus in me . . .

1 **LOOK IN GOD'S WORD:**
Feel free to underline, circle, or otherwise mark text if it will aid your study.

2 **LIST THE FACTS:**
Make a verse-by-verse list of the most obvious facts. What does the passage say? Do not paraphrase.

JOHN 7:37–39

37 On the last and greatest day of the
Feast, Jesus stood and said in a loud
voice, "If anyone is thirsty, let him
come to me and drink. **38** Whoever
believes in me, as the Scripture has
said, streams of living water will flow
from within him." **39** By this he
meant the Spirit, whom those who
believed in him were later to receive.
Up to that time the Spirit had not
been given, since Jesus had not yet
been glorified.

3 **LEARN THE LESSONS:**
What lessons can be learned from these facts? What do the facts mean? Is there an example to follow? Warning to heed? Promise to claim? Command to obey?

4 **LISTEN TO HIS VOICE:**
What does this passage mean to you? Rewrite the lessons from Step 3 in the form of a question to ask yourself or another.

5 **LIVE IT OUT:**
Pinpoint what God is saying to you from the passage. How will you respond? Write down today's date and what you will do now to live it out.

1 LOOK IN GOD'S WORD:

JOHN 14:15–18

15 "If you love me, you will obey what
I command.**16** And I will ask the
Father, and he will give you another
Counselor to be with you forever—
17 the Spirit of truth. The world cannot accept him, because it neither sees
him nor knows him. But you know
him, for he lives with you and will be
in you. **18** I will not leave you as
orphans; I will come to you."

2 LIST THE FACTS:

3 **LEARN THE LESSONS:**

4 **LISTEN TO HIS VOICE:**

5 **LIVE IT OUT:**

1 LOOK IN GOD'S WORD:

2 LIST THE FACTS:

JOHN 14:19–21

19 "Before long, the world will not see
me anymore, but you will see me.
Because I live, you also will live. **20**
On that day you will realize that I am
in my Father, and you are in me, and I
am in you. **21** Whoever has my commands and obeys them, he is the one
who loves me. He who loves me will
be loved by my Father, and I too will
love him and show myself to him."

3 **LEARN THE LESSONS:**

4 **LISTEN TO HIS VOICE:**

5 **LIVE IT OUT:**

1 **LOOK IN GOD'S WORD:**

2 **LIST THE FACTS:**

JOHN 14:22–24

22 Then Judas (not Judas Iscariot)
said, "But, Lord, why do you intend to
show yourself to us and not to the
world?" **23** Jesus replied, "If anyone
loves me, he will obey my teaching.
My Father will love him, and we will
come to him and make our home
with him. **24** He who does not love
me will not obey my teaching. These
words you hear are not my own; they
belong to the Father who sent me."

3 **LEARN THE LESSONS:**

4 **LISTEN TO HIS VOICE:**

5 **LIVE IT OUT:**

1 LOOK IN GOD'S WORD:

2 LIST THE FACTS:

John 14:25–26
25 "All this I have spoken while still
with you. **26** But the Counselor, the
Holy Spirit, whom the Father will
send in my name, will teach you all
things and will remind you of everything I have said to you."

3 LEARN THE LESSONS:

4 LISTEN TO HIS VOICE:

5 LIVE IT OUT:

COMMITMENT:

What was the most meaningful lesson to you from each day's study this week?

Study #1

Study #2

Study #3

Study #4

Study #5

As you reflect on all the lessons, what one thing has God seemed to say to you from John 7:37–39; 14:15–26? Take a moment now to write out what He has said.

What has been your response?

Is there anything else you need to do in order to follow through completely?

Date your answer—then do it. Be committed!

CHAPTER 9

Jesus Makes Suffering Understandable . . . to the Observer

The problem of pain and questions about suffering are as old as the human race. But they remain the clinical subject of philosophical theories and intellectual sparring and theological debate until they become personal, until it's *our* homes or *our* children or *our* loved ones who are hurting. Then we simply have desperate questions that need direct answers.

The disciples had been so sure that suffering was a punishment for someone's fault that it was a totally new thought to consider suffering as a powerful and personal opportunity to glorify God . . .

1

LOOK IN GOD'S WORD:
Feel free to underline, circle, or otherwise mark text if it will aid your study.

2

LIST THE FACTS:
Make a verse-by-verse list of the most obvious facts. What does the passage say? Do not paraphrase.

JOHN 9:1–7

1 As he went along, he saw a man
blind from birth. **2** His disciples asked
him, "Rabbi, who sinned, this man or
his parents, that he was born blind?" **3**
"Neither this man nor his parents
sinned," said Jesus, "but this happened
so that the work of God might be displayed in his life. **4** As long as it is
day, we must do the work of him who
sent me. Night is coming, when no
one can work. **5** While I am in the
world, I am the light of the world." **6**
Having said this, he spit on the
ground, made some mud with the
saliva, and put it on the man's eyes. **7**
"Go," he told him, "wash in the Pool
of Siloam" (this word means Sent). So
the man went and washed, and came
home seeing.

3 **LEARN THE LESSONS:**
What lessons can be learned from these facts? What do the facts mean? Is there an example to follow? Warning to heed? Promise to claim? Command to obey?

4 **LISTEN TO HIS VOICE:**
What does this passage mean to you? Rewrite the lessons from Step 3 in the form of a question to ask yourself or another.

5 **LIVE IT OUT:**
Pinpoint what God is saying to you from the passage. How will you respond? Write down today's date and what you will do now to live it out.

1 LOOK IN GOD'S WORD:

2 LIST THE FACTS:

JOHN 9:8–16

8 His neighbors and those who had
formerly seen him begging asked,
"Isn't this the same man who used to
sit and beg?" **9** Some claimed that he
was. Others said, "No, he only looks
like him." But he himself insisted, "I
am the man." **10** "How then were
your eyes opened?" they demanded. **11**
He replied, "The man they call Jesus
made some mud and put it on my
eyes. He told me to go to Siloam and
wash. So I went and washed, and then
I could see." **12** "Where is this man?"
they asked him. "I don't know," he
said. **13** They brought to the Pharisees
the man who had been blind. **14** Now
the day on which Jesus had made the
mud and opened the man's eyes was a
Sabbath. **15** Therefore the Pharisees
also asked him how he had received
his sight. "He put mud on my eyes,"
the man replied, "and I washed, and
now I see." **16** Some of the Pharisees
said, "This man is not from God, for
he does not keep the Sabbath." But
others asked, "How can a sinner do
such miraculous signs?" So they were
divided.

3 LEARN THE LESSONS:

4 LISTEN TO HIS VOICE:

5 LIVE IT OUT:

1 LOOK IN GOD'S WORD:

2 LIST THE FACTS:

John 9:17–25

17 Finally they turned again to the
blind man, "What have you to say
about him? It was your eyes he
opened." The man replied, "He is a
prophet." **18** The Jews still did not
believe that he had been blind and had
received his sight until they sent for
the man's parents. **19** "Is this your son?"
they asked. "Is this the one you say was
born blind? How is it that now he can
see?" **20** "We know he is our son," the
parents answered, "and we know he
was born blind. **21** But how he can see
now, or who opened his eyes, we don't
know. Ask him. He is of age; he will
speak for himself." **22** His parents said
this because they were afraid of the
Jews, for already the Jews had decided
that anyone who acknowledged that
Jesus was the Christ would be put out
of the synagogue. **23** That was why his
parents said, "He is of age; ask him."
24 A second time they summoned the
man who had been blind. "Give glory
to God," they said. "We know this man
is a sinner." **25** He replied, "Whether
he is a sinner or not, I don't know.
One thing I do know. I was blind but
now I see!"

3 **LEARN THE LESSONS:**

4 **LISTEN TO HIS VOICE:**

5 **LIVE IT OUT:**

1 LOOK IN GOD'S WORD:

2 LIST THE FACTS:

JOHN 9:26–34
26 Then they asked him, "What did
he do to you? How did he open your
eyes?" **27** He answered, "I have told
you already and you did not listen.
Why do you want to hear it again?
Do you want to become his disciples,
too?" **28** Then they hurled insults at
him and said, "You are this fellow's
disciple! We are disciples of Moses! **29**
We know that God spoke to Moses,
but as for this fellow, we don't even
know where he comes from." **30** The
man answered, "Now that is remarkable! You don't know where he comes
from, yet he opened my eyes. **31** We
know that God does not listen to sinners. He listens to the godly man who
does his will. **32** Nobody has ever
heard of opening the eyes of a man
born blind. **33** If this man were not
from God, he could do nothing." **34**
To this they replied, "You were
steeped in sin at birth; how dare you
lecture us!" And they threw him out.

3 **LEARN THE LESSONS:**

4 **LISTEN TO HIS VOICE:**

5 **LIVE IT OUT:**

1 LOOK IN GOD'S WORD:

JOHN 9:35–41

35 Jesus heard that they had thrown
him out, and when he found him, he
said, "Do you believe in the Son of
Man?" **36** "Who is he, sir?" the man
asked. "Tell me so that I may believe
in him." **37** Jesus said, "You have now
seen him; in fact, he is the one speaking with you." **38** Then the man said,
"Lord, I believe," and he worshiped
him. **39** Jesus said, "For judgment I
have come into this world, so that the
blind will see and those who see will
become blind." **40** Some Pharisees
who were with him heard him say this
and asked, "What? Are we blind too?"
41 Jesus said, "If you were blind, you
would not be guilty of sin; but now
that you claim you can see, your guilt
remains."

2 LIST THE FACTS:

3 LEARN THE LESSONS:

4 LISTEN TO HIS VOICE:

5 LIVE IT OUT:

COMMITMENT:

What was the most meaningful lesson to you from each day's study this week?

Study #1

Study #2

Study #3

Study #4

Study #5

As you reflect on all the lessons, what one thing has God seemed to say to you from John 9:1–41? Take a moment now to write out what He has said.

What has been your response?

Is there anything else you need to do in order to follow through completely?

Date your answer—then do it. Be committed!

CHAPTER 10

Jesus Makes Suffering Understandable . . . to the Sufferer

Do you have a prayer that has remained unanswered? Does God seem to be hiding Himself from you? *Why does He delay?* Why does He allow you and your loved ones to suffer so? One reason for His delay seems to be to allow us time to exhaust every other avenue of help until we come to the conclusion, without any doubt, that we are totally helpless without Him, and we rest our faith in Him and Him alone.

Jesus' delay in answering our prayers is never due to preoccupation or indifference with other things or an inability to act. His delay has a purpose.

Jesus patiently persisted in developing Martha's faith until it was focused on Him, and Him alone. With eyes that must have seemed to penetrate past her doubting mind and into her bleeding heart to the very depths of her being, He replied with words that have resonated through the centuries, giving hope at the gravesides of thousands of believers of every generation, "I am the resurrection and the life. He who believes in me will live, even though he dies; and whoever lives and believes in me will never die. Do you believe this?" (John 11:25–26) *Do you believe this . . . ?*

1 **LOOK IN GOD'S WORD:**
Feel free to underline, circle, or otherwise mark text if it will aid your study.

2 **LIST THE FACTS:**
Make a verse-by-verse list of the most obvious facts. What does the passage say? Do not paraphrase.

JOHN 11:1–6
1 Now a man named Lazarus was
sick. He was from Bethany, the village
of Mary and her sister Martha. **2** This
Mary, whose brother Lazarus now lay
sick, was the same one who poured
perfume on the Lord and wiped his
feet with her hair. **3** So the sisters sent
word to Jesus, "Lord, the one you love
is sick." **4** When he heard this, Jesus
said, "This sickness will not end in
death. No, it is for God's glory so that
God's Son may be glorified through
it." **5** Jesus loved Martha and her sister and Lazarus. **6** Yet when he heard
that Lazarus was sick, he stayed where
he was two more days.

3 **LEARN THE LESSONS:**
What lessons can be learned from these facts? What do the facts mean? Is there an example to follow? Warning to heed? Promise to claim? Command to obey?

4 **LISTEN TO HIS VOICE:**
What does this passage mean to you? Rewrite the lessons from Step 3 in the form of a question to ask yourself or another.

5 **LIVE IT OUT:**
Pinpoint what God is saying to you from the passage. How will you respond? Write down today's date and what you will do now to live it out.

1 LOOK IN GOD'S WORD:

2 LIST THE FACTS:

JOHN 11:7–16

7 Then he said to his disciples, "Let
us go back to Judea." **8** "But Rabbi,"
they said, "a short while ago the Jews
tried to stone you, and yet you are
going back there?" **9** Jesus answered,
"Are there not twelve hours of daylight? A man who walks by day will
not stumble, for he sees by this
world's light. **10** It is when he walks
by night that he stumbles, for he has
no light." **11** After he had said this, he
went on to tell them, "Our friend
Lazarus has fallen asleep; but I am
going there to wake him up." **12** His
disciples replied, "Lord, if he sleeps, he
will get better." **13** Jesus had been
speaking of his death, but his disciples
thought he meant natural sleep. **14** So
then he told them plainly, "Lazarus is
dead, **15** and for your sake I am glad I
was not there, so that you may believe.
But let us go to him." **16** Then
Thomas (called Didymus) said to the
rest of the disciples, "Let us also go,
that we may die with him."

3 LEARN THE LESSONS:

4 LISTEN TO HIS VOICE:

5 LIVE IT OUT:

1 LOOK IN GOD'S WORD:

2 LIST THE FACTS:

JOHN 11:17–27

17 On his arrival, Jesus found that Lazarus had already been in the tomb for four days. **18** Bethany was less than two miles from Jerusalem, **19** and many Jews had come to Martha and Mary to comfort them in the loss of their brother. **20** When Martha heard that Jesus was coming, she went out to meet him, but Mary stayed at home. **21** "Lord," Martha said to Jesus, "if you had been here, my brother would not have died. **22** But I know that even now God will give you whatever you ask." **23** Jesus said to her, "Your brother will rise again." **24** Martha answered, "I know he will rise again in the resurrection at the last day." **25** Jesus said to her, "I am the resurrection and the life. He who believes in me will live, even though he dies; **26** and whoever lives and believes in me will never die. Do you believe this?" **27** "Yes, Lord," she told him, "I believe that you are the Christ, the Son of God, who was to come into the world."

3 **LEARN THE LESSONS:**

4 **LISTEN TO HIS VOICE:**

5 **LIVE IT OUT:**

1 LOOK IN GOD'S WORD:

2 LIST THE FACTS:

JOHN 11:28–37

28 And after she had said this, she
went back and called her sister Mary
aside. "The Teacher is here," she said,
"and is asking for you." **29** When
Mary heard this, she got up quickly
and went to him. **30** Now Jesus had
not yet entered the village, but was
still at the place where Martha had
met him. **31** When the Jews who had
been with Mary in the house, comforting her, noticed how quickly she
got up and went out, they followed
her, supposing she was going to the
tomb to mourn there. **32** When Mary
reached the place where Jesus was and
saw him, she fell at his feet and said,
"Lord, if you had been here, my
brother would not have died." **33**
When Jesus saw her weeping, and the
Jews who had come along with her
also weeping, he was deeply moved in
spirit and troubled. **34** "Where have
you laid him?" he asked. "Come and
see, Lord," they replied. **35** Jesus wept.
36 Then the Jews said, "See how he
loved him!" **37** But some of them said,
"Could not he who opened the eyes of
the blind man have kept this man
from dying?"

3 **LEARN THE LESSONS:**

4 **LISTEN TO HIS VOICE:**

5 **LIVE IT OUT:**

1 LOOK IN GOD'S WORD:

2 LIST THE FACTS:

JOHN 11:38–44

38 Jesus, once more deeply moved,
came to the tomb. It was a cave with a
stone laid across the entrance. **39**
"Take away the stone," he said. "But,
Lord," said Martha, the sister of the
dead man, "by this time there is a bad
odor, for he has been there four days."
40 Then Jesus said, "Did I not tell you
that if you believed, you would see the
glory of God?" **41** So they took away
the stone. Then Jesus looked up and
said, "Father, I thank you that you
have heard me. **42** I knew that you
always hear me, but I said this for the
benefit of the people standing here,
that they may believe that you sent
me." **43** When he had said this, Jesus
called in a loud voice, "Lazarus, come
out!" **44** The dead man came out, his
hands and feet wrapped with strips of
linen, and a cloth around his face.
Jesus said to them, "Take off the grave
clothes and let him go."

3 **LEARN THE LESSONS:**

4 **LISTEN TO HIS VOICE:**

5 **LIVE IT OUT:**

COMMITMENT:

What was the most meaningful lesson to you from each day's study this week?

Study #1

Study #2

Study #3

Study #4

Study #5

As you reflect on all the lessons, what one thing has God seemed to say to you from John 11:1–44? Take a moment now to write out what He has said.

What has been your response?

Is there anything else you need to do in order to follow through completely?

Date your answer—then do it. Be committed!

CHAPTER 11

Jesus Makes Sin Forgivable . . . for Anyone

Not only are we hopelessly doomed in our sin and guilt, not only did God the Father send His only Son to save us, not only did the Son give His life to do so, but we also shrugged off His sacrifice and said it wasn't necessary, boasting, "I can save myself by my own activity, or morality, or religiosity, or sincerity. I don't need a Savior."

We are oblivious to what God's Son did for us. We don't realize we need a Savior, much less have any gratitude for our salvation. But God demonstrated His love for us before we were even born by sending His Son to be our Savior. His Son is Jesus, Who makes sin forgivable for anyone. Even you. Even me. Even Judas . . .

Pilate missed the opportunity of a lifetime—to ask the Truth to explain Himself. Pilate had found the source of all Truth, the summation of all truth, the supremacy of all truth, yet he had casually dismissed Him as irrelevant! The Truth was staring him in the face, but Pilate wasn't interested. Pilate has many ideological children today who spend their lives and a lot of money searching for the truth while dismissing the gospel as irrelevant. The climate today, even within the church, can be so pragmatic, so political, so psychological, so philosophical, that we casually dismiss the Truth as an unnecessary complication to our plans and programs . . .

Note: Some Scripture verses were omitted on the worksheets for this chapter due to space restraints. But you are encouraged to go back and study the entire passage for the fullest blessing.

1 **LOOK IN GOD'S WORD:**
Feel free to underline, circle, or otherwise mark text if it will aid your study.

2 **LIST THE FACTS:**
Make a verse-by-verse list of the most obvious facts. What does the passage say? Do not paraphrase.

JOHN 18:1–8
1 When he had finished praying, Jesus
left with his disciples and crossed the
Kidron Valley. On the other side there
was an olive grove, and he and his disciples went into it. 2 Now Judas, who
betrayed him, knew the place, because
Jesus had often met there with his
disciples. 3 So Judas came to the
grove, guiding a detachment of soldiers and some officials from the chief
priests and Pharisees. They were carrying torches, lanterns and weapons.
4 Jesus, knowing all that was going to
happen to him, went out and asked
them, "Who is it you want?" 5 "Jesus
of Nazareth," they replied. "I am he,"
Jesus said. (And Judas the traitor was
standing there with them.) 6 When
Jesus said, "I am he," they drew back
and fell to the ground. 7 Again he
asked them, "Who is it you want?"
And they said, "Jesus of Nazareth."
8 "I told you that I am he," Jesus
answered. "If you are looking for me,
then let these men go."

3 LEARN THE LESSONS:

What lessons can be learned from these facts? What do the facts mean? Is there an example to follow? Warning to heed? Promise to claim? Command to obey?

4 LISTEN TO HIS VOICE:

What does this passage mean to you? Rewrite the lessons from Step 3 in the form of a question to ask yourself or another.

5 LIVE IT OUT:

Pinpoint what God is saying to you from the passage. How will you respond? Write down today's date and what you will do now to live it out.

1 LOOK IN GOD'S WORD:

2 LIST THE FACTS:

JOHN 18:12–14; 19–24

12 Then the detachment of soldiers
with its commander and the Jewish
officials arrested Jesus. They bound
him **13** and brought him first to
Annas, who was the father-in-law of
Caiaphas, the high priest that year.
14 Caiaphas was the one who had
advised the Jews that it would be
good if one man died for the people.

19 Meanwhile, the high priest questioned Jesus about his disciples and
his teaching. **20** "I have spoken openly
to the world," Jesus replied. "I always
taught in synagogues or at the temple,
where all the Jews come together. I
said nothing in secret. **21** Why question me? Ask those who heard me.
Surely they know what I said." **22**
When Jesus said this, one of the officials nearby struck him in the face. "Is
this the way you answer the high
priest?" he demanded. **23** "If I said
something wrong," Jesus replied, "testify as to what is wrong. But if I spoke
the truth, why did you strike me?" **24**
Then Annas sent him, still bound, to
Caiaphas the high priest.

3 **LEARN THE LESSONS:**

4 **LISTEN TO HIS VOICE:**

5 **LIVE IT OUT:**

1 LOOK IN GOD'S WORD:

JOHN 18:25–32

25 As Simon Peter stood warming
himself, he was asked, "You are not one
of his disciples, are you?" He denied it,
saying, "I am not." **26** One of the high
priest's servants, a relative of the man
whose ear Peter had cut off, challenged him, "Didn't I see you with
him in the olive grove?" **27** Again
Peter denied it, and at that moment a
rooster began to crow. **28** Then the
Jews led Jesus from Caiaphas to the
palace of the Roman governor. By
now it was early morning, and to
avoid ceremonial uncleanness the Jews
did not enter the palace; they wanted
to be able to eat the Passover. **29** So
Pilate came out to them and asked,
"What charges are you bringing
against this man?" **30** "If he were not a
criminal," they replied, "we would not
have handed him over to you." **31**
Pilate said, "Take him yourselves and
judge him by your own law." "But we
have no right to execute anyone," the
Jews objected. **32** This happened so
that the words Jesus had spoken indi-
cating the kind of death he was going
to die would be fulfilled.

2 LIST THE FACTS:

3 LEARN THE LESSONS:

4 LISTEN TO HIS VOICE:

5 LIVE IT OUT:

1 LOOK IN GOD'S WORD:

JOHN 18:33–40
33 Pilate then went back inside the
palace, summoned Jesus and asked
him, "Are you the king of the Jews?"
34 "Is that your own idea," Jesus asked,
"or did others talk to you about me?"
35 "Am I a Jew?" Pilate replied. "It was
your people and your chief priests who
handed you over to me. What is it you
have done?" **36** Jesus said, "My kingdom is not of this world. If it were, my
servants would fight to prevent my
arrest by the Jews. But now my kingdom is from another place." **37** "You
are a king, then!" said Pilate. Jesus
answered, "You are right in saying I
am a king. In fact, for this reason I was
born, and for this I came into the
world, to testify to the truth. Everyone
on the side of truth listens to me." **38**
"What is truth?" Pilate asked. With
this he went out again to the Jews and
said, "I find no basis for a charge
against him. **39** But it is your custom
for me to release to you one prisoner
at the time of the Passover. Do you
want me to release 'the king of the
Jews'?" **40** They shouted back, "No, not
him! Give us Barabbas!" Now
Barabbas had taken part in a rebellion.

2 LIST THE FACTS:

3 LEARN THE LESSONS:

4 LISTEN TO HIS VOICE:

5 LIVE IT OUT:

1 LOOK IN GOD'S WORD:

2 LIST THE FACTS:

JOHN 19:6–12
6 As soon as the chief priests and
their officials saw him, they shouted,
"Crucify! Crucify!" But Pilate
answered, "You take him and crucify
him. As for me, I find no basis for a
charge against him." 7 The Jews
insisted, "We have a law, and according to that law he must die, because
he claimed to be the Son of God." 8
When Pilate heard this, he was even
more afraid, 9 and he went back
inside the palace. "Where do you
come from?" he asked Jesus, but Jesus
gave him no answer. 10 "Do you
refuse to speak to me?" Pilate said.
"Don't you realize I have power either
to free you or to crucify you?" 11 Jesus
answered, "You would have no power
over me if it were not given to you
from above. Therefore the one who
handed me over to you is guilty of a
greater sin." 12 From then on, Pilate
tried to set Jesus free, but the Jews
kept shouting, "If you let this man go,
you are no friend of Caesar. Anyone
who claims to be a king opposes
Caesar."

3 **LEARN THE LESSONS:**

4 **LISTEN TO HIS VOICE:**

5 **LIVE IT OUT:**

COMMITMENT:

What was the most meaningful lesson to you from each day's study this week?

Study #1

Study #2

Study #3

Study #4

Study #5

As you reflect on all the lessons, what one thing has God seemed to say to you from John 18:1–19:16? Take a moment now to write out what He has said.

What has been your response?

Is there anything else you need to do in order to follow through completely?

Date your answer—then do it. Be committed!

CHAPTER 12

Jesus Makes Sin Forgivable . . . for Everyone

The pervasive misconception today is that since Jesus died as a sacrifice for the sins of the world, then we are all automatically forgiven. But we overlook the vital truth that we must grasp the Lamb with our hands of faith and confess our sins. We then must acknowledge that He was slain for our sins as surely as if we had plunged the knife into His heart. At that moment, the Lamb becomes our High Priest and offers His own blood on the altar of the cross on our behalf. And, wonder of wonders! God accepts the sacrifice, and we are forgiven! Our guilt is atoned for! We are made right in God's sight! Jesus, the Lamb of God, makes sin forgivable for everyone!

1 **LOOK IN GOD'S WORD:**
Feel free to underline, circle, or otherwise mark text if it will aid your study.

2 **LIST THE FACTS:**
Make a verse-by-verse list of the most obvious facts. What does the passage say? Do not paraphrase.

JOHN 19:17–18
17 Carrying his own cross, he went
out to the place of the Skull (which in
Aramaic is called Golgotha). **18** Here
they crucified him, and with him two
others—one on each side and Jesus in
the middle.

3 LEARN THE LESSONS:

What lessons can be learned from these facts? What do the facts mean? Is there an example to follow? Warning to heed? Promise to claim? Command to obey?

4 LISTEN TO HIS VOICE:

What does this passage mean to you? Rewrite the lessons from Step 3 in the form of a question to ask yourself or another.

5 LIVE IT OUT:

Pinpoint what God is saying to you from the passage. How will you respond? Write down today's date and what you will do now to live it out.

1 LOOK IN GOD'S WORD:

2 LIST THE FACTS:

JOHN 19:19–22

19 Pilate had a notice prepared and
fastened to the cross. It read: JESUS OF
NAZARETH, THE KING OF THE
JEWS. 20 Many of the Jews read this
sign, for the place where Jesus was
crucified was near the city, and the
sign was written in Aramaic, Latin
and Greek. 21 The chief priests of the
Jews protested to Pilate, "Do not write
'The King of the Jews,' but that this
man claimed to be king of the Jews."
22 Pilate answered, "What I have
written, I have written."

3 **LEARN THE LESSONS:**

4 **LISTEN TO HIS VOICE:**

5 **LIVE IT OUT:**

1 LOOK IN GOD'S WORD:

2 LIST THE FACTS:

JOHN 19:23–24
23 When the soldiers crucified Jesus,
they took his clothes, dividing them
into four shares, one for each of them,
with the undergarment remaining.
This garment was seamless, woven in
one piece from top to bottom. 24
"Let's not tear it," they said to one
another. "Let's decide by lot who will
get it." This happened that the scripture might be fulfilled which said,
"They divided my garments among
them and cast lots for my clothing."
So this is what the soldiers did.

3 **LEARN THE LESSONS:**

4 **LISTEN TO HIS VOICE:**

5 **LIVE IT OUT:**

1 LOOK IN GOD'S WORD:

2 LIST THE FACTS:

John 19:25–27
25 Near the cross of Jesus stood his
mother, his mother's sister, Mary the
wife of Clopas, and Mary Magdalene.
26 When Jesus saw his mother there,
and the disciple whom he loved
standing nearby, he said to his mother,
"Dear woman, here is your son," **27**
and to the disciple, "Here is your
mother." From that time on, this disciple took her into his home.

3 LEARN THE LESSONS:

4 LISTEN TO HIS VOICE:

5 LIVE IT OUT:

1 LOOK IN GOD'S WORD:

2 LIST THE FACTS:

JOHN 19:28–30

28 Later, knowing that all was now
completed, and so that the Scripture
would be fulfilled, Jesus said, "I am
thirsty." **29** A jar of wine vinegar was
there, so they soaked a sponge in it,
put the sponge on a stalk of the hyssop plant, and lifted it to Jesus' lips. **30**
When he had received the drink, Jesus
said, "It is finished." With that, he
bowed his head and gave up his spirit.

3 **LEARN THE LESSONS:**

4 **LISTEN TO HIS VOICE:**

5 **LIVE IT OUT:**

COMMITMENT:

What was the most meaningful lesson to you from each day's study this week?

Study #1

Study #2

Study #3

Study #4

Study #5

As you reflect on all the lessons, what one thing has God seemed to say to you from John 19:17–30? Take a moment now to write out what He has said.

What has been your response?

Is there anything else you need to do in order to follow through completely?

Date your answer—then do it. Be committed!

CHAPTER 13

Jesus Makes Heaven Available . . . to the Sinner

After the long journey of life, we are going to look up and see heaven. We're going to hear voices lifted in songs of praise. We're going to see the glory of God radiating from within, and we're going to long for home. But we will be forbidden to enter. Heaven is closed to us because we are too dirty in our sin to enter it.

However, because Jesus found us in our hopeless, helpless state and offered us His hand at the cross, we can be welcomed into heaven. If we accept His offer and put our hand of faith in His, He will walk with us hand in hand, not only through the remainder of our journey, but through the gates of heaven that will be opened wide for us. We will be as welcomed and accepted in heaven as He is, solely because of our relationship and identification with Him. Praise God! Jesus is the One, and the only One, who opens heaven to the sinner, not only through the cross, but also through His resurrection. Come and see the facts . . .

1 **LOOK IN GOD'S WORD:**
Feel free to underline, circle, or otherwise mark text if it will aid your study.

2 **LIST THE FACTS:**
Make a verse-by-verse list of the most obvious facts. What does the passage say? Do not paraphrase.

JOHN 19:38–42
38 Later, Joseph of Arimathea asked
Pilate for the body of Jesus. Now
Joseph was a disciple of Jesus, but
secretly because he feared the Jews.
With Pilate's permission, he came and
took the body away. **39** He was
accompanied by Nicodemus, the man
who earlier had visited Jesus at night.
Nicodemus brought a mixture of
myrrh and aloes, about seventy-five
pounds. **40** Taking Jesus' body, the two
of them wrapped it, with the spices, in
strips of linen. This was in accordance
with Jewish burial customs. **41** At the
place where Jesus was crucified, there
was a garden, and in the garden a new
tomb, in which no one had ever been
laid. **42** Because it was the Jewish day
of Preparation and since the tomb was
nearby, they laid Jesus there.

3 LEARN THE LESSONS:

What lessons can be learned from these facts? What do the facts mean? Is there an example to follow? Warning to heed? Promise to claim? Command to obey?

4 LISTEN TO HIS VOICE:

What does this passage mean to you? Rewrite the lessons from Step 3 in the form of a question to ask yourself or another.

5 LIVE IT OUT:

Pinpoint what God is saying to you from the passage. How will you respond? Write down today's date and what you will do now to live it out.

1 LOOK IN GOD'S WORD:

2 LIST THE FACTS:

JOHN 20:1–2

1 Early on the first day of the week,
while it was still dark, Mary
Magdalene went to the tomb and saw
that the stone had been removed from
the entrance. **2** So she came running
to Simon Peter and the other disciple,
the one Jesus loved, and said, "They
have taken the Lord out of the tomb,
and we don't know where they have
put him!"

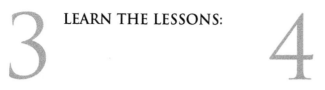

3 **LEARN THE LESSONS:**

4 **LISTEN TO HIS VOICE:**

5 **LIVE IT OUT:**

1 LOOK IN GOD'S WORD:

2 LIST THE FACTS:

JOHN 20:3–9

3 So Peter and the other disciple
started for the tomb. **4** Both were running, but the other disciple outran
Peter and reached the tomb first. **5** He
bent over and looked in at the strips
of linen lying there but did not go in.
6 Then Simon Peter, who was behind
him, arrived and went into the tomb.
He saw the strips of linen lying there,
7 as well as the burial cloth that had
been around Jesus' head. The cloth
was folded up by itself, separate from
the linen. **8** Finally the other disciple,
who had reached the tomb first, also
went inside. He saw and believed. **9**
(They still did not understand from
Scripture that Jesus had to rise from
the dead.)

3 **LEARN THE LESSONS:**

4 **LISTEN TO HIS VOICE:**

5 **LIVE IT OUT:**

1 LOOK IN GOD'S WORD:

2 LIST THE FACTS:

JOHN 20:10–14

10 Then the disciples went back to
their homes, **11** but Mary stood outside the tomb crying. As she wept, she
bent over to look into the tomb **12**
and saw two angels in white, seated
where Jesus' body had been, one at the
head and the other at the foot. **13**
They asked her, "Woman, why are you
crying?" "They have taken my Lord
away," she said, "and I don't know
where they have put him." **14** At this,
she turned around and saw Jesus
standing there, but she did not realize
that it was Jesus.

3 **LEARN THE LESSONS:**

4 **LISTEN TO HIS VOICE:**

5 **LIVE IT OUT:**

1 LOOK IN GOD'S WORD:

2 LIST THE FACTS:

JOHN 20:15–18

15 "Woman," he said, "why are you
crying? Who is it you are looking
for?" Thinking he was the gardener,
she said, "Sir, if you have carried him
away, tell me where you have put him,
and I will get him." **16** Jesus said to
her, "Mary." She turned toward him
and cried out in Aramaic, "Rabboni!"
(which means Teacher). **17** Jesus said,
"Do not hold on to me, for I have not
yet returned to the Father. Go instead
to my brothers and tell them, 'I am
returning to my Father and your
Father, to my God and your God.'" **18**
Mary Magdalene went to the disciples
with the news: "I have seen the Lord!"
And she told them that he had said
these things to her.

3 **LEARN THE LESSONS:**

4 **LISTEN TO HIS VOICE:**

5 **LIVE IT OUT:**

COMMITMENT:

What was the most meaningful lesson to you from each day's study this week?

Study #1

Study #2

Study #3

Study #4

Study #5

As you reflect on all the lessons, what one thing has God seemed to say to you from John 19:38–20:18? Take a moment now to write out what He has said.

What has been your response?

Is there anything else you need to do in order to follow through completely?

Date your answer—then do it. Be committed!

CHAPTER 14

Jesus Makes Heaven Available . . . to the Failure

Peter was a failure. He had failed miserably to grasp the will of God when it was revealed to him, and he had brashly told Jesus He wasn't going to the cross. He had slept when he should have prayed, and he had almost provoked a massacre in the garden when he single-handedly tried to take on the Roman army and sliced off Malchus's ear. He had repeatedly sworn that even if all the other disciples forsook Jesus, he would die for Him—then he denied three times that very day that he even knew Him. There was no doubt in his mind or anyone else's that he was a miserable, habitual failure.

Do you feel like a failure? Have you been discouraged in your Christian life or your Christian leadership to the point of quitting? Do you feel you're just not cut out for this sort of thing? Then praise God! Failure is not final! He has a place for you in His kingdom because Jesus makes heaven available to the failure . . .

Note: Some Scripture verses were omitted on the worksheets for this chapter due to space restraints. But you are encouraged to go back and study the entire passage for the fullest blessing.

1 **LOOK IN GOD'S WORD:**
Feel free to underline, circle, or otherwise mark text if it will aid your study.

2 **LIST THE FACTS:**
Make a verse-by-verse list of the most obvious facts. What does the passage say? Do not paraphrase.

John 21:1–3

1 Afterward Jesus appeared again to
his disciples, by the Sea of Tiberias. It
happened this way: 2 Simon Peter,
Thomas (called Didymus), Nathanael
from Cana in Galilee, the sons of
Zebedee, and two other disciples were
together. 3 "I'm going out to fish,"
Simon Peter told them, and they said,
"We'll go with you." So they went out
and got into the boat, but that night
they caught nothing.

3

LEARN THE LESSONS:

What lessons can be learned from these facts? What do the facts mean? Is there an example to follow? Warning to heed? Promise to claim? Command to obey?

4

LISTEN TO HIS VOICE:

What does this passage mean to you? Rewrite the lessons from Step 3 in the form of a question to ask yourself or another.

5

LIVE IT OUT:

Pinpoint what God is saying to you from the passage. How will you respond? Write down today's date and what you will do now to live it out.

1 LOOK IN GOD'S WORD:

2 LIST THE FACTS:

JOHN 21:4–9
4 Early in the morning, Jesus stood on
the shore, but the disciples did not
realize that it was Jesus. **5** He called
out to them, "Friends, haven't you any
fish?" "No," they answered. **6** He said,
"Throw your net on the right side of
the boat and you will find some."
When they did, they were unable to
haul the net in because of the large
number of fish. **7** Then the disciple
whom Jesus loved said to Peter, "It is
the Lord!" As soon as Simon Peter
heard him say, "It is the Lord," he
wrapped his outer garment around
him (for he had taken it off) and
jumped into the water. **8** The other
disciples followed in the boat, towing
the net full of fish, for they were not
far from shore, about a hundred yards.
9 When they landed, they saw a fire
of burning coals there with fish on it,
and some bread.

3 **LEARN THE LESSONS:**

4 **LISTEN TO HIS VOICE:**

5 **LIVE IT OUT:**

1 LOOK IN GOD'S WORD:

JOHN 21:10–14

10 Jesus said to them, "Bring some of
the fish you have just caught." **11**
Simon Peter climbed aboard and
dragged the net ashore. It was full of
large fish, 153, but even with so many
the net was not torn. **12** Jesus said to
them, "Come and have breakfast."
None of the disciples dared ask him,
"Who are you?" They knew it was the
Lord. **13** Jesus came, took the bread
and gave it to them, and did the same
with the fish. **14** This was now the
third time Jesus appeared to his disciples after he was raised from the
dead.

2 LIST THE FACTS:

3 **LEARN THE LESSONS:**

4 **LISTEN TO HIS VOICE:**

5 **LIVE IT OUT:**

1 LOOK IN GOD'S WORD:

JOHN 21:15–17

15 When they had finished eating,
Jesus said to Simon Peter, "Simon son
of John, do you truly love me more
than these?" "Yes, Lord," he said, "you
know that I love you." Jesus said,
"Feed my lambs." **16** Again Jesus said,
"Simon son of John, do you truly love
me?" He answered, "Yes, Lord, you
know that I love you." Jesus said,
"Take care of my sheep." **17** The third
time he said to him, "Simon son of
John, do you love me?" Peter was hurt
because Jesus asked him the third
time, "Do you love me?" He said,
"Lord, you know all things; you know
that I love you." Jesus said, "Feed my
sheep."

2 LIST THE FACTS:

3 **LEARN THE LESSONS:**

4 **LISTEN TO HIS VOICE:**

5 **LIVE IT OUT:**

1 LOOK IN GOD'S WORD:

2 LIST THE FACTS:

JOHN 21:18–25a

18 "I tell you the truth, when you were
younger you dressed yourself and went
where you wanted; but when you are
old you will stretch out your hands,
and someone else will dress you and
lead you where you do not want to go."
19 Jesus said this to indicate the kind
of death by which Peter would glorify
God. Then he said to him, "Follow
me!" **20** Peter turned and saw that the
disciple whom Jesus loved was following them. (This was the one who had
leaned back against Jesus at the supper
and had said, "Lord, who is going to
betray you?") **21** When Peter saw him,
he asked, "Lord, what about him?"
22 Jesus answered, "If I want him to
remain alive until I return, what is that
to you? You must follow me." **23**
Because of this, the rumor spread
among the brothers that this disciple
would not die. But Jesus did not say
that he would not die; he only said, "If
I want him to remain alive until I
return, what is that to you?" **24** This is
the disciple who testifies to these
things and who wrote them down. We
know that his testimony is true. **25a**
Jesus did many other things as well.

3 **LEARN THE LESSONS:**

4 **LISTEN TO HIS VOICE:**

5 **LIVE IT OUT:**

COMMITMENT:

What was the most meaningful lesson to you from each day's study this week?

Study #1

Study #2

Study #3

Study #4

Study #5

As you reflect on all the lessons, what one thing has God seemed to say to you from John 21:1–25a? Take a moment now to write out what He has said.

What has been your response?

Is there anything else you need to do in order to follow through completely?

Date your answer—then do it. Be committed!

PRAYERS

PRAYERS

PRAYERS

PRAYERS

PRAYERS

REFLECTIONS

REFLECTIONS

REFLECTIONS

REFLECTIONS

REFLECTIONS

REFLECTIONS

CLASSIC BOOKS BY

ANNE GRAHAM LOTZ...

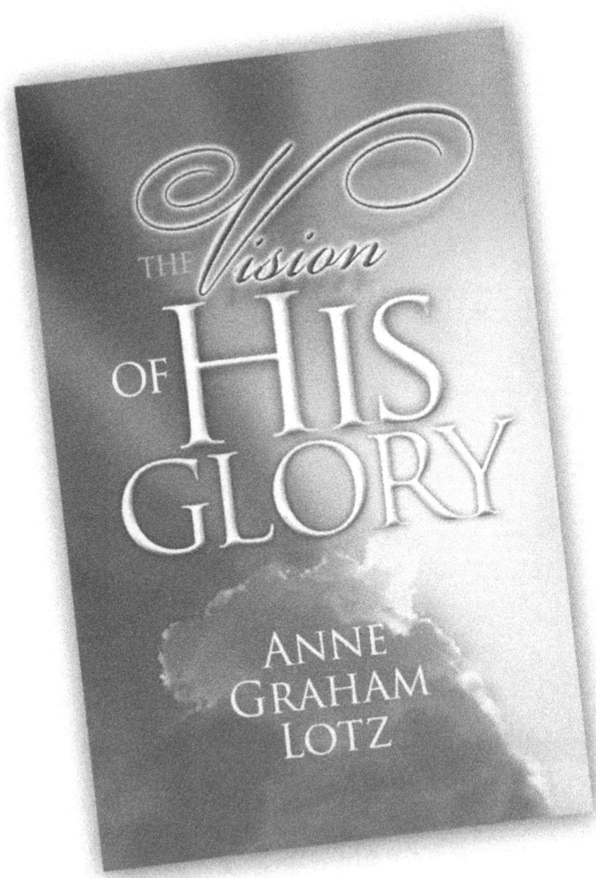

THE VISION OF HIS GLORY

With a focus on Jesus Christ, Anne Graham Lotz brings clarity and understanding to the book of Revelation.

GOD'S STORY

Find meaning for your life as you journey through the first 11 chapters of Genesis.

PURSUING MORE OF JESUS

Anne shares how a personal revelation of Jesus can change your life forever.

Additional resources from Anne Graham Lotz
are available at:

AnGeL Ministries
5115 Hollyridge Drive
Raleigh, NC 27612
Phone: 919-787-6606
www.AnneGrahamLotz.com

CPSIA information can be obtained
at www.ICGtesting.com
Printed in the USA
LVHW01s0744020118
561499LV00013B/239/P

9 780849 92093